TRANSNATIONAL CAPITAL AND CLASS FRACTIONS

Emerging in the late 1970s, the Amsterdam School's (AS) most distinctive contribution to international political economy was the systematic incorporation of the Marxian concept of capital fractions into the study of international politics. Contending that politics in advanced capitalist countries takes place in a fundamentally transnationalized space in which the distinction between 'domestic' and 'international' has blurred, it shows how in this space, politics is structured by competing comprehensive concepts of control.

Presenting a concise and instructive introduction to the origins, development and significance of this distinct approach, this book provides a unique overview of the School's contemporary significance for the field. Offering a new generation of critical scholars the opportunity to become acquainted at first hand with some of the contributions that have shaped the work of the AS, the contributions present critical commentaries, discussing the merits and shortcomings of the AS from a variety of perspectives, and undertake a (self-)critical evaluation of the current place and value of the AS framework in the broader landscape of approaches to the study of contemporary capitalism.

Written for scholars and students alike, it will be of interest to those working in international political economy, international relations and political science, political sociology, European studies and branches of academic economics such as regulation theory and institutional economics.

Bob Jessop is Distinguished Professor of Sociology and Co-Director of the Cultural Political Economy Research Centre at Lancaster University.

Henk Overbeek is Emeritus Professor of International Relations. He has taught international relations and international political economy at the Vrije Universiteit Amsterdam since 1999.

RIPE SERIES IN GLOBAL POLITICAL ECONOMY

Series editors:

James Brassett *(University of Warwick, UK)*, **Eleni Tsingou** *(Copenhagen Business School, Denmark)* and **Susanne Soederberg** *(Queen's University, Canada)*

The RIPE Series published by Routledge is an essential forum for cutting-edge scholarship in International Political Economy. The series brings together new and established scholars working in critical, cultural and constructivist political economy. Books in the RIPE Series typically combine an innovative contribution to theoretical debates with rigorous empirical analysis.

The RIPE Series seeks to cultivate:
- Field-defining theoretical advances in International Political Economy
- Novel treatments of key issue areas, both historical and contemporary, such as global finance, trade, and production
- Analyses that explore the political economic dimensions of relatively neglected topics, such as the environment, gender relations, and migration
- Accessible work that will inspire advanced undergraduates and graduate students in International Political Economy.

The *RIPE Series in Global Political Economy* aims to address the needs of students and teachers.

For more information about this series, please visit: www.routledge.com/RIPE-Series-in-Global-Political-Economy/book-series/RIPE

Securing Finance, Mobilizing Risk
Money Cultures at the Bank of England
John Hogan Morris

Affective Politics of the Global Event
Trauma and the Resilient Market Subject
James Brassett

Transnational Capital and Class Fractions
The Amsterdam School Perspective Reconsidered
Edited by Bob Jessop and Henk Overbeek

TRANSNATIONAL CAPITAL AND CLASS FRACTIONS

The Amsterdam School Perspective Reconsidered

Edited by Bob Jessop and Henk Overbeek

LONDON AND NEW YORK

First published 2019
by Routledge
2 Park Square, Milton Park, Abingdon, Oxon OX14 4RN

and by Routledge
711 Third Avenue, New York, NY 10017

Routledge is an imprint of the Taylor & Francis Group, an informa business

© 2019 selection and editorial matter, Bob Jessop and Henk Overbeek; individual chapters, the contributors

The right of Bob Jessop and Henk Overbeek to be identified as the authors of the editorial material, and of the authors for their individual chapters, has been asserted in accordance with sections 77 and 78 of the Copyright, Designs and Patents Act 1988.

All rights reserved. No part of this book may be reprinted or reproduced or utilised in any form or by any electronic, mechanical, or other means, now known or hereafter invented, including photocopying and recording, or in any information storage or retrieval system, without permission in writing from the publishers.

Trademark notice: Product or corporate names may be trademarks or registered trademarks, and are used only for identification and explanation without intent to infringe.

British Library Cataloguing in Publication Data
A catalogue record for this book is available from the British Library

Library of Congress Cataloging in Publication Data
Names: Jessop, Bob, editor. | Overbeek, Henk, editor.
Title: Transnational capital and class fractions: the Amsterdam School perspective reconsidered / edited by Bob Jessop and Henk Overbeek.
Description: Abingdon, Oxon ; New York, NY : Routledge, 2018. | Series: RIPE series in global political economy | Includes bibliographical references and index.
Identifiers: LCCN 2018008460| ISBN 9780815369592 (hardback) | ISBN 9781351251945 (e-book) | ISBN 9780815369608 (pbk.)
Subjects: LCSH: Capitalism--Political aspects. | Internationalrelations--Philosophy. | International economic relations. | Transnationalism--Political aspects. | Transnationalism--Economic aspects. | Marxian economics.
Classification: LCC HB501 .T7217 2018 | DDC 335.4--dc23
LC record available at https://lccn.loc.gov/2018008460

ISBN: 978-0-8153-6959-2 (hbk)
ISBN: 978-0-8153-6960-8 (pbk)
ISBN: 978-1-351-25194-5 (ebk)

Typeset in Bembo
by Taylor & Francis Books

We dedicate this book to the memory of our late colleagues Uwe Becker (1951–2014), Alex Fernandez Jilberto (1948–2010), Andre Mommen (1945–2017), Moishe Postone (1942–2018) and John Urry (1946–2016). They shared our commitment to critical political economy and died far too young.

CONTENTS

List of illustrations	*x*
Notes on contributors	*xi*
Foreword by Gerd Junne	*xix*
Original sources and acknowledgements	*xxi*
List of abbreviations	*xxii*

Introduction – political economy, capital fractions, transnational
class formation: revisiting the Amsterdam School   1
Henk Overbeek

PART I
The Amsterdam School: key contributions   **19**

1 The Dutch bourgeoisie between the two world wars (1979)   21
  Ries Bode

2 Class formation at the international level: reflections on the
  political economy of Atlantic Unity (1979)   58
  Kees van der Pijl

3 Finance capital and the crisis in Britain (1980)   79
  Henk Overbeek

4 The international corporate elite (1984)   100
  Meindert Fennema

viii Contents

5 Transnational class agency and European governance: the case
   of the European Round Table of Industrialists (2000)   119
   Bastiaan van Apeldoorn

6 Asymmetrical regulation and multidimensional governance in
   the European Union (2004)   145
   Otto Holman

PART II
Critical commentaries   **167**

7 Class fractions and hegemonic concepts of control   169
   Andreas Bieler and Adam David Morton

8 Losing control? The Amsterdam School travels east   175
   Dorothee Bohle

9 The Amsterdam School as a potential source of inspiration for
   Chinese scholars   180
   Bai Yunzhen

10 Reconsidering the 'dangerous liaisons' between China and
   neoliberalism and its impact in Latin America and Caribbean
   countries   185
   Leonardo Ramos and Javier Vadell

11 Saying goodbye? Tracing my itinerary from Amsterdam to
   Beijing   191
   Naná de Graaff

12 Reflections on the Amsterdam School and the transnational
   capitalist class   197
   William K. Carroll

13 Alternative perspectives on European integration   202
   Alan Cafruny and Magnus Ryner

14 Nationalist populism within the Lockean heartland   207
   Hans-Jürgen Bieling

15 Out of Amsterdam! Beyond the boundaries of (transnational)
   capitalist class formation   212
   Laura Horn and Angela Wigger

16 The Amsterdam School: gender as a blind spot   217
   Marianne H. Marchand

Contents ix

17 The Amsterdam School, critical realism and the study of 'deep
structures'   223
Hubert Buch-Hansen and Juan Ignacio Staricco

18 Confronting global governance after the historical turn in
International Relations   228
Samuel Knafo

19 Network analysis and the Amsterdam School: an unfulfilled
promise?   233
Eelke M. Heemskerk

PART III
**The Amsterdam School and the political economy of
contemporary capitalism**   **239**

20 A transnational class analysis of the current crisis   241
Kees van der Pijl

21 Putting the Amsterdam School in its place   263
Bob Jessop

Index   *293*

ILLUSTRATIONS

Figures

1.1	Capital fractions, fractions of the bourgeoisie, bourgeois political parties	34
4.1	Different types of interlock	107
4.2	Interlocking directorates according to the position of the multiple directors	111
20.1	Successive class constellations in the West, 'disruptive contingencies', and contender formations	243

Tables

1.1	Export and national income in millions of Dutch guilders	27
4.1	Distribution of international interlocks	106
4.2	Distribution of directorships among the international corporate elite	107
4.3	Distribution of positions over the populations of persons in interlock networks	108
4.4	Lines in the network according to their multiplicity	110
4.5	Distribution of interlocks over directors	115
5.1	Members of the ERT and their companies, May 1999	124
20.1	Key moments in the UK/US financial crisis, state intervention, and corruption, 2007–2008	252
21.1	Distinctive features of the Amsterdam School in global political economy	277

CONTRIBUTORS

Editors

Bob Jessop is Distinguished Professor of Sociology and Co-Director of the Cultural Political Economy Research Centre at Lancaster University. He is best known for his contributions to state theory, critical political economy, critical governance studies and social theory. His recent publications include *Towards a cultural political economy: Putting culture in its place in political economy* (co-authored with Ngai-Ling Sum, 2013) and *The state: Past, present, future* (2015). Recent journal articles derive from ESRC-funded research projects on crises of crisis management in relation to the North Atlantic financial crisis (2010–13) and on civil society as a mode of governance (2016–19). His work is accessible via Academia.edu, www.researchgate.net/profile/Bob_Jessop3 and bobjessop.org.

Henk Overbeek is Emeritus Professor of International Relations. He has taught international relations and international political economy at the *Vrije Universiteit Amsterdam* since 1999. Before joining the Vrije Universiteit he taught at the University of Amsterdam (1974–98) and Webster University in Leiden (1994–2004). His research interests focus on neoliberalism, the Eurozone crisis and the impact of the rise of China on the global political economy. His recent book publications are *The state-capital nexus in the global crisis: Rebound of the capitalist state* (co-edited with Bastiaan van Apeldoorn and Naná de Graaff, 2014), *Neoliberalism in crisis* (co-edited with Bastiaan van Apeldoorn, 2012) and *Globalisation and European integration: Critical approaches to regional order and international relations* (co-edited with Petros Nousios and Andreas Tsolakis, 2012). His work is accessible at https://research.vu.nl/en/persons/henk-overbeek, https://vu-nl.academia.edu/HenkOverbeek and www.researchgate.net/profile/Henk_Overbeek.

Contributors

Bastiaan van Apeldoorn is Reader in International Relations in the Department of Political Science at the Vrije Universiteit Amsterdam. His research centres on the role of transnational corporate elites in US foreign policy, European socio-economic governance and on the transformation of liberal world order. His publications include *Transnational capitalism and the struggle over European integration* (2002), *Contradictions and limits of neoliberal Europe: From Lisbon to Lisbon* (co-edited with Jan Drahokoupil and Laura Horn, 2009), *The state-capital nexus in the global crisis: Rebound of the capitalist state* (co-edited with Naná de Graaff and Henk Overbeek, 2014) and *American grand strategy and corporate elite networks: The open door since the end of the Cold War* (co-authored with Naná de Graaff, 2016). His research can be accessed at https://research.vu.nl/en/persons/bastiaan-van-apeldoorn, https://vu-nl.academia.edu/BastiaanvanApeldoorn and www.researchgate.net/profile/Bastiaan_Apeldoorn.

Bai Yunzhen is Associate Professor of International Relations and Dean of the Department of International Politics at the Central University of Finance and Economics in Beijing. He is the author of *The evolution and transformation of contemporary Chinese diplomacy* and edits two book series: *Global political economy* and *China and global political economy*. Reflecting his research interests, Bai Yunzhen is currently writing *The Chinese foreign strategy in the age of economic power* and is involved in research programmes on Chinese financial strategy and policies, China–ASEAN development cooperation and China's 'Belt and Road Initiative'. His research can be accessed at www.researchgate.net/profile/Bai_Yunzhen.

Andreas Bieler is Professor of Political Economy and Fellow of the Centre for the Study of Social and Global Justice at the University of Nottingham. He is the author of *Globalisation and enlargement of the European Union: Austrian and Swedish social forces in the struggle over membership* (2000), *The struggle for a social Europe: Trade unions and EMU in times of global restructuring* (2006) and of *Global capitalism, global war, global crisis* (with Adam David Morton, 2018). With Bruno Ciccaglione, Ingemar Lindberg and John Hilary, he co-edited *Free trade and transnational labour* (2015) and, with Chun-Yi Lee, *Chinese labour in the global economy* (2017). His research can be accessed at www.nottingham.ac.uk/politics/people/andreas.bieler, http://andreasbieler.net/ and www.researchgate.net/profile/Andreas_Bieler.

Hans-Jürgen Bieling is Professor of Political Economy and Economic Didactics at the Institute of Political Science at the University of Tübingen, Germany. He previously taught at the Philipps-University Marburg as Junior Professor for European integration (2003–2008). In between there were shorter appointments at the University of Hamburg, the Technical University of Darmstadt and the University of Applied Sciences in Bremen. Bieling has published widely on financial markets, European crises dynamics, labour and social developments and the transformation of democratic participation and control. His current research focuses on European crisis management, its implications for European societies and national welfare regimes, and the rise of nationalist populism. His most recent book publication is *The political economy of the European Union* (2015). His research can be accessed at www.uni-tuebingen.de/en/faculties/economics-and-social-sciences/subjects/ifp/about-the-institute/lehrende/political-economy-and-economic-didactics-professor-bieling/staff/prof-dr-hans-juergen-bieling.html and www.researchgate.net/scientific-contributions/2034546949_Hans-Juergen_Bieling.

Ries Bode obtained his master's degree in social and political sciences at the University of Amsterdam (1976), where he was a teaching assistant in the Department of International Relations. Over the next few years, he taught personnel managers and labour market mediators at the Foundation of Education in Social Work in the city of Haarlem. This endeavour developed into the independent company Convia Opleidingen, which was bought by the Reed Elsevier publishing company in 1992. Bode continued with Elsevier for another three years. After a sabbatical in 1996 followed a period of diverse interim management assignments, he returned to academia in 2004 with a research position at the Vrije Universiteit Amsterdam. Here he worked on various research and consultancy projects in the field of sustainable energy policy, with a focus on, and a number of publications in, the field of hydrogen energy.

Dorothee Bohle is Professor of Political Science at the European University Institute, San Domenico di Fiesole, Italy, where she was previously a Fernand Braudel Fellow. She got her PhD from the Free University of Berlin. Her research focuses on social and political change and on comparative political economy with a special interest in Eastern Europe. She was previously a professor of political science at Central European University, Budapest, and from 1995 to 2001 a research fellow at the Social Science Research Center, Berlin. She is the author of *Europas neue Peripherie: Polens Transformation und transnationale Integration* (2002) and *Capitalist diversity on Europe's periphery* (co-authored with Béla Greskovits, 2012), as well as numerous journal articles and book chapters. Her current research focuses on responses to the European debt crisis. Her research can be accessed at www.eui.eu/DepartmentsAndCentres/PoliticalAndSocialSciences/People/Professors/Bohle and www.researchgate.net/profile/Dorothee_Bohle.

Hubert Buch-Hansen is Associate Professor at the Department of Business and Politics, Copenhagen Business School. His current research focuses on corporate networks and seeks to cross-fertilize insights from critical political economy and growth-critical scholarship (degrowth and steady-state economics). He is the author of several journal articles and books, including *The politics of European competition regulation: A critical political economy perspective* (2011), which was co-authored with Angela Wigger. His research can be accessed at www.cbs.dk/en/research/departments-and-centres/department-of-business-and-politics/staff/hbdbp, https://cbs.academia.edu/HubertBuchHansen and www.researchgate.net/scientific-contributions/2002768324_Hubert_Buch-Hansen.

xiv Contributors

Alan Cafruny is Henry Platt Bristol Professor of International Affairs at Hamilton College. He has written extensively on international political economy and European politics. His most recent books include *The European Union and global capitalism: Origins, development, crisis* (co-authored with Magnus Ryner, 2017), *The Palgrave handbook of critical political economy* (co-edited with Leila Simona Talani and Gonzalo Pozo Martin, 2016) and *Exploring the global financial crisis* (co-edited with Herman Schwartz, 2013). His research can be accessed at https://academics.hamilton.edu/government/faculty/alan-cafruny, https://hamilton.academia.edu/Alan Cafruny and www.researchgate.net/profile/Alan_Cafruny/publications.

William K. Carroll's research interests are in the areas of the political economy of corporate capitalism, social movements and social change, and critical social theory and method. A member of the Sociology Department at the University of Victoria since 1981, and Founding Director of the interdisciplinary programme in Social Justice Studies, his recent books include *The making of a transnational capitalist class* (2010), *Corporate power in a globalizing world* (2010) and *Expose, oppose, propose: Alternative policy groups and the struggle for global justice, a world to win* (with Kanchan Sarker, 2014), His current project, 'Mapping the power of the carbon-extractive corporate resource sector', is an interdisciplinary partnership of several universities and civil society organizations that traces various modalities of corporate power and resistance within the global political economy, focusing on fossil capital based in western Canada. His research can be accessed at www.uvic.ca/socialsciences/sociology/people/faculty/carrollwilliam.php and www.researchgate.net/profile/William _Carroll8.

Naná de Graaff is Assistant Professor in International Relations at the Department of Political Science and Public Administration at the Vrije Universiteit Amsterdam. Her main research interests are the globalization of Chinese firms and elites, US foreign policy and corporate elite networks, the geopolitical economy of energy and emerging powers and social network analysis. She publishes in leading journals in international relations, international political economy and sociology. Her latest books are *American grand strategy and corporate elite networks* (with Bastiaan van Apeldoorn, 2016) and *The state-capital nexus in the global crisis* (co-edited with Bastiaan van Apeldoorn and Henk Overbeek, 2014). Her research can be accessed at https://research.vu.nl/en/persons/na-de-graaff and www.researchgate.net/profile/Nana_Graaff.

Meindert Fennema is Emeritus Professor in Political Theory at the University of Amsterdam. He published extensively on anti-immigration parties, ethnic mobilization, political theory and political violence. His work on Dutch political history and his work on the analysis of interlocking directorates in global business has also resulted in numerous publications, including *International networks of banks and industry* (1982), *Het Nederlands Belang bij Indië* (with H. Baudet, 1983), *Hans Max Hirschfeld. Man van het Grote Geld* (with John Rhijnsburger, 2007), *Nieuwe*

Netwerken. De ondergang van NV Nederland (with Eelke Heemskerk, 2008), and as contributing author, *The making of a transnational capitalist class* (2010, with W.K. Carroll, C. Carson, E. Heemskerk and J.P. Sapinski). His research can be accessed at www.uva.nl/profiel/f/e/m.fennema/m.fennema.html?page=1&pageSize=200& origin=wRMmARqSQFWPuRKx9zHQ7w, https://uva.academia.edu/Meindert Fennema and www.researchgate.net/profile/Meindert_Fennema/publications.

Eelke M. Heemskerk is Associate Professor of Political Science at the University of Amsterdam (UvA). He received his PhD at the Amsterdam School for Social Science Research in 2006. He has been a research fellow at the Germany Institute and AIAS, both at UvA, and was visiting fellow at the Institute for Strategic Management, Ludwig Maximilians Universität and the Center on Organizational Innovation, Columbia University. Eelke has published widely on corporate power and governance, corporate elites, social networks and institutional reform in the Netherlands and Europe. His book publications include *Decline of the corporate community* (2007). He is currently Principal Investigator of the ERC-funded CORPNET research group which uncovers, investigates and aims to understand global networks of corporate control in contemporary global capitalism. For more information visit his personal website www.eelkeheemskerk.nl, or the CORPNET.uva.nl website.

Otto Holman is Reader in International Relations and European Integration Studies in the Department of Political Science and member of the Amsterdam Institute for Social Science Research, both at the University of Amsterdam. Previous positions include staff member at the Netherlands Scientific Council for Government Policy (1994–95), *professeur invité* at the University of Lausanne (2009–15, fall terms) and visiting professor at the University of Granada (2017). His research has focused on the role of transnational social forces in emerging patterns of European governance, peripheral capitalism and the enlargement of the European Union (EU) (the Mediterranean enlargement in the 1980s and the 2004–2007 big bang incorporation of Central and Eastern Europe), the social and regional impact of core-periphery relations in Europe, and Spanish politics. His current research concentrates on the multidimensionality of crisis and core-periphery dynamics within the EU and in its external relations with neighbouring countries and the developing world. He is working on a book on the foreign relations of the EU. See www.uva.nl/profiel/h/o/o.h.holman/o.h. holman.html and www.researchgate.net/scientific-contributions/2010029920_ Otto_Holman.

Laura Horn is Associate Professor in the Department of Social Science and Business, Roskilde University. Her main research area is the critical political economy of Europe. Her publications include *Regulating corporate governance in the EU* (2011), *Contradictions and limits of neoliberal European governance* (co-edited with Bastiaan van Apeldoorn and Jan Drahokoupil, 2008) and articles published in several journals. See http://forskning.ruc.dk/site/en/persons/laura-horn(8d17a6a

xvi Contributors

5-aee0–42d3–92cf-d152b46cae48).html and https://ruc-dk.academia.edu/Laura Horn.

Samuel Knafo is Senior Lecturer in the Department of International Relations at the University of Sussex. He is the author of *The Making of modern finance: Liberal governance and the gold standard* (Routledge, 2013), which was awarded the 2014 IPEG book prize. He has also published various articles on critical methodology, financial speculation and neoliberal governance. His work can be found at www.sussex.ac.uk/profiles/165982, https://sussex.academia.edu/SamuelKnafo and www.researchgate.net/scientific-contributions/2027125872_Samuel_Knafo.

Marianne H. Marchand holds a chair in international relations at the Universidad de las Américas Puebla, Mexico, where she directs the Canadian Studies Program. In 2013 she was promoted to the highest level of the National System of Researchers. In addition to her academic activities in Mexico she has worked at or been affiliated with universities in Canada, the US, the Netherlands, Norway, Denmark, Sweden, Surinam and Trinidad and Tobago. She has published widely about such themes as globalization, gender, migration, development, resistance and transnational movements. Her research can be accessed at www.researchgate.net/profile/Marianne_Marchand.

Adam David Morton is Professor of Political Economy in the Department of Political Economy at the University of Sydney. His research interests are shaped through interdisciplinary concerns across political economy, state theory, development, geographical studies and historical sociology. He is the author of *Unravelling Gramsci: Hegemony and passive revolution in the global political economy* (2007), *Revolution and state in modern Mexico: The political economy of uneven development* (2011), which was awarded the 2012 Book Prize of the British International Studies Association International Political Economy Group, and of *Global capitalism, global war, global crisis* (with Andreas Bieler, 2018). See www.researchgate.net/profile/Adam_Morton2 and http://sydney.edu.au/arts/political_economy/staff/profiles/adam.morton.php.

Kees van der Pijl taught international relations at the University of Amsterdam from 1973 to 1999. In January 2000, he moved to the University of Sussex, retiring from teaching in 2012. Today he is Fellow of the Centre for Global Political Economy at Sussex and Emeritus Professor of International Relations. His work deals with transnational class formation and global political economy. He has published *The making of an Atlantic ruling class* (1984, republished with new introduction, 2012), *Transnational classes and international relations* (1998), *Global rivalries from the Cold War to Iraq* (2006) and other work. In 2006 he was awarded a Leverhulme Major Research Fellowship that supported the publication of the Deutscher Prize-winning trilogy, *Modes of foreign relations and political economy* (a critique of the 'clash of civilizations' argument and mainstream international relations) between 2007 and 2014. In 2015 he edited the *Handbook on the international political economy of production*. His book, *Flight MH17, Ukraine and the New Cold War*, was published in 2018 in English, German and Portuguese. See www.sussex.ac.uk/profiles/114421/publications, https://sussex.academia.edu/KeesVanderPijl, en.wikipedia.org/wiki/Kees_van_der_Pijl and www.researchgate.net/scientific-contributions/2002971273_Kees_van_der_Pijl.

Leonardo Ramos is Senior Lecturer at the Department of International Relations, Pontificia Universidade Católica de Minas Gerais, Brazil. His research interests include the theory of international relations, Gramsci, hegemony, globalization, G7/8 and the G20. Together with Javier Vadell, he directs the Grupo de Pesquisa dos Países Emergentes (https://potenciasmedias.com/). His publications include *Hegemonia, revolução passive e globalização: O sistema G7/8* (2013).

Magnus Ryner is Professor of International Political Economy and Head of Department at King's College London. His publications include *Capitalist restructuring, globalisation and the Third Way* (2002) and *A ruined fortress? Neoliberal hegemony and transformation in Europe* (with Alan Cafruny, 2003), *Europe at bay: In the shadow of US hegemony* (2007) and *The European Union and global capitalism: Origins, development, crisis* (2017). See www.kcl.ac.uk/sspp/departments/european-studies/people/staff/academic/rynerm.aspx and www.researchgate.net/profile/Magnus_Ryner.

Juan Ignacio Staricco is a postdoctoral fellow at the Management Institute of the School of Economics (National University of Córdoba) and Argentina's National Scientific and Technical Research Council. His current research employs international political economy perspectives – combining contributions from the Amsterdam School, the regulation approach and the international food regimes literature – to critically examine the capacity of voluntary forms of governance to advance the agri-food sector in the direction of social, economic and environmental sustainability. See https://cordoba.academia.edu/JuanIgnacioStaricco and www.researchgate.net/profile/Juan_Staricco.

Javier Vadell is Adjunct Professor at the Department of International Relations of the Pontifical Catholic University of Minas Gerais, PUC Minas, Brazil. He is also Visiting Professor at the National University of Rosario, Argentina, and Professor of International Relations at the State University of Paraíba. Vadell serves as Coordinator of the Middle Powers Research Group at PUC Minas. His research interests include international political economy, South American international relations, political and economic integration, Mercosur and Unasur, BRICS and emerging powers, Chinese social and economic development and China–Latina American relations. See http://portal.pucminas.br/pos/ri/index-link.php?arquivo=docente&pagina=4198&id=112&PHPSESSID=1ccf831d2be7fda81c6a7a1ea9a7417c, https://pucminas.academia.edu/JavierVadell and www.researchgate.net/profile/Javier_Vadell2.

xviii Contributors

Angela Wigger is Associate Professor of Global Political Economy at the Institute of Management Research at the Radboud University Nijmegen. Angela specializes in the transnational political economy of the European Union with a special focus on competition, industrial policy and debt-led accumulation patterns from a critical (historical-materialist) perspective. Her most recent research focuses on the global economic crisis, crisis responses and power configurations regarding political resistance. The European Union's 'competitiveness' fetish, the issue of debt and how the 2008- crisis is (de)politicized constitutes a focal point. Angela Wigger co-authored *The politics of European competition regulation: A critical political economy approach* (with Hubert Buch-Hansen, 2011) and publishes widely in leading journals. Her research can be accessed at www.ru.nl/personen/wigger-a/, https:// radboud.academia.edu/AngelaWigger and www.researchgate.net/profile/Angela_ Wigger.

FOREWORD

Gerd Junne

The Amsterdam School took shape in the last decade of the Cold War, when the East–West conflict no longer dominated all aspects of international relations and their study. The 1970s saw a fast process of European integration, which formed the background for the study of integration and disintegration in the world system. This became a prominent theme in the Amsterdam School, which, in a time of heated Brexit discussions, is as actual now as it was when the groundwork of the Amsterdam School was laid down in the 1980s. Thus, inspired by Kees van der Pijl's work on the making of an Atlantic ruling class, Henk Overbeek analysed the development of Britain's political economy after the United Kingdom's entry into the European Community and its shaping over decades by financial capital. Similarly, Otto Holman researched the struggle within Spain about whether to join the Common Market and, later, extended his work to Eastern and Central Europe. Some arguments in contemporary Europe seem to be replaying these debates.

Ries Bode's earlier developed notion of a 'comprehensive concept of control', which is at the heart of his chapter in this volume, was a first step in elaborating what became a shared neo-Gramscian approach. When I joined the University of Amsterdam in 1979, it was easy for me to blend in, given the similarities with discussions in which I took part in the early 1970s in Berlin. These concerned the *Herrschaftssynthese* of dominant social forces that coalesce around a common approach to prevailing challenges in the international system. This concept denotes a synthesis of structural processes and strategic orientations that create and sustain a specific mode of intra and international integration that link different formally sovereign national states into a hegemonic configuration. During the 1980s there was a clear trend for studies focused on European and Atlantic affairs to expand into wider studies of the 'world system'. Robert W. Cox's analysis of *Production, power, and world order* became a crucial source for many critical scholars here, including those in Amsterdam. Kees van der Pijl's distinction between a Lockean heartland and a Hobbesian periphery also proved to have more explanatory power than the usual categories of centre and periphery. More generally, the Amsterdam School's early study of transnational class formation transcended the classical distinction between international relations and domestic politics. Globalization was not regarded as a natural force. Instead, the dominant actors driving this process forward were studied assiduously.

Globalization has continued since then. However, the fast globalization in the past decades has unleashed a dialectical reaction that Amsterdam School authors fully recognized at the time. Globalization has increased inequality within societies around the world. It also accelerated technological development, which has strengthened this effect. For, while most of the better educated with higher incomes in urban agglomerations have benefitted from globalization, those with less education and lower incomes in more peripheral areas did not see similar improvement in their situation. While social mobility was relatively high in the immediate post-war decades, it has declined since the turn of the century. The resulting backlash to globalization and the rise of 'identity politics' is largely a class-based reaction.

Today, as in the 1970s and 1980s, a hegemonial struggle is occurring between the 'concepts of control' of protagonists of a neo-liberal world order and a conglomerate of challenging forces – although the main actors on each side have changed somewhat. At governmental level, the most important switch has been that of the Chinese government. It has become a crucial supporter of free world markets, though it is setting up its own alternative set of less liberal international institutions. Conversely, the US government has become a less reliable defender of the neo-liberal order. The end of the hegemony of the US has been announced for decades. But this is reminiscent of Mark Twain's remark that 'reports of my death have been greatly exaggerated'. With politics in the US polarized and often paralysed, the main power no longer lies with government but, increasingly, with the large tech companies. Companies like Google and Facebook know more about billions of citizens around the world than any secret service, and knowledge is power. 'Information capital' can be seen as a new capital fraction that did not exist in this way two decades ago. The most influential tech companies are still American, though their Chinese counterparts like Baidu, Alibaba and Tencent are quickly catching up. Together, these companies probably have contributed more to transnational class formation than any other previous social force. Likewise, at the level of political parties and civil society, quite dramatic shifts have also taken place. A few decades ago, leftist parties were the most important challengers of the neo-liberal order. Right-wing populist movements have now largely assumed this role.

So, while the protagonists of competing concepts of world order have changed, the questions raised by the authors of the Amsterdam School and their distinctive analytical concepts retain their heuristic power in structuring the analysis of the dialectics of national politics and international relations. This makes re-reading the earlier work inspiring and is likely to provoke new questions and new challenges.

ORIGINAL SOURCES AND ACKNOWLEDGEMENTS

Chapter 1: Ries Bode (1979). De Nederlandse bourgeoisie tussen de twee wereldoorlogen. *Cahiers voor de politieke en sociale wetenschappen* 2(4): 9–50.★

Chapter 2: Kees van der Pijl (1979). Class formation at the international level. *Capital & Class* 9(Autumn): 1–21. (Permission granted by SAGE.)

Chapter 3: Henk Overbeek (1980). Finance capital and the crisis in Britain. *Capital & Class* 11(Summer): 99–120. (Permission granted by SAGE.)

Chapter 4: Meindert Fennema (1982). The international corporate elite. In Meindert Fennema, *International networks of banks and industry* (pp. 83–102). The Hague: Martinus Nijhoff. (Permission granted by Springer.)

Chapter 5: Bastiaan van Apeldoorn (2000). Transnational class agency and European governance: The case of the European round table of industrialists. *New Political Economy* 5(2): 157–81. (Permission granted by T&F.)

Chapter 6: Otto Holman (2004). Asymmetrical regulation and multidimensional governance in the European Union. *Review of International Political Economy* 11 (4): 714–35. (Permission granted by T&F.)

Referencing practice in the reprinted articles has been left unchanged from the original.

★ The editors thank Pascal van Opzeeland for translating the article by Ries Bode.

Note on spelling of author names

Throughout this book, the editors have chosen to follow Dutch practice when spelling and alphabetically ordering author names. Therefore, for instance, Kees van der Pijl is referred to as van der Pijl, not Van der Pijl; in the lists of references following each chapter, he is ranked under the P, not under the V.

ABBREVIATIONS

AC	Asian Consensus
AKU	Algemene Kunstzijde Unie (General Artificial Silk Union)
AMUE	Association for Monetary Union of Europe
AP	Amsterdam Project
ARP	Anti-Revolutionaire Partij (Anti-Revolutionary Party)
AS	Amsterdam School
BRIC	Brazil, Russia, India, China
CAG	Competitiveness Advisory Group
CCC	comprehensive concept of control
CEO	chief executive officer
CHU	Christelijk-Historische Unie (Christian Historical Union)
CPE	critical political economy
EC	European Commission
ECJ	European Court of Justice
EEC	European Economic Community
EMU	Economic and Monetary Union
EU	European Union
ERT	European Roundtable of Industrialists
GATT	General Agreement on Tariffs and Trade
IPE	International Political Economy (as discipline)
IR	International Relations (as discipline)
LAC	Latin America and the Caribbean
MLG	multi-level governance
MPS	Mont Pèlerin Society
NATO	North Atlantic Treaty Organization
NHM	Nederlandse Handel-Maatschappij (Dutch Trading Company)

NOT	Nederlandse Overzee Trustmaatschappij (Dutch Overseas Trust Society)
NUM	Nederlandse Uitvoermaatschappij (Dutch Export Society)
RKWV	Rooms-Katholiek Werkgeversvereniging (Roman Catholic Employers Association)
RPV	reproductive, productive, and virtual
TCC	transnational capitalist class
THM	transnational historical materialism
TNC	transnational corporation
VB	Vrijheidsbond (Freedom League)
VNF	Verbond van Nederlandse Fabrikantenverenigingen (Dutch Manufacturers' Association)
VNW	Vereniging van Nederlandse Werkgevers (Dutch Employers' Union)
WWI	World War I
WWII	World War II

INTRODUCTION – POLITICAL ECONOMY, CAPITAL FRACTIONS, TRANSNATIONAL CLASS FORMATION

Revisiting the Amsterdam School

Henk Overbeek

Why this book?

The RIPE Series in Global Political Economy celebrates its twentieth anniversary in 2018. The series was created and – during its first five years – edited by three scholars based at the University of Amsterdam: Marianne Marchand, Otto Holman, and Henk Overbeek (later joined by Marianne Franklin). The first title in the series was *Transnational Classes and International Relations* by Kees van der Pijl (1998), one of the founding members of what was known as the Amsterdam School (AS). Most of its erstwhile authors are still active, and their work continues to provoke debate (e.g. Staricco 2016; Jessop and Sum 2017).

The AS emerged from the Department of International Relations at the University of Amsterdam in the 1970s. Its most distinctive contribution was the systematic incorporation of the Marxian concept of *capital fractions* into the study of international politics. Politics in advanced capitalist countries, as the AS has argued, occurs in a fundamentally transnationalized space in which the distinction between 'domestic' and 'international' has blurred. In this transnational space, politics is structured by competing *comprehensive concepts of control*, or hegemonic projects, formed around the fundamental interests of specific configurations of class fractions that successfully claim to represent the *general interest*. The emergence and further development of this paradigm has been recounted at several moments by its protagonists as well as by some outsiders keen on putting the AS in its place in the critical political economy landscape (see in particular van der Pijl 1998: 1–6; Overbeek 2000, 2004; van Apeldoorn 2004a; Jessop 1990; Jessop and Sum 2005; Sum and Jessop 2013).

The purpose of this book is not to repeat this exercise. Rather, the objective is threefold:

2 Henk Overbeek

1. Provide a new generation of critical scholars an opportunity to become acquainted at first hand with some of the most representative contributions that have shaped the work of the AS (Chapters 1–6).
2. Present critical commentaries, discussing the merits and shortcomings of the AS from a variety of perspectives (Chapters 7–19).
3. Undertake a (self-)critical evaluation of the current place and value of the AS framework in the broader landscape of approaches to the study of contemporary capitalism (this introduction and Chapters 20 and 21).

First, the selection of original contributions constitutes a unique collection of papers. Although most are easily obtained by those with access to the electronic collections of university libraries, not all of them are. Moreover, the foundational article by Ries Bode (Chapter 1) is being made available in English for the first time, nearly 40 years after it appeared in Dutch.[1]

Second, the set of commentaries provides not only a sobering reminder of the weaknesses in the approach but also offers a particularly valuable didactic tool. Together, the commentaries evaluate the conceptual framework of the AS, its underlying ontological assumptions, its methodological strengths and weaknesses, and, finally, its empirical reach. These appraisals are clearly and eloquently formulated and eminently display what constructive academic critique must involve: the critical interrogation of meta-theoretical assumptions, theoretical blind spots and omissions, methodological rigour, reliability of empirical statements, and validity of conclusions.

Third, after over 40 years it is clearly necessary to ask what has become of the 'School' after all these years and to ponder the continuing relevance of the AS's conceptual framework.

The place of the Amsterdam School[2]

When we go back to the early days, i.e. to the second half of the 1970s (see especially Chapters 1–4), it is obvious that the thinking of those making up the group, all working at the time at the Department of International Relations at the University of Amsterdam, was firmly based in the Marxist tradition: starting with Marxist theories of imperialism (Rudolf Hilferding, Rosa Luxemburg, Nikolai Bukharin, Vladimir Lenin, Leon Trotsky), (re)turning to the classic texts by Karl Marx and Friedrich Engels and simultaneously relating to the revival of Marxism taking place in the West in the late 1960s and 1970s. As recounted elsewhere (Overbeek 2000, 2004), the group engaged with the various debates waging in Western Marxism at the time, which often echoed divisions in the earlier debates of the 1910s (see below for details). These debates gradually sharpened the understanding of capital as an inherently *transnational* force (i.e. transcending – but not obliterating – the boundaries of national spaces and polities), but also raised important questions about what its transnational character implied for the critique of political economy and political practice. In certain respects, this growing awareness resonated

Introduction: revisiting the Amsterdam School **3**

with the emergence of dependency theory and world systems theory during the same years, even if most AS scholars kept their distance from some of the more deterministic and mechanistic dimensions of world systems theory.

In the early years, into the 1980s, references to Antonio Gramsci remained very limited (for an account see Overbeek 2000: 171; 2004: 125); they were exclusively to Gramsci's famous notebook on *Americanism and Fordism* (1971: 279–318). This was no coincidence as this masterpiece foreshadowed in many ways the debate between Mandel and Poulantzas about the form and impact of the penetration of US capital into Europe. However, a fuller processing of Gramsci's thought only came later.

So, the AS was already firmly established as a distinctive approach to the study of (international) politics when the 'Gramscian turn' materialized in international political economy (IPE), most notably with the publication of Robert Cox's magnum opus (1987) and the textbook by Stephen Gill and David Law (1988). Subsequently, a period of animated exchange of ideas developed between the AS and the Toronto School,[3] leading to the widespread recognition of Amsterdam and Toronto as the two leading poles in what became increasingly referred to as Transnational Historical Materialism (THM) (Gill 1993; Overbeek 1993b, 2000).[4]

In 1990, the term 'Amsterdam School' entered the professional literature. Until then, the term had circulated as a joke (Overbeek 1993b: x) at international conferences where the Amsterdam crowd conducted an ongoing debate with its critics. In 1990, Bob Jessop and Stephen Gill each published an article in which the existence of a distinct 'Amsterdam School' was noted for the first time (Gill 1990; Jessop 1990).[5] Both identify the AS as related to the French Regulation School (subdivided by Jessop into Parisian and Grenoblois branches, together with a particular current in the Parti Communiste Français associated with Paul Boccara, its chief economist; see also Jessop's chapter in this book), as both 'schools' were driven by a concern to understand the nature of the crisis in international capitalism of the 1970s and responses thereto, including the rise of neoliberalism.

From 2000 onwards, THM came to be partly subsumed under the newly coined term Critical IPE. The term 'critical theory' is, of course, a reference (usually implicit) to the legacy of the early *Frankfurter Schule* (Theodor Adorno, Max Horkheimer, Herbert Marcuse, and others), which was given a new lease of life by Robert Cox's oft-quoted distinction between problem solving and critical theory (Cox 1981: 128–30). Critical theory claims to combine analytical critique with a normative concern with emancipation. In line with the critique by the Frankfurt School not just of (liberal) capitalism but equally of (Soviet) Marxism, contemporary critical theory is no longer exclusively (if at all) based on classical Marxism. Rather, as Alan Cafruny (2016) notes, it draws its inspiration from such diverse sources as social constructivism, feminism, and post-modernism, making the Critical IPE community much wider than either THM or AS were up to that point.

Summing up: the AS has today become one small, relatively old, member of a much bigger heterodox family of approaches to understanding the global economy. Or, alternatively formulated, AS forms part of two overlapping, internally nested

4 Henk Overbeek

sets of approaches, the one being 'Marxism', the other being 'Critical IPE', where the subfamily THM constitutes the bridge between the two sets.

Does the Amsterdam School qualify as a school?

Let us now briefly address the question whether the AS can really be considered a proper school. If we search the internet with the term 'Amsterdam School', we do not immediately end up on the websites of the University of Amsterdam or the Vrije Universiteit Amsterdam. Instead, we encounter the following reference: 'The Amsterdam School is a style of architecture that arose from 1910 through about 1930 in the Netherlands. The Amsterdam School movement is part of international Expressionist architecture, sometimes linked to German Brick Expressionism.'[6] So, in the greater scheme of things, the AS existed but has nothing to do with global political economy (cf. Horn and Wigger, Chapter 15, this volume).

This apart, returning to (social) science, what constitutes a school of thought,[7] and what determines its success both in terms of following and over time?

The intellectual specificity of the Amsterdam School

McKinley et al. (1999) identified three determining factors for the consolidation of a school: *novelty, continuity*, and *scope*. Everything begins with the novel ideas proposed, the distinctiveness of the concepts and propositions expounded, the shared intellectual history. For a body of thought to be possibly considered a school, its theoretical contribution must be original and innovative, relatively coherent, and built on an intellectual heritage shared by the putative members of the school.

On this criterion, a good case can be made for considering the AS a school. Let me explain.

Firstly, in the early years, the group of scholars seen as belonging to it (Bode, Fennema, Holman, Overbeek, van der Pijl) was close-knit: all started working in the University of Amsterdam Department of International Relations and International Law in the mid-1970s (Fennema soon moved to the sister Department of Political Science; Bode left academia in 1979–80; Holman joined the department as a teaching assistant in 1983).

Secondly, all started out from a shared philosophical and theoretical heritage, namely classical Marxism, as indicated above. Thus, in the early work (see, in particular, Chapters 1–4) we see clear influences of Marx (emphasizing the ontological primacy of class and social relations of production over states), Marx and Hilferding (the focus on capital fractions and particularly on finance capital in its various manifestations), Luxemburg and Lenin (as more general proponents of classical theories of imperialism), and, somewhat later, Gramsci (especially in the thinking about hegemony and 'comprehensive concepts of control').

Thirdly, this common framework was gradually extended by the incorporation of more recent debates in the Marxist tradition: the debate between Ralph Miliband, Nicos Poulantzas, and Louis Althusser on the nature of the state in capitalism; the debate between, among others, Ernest Mandel, Johan Galtung, and Poulantzas on the nature of the European Community and its relationship to the US; theoretical and empirical work in Germany (Claudia von Braunmühl, Klaus Busch, Christian Deubner, Christel Neusüß), France (Christian Palloix, Wladimir Andreff), and the UK (Robin Murray) on the internationalization of capital; the character of the most recent phase of capitalism (Paul Baran and Paul Sweezy, Mandel, and others); the Parisian Regulation School (in the first place Michel Aglietta and Alain Lipietz); the debates around dependency and world systems theories (in particular Andre Gunder Frank and Immanuel Wallerstein); and finally the work of Robert Cox and his close associate for many years, Stephen Gill.

Fourthly, the early AS developed a coherent – albeit emerging and therefore necessarily incomplete and unstable – set of concepts, grounded in the (neo-) Marxist tradition elaborated above: capital fractions, fractions of the bourgeoisie, comprehensive concepts of control, hegemony, transnational ruling class, and Lockean heartland versus Hobbesian contenders.[8]

Fifthly, this framework was fruitfully applied to three well-defined, broad, (and interrelated) empirical domains: first, European integration; second, transnational (ruling) class formation and transnational relations; and, third, the critique of neo-liberalism (see the Appendix to this chapter for references to the main AS publications, and Chapter 21).

Finally, the AS applied and partly developed little used or new research methods. Several members engaged in forms of network analysis (especially in the form of the analysis of interlocking directorates), with Fennema becoming a leading contributor to the further development of the theory, methodology, and software for Social Network Analysis (see Chapter 19 by Heemskerk in this volume). Some years later, Holman and then van Apeldoorn introduced the use of elite interviewing in their work on the European Roundtable of Industrialists. Together, these two research methods, though by no means unique to the AS, definitely solidified the empirical basis of the AS (though not to the degree that several of the critical commentaries below would have considered desirable or even necessary).

However, intellectual specificity, theoretical innovation, and empirical productivity are not enough to seriously speak of a *theoretical school*.

What would make the AS into a true theoretical school?

For a school of thought to become established and serve as a reference point in ongoing debates, more is needed. McKinley et al. (1999) identified two further determining factors for the consolidation of a school in addition to novelty: *continuity* and *scope*.

Firstly, there must be *continuity*: for the new ideas to appeal to growing numbers of scholars in the field, they must not stray too far from established conceptions. Otherwise, the would-be school runs the danger of being seen as an oddity, and then marginalized. Further, the school must have sufficient *scope* – it must encompass a wide range of phenomena to be able to generate ample empirical studies building

6 Henk Overbeek

up the body of thought comprising the school. If we hold up the record of the AS against these criteria, we may conclude that, while the AS scores well in terms of scope, it has largely failed the criterion of continuity. This can be partly attributed to the choices made by the AS in the early years. By adopting an explicitly Marxist frame, and deeply critiquing established theoretical approaches in European integration studies and more generally in IR and IPE, the AS arguably placed itself so far outside the mainstream that continuity had become impossible.

However, whether a body of thought can develop into a school depends on more than its content. Whether a particular position is too far outside the mainstream as to preclude some minimal continuity also hinges, of course, on the attitude of mainstream scholars themselves, and on more abstract institutional and structural factors. This extension was proposed by Ofori-Dankwa and Julian (2005) in their reaction to McKinley et al. They argue that context-based factors are equally influential, especially the reputation and scholarly audience of the main publication outlets, the reputation and persistence of the theory's originators, and the reputation and institutional back-up of the university of origin. Now, of course each of these factors strongly interacts with and depends on the content-based factors identified by McKinley et al. The selection of publication outlets is not a free choice but also very much depends on the selection criteria imposed by leading journals and publishing houses. Equally, whether an author can be persistent in a negative or possibly even hostile institutional environment is highly questionable, if that means being mostly shut out from research funding and career perspectives.

Likewise, the level of support that the university gives scholars is determined not only by available resources or the reputation and persistence of the scholars but also by the biases and perceptions of the university authorities in question. It is here that the AS encountered severe obstacles that made it very difficult to consolidate as a school in a friendly and supportive institutional context. This became especially clear with the acceleration of neoliberal reforms in the Dutch university system starting in the early 1990s, with the concomitant pressure to produce 'normal science' in an increasingly 'professionalized' institutional setting.[9] In the same vein, the so-called mainstream in IPE has largely ignored critical IPE (including Robert Cox), and completely snubbed the AS.[10]

Other determinants of school formation may be identified. One is the degree to which the original thought of the school is consolidated and reproduced through solid institutional foundations and the development of its own textbook(s), journals, and book series. A second determinant would be reproduction through the proliferation of new generations of scholars who identify with the school, through PhD training or otherwise.

Regarding the first, during the 1980s and early 1990s, the AS seemed to be on its way to consolidation. It was becoming increasingly productive, and a growing number of scholars identified with the core concepts of the AS (see for instance Overbeek 1993a). In April 1990, it organized a major international conference (*After the Crisis*) with Robert Cox as the keynote speaker, and with some two dozen prominent participants. It also for some years published two working paper series (*Amsterdam International Studies* and *After the Crisis*) and created the Research Centre for International Political Economy (RECIPE) offering a post-graduate MPhil degree. The creation of RECIPE briefly held the promise of creating the right environment for attracting high-calibre talent interested in seriously engaging with AS scholars.[11] Additionally, the link with York University brought some promising post-doc researchers to Amsterdam, all of whom made a major contribution to the intellectual climate in the department before moving on to successful academic careers.[12]

But, as indicated above, by the mid-1990s, conditions gradually changed. There were several factors involved here.

First, the end of the Cold War fundamentally changed the room for manoeuvre for Marxist scholarship in Western academia. Communism, and Marxism with it, was radically discredited in public opinion but also within the academic world, where this change of climate was reinforced by the effects of the rise of New Public Management in university administrations. In the University of Amsterdam, this process led to the merger of the Department of International Relations with the Departments of Political Science and of Public Administration into one big Department of Political Science and the forced amalgamation of RECIPE into the much bigger faculty-wide graduate school.

The deteriorated climate also led to worsening interpersonal relations within the department. In the end, Henk Overbeek left for the Vrije Universiteit in 1999 and Kees van der Pijl went to Sussex University in 2000.

With hindsight, we can say that these developments effectively led to the demise of the AS as a true group, small as it was. The lack of daily contact and the pressures of diverse institutional environments led over time to a considerable weakening of the sense of common identity. Also, the situation with respect to the recruitment and training of doctoral students stood in the way of an effective reproduction through that channel. First, there were then and remain today very few funding opportunities for PhD students, especially if funding is sought for critical projects. And, second, the extremely hierarchical Dutch system where only full professors are officially authorized to serve as PhD supervisors made it difficult for the AS members to attract PhD students interested in engaging with the group's theoretical work.[13]

By the start of the new millennium, the AS was thus clearly in decline in institutional terms. In this sense, the special issue of *Journal of International Relations and Development* that Bastiaan van Apeldoorn edited (2004b) might perhaps be read as the de facto obituary for the school. The individual scholars had gradually moved on to other empirical topics, incorporating other theoretical perspectives into their work and becoming more eclectic in their theoretical profile.[14]

However, the gradual disappearance of a localized, institutionalized 'school' – in which the founding thoughts are continuously being codified and further developed through a process of generational reproduction – need not imply the loss of interpretive and explanatory power of the original conceptual framework. To recognize this one needs only to consider the focus on the strategic divisions within the

8 Henk Overbeek

transnational ruling class; on the variations in terms of relative power positions of different fractions across countries and across macro-regions; on the dialectical interplay between the ebb and flow of the power struggles between rival ruling class fractions, the dynamics of capital accumulation on a world scale, and the evolving geo-political power relations between the Lockean heartland of capitalism and Hobbesian challengers.[15] These foci continue to produce a distinctive and very fruitful perspective on the contemporary global (geo-)political economy, as is exemplified in this volume by the new chapter by Kees van der Pijl (Chapter 20).

Structure of this book

In Part I, we present six original papers, published in the years 1979–2004. As explained at the beginning of this introduction, one of the motives for putting together this volume was the desire to provide a platform for the publication of an English translation of Bode's paper on Dutch politics in the 1930s and 1940s that, to most readers of AS work, must have appeared obscure and inaccessible in the best of cases (Chapter 1). However, Ries Bode made a decisive contribution by coining the term 'comprehensive concept of control', with which he provided a conceptual tool to analytically bridge the gap between structure and agency, or more precisely, between the structural sphere of capital accumulation and the agential sphere of political practice and ideological struggle. In addition to the notion of 'capital fraction' (which derives from the second volume of Marx's *Das Kapital*), he also introduced the concept of 'fraction of the bourgeoisie'. This conceptual couplet embodies the same duality of structure and agency, capital fraction referring to the position of specific groups of individual capitals in the overall process of reproduction of capital, and fraction of the bourgeoisie referring to configurations of interest groups and political forces that coalesce around broad political programmes transcending simple party lines: comprehensive concepts of control.

These insights, developed by Bode in his account of the development of interbellum politics in the Netherlands, were taken up and fine-tuned by van der Pijl and Overbeek in their *Capital & Class* papers (Chapters 2 and 3). These two papers were also the product of the same collective research and teaching programme initiated a few years earlier. Together they clarify how this project had moved from the analysis of political and economic developments in selected European countries in the 1930s–1950s, to the analysis of how these 'national' developments were embedded in broader dynamics at the transatlantic level. They also make clear how the thinking about what 'comprehensive concepts of control' were advanced: in particular, the distinction between the two ideal-typical forms (the money capital concept and the productive capital concept) enables us to structure the range of real-life 'concepts of control' that are put forward and pushed to become truly comprehensive and hegemonic. In both cases, we can discern in these early papers the first contours of the doctoral dissertations and then revised book-length publications that resulted from these efforts (i.e. van der Pijl 1984 and Overbeek 1990).

Chapter 4 contains a key chapter from the dissertation by Meindert Fennema. As recounted above, because Meindert moved on very early to new areas of research, notably political participation by immigrant groups and the nature of right-wing nationalist parties, both nationally and from an international comparative perspective, he was never considered as a member of the AS. Nevertheless, his inclusion in this volume is warranted for two related reasons. First, Fennema and the other 'first generation' AS scholars closely interacted during the early formative years, as is clearly seen from the cross-references, e.g. in Bode and van der Pijl. There was a clear process of mutual influence. Second, Fennema became one of the scholars laying the foundations for what has since then developed into an advanced branch of empirical research methodology making extensive use of computer-aided techniques for the analysis of social networks (see also the commentaries by Carroll, de Graaff, and Heemskerk). Chapter 4 presents the early foundations of this research line which has continued throughout the years to inspire AS thinking as well as recruiting a new generation of scholars.

Finally, Chapters 5 and 6 present two representative papers that exemplify the continued productiveness of the early focus on the sources of European integration. Bastiaan van Apeldoorn, building on work he undertook together with his master thesis supervisor, Otto Holman, focused his doctoral research on the role of the European Roundtable of Industrialists in breaking the impasse in the progress of the European integration process since the so-called empty-chair crisis of 1965 through launching the Internal Market programme in the mid-1980s. Otto Holman's well-known early contribution to the work of the AS concerned the analysis of the European Union (EU)'s southern enlargement in the 1980s, later followed by his work on the eastern big bang enlargement during the 2000s (cf. Bieler and Morton as well as Bohle in this volume). The second strand in his work concerned, and continues to concern, the contradictory relationship between the neoliberal nature of socio-economic regulation and the deficient quality of democratic governance in the EU. Holman's 2004 article reprinted here is remarkably prophetic in its astute analysis of the contradictions in the EU architecture which were later acutely brought to the surface under the impact of the global financial crisis from 2008.

In Part II, we bring together 13 commentaries by 18 authors. All contributors were invited to reflect on the strengths and weaknesses of the AS as they saw fit. For a variety of personal reasons, four of those initially invited had to bow out; later we invited one further contribution. The selection provides a balance between established scholars and young and rising ones. Additionally, we attempted (but succeeded only partially) to secure a gender balance and to include scholars from outside the circle of 'usual suspects'. During the editorial process we have pushed the authors to clarify their arguments, but in the end the authors were left free to present their arguments in the way they thought best. Taken together, the commentaries provide a broad range of viewpoints, inviting the reader to assess for themselves how credible the concerns are, and how serious they should be taken.

Several themes run through the commentaries, surfacing in different forms in multiple contributions. They often echo themes that have been raised in the past

10 Henk Overbeek

but also raise new issues, especially where it relates to emerging new trends in the global political economy.

A first theme raises *ontological concerns*. Several contributors signal that AS work is typically too elite-oriented and call for more explicit incorporation of the role of subaltern forces and of social and political resistance (Bieler and Morton, Bohle, and Horn and Wigger). Others criticize the almost total neglect by AS authors of the role of gender and of race/ethnicity alongside class in the structuring of politics (Horn and Wigger, and Marchand). Marianne Marchand develops this point most comprehensively by arguing for the necessity of taking the literature on inter-sectionality seriously.

A second theme combines numerous comments on the *substantive focus* of the AS, and the need to encompass phenomena and dynamics that are key to the global political economy but are underdeveloped or even absent in AS work. Several authors point out that the AS has too little to offer on the subject of emerging right-wing nationalism and populism (in particular Bohle and Bieling). Bieling argues that the current crisis tendencies reveal both inherent and contingent limits of neoliberalism even in its core region. According to Bieling this would necessitate more emphasis on contradictions and hegemonic struggles in national settings of capitalism and on the new discursive cleavage between neoliberal cosmopolitanism and nationalist populism within the Lockean heartland. We may also place Carroll's observation that the ongoing climate crisis is not getting enough attention in the same category. A second set of comments in this category deals with the overemphasis in the work of the AS on the Lockean heartland, and the neglect of the role of Hobbesian contender states (Bieling, de Graaff). In particular, it is argued by several contributors that the AS urgently needs to pay more attention to the rise of China as a contender state, and do more empirical and theoretical work on this (Bai, Ramos and Vadell, de Graaff). Other themes that are identified as in need of more attention in the work of the AS are the theory of uneven and combined development and its understanding of the relationship between emerging capitalism and the pre-existing state system (Bieler and Morton), and the particular form of the asymmetric power relation between the US and Europe, or rather between leading US corporate capital and European capital (Cafruny and Ryner).

A third cluster of comments deals with *theoretical and methodological issues*. Several authors are of the opinion that the AS suffers from, or is in danger of suffering from, a closed mind or a lack of openness towards new theoretical contributions in the broader field of critical IPE (Bieler and Morton, Heemskerk, Horn and Wigger, Knafo). A related concern is that the AS's theoretical framework assumes too much coherence in ruling class politics, and leaves too little room for detailed attention to the local, to politics 'on the ground' (Bieler and Morton, Bohle, de Graaff, Horn and Wigger, Knafo). Samuel Knafo places this latter comment in the context of his view that the AS has missed, or risks missing, the Historical Turn and imputes too much explanatory power to its abstract theoretical framework, where more detailed analysis of the concrete, and largely contingent, historical process would be called for. Finally, several commentators argue that the AS has neglected the use of more rigorous empirical social science research techniques to back up its theoretically derived claims. Thus, de Graaff, Heemskerk, and Buch-Hansen and Staricco argue that the AS framework lends itself to much more serious use of Social Network Analysis. Buch-Hansen and Staricco put this call in the context of their plea for more explicit engagement by the AS with the literature of critical realism to strengthen its meta-theoretical reflexivity.

Finally, Part III offers two original contributions from within (Kees van der Pijl) and from the 'near abroad' (Bob Jessop).

Kees van der Pijl analyses the contemporary condition of global capitalism, investigating how the original ideas of the AS can still inspire original and stimulating insights into the workings of our social system. Taking the post-crisis period as his starting point, van der Pijl revisits the AS theory of neoliberalism, and reformulates and refines it in light of the post-2008 experience. The future of neoliberalism was widely expected to be short-lived as the financial crisis seemed to embody the bankruptcy of the finance-led accumulation model that had brought financial capital to the apex of the global power structure. However, restoration was swift and neoliberalism has since regained its dominant position, if not its hegemony. In vintage AS style, van der Pijl argues that underneath the surface the financial crisis has brought out into the open an important shift (which had its roots in the early 1990s when the Soviet Union collapsed) in terms of the fraction of capital directing the renovated neoliberal concept of control. Whereas neoliberalism Mark I – dubbed *systemic neoliberalism* by van der Pijl – was directed by a coalition of asset-owning middle classes and top management, interested first of all in radical deregulation of all constraints on production (labour markets, state support, capital controls), a shift occurred from the 1990s with the full liberalization of financial markets, bringing to power money-dealing capital (or speculative capital invested in financial assets), cementing its own concept of control, neoliberalism Mark II, which van der Pijl characterizes as *predatory neoliberalism*. Supported by a wealth of evidence, van der Pijl traces the ascendancy of money-dealing capital, analysing the sombre perspectives of the increasingly authoritarian and rapacious mode of accumulation as it has emerged over the past two decades.

Bob Jessop, finally, explores the particular contribution of the AS to the field of critical political economy, both in its original form of the late 1970s and in its current manifestations. He begins by situating the AS in four fields of literature: the field of regulation theories (Jessop's 1990 article cited above pioneered this perspective); the field of European integration studies (the origin of the AS at the University of Amsterdam in the 1970 and 1980s); the more recent field of THM (sometimes equated with neo-Gramscianism); and, finally, the field of approaches to neoliberalism. Subsequently, Jessop highlights a number of distinctive theoretical and methodological features of the work of the AS. Finally, Jessop surveys the prospects for the development of new avenues of research and theory building within, but innovatively extending, the fundamental framework of the AS.

Notes

1 In fact, the insistence by Bob Jessop that Bode's article be made available to English-reading audiences first gave rise to the idea to produce what eventually became this book.
2 This section inevitably shows overlap with Bob Jessop's chapter (Chapter 21). However, this need not be problematic. First, returning to some of these thoughts after having gone through the main body of the book can only be productive for the reader. But, second, each of us presents a different perspective, influenced by our respective intellectual trajectories (namely, state theory and International Relations) towards IPE, where our interpretations are moreover inevitably coloured by the fact that Jessop looks at these issues as an outside observer while I have been an active participant.
3 Stephen Gill moved from Wolverhampton Polytechnic to York University in Toronto, the home base of Robert Cox, in 1990. In the early 1990s, several University of Amsterdam master students spent a semester studying as exchange students at York. Among them was Bastiaan van Apeldoorn.
4 In his comprehensive textbook, Knud Erik Jørgensen distinguishes three schools within 'Marxist IPE', namely the Amsterdam School, the Toronto School, and the World Systems Theory School (2010: 138–9). While several comments could be made on this taxonomy, constraints of space and focus allow just one: both Cox and Wallerstein have consciously avoided self-identifying as 'Marxists'. But here they are in the company of none other than Karl Marx himself, who once commented that 'all I know is that I am not a Marxist' (quoted in Engels 1890).
5 In all, Google Scholar (accessed 15 January 2018) gives a total of 178 hits for the combination 'Amsterdam School' and 'van der Pijl', showing a gradually increasing frequency of usage of the term. Only 3 per cent (six to be precise) are self-references.
6 https://en.wikipedia.org/wiki/Amsterdam_School; for more on this jewel of social-democratic emancipation: www.amsterdam.info/architecture/amsterdam-school/
7 In these pages I disagree with Adam Morton (2001; see also his contribution with Andreas Bieler to this volume), who regards the formation of 'schools' as a threat to open dialogue and creative thinking and therefore rejects any tendency towards school formation. As the following pages will make clear, to the extent that the AS was ever on the way to becoming a school, it was never intended to become and, indeed, never became the kind of mentally closed shop envisaged by Morton. As the key contributions in Part I already indicate, the core members have somewhat different theoretical positions, research interests, and sources of inspiration and engage in open dialogue with other currents in International Relations (IR) and IPE. Likewise, their 'pupils' do not explicitly identify with the AS label nor, given their commitment to fruitful exchange and mutual critique as well as recognition of the embeddedness of academic research in wider social contexts, would the 'masters' have attempted to force them to do so.
8 For fuller representations of the AS framework, refer to earlier overviews, e.g. Overbeek and van der Pijl 1993; van Apeldoorn 2004a; Overbeek 2000, 2004.
9 I discussed this theme both in my inaugural lecture (2005) and farewell lecture (2014).
10 As illustrated in Overbeek 2000: 169, 181n.
11 To be clear, although we definitively entertained illusions of greatness, all the activities referred to here were always conceived and undertaken in a spirit of openness and inclusiveness, as can be seen from the range of participants and the subsequent academic careers of the post-graduate students.
12 These post-docs were André Drainville, Hélène Pellerin, and Magnus Ryner.
13 The legal requirement of full professorship to qualify for PhD supervision was only lifted from 2018.
14 By the end of the 1980s, Fennema had completely turned to political theory and to the study of right-wing parties and of ethnic political participation, in which field he gained a chair in 2002. Van der Pijl became full professor when appointed at Sussex in 2000; Overbeek was promoted to full professor at the Vrije Universiteit in 2004. Holman was never granted promotion to full professor. In the end, only van Apeldoorn, a former

master student at the University of Amsterdam, identified fully with the AS. He took his PhD at the European University Institute in Florence, where Colin Crouch was his main supervisor, and joined the Vrije Universiteit Department of Political Science in 2000. Many PhD students supervised by AS members (among them several contributors to this volume: Heemskerk (Fennema), Wigger, Horn, de Graaff (Overbeek and van Apeldoorn)) are doing academic work close to the core of AS thought but, as some commentaries indicate, none identifies explicitly with the AS.

15 Such as Iran (in the Middle East), Russia (in Europe and the Middle East), and China (in East and Southeast Asia, Sub-Saharan Africa, and South America but increasingly also in Eastern Europe).

Appendix

Selected chronological list of publications by Bastiaan van Apeldoorn, Ries Bode, Meindert Fennema, Otto Holman, Henk Overbeek, and Kees van der Pijl

Included are all books, edited volumes and edited special issues, plus the first English-language journal article per author (for Bode the 1979 Dutch original of Chapter 1 in this volume).

Fennema, M. (1975). *De multinationale onderneming en de nationale staat*. Amsterdam: Socialistische Uitgeverij Amsterdam.

Fennema, M. and Schijf, H. (1978). Analysing interlocking directorates: Theory and methods. *Social Networks* 1: 297–332.

van der Pijl, K. (1978). *Een Amerikaans plan voor Europa. Achtergronden van het ontstaan van de EEG*. Amsterdam: Socialistische Uitgeverij Amsterdam.

Bode, R. (1979). De Nederlandse bourgeoisie tussen de twee wereldoorlogen. *Cahiers voor de politieke en sociale wetenschappen* 2(4): 9–50.

van der Pijl, K. (1979). Class formation at the international level: Reflections on the political economy of Atlantic unity. *Capital & Class* 3: 1–21.

Overbeek, H. (1980). Finance capital and the crisis in Britain. *Capital & Class* 11: 99–120.

Crone, F. and Overbeek, H. (Eds) (1981). *Nederlands kapitaal over de grenzen, Verplaatsing van produktie en de gevolgen voor de nationale ekonomie*. Amsterdam: SUA.

Fennema, M. (1982). *International networks of banks and industry*. The Hague/Boston, MA: Martinus Nijhoff.

Baudet, H. and Fennema, M. (1983). *Het Nederlands belang bij Indië*. Utrecht: Spectrum.

van der Pijl, K. (1983). *Marxisme en internationale politiek*. Amsterdam: Instituut voor Politiek en Sociaal Onderzoek.

van der Pijl, K. (1984). *The making of an Atlantic ruling class*. London: Verso (2nd rev. edition 2014).

Fennema, M. and van der Pijl, K. (1987). *El triunfo del neoliberalismo* (in collaboration with J. Ortega). Santo Domingo: Ediciones de Taller.

Holman, O. (1987). Semiperipheral Fordism in Southern Europe: The national and international context of socialist-led governments in Spain, Portugal and Greece, in historical perspective. *International Journal of Political Economy* 17(4): 11–55.

van der Pijl, K. (Ed.) (1989). Transnational relations and class strategy, special issue. *International Journal of Political Economy* 19(3).

Overbeek, H. (1990). *Global capitalism and national decline: The Thatcher decade in perspective.* London: Unwin Hyman.

Holman, O. (Ed.) (1992). European unification in the 1990s: Myth and reality, special issue. *International Journal of Political Economy* 22(1).

Overbeek, H. (Ed.) (1993). *Restructuring hegemony in the global political economy: The rise of transnational neo-liberalism in the 1980s.* London: Routledge.

Holman, O. (1995). *Transformatieprocessen in Midden-en Oost-Europa: De internationale dimensie.* Den Haag: Wetenschappelijke Raad voor het Regeringsbeleid.

Holman, O. (1996). *Integrating Southern Europe: EC expansion and the transnationalization of Spain.* London: Routledge.

van der Pijl, K. (1996). *Vordenker der Weltpolitik: Einführung in die internationale Politik aus ideengeschichtlicher Perspektive.* Opladen: Leske and Budrich.

Holman, O. (Ed.) (1997). *Democratie, werkgelegenheid, veiligheid, immigratie. Europese dilemma's aan het einde van de 20ste eeuw.* Amsterdam: 't Spinhuis.

Holman, O., Overbeek, H., and Ryner, M. (Eds) (1998). Neoliberal hegemony and the political economy of European restructuring (2 vols), special issue. *International Journal of Political Economy* 28(1–2).

van Apeldoorn, B. (2000). Transnational class agency and European governance: The case of the European Round Table of Industrialists. *New Political Economy* 5 (2): 157–81.

van Apeldoorn, B. (2002). *Transnational capitalism and the struggle over European integration.* London: Routledge.

Overbeek, H. (Ed.) (2003). *The political economy of European employment: European integration and the transnationalization of the (un)employment question.* London: Routledge.

van Apeldoorn, B. (Ed.) (2004). Transnational historical materialism: The Amsterdam international political economy project, special issue. *Journal of International Relations and Development* 7(2).

van der Pijl, K. (2006). *Global rivalries from the Cold War to Iraq.* London: Pluto.

Fennema, M. and Rhijnsburger, J. (2007). *Dr. Hans Max Hirschfeld. Man van het grote geld.* Amsterdam: Bert Bakker.

Overbeek, H., van Apeldoorn, B., and Nölke, A. (Eds) (2007). *The transnational politics of corporate governance regulation.* London: Routledge.

van der Pijl, K. (2007). *Nomads, empires, states: Modes of foreign relations and political economy,* vol. 1. London: Pluto.

Fennema, M. and Heemskerk, E.M. (2008). *Nieuwe netwerken. De ondergang van NV Nederland.* Amsterdam: Bert Bakker.

Overbeek, H. (2008). *Rivalität und ungleiche Entwicklung. Einführung in die internationale Politik aus der Sicht der Internationalen Politischen Ökonomie.* Wiesbaden: Verlag für Sozialwissenschaften.

van der Pijl, K. (2009). *A survey of global political economy*, available at https://libcom.org/library/survey-global-political-economy

Carroll, W.K., Carson, C., Fennema, M., Heemskerk, E., and Sapinski, J.P. (2010). *The making of a transnational capitalist class: Corporate power in the twenty-first century.* London: Zed.

van der Pijl, K. (2010). *The foreign encounter in myth and religion: Modes of foreign relations and political economy*, vol. 2. London: Pluto.

van Apeldoorn, B., de Graaff, N., and Overbeek, H. (Eds) (2012). The rebound of the capitalist state: The re-articulation of state-capital relations in the global crisis, special issue. *Globalizations* 9(4).

Nousios, P., Overbeek, H., and Tsolakis, A. (Eds) (2012). *Globalisation and European integration: Critical approaches to regional order and international relations.* London: Routledge.

Overbeek, H. and van Apeldoorn, B. (Eds) (2012). *Neoliberalism in crisis.* London: Palgrave Macmillan.

van Apeldoorn, B., de Graaff, N., and Overbeek, H. (Eds) (2014). *The state–capital nexus in the global crisis: Rebound of the capitalist state.* London: Routledge.

van der Pijl, K. (2014). *The discipline of western supremacy: Modes of foreign relations and political economy*, vol. 3. London: Pluto.

van Apeldoorn, B. and de Graaff, N. (2015). *American grand strategy and corporate elite networks: The open door and its variations since the end of the Cold War.* London: Routledge.

van der Pijl, K. (Ed.) (2015). *Handbook of the international political economy of production.* Cheltenham: Edward Elgar.

Parmar, I., van Apeldoorn, B., de Graaff, N., and Ledwidge, M. (Eds) (2017). Elites and American power, special issue. *International Politics* 54(3).

van der Pijl, K. (2018). *Flight MH17, Ukraine and the new Cold War: Prism of disaster.* Manchester, Manchester University Press. A German edition will appear as: *Der Abschuss. Flug MH 17, die Ukraine und der neue Kalte Krieg.* Köln: Papyrossa. A Brazilian-Portuese edition is under preparation.

References

Abbott, J. and Worth, O. (Eds) (2002). *Critical perspectives on international political economy.* Basingstoke: Palgrave Macmillan.

van Apeldoorn, B. (2004a). Theorizing the transnational: A historical materialist approach. *Journal of International Relations and Development* 7(2): 142–176.

van Apeldoorn, B. ed. (2004b). Transnational historical materialism: The Amsterdam International Political Economy Project. Special issue of *Journal of International Relations and Development* 7(2).

van Apeldoorn, B., Bruff, I., and Ryner, M. (2010). The richness and diversity of critical International Political Economy perspectives: Moving beyond the debate on the 'British School'. In N. Phillips and C. Weaver (Eds), *International political economy: Debating the past, present and future* (pp. 215–222). London: Routledge.

Cafruny, A. (2016). Introduction. In A. Cafruny, L.S. Talani, and G. Pozo Martin (Eds), *The Palgrave handbook of critical political economy: Theories, issues and regions* (pp. 1–6). London: Palgrave Macmillan.

Cox, R.W. (1981). Social forces, states and world orders: Beyond international relations theory. *Millennium: Journal of International Studies* 10(2): 126–155.

Cox, R.W. (1987). *Production, power and world order: Social forces in the making of history*. New York: Columbia University Press.

Engels, F. (1890). *Letter to Conrad Schmidt in Berlin*, 5 August. www.marxists.org/archive/marx/works/1890/letters/90_08_05.htm (accessed 14 January 2018).

Gill, S.R. (1990). Intellectuals and transnational capital. *Socialist Register 1990* (pp. 290–310). London: Merlin. www.socialistregister.com/index.php/srv/article/view/5584/2482#.Wlw79ksiGCQ

Gill, S.R. (Ed.) (1993). *Gramsci, historical materialism and international relations*. Cambridge: Cambridge University Press.

Gill, S.R. and Law, D. (1988). *The global political economy: Perspectives, problems and policies*. London: Harvester Wheatsheaf.

Gramsci, A. (1971). *Selections from the Prison Notebooks* (pp. 279–318). New York: International Publishers.

Jessop, B. (1990). Regulation theories in retrospect and prospect. *Economy & Society* 19(2): 153–216.

Jessop, B. and Sum, N.L. (2005). *Beyond the regulation approach: Putting the economy in its place in political economy*. Cheltenham: Edward Elgar.

Jessop, B. and Sum, N. (2017). Putting the Amsterdam School in its rightful place: A reply to Juan Ignacio Staricco's critique of cultural political economy. *New Political Economy* 73 (6): 342–353.

Jørgensen, K.E. (2010). *International relations theory: A new introduction*. Basingstoke: Palgrave Macmillan.

McKinley, W., Mone, M.A., and Moon, G. (1999). Determinants and development of schools in organization theory. *Academy of Management Review* 24(4): 634–648.

Morton, A.D. (2001). The sociology of theorising and neo-Gramscian perspectives: The problems of 'school' formation in IPE. In A. Bieler and A. D. Morton (Eds), *Social forces in the making of the 'New Europe': The restructuring of European social relations in the global political economy* (pp. 137–157). Basingstoke: Palgrave.

Ofori-Dankwa, J. and Julian, S.D. (2005). From thought to theory to school: The role of contextual factors in the evolution of schools of management thought. *Organization Studies* 26(9): 1307–1329.

Overbeek, H. (1990). *Global capitalism and national decline: The Thatcher decade in perspective*. London: Unwin Hyman.

Overbeek, H. (1993a). Preface. In H. Overbeek (Ed.), *Restructuring hegemony in the global political economy: The rise of transnational neoliberalism in the 1980s* (pp. ix–xi). London: Routledge.

Overbeek, H. (Ed.) (1993b). *Restructuring hegemony in the global political economy: The rise of transnational neoliberalism in the 1980s*. London: Routledge.

Overbeek, H. (2000). Transnational historical materialism: Theories of transnational class formation and world order. In R. Palan (Ed.), *Global political economy: Contemporary theories* (pp. 168–183). London: Routledge.

Overbeek, H. (2004). Transnational class formation and concepts of control: Notes towards a genealogy of the Amsterdam Project in international political economy. *Journal of International Relations and Development* 7(2): 113–141.

Overbeek, H. (2005). *Cultuurgoed of koopwaar? Over hoger onderwijs, globalisering en de leer der internationale betrekkingen.* Inaugural address, Vrije Universiteit Amsterdam.

Overbeek, H. (2014). *Over ongelijkheid, internationale politiek en de universiteit. Veertig jaar academische praktijk in perspectief.* Farewell lecture, Vrije Universiteit Amsterdam.

Overbeek, H. and van der Pijl, K. (1993). Restructuring capital and restructuring hegemony: Neo-liberalism and the unmaking of the post-war order. In H. Overbeek (Ed.), *Restructuring hegemony in the global political economy: The rise of transnational neoliberalism in the 1980s* (pp. 1–27). London: Routledge.

van der Pijl, K. (1984). *The making of an Atlantic ruling class.* London: Verso.

van der Pijl, K. (1998). *Transnational classes and international relations.* London: Routledge.

Shields, S., Bruff, I., and Macartney, H. (Eds) (2011). *Critical international political economy: Dialogue, debates and dissensus.* London: Palgrave Macmillan.

Staricco, J.I. (2016). Putting culture in its place? A critical engagement with cultural political economy. *New Political Economy* 22(3): 1–14.

Sum, N.L. and Jessop, B. (2013). *Towards a cultural political economy: Putting culture in its place in political economy.* Cheltenham: Edward Elgar.

PART I

The Amsterdam School

Key contributions

1

THE DUTCH BOURGEOISIE BETWEEN THE TWO WORLD WARS (1979)

Ries Bode

Introduction

This article aims to highlight the changes in domestic and foreign policy orientations within the most important segments of the Dutch ruling class during the interwar period (1918–39).[1] Careful research into such segments is especially relevant because this field has been dominated for too long by a Marxist school of thought influenced by vulgar materialism. The latter holds that bourgeois politicians, as far as they enter politics from specific enterprises, would be directly motivated by the immediate commercial interests of these enterprises. In this view, identifying the personal connections between politicians and corporations suffices to support the thesis that the state has become the instrument of specific monopolies. This so-called *Stamokap*-theory,[2] which evolved especially in the German Democratic Republic and France, has been applied to the Dutch situation by Baruch (1962).

Without excluding the possibility of direct intervention, this article assumes that the political currents[3] within the bourgeoisie, although exposed to outside influences, cannot be reduced to their importance to specific group interests. Accordingly, the article analyses changes in national and foreign policy orientation against the background of traditions associated with specific segments, because these appear to form the interpretive and calculative framework for leading politicians. The article furthermore attempts to place these changes within a global overview of developments in Dutch capitalism within the interwar period that is the focus of this study. Because, even though they are caught within their own inherited ways of thinking, different currents in the bourgeoisie must always be able, on an ideological level as well, to provide answers to the problems of the day in capital accumulation. After all, the ideational insofar as it is characteristic of a certain segment within the ruling class is an integral part of the mode of production. This does not just change simply through revolutions in production technology. Rather, a continuous process of

22 Ries Bode

change takes place, sometimes slow, other times rapid, shaking up the totality of economic, social, and cultural relations. The reorganization of production is accompanied by changes in all other aspects of this totality. This explains why the restructuring of capital must be interpreted 'not just in logical terms, but as a constant struggle of the bourgeoisie to reorganize this whole complex of social conditions in the interests of continued capital accumulation' (Holloway and Picciotto 1980: 132). Thus, any treatise on the development of capitalism or on the ideas and actions of the ruling class should allocate a central role to concrete history.

With this in mind, this article is structured as follows. The first part covers some key structural characteristics of the Dutch economic situation after World War I (WWI). The second part discusses possible theoretical distinctions regarding capital and the bourgeoisie, highlighting that between *capital fractions* and *fractions of the bourgeoisie*. It then covers various orientations within the bourgeoisie as well as their development in response to the crisis of the 1930s.

Structural changes in Dutch capitalism

War profits and reconstruction credit

WWI proved lucrative for Dutch capital. Already in April 1916, the London *Economist* estimated Dutch war profits to be around 2.4 billion Dutch guilders, judging this as 'not unsatisfactory for a nation of six million people' (cited by Smit 1975: 9).

The profits were vast indeed, especially for agricultural exporters, banks, trading companies, shipping, and colonial capital. Despite their oftentimes sharply conflicting interests, these businesses managed to jointly circumvent the British- and German-imposed limitations on deliveries from the Netherlands to the respective warring states. Food exports to Germany, for example, risked being raised to such an extent that there was a threat of famine within the Netherlands itself (Roland Holst 1971 [1932] II: 118–19).

Behind the façade of profitable neutrality, however, the government clashed with the supervising bodies that were created at the instigation of the warring parties: the Dutch Oversea Trust Society (Nederlandse Overzee Trustmaatschappij, NOT) and the Dutch Export Society (Nederlandse Uitvoermaatschappij, NUM). Within the government, an intense struggle took place over the control of the NUM between the ministers Treub and Posthuma. The former represented the pro-English shipping interests, while the latter represented the major agricultural exporters and was supported by the powerful grain trader Kröller. When Treub managed to centralize exports to Germany in the NUM, with the purpose of imposing stricter controls, Posthuma responded by redirecting control of export policies into the hands of the so-called 'Commission of Assistance to Execution of the Distribution Law 1916' (Commissie van Bijstand tot Uitvoering van de Distributiewet 1916) – and thus into the hands of none other than Kröller (Smit 1975: 33). In contrast, the NOT predominantly favoured the Allies.

The most explosive clash between pro-English and pro-German elements followed the seizure of Dutch merchant ships by the United States, which had only recently joined the war. Heldring recounts how the Cabinet, in the absence of Treub, had decided to declare war on the Allies. When Treub found out, his threats to step down combined with the unfavourable news reports about the progress of the German war effort tipped the scales towards revoking the decision (Heldring 1970: 682–3; cf. Smit 1975: 144).

After the war, the capital accumulated during it was invested primarily in defeated Germany. Class solidarity with the worn-out German bourgeoisie played a part here:

> The other neutrals are only interested in receiving recognition for their claims on Germany and do not consider extending the new credit that we, the Dutch, deem necessary to enable Germany to make the investments to get its industry back on the rails, thus putting a stop to Bolshevism.
>
> *(Heldring 1970: 328–9)*

The only difference of opinion concerned whether the credit extensions to Germany should be bilateral or occur in the context of an international arrangement (Heldring 1970: 345).

Hardly any conditions were attached to these credits. Thus, Dutch industry could hardly reap any benefits from export advantages, which, according to Bosch (1948: 648), indicated weak ties between bankers and industrialists. This occurred even though, during the war, the Germans had imposed tight conditions on, for example, the delivery of steel. This had been one of the reasons for trade and shipping capitalists to support the creation of the leading Dutch iron and steel works, *Hoogovens*[4] (see van der Pijl 1978: 13). Industrialists, on the other hand, severely criticized these credit policies, such as the May 1920 Credit and Coal Agreement, which was intended to finance raw material supply to German industry (Blaisse 1952: 79).

Dutch credits to Germany amounted to around 200 billion Marks. The significance of this number becomes apparent when one considers the total value of outstanding loans of the four largest German banks in 1922: 269 billion marks (Blaisse 1952: 79). The generous credit extension to Germany even culminated in a situation in 1920 that obliged several Dutch enterprises to turn to the American capital market (Bosch 1948: 294). Reinforced by the fact that the government was also resorting to the capital market, interest rates in the Netherlands quickly rose to an unprecedented level. In contrast, German profit rates dropped sharply after 1920 because of social unrest, a global crisis, and runaway inflation – which rendered a large chunk of the Dutch investments worthless.

Industrialization and economic cycles

A familiar situation was now developing in the Netherlands. The low profit rates from overseas investments redirected the interest of bank capital to financing

24 Ries Bode

national industry. This had also occurred during the period of the long, stagnating wave from 1873 to 1890. As then, the Rotterdam Bank took the lead.

Of course, Dutch industrialization after WWI must be seen against the backdrop of international conjunctural developments. These can be periodized as follows:

1. A boom from the beginning of 1919 until the end of 1920, which was primarily due to reconstruction efforts in the war-damaged countries. As far as Dutch domestic investments are concerned, the boom can be ascribed to attempts to reduce the dependency on the import of strategically important raw materials, as well as to the massive expansion of the merchant fleet (Bosch 1948: 290).
2. A downturn from 1920 until the summer of 1923, caused by economic and social developments in Germany. Dutch exports were troubled by so-called currency competition, and large losses were incurred on the capital transferred from the Dutch East Indies to Germany.
3. The stabilization of international capitalism from 1923 onwards resulted in another boom, which lasted for six years. Backed by American and (as a good second) Dutch capital, large investments were made in Germany. The speculative character of this boom expressed itself in the 1929 Wall Street crash. The European banks were in rough waters as well, either because they had used short-term credits as a basis for medium- and long-term industrial financing or because they were caught up in bankruptcies elsewhere as a result of the internationalization of credit relations. An example of the latter was Hope & Co., which had a large claim on a Dutch daughter company of the failing Österreichische Kredit Anstalt (Austrian Credit Institution) (Heldring 1970: 928).
4. The crisis at the start of the 1930s. Its absolute low for the Netherlands can be placed around 1933, although the crisis continued unevenly across various industries, and stagnation lasted in certain respects until 1936 (de Graaff 1952: 27; Keesing 1952: 303).

The two booms were marked by large-scale industrialization. From 1923 onwards, the expanded investments by existing enterprises became especially important in this respect (Bosch 1948: 299; de Graaff 1952: 24). Directly after WWI, and in some cases even before its end, many new enterprises were established in industrial raw materials and basic products sectors (such as Hoogovens, Koninklijke Zout, and Limburg coal mining). As far as financing was concerned, these projects copied the old tradition of the Dutch East India Company (Vereenigde Oost-Indische Compagnie) and the Dutch Trading Company (Nederlandsche Handel-Maatschappij, NHM): several lenders undertake a joint project and minimize the risk by means of state participation.

The need for an independent supply of raw materials was broadly acknowledged in the light of the dependency that had become apparent during the war. So, the founding of Hoogovens dovetailed with the interests of 'capital in general', although the breadth of the initiative would lead to sharp contradictions within its leadership. These contradictions, in turn, were exploited by foreign interests. The most important point remained, however, that in contrast to the situation in England, Germany, or the United States, no autonomous fraction of capital developed within the heavy industries sector (Bode 1978: 148 and 63; van der Pijl 1978: 151–9). Apart from this specifically Dutch development of the – preferably state-backed – founding of an independent raw materials and semi-finished goods production base, another element in the industrialization of the Netherlands during this period was the 'catching up' with the so-called second industrial revolution, which involved the generalized application of mechanically produced electric and combustion engines (Mandel 1972: 120–1).

This especially applies to the 1923–29 boom. As far as new technologically advanced production picked up steam, it did so in industrial branches that had already been developed in other capitalist countries in the 20 years before WWI. Opportunities for Dutch industry opened up mainly as a result of international political developments that had disrupted the traditional division of labour between Dutch and German capital. The long-term difficulties of German capitalism enabled companies like Philips to capture a fair market share from the German electro-technical industry – albeit temporarily (Teulings 1975: 71, 74).

We should now consider the consequences of two aspects of this emerging situation on the relations between Dutch industrial capital and international capital: on the one hand, the political-strategic background to industrialization in the raw materials sector and, on the other, the fact that a large part of industrialization was occurring in areas that had already been exploited abroad for some time. Two outcomes are significant.

First, a lack of effective state protection forced Dutch industrialists to produce on the same technical level and scale at which their foreign competitors were operating. Where this was not achieved, technological backwardness had to be compensated through a relatively stronger exploitation of labour. This also explains why, in this modern industry, you would find relatively few medium-sized enterprises, apart from several enterprises in sectors characteristic of the second industrial revolution that were huge for Dutch standards (Klein 1975: 156).

Second, it puts the early internationalization of the Netherlands in perspective. The participation of a company like Philips in international cartel agreements resulted not from a position of power, but because it was tolerated and exploited by the major American, British, and German electro-technical conglomerates (Teulings 1975: 21). Similarly, one can only explain the international character of multinational companies like Unilever and Royal Shell (including their binational ownership structure, which remained unique right up to the 1970s) by the relative weakness of their Dutch constituents. This weakness resulted from technological limitations but especially from the incapability of the Dutch state to protect the longer-term colonial interests of these enterprises.

The development from 1929 until 1940

Despite the general malaise of the 'crisis years', industrialization continued in the 1930s. This time it did not concern extensive investment but involved two new forms of intensive development: a redirection of the industrialization process and, notably, the *mechanization* of production. Another difference from the 1920s was that, instead of being concentrated in upturns, investments were now concentrated in a period of recession (de Graaff 1952: 22–3). Because mechanization was largely financed through depreciation, it did not appear as such in the investment statistics. The results, however, *were* visible: frequent bankruptcies of labour-intensive enterprises and lay-offs by companies that attempted to minimize losses. De Graaff concluded:

> The crisis of 1930 was the crisis of labour, the crisis of mechanization. Never before did mechanization gain so much ground as in those years. Never before did so many workers end up outside the factories as after 1930, not because of diminished demand, but because machines replaced human labour.
>
> *(1952: 207)*

Just as the large industrial enterprises that emerged during the period of relative expansion in the first decade after WWI shared several characteristics resulting from that period, so the enterprises emerging in the 1930s also had common features that reflected the general situation of Dutch capitalism at this time. The General Rayon Union (AKU, Algemene Kunstzijde Unie) and C&A[5] exemplify this. If these companies were not already targeting domestic household consumption, they were at least aiming to protect sales in the internal market as a precondition for a favourable export position and/or as a basis for foreign investment in equally protected markets.

This reorientation, as well as the rationalization of production, proceeded unevenly across industrial sectors. Older industries, such as textiles, focused less on exports, thanks to international competition and a movement toward increased protection. In other sectors, like the electro-technical industry, there was a shift to production for domestic needs. This led to a reduction of specialization through import substitution, of which the increased production of vacuum cleaners during the crisis years is a good example (Blaisse 1952: 188). Other firms already had a semi-monopolistic position on the domestic market, like Unilever. As its former president put it: 'Unilever was in fact not experiencing difficulties. It comes down to the fact that Unilever concentrated on first necessities. Sales figures were thus actually no cause for concern, not even during the worst of the crisis years' (Rijkens 1965: 69).

The new industrial sectors mentioned earlier, such as those for artificial fabrics and clothing, arose as crisis industries, producing relatively cheap goods for mass consumption.

Together, these three forms of reorientation of the Dutch industry taken as a whole were expressed in an increasing orientation on the domestic market, and a diminished orientation on exports. This poses two questions: how far this was just the result of the general collapse of world trade; and whether – and how far – the decline in export orientation was due to a substantial process of import substitution. Table 1.1 sheds some light on this. These numbers show that the fall in exports was not associated with a proportional fall in national income. It appears that new, compensating sources of

Dutch bourgeoisie between the two world wars 27

TABLE 1.1 Export and national income in millions of Dutch guilders

Year	Export (X)	National income (Y)	X as % of Y
1929	2005	6469	31
1930	1728	6237	28
1931	1315	5490	24
1932	850	4928	17
1933	754	4779	16
1934	736	4754	15
1935	711	4682	15
1936	796	4807	17
1937	1204	5310	23
1938	1079	5305	20
1939	1006	5743	18

Source: Centraal Bureau voor de Statistiek (1975: 85)

income were found. Concerning these sources, one should obviously look at the sectors protected through tariffs. Through this protection against foreign competition, these sectors could capture a share of the domestic market.

All of this thoroughly changed the structure of the Dutch economy. Based on data regarding the structure of the labour force one can conclude that manufacturing strongly gained in importance in the period 1930–50, at the cost of, in particular, agriculture, trade, and transportation.

While the number of people employed in industry rose by 58.1 percent, the increases for trade and transport were a mere 14.9 and 13.8 percent, respectively (Elshof 1973, numbers based on the Second General Business Census of 1950). The significance of the numbers relating to the composition of the labour force is further accentuated when one compares them to the developments during the first wave of industrialization in the Netherlands (1900–10) and again the 1920s. In both periods, from 1900–10 and from 1920–30, the growth percentages for 'trade and transport' were higher than those of 'industry' (Lieftinck 1938: 3).

Agriculture also fell behind, even though the big shift took place here after 1945. During the crisis years agriculture grew mainly extensively; (intensive development based on) rationalization only took off after World War II (hereafter WWII).

Concerning trade and shipping, one can conclude that the results of increased protection on a global scale were far-reaching for these cyclically sensitive sectors. For them, the big blow definitely came in the midst of the crisis years. From 1929 until 1933, the volume of total port traffic fell by 40 percent and, due to falling profits, 38 percent of the available deadweight had already been taken out of business by the autumn of 1932 (Keesing 1952: 121–2).

We can summarize the changes in the Dutch industrial structure resulting from the crisis as follows:

28 Ries Bode

1. Further *concentration* and *centralization* of capital. Alas, unlike for example the United States, the Dutch government refused to collect any systematic data on concentration trends in the 1930s. Because of this an overview cannot be provided, except for a partial overview of just one aspect of the centralization process: the development of the cartels (for a summary, see Blaisse 1952: 180).
2. *Mechanization.* Even though here, too, direct data are missing, there are clues pointing to an essential development in this area. According to Keesing, 'concerning those industry sectors for which production statistics exist, it transpires that the wage sum paid per used unit of raw material fell by around 25 percent between 1922 and 1930. During the same period, the mechanical power per worker rose by around 45 percent. Both numbers illustrate the continuing mechanization without, of course, offering a detailed insight into this development. So, there are reasons to assume that this process of mechanization and rationalization proceeded significantly faster between 1920 and 1929 than during the preceding decades' (Keesing 1952: 82).
3. An increased focus on production for *domestic use* (for data, see Blaisse 1952: 185).
4. The development of a few large industrial enterprises, which focused from the start on production for the domestic market, with few foreign competitors. Examples are AKU and the clothing industry (de Graaff 1952: 152, 156).
5. *Internationalization of production.* Besides the internationalization of ownership structures (for example Unilever and Shell), foreign direct investment emerged in the 1930s. To the extent that these direct investments occurred, they were mostly the result of increasing international protection. Tariff walls were jumped over (Busch 1974: 90f.). Thus, an international orientation of several large industrial enterprises in the sense of relocating production abroad does not necessarily imply an 'international' orientation in the sense of being advocates of free trade. On the contrary, the 'hommes politiques' of enterprises like Philips and AKU were known as convinced protectionists. We return to this in more detail in the last part of this article.

Capital fractions and fractions of the bourgeoisie

The bourgeoisie can be categorized based on various criteria. One is the position that the capitalists in question take within the production and circulation process. For example:

1. Capitalists that primarily base themselves on the aspect of the *transformation process* that capital goes through: industry, trade, and bank capital (and optionally capital invested in land) (see Marx 1978: 128f.). Commenting on this, for example, Ernest Mandel notes how '[t]he different sections of the bourgeoisie opposed and fought each other because of the predominant form assumed by the capital of each section respectively: landed property, banks, industrial or commercial property' (1971: 70).

2. Capitalists that have their prime activity in a certain part of the *process of social metabolism* based on the use value of the products: producers of consumer goods (Department II) and of raw materials and investment goods (Department I). Further nuances can be made here. Some capitalists, for example, are primarily active in the production of non-reproductive goods, which means that these would not be changed into investment goods or consumed by labourers: luxury goods, weapons, etc. (Department III) (Cogoy 1973: 152). In addition, capitalists can produce for Departments I and II simultaneously.

3. Capitalists operating within a certain sector at different *levels of productivity* and who are simultaneously subject to the workings of the law of value between different sectors, both nationally and internationally (Busch 1974: 90–1, explores the trade and monetary-political consequences of the workings of the law of value on the international level).

4. Capitalists who, given the technical nature of the production process they control directly, need different forms of *labour* (highly skilled labour, unskilled labour, etc.), thus developing diverging attitudes toward the working class (Sohn-Rethel 1975: 47).

5. Capitalists with either conflicting or shared interests regarding the *geographical orientation*, as far as the sale of goods and the supply of raw materials are concerned. This aspect has gained in importance under monopoly-capitalist conditions, under which potential future markets and sources for raw materials also play a role. Against this background, Fennema distinguishes an Atlantic and a European fraction of the bourgeoisie [using this term differently from my proposal below] in the Netherlands: 'On the one hand there are several international capital groups that depend on the supply of raw materials from the Third World and, thus, on a good relationship with the United States, as long as this power dominates the largest part of that Third World ... On the other hand, there are corporations that are more oriented towards Germany and the EEC. The needs of these companies lie more on the terrain of technology and support for sales' (Fennema 1975: 92–3).

Now, the problem with all these distinctions is that they are economic in nature and, in principle, can be described as such, regardless of how, if at all, they translate into political divisions. To me, however, it *only seems useful to talk about capital fractions when these differences in position also get expressed in political struggle*. In other words, it makes sense to refer to capital fractions only when it is possible to connect the political antagonisms within the ruling class and the above-mentioned material bases. This is also why 'capital fraction' (as employed hereafter) is not interpreted as a fraction in terms of its role in the capitalist production process but in terms of its distinctive political orientation. Shortly, I will also distinguish between capital fraction and fraction of the bourgeoisie.

What, then, is the difference between normal competition between particular capitals and the struggle among different capital fractions?

30 Ries Bode

Competition concerns the struggle between particular capitals on the same (economic) terrain. The form of such competitive battles has been subject to marked changes over the years. Price competition was the most important form in the early phases of capitalist development and, before that, it also characterized social formations in which petty commodity production developed. Nowadays, price competition mainly prevails in relatively backward sectors. Conversely, a plethora of monopolistic and oligopolistic types of competition are characteristic, like brand competition, product differentiation, etc. (Baran and Sweezy 1966: 57). The essence of this competition is, and always has been, the struggle between capitals concerning the redistribution of the total surplus value of societal production, as ultimately expressed in the rate of profit.

The battle between different *fractions of capital* is ultimately, of course, also a question of the redistribution of surplus value. *This struggle, however, does not occur within the general framework conditions of capitalist production, but concerns these conditions themselves* and how they come to be established through political action.

Classical Marxist theories consider the state as the central institution of the bourgeoisie, with the task of guaranteeing the continuity of the capitalist system of production wherever this (profit-oriented, market-mediated) process itself falls short of doing so. Concretely, its tasks include limiting the conflicts between individual capitalists, the antagonisms between different classes, protecting domestic capitalists from foreign competition, etc. The state thus intervenes when, and to the extent that, the overall conditions for the reproduction of capital are no longer produced by the automatic laws of production operating behind the backs of the producers.

This is where two important issues come into play. First, the direction of the state's general intervention results from the political struggle among different parts of the ruling class(es).

> This means that – just as the bourgeois state emerged historically not through the conscious agency of a society or a class pursuing its 'general will' (*allgemeines Willen*) but as the result of often contradictory and narrow-minded class conflicts and struggles – its specific operational mechanisms develop in the context of antagonistic interests and societal conflicts.
>
> *(Hirsch 1974: 26; editors' translation)*[6]

Here it is important to note that the given framework within which the bourgeoisie aims to solve accumulation problems, namely the development of productive forces and the conjuncture of the class struggle, does not entirely determine the space available to the ruling class to develop its strategy; this strategy precisely serves the purpose of changing that space.

Second, the *general* measures taken by the state have direct effects that can benefit or hurt particular capitalists. These specific effects of state intervention are also contested. Certain group interests can be the *direct* basis for a certain policy propagated by a certain group. The support of heavy industry for fascism is an example, but it simultaneously shows that the pursuit of narrow group interests cannot offer a

Dutch bourgeoisie between the two world wars 31

long-term solution for the fundamental problems of capitalism as a whole in these countries (Bettelheim 1946: 255). However, the relationship between specific group interests and political programmes can also proceed in a less *direct* manner.

In this case, we speak of *comprehensive concepts of control*: comprehensive political answers to the question of how societal contradictions (between classes, between different parts of the bourgeoisie, between national and foreign bourgeoisies) should be managed. Such comprehensive concepts of control are the result of class and fractional struggles and are conditioned by contemporary problems of accumulation. They can be interpreted as variants within the overarching ideology of the ruling class.

Based on this distinction between types of political demands, we can now distinguish between *capital fractions* and *fractions of the bourgeoisie* in terms of their respective concern with immediate interests or comprehensive concepts of control that are at the most influenced by specific economic positions. Thus, fraction of the bourgeoisie denotes the capitalists who, together with their ideological and political functionaries, have articulated various specific group interests into a conception of 'the general interest'.

The lines of demarcation that, according to this definition, can be drawn within the bourgeoisie run partly parallel with the political demarcations between the various political parties. They are not identical, however. As explained in Part III, in the 1930s the similarities between a given current extending across different Dutch bourgeois parties were often stronger than those between different wings of individual parties. Especially at the level of the 'inner circle' of the bourgeoisie – the relatively small group of people with significant political influence – fractional lines of division run straight through several political parties. This is hardly surprising because, especially in periods of rapid societal changes, the party-based political crystallization of societal opinions and interests can lag behind the development of new comprehensive concepts.

The second reason behind the fractional structure that cuts across the structure of the bourgeois parties is a practical one. From the viewpoint of the bourgeoisie, the success of comprehensive concepts of control depend critically on the presence of its representatives in multiple political parties. The shipping magnate Ernst Heldring, whose diaries are an invaluable source of insight into the inner workings of thought and labour in higher bourgeois circles, mentions the creation of a fund that included Waller, August Philips and himself, which was aimed at defending the interests of employers in politics. The purpose was to promote getting representative members in the Second Chamber[7] on whose proper insights and character one could count (Heldring 1970: 684). He explicitly adds:

> while for the time being only the weak Freedom League (Vrijheidsbond, VB) is supported, this is not the fund's sole intention. In principle, other parties are eligible for support as well – especially the Christian Historical Union (CHU), if they would not follow the Catholics in their votes so often.
> *(Heldring 1970: 684; this foundation would later grow into the Vereeniging voor Economische Politiek (Association for Economic Policy))*

32   Ries Bode

It would be incorrect, however, to describe these processes one-sidedly in terms of individuals and their intrigues. It is more meaningful to try to indicate the relations that exist between, on the one hand, particular interest structures – in a changing global constellation that modifies (embedded/associated) interest structures in turn – and, on the other hand, the political crystallization of comprehensive concepts of control. Of course, pressure groups play a role here. As we will see, however, they do not control these processes, despite oftentimes wielding significant, notably financial, influence. Rather, this process of crystallization results from competing pressures of quite a different kind.

Summarizing, we propose two main modes of struggle within the bourgeoisie. First, *competition* is a mode of struggle over the redistribution of the total socially produced surplus value. This occurs among individual (particular) capitals *within* the framework formed by the prevailing boundary conditions of the capitalist mode of production. What one would commonly refer to as 'politics' does not play a role here. But certain aspects of monopolistic competition *sometimes* do already touch these boundary conditions, because the struggle among monopolies often concerns an exclusivity that is guaranteed by the state.

Second, there is *the struggle over the nature of state intervention* regarding boundary conditions. This has two variants. One is very similar to competition: this is where capitalists fight each other over the *concrete economic effects* [positive or negative] of state intervention. We can speak here of *capital fractions* (as opposed to individual/ particular capitals) to the extent that economic interests depend on specific kinds of political framework conditions, policy interventions, and other state measures. We speak of capital fractions to the extent that the economic interest of particular capitals or capitalist sectors turns into political action. The other variant concerns the *general direction* of state intervention. Here we speak of the rival *fractions of the bourgeoisie* that wage a political battle conducted [strategically] from the vantage point of their respective comprehensive concepts of control. Transitional forms, as well as contradictions, can certainly arise between these variants. The Amsterdam trade and shipping circles, for example, supported the free trade policies of Thorbecke[8] (Chamber of Commerce Amsterdam 1936, I: 31), which did not, however, prevent the same capitalists from uniting as a capital fraction against the shipping laws of 1850, which ended the protection from foreign competition in the shipping sector (Brugmans 1976: 216; Blaisse 1952: 45).

This conceptualization will be helpful in the analysis of the different orientations within the Dutch bourgeoisie and the changes resulting from the crisis in the 1930s.

Competition and fractional struggle in the Dutch bourgeoisie in the interwar period

In assessing Dutch politics in the 1930s it is important to note that no fraction of the bourgeoisie managed to win hegemony over *all* areas of policy. That is why Dutch crisis policies lacked what Hirschfeld called 'a grand political conception' (Hirschfeld 1946: 60). This will be elaborated below through an analysis of currents concerning trade, finance, and social policy. To guide this analysis, I provide an overview of the most important capital fractions, fractions of the bourgeoisie (in the years 1918–30 and the first half of the 1930s, respectively), and bourgeois political parties (see Figure 1.1). Parties that operated independently only due to coalition-political considerations, like the *Liberal Democratic Union* (Vrijzinnige Democratische Bond, VDB), have been omitted.

Currents regarding trade policies

Compared to other sectors in the Dutch economy, industry has traditionally been weak. Even when industrialization had proceeded substantially during the global crisis of 1879–90, Dutch industrialists could not form a strong political front. The campaign for protectionist policies was led in the 1880s by the protectionist Union of and for Dutch Industrialists (Vereeniging van en voor Nederlandse Industriëlen, which was established in 1862 and from which industrialists in Twente[9] happened to keep aloof because of its protectionist orientation) in conjunction with several sector organizations. Yet the campaign ended in failure. It was only at the start of the twentieth century that industry organized itself in politically representative institutions but (at this stage) always as a representation of common industrial, trade, and bank interests. An example was the Commission for Trade Policies (Commissie voor Handelspolitiek), an advisory committee for the government founded in 1891 (de Jonge 1976: 33). Only with the rise and increasing power of the Calvinists emancipating from the conservative party and Catholics breaking away from the liberal party did these relationships change somewhat. But even though this expressed resistance against the free trade orientation of the liberal 'establishment' – also against the background of the agricultural crisis of 1890 – the right-wing governments that emerged from it would stay powerless or be forced to make concessions regarding trade policies for a long time.

Nevertheless, trade policy was contested from the beginning of the twentieth century. Trade and industry, which in the Netherlands remained in the hands of separate capitalists for a long time, did not just limit themselves to competition, but also engaged in struggles on trade policy as capital fractions. Whenever an economic recession occurred, the call for protection from the side of industry and certain circles of agriculture strengthened. Trade capital, on the other hand, was increasingly forced to organize itself in committees and the like to mobilize the resistance against this call. Already before WWI, ministers Kolkman and Harte had proposed to legally open the possibility for raising protective tariffs. These propositions had been refused due to strong resistance in both Chambers of Parliament, backed by the Anti-Tariff Law Committee (Anti-Tariefwet Comité), established by Heldring and others. The elections of 1913 were strongly marked by this question (Heldring 1970: 180).

After the war, during the post-war crisis of 1920–23, import restrictions came to the fore again, this time against the so-called monetary competition from Germany. An 'imbecile notion' according to Heldring (1970: 392), but the

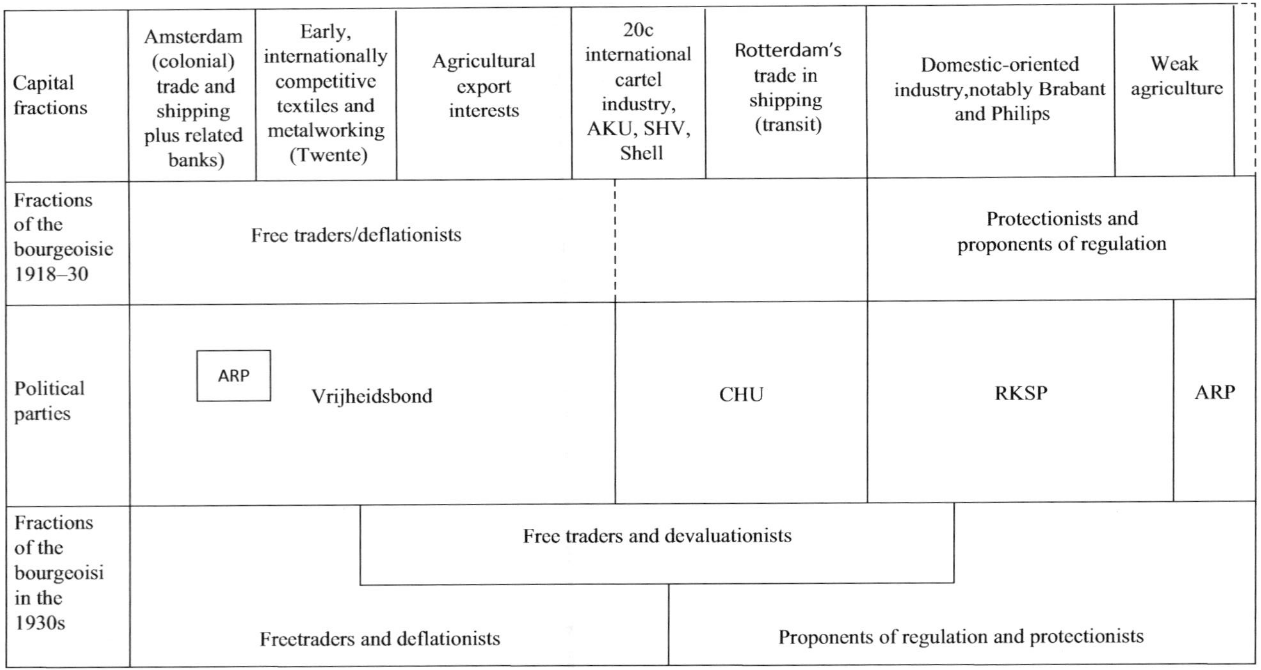

Capital fractions	Amsterdam (colonial) trade and shipping plus related banks)	Early, internationally competitive textiles and metalworking (Twente)	Agricultural export interests	20c international cartel industry, AKU, SHV, Shell	Rotterdam's trade in shipping (transit)	Domestic-oriented industry, notably Brabant and Philips	Weak agriculture
Fractions of the bourgeoisie 1918–30	Free traders/deflationists					Protectionists and proponents of regulation	
Political parties	ARP Vrijheidsbond			CHU		RKSP	ARP
Fractions of the bourgeoisi in the 1930s	Free traders and devaluationists						
	Freetraders and deflationists			Proponents of regulation and protectionists			

FIGURE 1.1 Capital fractions, fractions of the bourgeoisie, bourgeois political parties

Note: the Anti-Revolutionary Party (ARP) has an extremely heterogeneous class basis, which led to a complete reorientation after WWI. This explains the double placement of the ARP in the schema; SHV = Steenkolen Handels Vereniging (Coal Trading Society).

Dutch bourgeoisie between the two world wars **35**

protectionist movement had now grown stronger within the governmental advisory bodies. The sub-committee of the Commission for Economic Policy (Commissie voor Economische Politiek), tasked with delivering advice on this matter, declared itself in favour of protection. This sub-committee included, among others, Treub, Visiting, Bonger, and Kortenhorst. The Commission itself, however, advised against this: 'the liberal stronghold ... should not be overthrown here' (Blaisse 1952: 61).

Nevertheless, capitalists in trade, shipping, and sometimes industry as well, felt pressed to counteract the growing protectionist currents through more permanent public campaigning. The Free Trade Society (Vereniging Het Vrije Ruilverkeer) had been established in 1914, but had been considered too academic by Heldring, and was converted into the Union for Free Trade (Vrije Handelsbond) in 1925. It was not considered sufficiently combative, however, which gave rise to the revival of the above-mentioned Anti-Tariff Law Committee. Despite 'clerical slander', its funds originated not from abroad but from colonial trade and manufacturing, finance, and shipping (Heldring 1970: 180).

Obviously, the fight against tariff increases during economic crises called for alternative anti-crisis policies. The recipe of the free trade interests was to economize on social expenses, to lower salaries, and to prolong the working day. In other words, to reverse the concessions to the workers' revolt of November 1918. What is more, they called for a proportional reduction of military spending (Heldring 1970: 410; Oud 1948–51, II: 5ff.).

The latter was expressed in the conflict about the plans to expand the surface and submarine naval fleet after WWI through the fleet law. It was the reason the Minister of Finance, de Geer, who opposed rapid introduction of the fleet law, resigned in July 1923. But although his successor, Colijn, was suspected by Heldring to have made a deal with the Catholics (protection in exchange for their voting for the fleet law) (Heldring 1970, I: 492), the law was finally voted down by a small margin (Oud 1948–51, II: 136). A popular petition initiative collected 1.3 million signatures against the extension of the naval fleet had reminded the liberals once more that their proposed budget cuts could only be realized if military spending were cut too. And indeed, spending cuts followed, also under Colijn. Civil servant salaries were cut by 20 percent, the obligatory school age was lowered from 14 to 12 years, and the seventh school year was abolished. The last two measures cost 5500 teachers their jobs. During the crisis of 1920–23, those advocating free trade and austerity at any cost had won the day. During the next recession, which would prove more severe, the struggle between the fractions of the bourgeoisie would also become more severe.

If we wish to categorize the bourgeoisie in terms of their position regarding free trade or protection, we need to distinguish between the traditional bearers of free trade ideology – who maintained their position from Thorbecke up to WWII – and those interests that favoured free trade during prosperous cycles but rallied around the permanent protectionists during times of recession.

Foremost among the latter was the central body of the Roman Catholic Employers Association (R.K. Werkgeversvereniging, RKWV), which strongly favoured protection both before and after WWI (Blaisse 1952: 67). This was also the case for political representatives of the Catholic entrepreneurs, like Kortenhorst, 'our influential Catholic protectionist' (Heldring 1970: 502).

Regarding the other employer organizations, the positions within the Union of Dutch Manufacturers' Association (Verbond van Nederlandse Fabrikantenverenigingen, VNF) were less clear. During the crisis of 1920/23, however, the VNF, together with the Catholic employers, agitated against the prevailing free trade policy of the time (Blaisse 1952: 67).

Overall, the Dutch Employers' Union (Vereniging van Nederlandse Werkgevers, VNW) adopted an anti-protectionist position. This is not surprising, because besides industrialists it also represented trade and shipping capitalists. And the industrialists in the VNW were again the textile barons from Twente, who were committed free traders until around 1933. (With the merger between the VNF and the VNW in 1926, trade policy was declared to be an open issue.)

Several personal links existed between the leaderships of the VNW and the VB. Verster, a high-ranking official of the VNW, was at the same time the chairman of the Anti-Tariff Law Committee, and leading figures within the VNW were, in their turn, repeatedly supported (financially or otherwise) by the Union for Economic Policy (Heldring 1970: 179, 1001).

The Union for Economic Policy was a pressure group within the Vrijheidsbond to combat, on the one hand, liberal agricultural interests, when these started to sway over toward protectionism in the 1930s, and, on the other, 'politicization', the effort to make liberal principles negotiable in the context of parliamentary coalition politics. In some periods, the VNF contributed over two thirds of the VB's party income. But the 1930s, notably, witnessed the development of some sharp conflicts between party and Union, which led to a temporary interruption in the flow of subsidies (Heldring 1970: 963, 1591).

Besides the VB, those in favour of free trade were especially organized in the Christian Historical Union (CHU), notably some Rotterdam personalities associated with trade and shipping. One of the major financial supporters was the NHM banker Van Aalst. Although from Amsterdam, his increasingly pro-German orientation aligned more with the opinions of Rotterdam trade and shipping interests. During the 1920s, it was the CHU that, operating within successive right-wing cabinets, systematically resisted the protectionist measures demanded by the Catholics (especially the employer representatives) and by parts of the ARP (a Protestant Christian-Democratic party). For this, the CHU had to suffer the necessary theological blows from the prominent Anti-Revolutionary Party protectionist Diepenhorst, who had concluded that 'free trade is based on a deistic philosophy' (Vleeschhouwer 1927: 139; Oud 1948–51, III: 265, 268).

The final important pillar of the free trade bloc that must be mentioned is the Royal Dutch Agriculture Committee (Koninklijk Nederlands Landbouwcomité). Within this committee, the interests of the meat-producing and wheat-growing farmers, who suffered from import competition, were entirely overpowered by the export interests of the other agricultural sectors (Blaisse 1952: 69).

Concerning the *permanent protectionists*, the Catholic employers were mentioned above. The Catholics at the time did not have as long a tradition as for example the Anti-Revolutionary protectionists, because at the end of the nineteenth century the [religious] tolerance from the Liberals had still weighed heavier for them than a possible trade alliance with the ARP. This persisted when they turned away from the liberals, and the right-wing, exclusively confessional cabinets came to the fore (from 1888 onwards). 'The Catholics were the ... most passive supporters of the religious coalition. Afraid to expose themselves to anti-papal reaction, they were generally satisfied to be a follower rather than a leader in the religious coalition' (Daalder 1966: 203).

Universal suffrage and proportional representation increased the importance of the Catholic role in government, especially because the Catholics had a comprehensive answer to the increasing social tensions. During the 1920s, in relatively rare cases of problems within a certain sector concerning foreign competition, they took centre stage in the Chamber. The parliamentary leader, Nolens, as well as specific employer representatives in the party (like Blomjous, Kortenhorst, and van Spaendonck en Steenberghe, who had all previously served in the RKWV), came out fighting (Oud 1948–51, III: 273–9).

At the end of the nineteenth century, the Anti-Revolutionaries were principled defenders of protectionist trade policies. This was primarily inspired by industrial development in Germany. They abandoned this position, however, after WWI. One could probably argue that after the split with the CHU in 1894, an 'haute bourgeois' wing had developed anew in the ARP. Embodied by figures like Colijn, this wing opposed the economic policies that were traditionally inspired by the 'Kleine Luyden' ('little people'), the small producers, lower middle class and farmers, as well as that part of the working class that was integrated in the Protestant pillar.

Regarding pressure groups, the main counterpart of the Association for Free Exchange (Vereniging voor Vrij Ruilverkeer) and the Association for Free Trade (Vereniging voor Vrijhandel), was the Association for Active Trade Policy (Vereniging voor Actieve Handelspolitiek), founded in 1926 (Blaisse 1952: 11). Catholic and Protestant entrepreneurs in particular were well represented in this organization. Some of its prominent figures included Diepenhorst, van Spaendonck (then secretary of the RKWV), and Kortenhorst (Brugmans 1976: 513; Vleeschhouwer 1927: 139). In general, Dutch industrialists – with the exception of the oldest generation (textile, shipping, and metalworking) – supported protection and regulation, especially in times of economic downturn.

Yet there were exceptions. In 1930, for example, a committee was established from inside the VNW, named after Sydney van den Bergh, member of the Vrijheidsbond and director of Unilever. As its objective, this committee set out to 'organize the Dutch industries' solidarity toward foreign nations' and attempted to get rid of the sharp edges around the numerous boycotts initiated by agriculture, but also by Philips (Blaisse 1952: 109).

From within Shell as well, attempts were launched to counter the increasing protectionist tendencies. In 1936, for example, Henri Deterding invested 10 million guilders from his own pocket to export additional Dutch agricultural crops to

Germany, outside of the normal clearing arrangements. According to Blaisse, this gesture 'also expressed a propagandistic tendency ... and was intended as a hint toward aligning Dutch trade policies with the resurrected European economic bloc led by Germany' (1952: 343).

According to Hirschfeld, Deterding's stunt was motivated by fiscal considerations (Hirschfeld 1959: 92). It is remarkable that Shell and Unilever attempted to counter the call by Dutch industry for protection in the 1930s. Especially Unilever fulfilled a bridge function between orthodox liberals and industrialists. The attitudes of these two firms can be explained by the fact that they were vertically integrated internationally, and because they had almost no competition from other companies. Shell lacked competition because of the stable market agreements between the large oil companies; Unilever lacked competition because, within Europe, no corporations active in this sector had a similar market power. Philips and AKU, on the other hand, did support the protectionist ambition.

To explain the *change of course in Dutch policy* toward protectionism, it would be logical to look at the 'changers', those who switched from a free trade toward a protectionist point of view. The two most important changers in the 1920s and early 1930s were the farmers' organizations and the textile industry from Twente.

> The huge blows that hit the cotton industry through the collapse of the pound, the abnormal development of Oriental competition [from Japan, RB] and the increasing lock-out from its normal export markets made it a matter of life and death to protect its access to the domestic and Indonesian markets. With that, the free trade movement in the Netherlands lost one of her prime pillars.
>
> *(Blaisse 1952: 138)*

For agriculture, this switch had already come about around 1925 under the influence of the German protectionist measures. But it was not primarily the 'changers' who were responsible for the switch in Dutch trade policy. More important was the fact that the traditional protectionists grew more important than the traditional free traders within the total economic structure. Three developments played a part here:

1. Developments on the world market, which in reaction to the capitalist world crisis were leading to increased protection and state intervention.
2. The growing relative importance of activities that relied more on protection and state intervention than others. In the Netherlands, this was industrial development at the cost of the societal weight of the trade and financial activities not allied to the Dutch industry.
3. The constellation of interests that was changing in terms of capital fractions and fractions of the bourgeoisie resulting from the previous developments.

From 1925 onwards, protectionism was rapidly rising in the world. The call for protection by prominent Dutch enterprises was not so much directed at tariff policies for protecting the domestic market; oftentimes, it was about creating options to retaliate in case of foreign tariff measures, or to prevent such foreign actions through *the threat* of such retaliation. On this issue, there was broad consensus. Disagreement started with the question of which instruments should be used in bargaining, and how actively these should be used. This is illustrated by the reaction within the Netherlands to the termination of the Entente powers' control over German trade policies in 1925, and following Germany's turn to protectionism. These policies especially affected the ports of Amsterdam and Rotterdam, as well as agriculture. In response, agriculture demanded a reaction based on reciprocity as did the liberal Royal Dutch Agriculture Committee.

Posthuma even established a permanent lobby, the Committee for Economic Defence (Comité tot Economisch Verweer). Shipping and port capital, however, which had been hit just as hard by German policies, reacted in a considerably less combative fashion. Perhaps it did not oppose retaliatory measures, but these should not take the form of higher tariffs; it preferred the use of credit extension to Germany as a pressure tool. This view was also expressed by S. van den Bergh, who, as a member of parliament, was a proponent of the government influencing the big Amsterdam financiers to this effect (Blaisse 1952: 108). At the same time, these interests went to extreme lengths to prevent such a threat with equal counter-measures – and even a boycott of German products (as proposed by Philips, among others, Blaisse 1952: 108) – to be realized. This prevention was one of the main purposes of the van den Bergh committee.

Around 1925, these developments announced a debate that through constant hardening of positions would last until well into the 1930s. And even though those who opposed 'active trade policy' (read: protection) would still prosper for a while, the incubation time of the eventual 1931 switch in trade policy started in 1925. The number of measures not yet implemented during this period does not change the fact that they were being prepared.

The contradictions that existed within the business world, and which were expressed within and between political parties, could also be witnessed at the level of government departments. In the period between 1929 and 1934, a large reorganization of tasks and powers took place within various ministries. This was an expression of the power struggle between different fractions of the bourgeoisie. The problems regarding protection and state intervention took on a central role in all ministerial reorganizations. This also held true for the competence battle over foreign economic relations between the Ministry of Foreign Affairs, predominantly in favour of free trade in the old tradition of patrician liberalism, and the Ministry of Economic Affairs (named the Ministry of Agriculture, Industry, and Trade until 1932), predominantly in favour of protectionism. The fact that the lead in trade policy was taken by Economic Affairs in 1933 can be interpreted as an expression of the gradual victory of the protectionists in the battle over trade policy (Hirschfeld 1946: 42 ff.; Heldring 1970: 852, 897 ff.).

A similar long-term competence struggle was waged between the Ministries of Finance and Economic Affairs concerning monetary policy and the final say in

40 Ries Bode

tariff policies. Traditionally, tariff policy fell under the competence of the Ministry of Finance, as the prime function of tariffs had been fiscal in nature until around 1930, as an instrument to generate state revenue (Hirschfeld 1946: 42–3).

Similarly, another battle had been waged over what should fall within the realm of the Ministry of Agriculture, Industry, and Trade. Under the influence of the occasionally strong conflicts between agricultural and industrial interests, it was finally decided in 1932 to split this ministry into a Ministry of Agriculture and a Ministry of Economic Affairs – a victory primarily for the agricultural export interests (Hirschfeld 1946: 52). After all, agriculture and industry developed conflicts on different terrains. Concerning trade policies, for example, protectionist industry nevertheless feared agricultural protection, as this drove up prices for basic necessities and hence wages. At the same time, increasing bilateralism in international trade led to a practice of 'package deals' in which larger quotas for agricultural exports automatically led to smaller quotas for industrial exports (Plate 1936: 9; Blaisse 1952: 312–4; Hirschfeld 1946: 93).

In 1931, Dutch trade policy, under the influence of Britain's abandonment of the Gold Standard but without following it, finally switched towards protectionism. Heldring notes in September 1932: 'With all that, I believe that it will take a long time before the majority in parliament will return to a liberal policy, even though its foundations are vindicated daily' (Heldring 1970: 994). Within the Vrijheidsbond and the CHU, conflicts arose when agricultural export interests were threatened. The traditionally liberal agricultural interests demanded protection by import quotas as well as by an active government stance in international negotiations concerning these matters. People like Lovink, van Rappard, and Bierema represented this tendency in the Liberal Party. The fact that the liberals often voted against their principles and in favour of agricultural protection resulted from the fear that liberal agricultural interests would otherwise start a new farmers' party. This would have reduced the vote for the Vrijheidsbond even further, which had already significantly shrunk since the introduction of universal suffrage after 1919. The trade and shipping interests, however, did stick to their principles and enforced their orthodoxy by occasionally suspending their contributions to the Vrijheidsbond (Heldring 1970: 1084).

The final question then concerns the extent to which the struggle between the different wings in the Vrijheidsbond and the CHU resulted from political-strategic motives or from motives that can be reduced to capital interests. It does seem obvious that as far as capital fractions that were increasingly oriented toward protectionist and interventionist policies were represented within these parties, these fractions strengthened the tendency towards a rapprochement with the Catholics for party political reasons.

Foreign policy

At the level of fractions of the Dutch bourgeoisie, the distinction between a free trade and a protectionist wing corresponded to the distinction between a *pro-English* and a *pro-German* wing. One can generally say that the protectionist groups within the Dutch bourgeoisie were also pro-German, while those in favour of free trade

Dutch bourgeoisie between the two world wars **41**

gravitated toward England. This correspondence, which continued up until WWI, had two exceptions: the Germany-oriented trade and shipping capital from Rotterdam, and the agricultural export interests. These were pro-German as well as pro-free trade – albeit somewhat depending on the business cycle. In addition, the Catholic bourgeoisie had an ambiguous position regarding Germany; as far as trade policy was concerned, we have already noted that it was protectionist in nature (apart from the textile sector from Twente).

There is an obvious connection between a pro-English attitude and the free trade sentiments of particularly Amsterdam trade, shipping and colonial capital, the textile industry from Twente, and the metal-processing industry. The safeguarding of the Dutch East Indies was of utmost importance for this fraction of the bourgeoisie, and for this the support of Great Britain, the mightiest colonial power, was necessary. The only way to secure that support was an open-door policy vis-à-vis English capital; this policy was made official through the 1871 Sumatra Treaty.

These currents should however also be placed within the context of the general Dutch foreign policy of neutrality – of which they were nuances. Neutrality had been the official policy paradigm since the founding of the Kingdom of the Netherlands in 1815.

> It consisted of striving to stay out of the conflicts among other states. To achieve this, alliances were avoided, as well as any permanent alliance with a specific power or group of powers. The Dutch state could only lose by participation in wars. Further, in the absence of war, it counted on the antagonisms between the largest powers in the world [to stay outside the alliance system, RB].
>
> *(de Leeuw 1975 [1936]: 17)*

In various circles, however, there was a sharp awareness that Dutch neutrality was only possible due to the interest of England in a strong and independent Kingdom of the Netherlands. Against France right after Napoleonic times; later, as a buffer against the German Empire. The support that the English offered to the Belgian movement for independence was somewhat in conflict with this. This was related, however, to the fact that the English textile exports were experiencing serious difficulties as a result of, firstly, the limited industrial protection that King Willem I had imposed for Belgium and, secondly, the right that was granted to the Belgians to export their textile production to the Dutch East Indies. What is more, in contravention of the trade agreement between England and the Netherlands, the so-called Linen Fabric Regulation (Lijnwaadverordening) of 1824 had imposed a trade barrier against English textile exports to the Dutch East Indies.

With the growth of German unity during the nineteenth century, the conflicts within the Dutch bourgeoisie concerning foreign trade policy were growing as well. A part of commercial capital was increasingly oriented toward transit trade with the German hinterland. A division of labour also developed among the banks, which, as we know, were mostly focused on financing trade activities between, broadly speaking, those focused on the Dutch East Indies trade (and, later,

42 Ries Bode

financing the plantations there) and those that focused on the financing of the transit trade to the rapidly industrializing Ruhr area.

A similar division of labour existed within the shipping sector, although this was less sharp because the large Rotterdam and Amsterdam shipowners controlled both the oceanic trade and the trade along the Rhine. An important difference, however, was that in Amsterdam the overseas supply and the transit trade to Germany were in the same (Dutch) hands, allowing 'the port' sector to act as one bloc against the interests of German importers (Heldring 1970, appendix 2: 1501–2). In Rotterdam, however, a large part of the cargo was, upon release, directly in German hands or controlled by Dutch enterprises acting as agents for German trade and shipping enterprises. Because of this, the Rotterdam port economy was penetrated by German interests much more strongly than its Amsterdam counterpart, even though the Germans did attempt to gain a foothold there, too, for example by founding the Amsterdam Bank in 1870 (80 percent German capital, according to Brugmans 1976: 267). The penetration of German capital in the Rotterdam port cannot be seen in isolation from the pro-German policies advocated by the Rotterdam trade interests.

That such connections need not be permanent is illustrated by the orientation of the agricultural export sector. Even though it was also highly interested in good relations with its most important market, and even though its representative in the government, Posthuma, proposed a pro-Germany policy during WWI, things changed when Germany turned to agricultural protection in 1925. Posthuma, of all people, turned into a strongly anti-German politician (Smit 1975: 33: Blaisse 1952: 106; Heldring 1970: 222; Hirschfeld 1946: 51).

Of course, these economically based orientations could only gain vigour within the framework of larger societal, often ideological, developments. The Boer War, for example, triggered a strong anti-English popular movement, while the liberal Pierson government (1896–1901) refrained from criticism. 'The number one code of conduct for this government of the old liberal party, meaning of old trade and colonial capital, was to do nothing that could put the Netherlands in conflict with the British empire' (de Leeuw 1975 [1936]: 23). Riding the waves of this anti-English movement, which he had started himself, Abraham Kuyper came into office in 1901. But his pro-German course could hardly endure due to the resistance from the old liberals and the civil service of the Department of Foreign Affairs (see de Leeuw 1975 [1936]).

Thus, the essentially pro-English neutrality policy remained the main starting point for Dutch foreign policy during WWI and the years that followed. The Netherlands' accession to the League of Nations was intended to reinforce the trends toward 'international law', but also as a means to appease France and England; if they would not annex parts of the Netherlands, the loss of strategically important areas like the Scheldt estuary and South Limburg could be prevented (Heldring 1970: 305; Vandenbosch 1959: ch. 13).

A second factor causing fraternization within the ruling circles during the first postwar years was of a domestic nature, namely the revolutionary threat of 1917/ 18. This drove the Dutch bourgeoisie *en bloc* into the arms of the allied victors. In

November 1918, Fentener van Vlissingen handed to ter Meulen (of Hope & Co. merchant bank) a request to be handed over to the English, asking them:

> in the name of a number of prominent men in our dear fatherland ... Kröller, Van Leeuwen, (De Savornin) Lohman, Dresselhuys and Nolens ... to attempt to influence Henderson via either Smuts or Barnes, so that they [the English socialists, RB] would persuade [their Dutch comrade, RB] Troelstra to abandon his revolutionary plans before Sunday, by pointing out to him that deliveries of food supplies etc. would not be possible if as a result of riots a proper distribution could not be guaranteed.
>
> *(Heldring 1970: 264–5)*

In addition, several 'prominent' Dutch figures are said to have asked the English to undertake an armed intervention in case of revolution. Considering their pro-German reputation, Heldring went on to qualify the positions of Kröller and Fentener van Vlissingen in these matters as 'incomprehensible'.

An important turn in the overall foreign policy orientation of political parties was made by the ARP. Already before the start of WWI, the party realized that its traditional protectionist course was an insufficient guarantee for electoral success. From being reticent on tariff matters right before WWI, the ARP turned into a pillar of support for free trade afterwards. This switch was facilitated by the favourable business cycle dating from before WWI (Blaisse 1952: 55). At the same time, the ARP developed from a pro-German (under Kuyper) into a pro-English party under the leadership of Colijn. Colijn's foreign policy clarifies the extent to which domestic policy alternatives, trade policy, and foreign policy mutually influence each other.

Colijn's efforts for coming to agreements on multilateral tariff reductions, in which he invested much of his prestige in his role as an international intermediary, counteracted other attempts at containing the crisis internationally. These 'other attempts' were led by

> the industrialists of the great countries, especially France, Germany, and Italy, who oppose tariff reductions in principle and make it appear as if Europe's salvation lies in cartellization. Loucheur[10] defended this position time and again at Geneva, and in the International Chamber of Commerce it was Duchemin who strongly warned against hasty tariff reductions, as if that were the case.
>
> *(Heldring 1970: 822)*

What matters is that these attempts to find international solutions to the crisis are aligned with the proposed domestic solutions. International private cartel agreements presuppose 'disciplined' domestic markets; in other words, regulation. A deflationary, 'liberal', anti-crisis policy implies mutual tariff reductions, either on a global scale or in blocks of countries. Even when all attempts at mutual tariff reductions on a European level had failed, these still served as an

44 Ries Bode

imaginary keystone to Colijn's deflation policy (cf. his 1935 speech to the Industrial Club discussed below).

The same contradiction played a role in the so-called pan-European movement, in which the same Loucheur was chairman of the French Pan-Europe Committee (Heldring 1970: 903). The most important confrontation took place during the preparations of the Geneva conference, and it was Colijn who lost. The Dutch industrialists certainly did not appreciate Colijn's activities; nor did the Catholics or internationally oriented industrialists like Philips and Fentener van Vlissingen (AKU and Steenkolen Handels Vereniging – or Coal Trading Society), who were especially active in shaping the Loucheur conception on the international stage – Fentener van Vlissingen, among others, as chairman of the International Chamber of Commerce and in a later period as 'governor-regulator' during the German occupation of the Netherlands (Martin 1950: 99, 136; Heldring 1970: 1040). Colijn was, however, highly appreciated by the 'pacifist international' of trade, shipping, and banking capitalists.

So, what was the result of this Dutch foreign policy orientation for resolving the crisis within the Netherlands itself? At the start of the current section, it was noted that none of the fractions of the Dutch bourgeoisie managed to gain hegemony over all policy terrains. As far as foreign policy was concerned, it was the orientation towards England that caused several contradictions within Dutch crisis policies. Hirschfeld argues that an English-style imperial preference system was impossible for the Netherlands because of the above-mentioned Sumatra Treaty of 1871 (Hirschfeld 1946: 56). The Dutch acceptance of the English demand to keep the Dutch East Indies open for English goods and capital – while England itself decided to partly close her colonial territories to other capitalist interests – can only be explained by the persistent interests of one specific fraction of the Dutch bourgeoisie, namely colonial trade, shipping, and finance capital, which presumed that Dutch sovereignty over the Dutch East Indies could only be preserved by means of English support.

A similar subordination to the interests of English imperialism can be witnessed in the developments around the so-called Convention of Ouchy. Instigated by the Dutch Ministry of Foreign Affairs, which was still in the hands of the free traders (trade policy there was the responsibility of J.A. Nederbragt), it attempted to reach agreement on mutual tariff reductions between the Netherlands, the Belgian–Luxembourg Union, and the Scandinavian countries. This resulted in the Convention of Oslo (December 1930) and the Convention of Ouchy (July 1932). But these attempts to breach the protection system that had developed, ruefully characterized by Hirschfeld as 'one of the last convulsions of the archaic conservative trade policy' (Hirschfeld 1946: 82), broke down due to resistance from both the British as well as the protectionists.

Controversies in monetary and financial policies

The successive Colijn governments attempted to absorb the devaluation of the English pound and the consequences of increasing foreign protection through adjustments of the domestic price level. A devaluation of the Dutch guilder had to be avoided at all costs. However, the pressure from various interest groups, especially agriculture and the predominantly Catholic-backed industrialists, led to a system of protection through quotas and regulation of competition. Among other things, this caused the price levels of the sectors under quotas to drop significantly less than sectors unaffected by them (Blaisse 1952: 173). As a result, 'adaptation' occurred in some sectors but not others; likewise, its burden was felt by some categories of people but not by others. Wages fell while the price levels of many primary consumer goods remained at the same level. Wages also fell in the sectors under quotas, albeit to a lesser extent. This resulted in higher profits, because prices did not fall proportionally. At the same time, the consumer goods industry suffered from lower sales.

> In this manner, as it were, two price levels developed, one of free market prices for export goods and products for which no restrictions were in place, and another of privileged higher prices, which arose in the markets protected by the government or the entrepreneurs. This disparity was also felt in the wages. The privileged prices played an important role in household budgets.
>
> *(de Graaff 1952: 12–13)*

The fact that this price rigidity was manifested precisely in economically weak but politically strongly represented sectors also caused a situation of maladjustment of economic structures and of competitive strength compared to global market developments. The profits went to (labour-saving) investments in structurally backward sectors, or they were not invested in productive activities at all. In 1938, for example, a director of the Twentsche Bank estimated the total of idle capital at 1 billion guilders (Bosch 1948: 321).

Portfolio investments abroad were another destination for profits. According to Bosch, the English devaluation led to a large-scale 'capital flight' from the Netherlands due to the changing exchange rates; this was further strengthened in 1934 and in the following years, because unlike in the Netherlands, abroad the economy recovered and profits rose (Bosch 1948: 311–12). The reason behind this capital flight is clear. The devaluation of both the dollar and the pound increased the purchasing power of the Dutch guilder, allowing for more investments to be made with Dutch capital – which were often necessary to make up for the losses incurred in regions hit by devaluation.

The capital flight from the Netherlands resulted in a paradoxical situation in which interest rates remained high despite the economic downturn. This situation obviously did not stimulate investments reliant on capital market finance; on the other hand, high interest rates made it difficult for the government to keep the level of taxation within limits.

Under the influence of growing protest from, among others, the industrialists, and because money capital profited excessively from this situation, the government was forced to take several – albeit often rather toothless – measures at the expense of money capital. The so-called 'emission embargo' established in 1933, for

46 Ries Bode

example, forbade new portfolio investment abroad, thus intending to push down interest rates. The Dutch Central Bank (De Nederlandse Bank) could make exceptions, however, and the interested parties were prominently represented in this institution (Bosch 1948: 313).

The eventual drop in interest rates was not so much caused by these measures, but by the devaluation of the guilder in 1936. Either right before or right after this devaluation – opinions are divided on this (Bosch 1948: 313; Keesing 1952: 300; Becker and van Oenen 1975: 31) – an economic boom took place in the Netherlands, which for the time being was primarily expressed in profit levels.

This led to a repatriation of capital to the Netherlands, a tendency that was reinforced by several other consequences of the devaluation. On the one hand, the assets of funds that were investing abroad strongly increased in value after the earlier losses incurred by the devaluations of the dollar and pound. On the other hand, the diminished purchasing power of the guilder made it less attractive to expand foreign portfolio investment. What is more, after the devaluation – which was unnecessary from a technical perspective – the Dutch guilder was kept at an artificially low value, setting in motion an enormous influx of gold. The fact that, despite the changed circumstances (sharply fallen interest rates), no measures were taken (e.g. revoking the embargo on sending capital abroad) says something about the altered power relations between money and industrial capital. It had turned in favour of the latter (Bosch 1948: 322).

Government also profited strongly from low interest rates. After 1936, conversion after conversion of the interest on government loans took place. It seemed that the era of direct influence on government policy by money capital – or at any rate, investment capital – was over. Insurance companies, pension funds, social insurance funds, and saving banks were even forced to organize themselves into an investment cartel, the so-called Consultation Committee on Investments (Commissie tot Overleg in Beleggingszaken) (Bosch 1948: 320).

Of course, this did not mean that the societal power of money capital had been broken as well. When Minister of Economic Affairs Steenberghe, confronted by the social consequences of the large number of bankruptcies, tried to limit the powers of foreclosure on mortgages on agricultural properties, his measure was quickly countered by a freeze on lending to agriculture, as can be read in the diary of a very satisfied Heldring (April 1935, Heldring 1970: 1112).

One of the main causes of the 1936 devaluation has probably been the pressure from the industrial and agricultural sectors to apply the deflationary policy to lending as well. Their goal of a redistribution of surplus value at the expense of money capital resulted in a steep drop in support for a consistent deflationary policy from money and commercial capital. 'It is my opinion that, *now that the government regards intervention in interest rates as necessary for further deflation*, the fight over the Gold Standard at its current level is turning into a waste of mental and national energy' (Heldring 1970: 1130 [italics added by RB]).

As with the aspects of the governmental policy considered earlier, we again see that economic policy (in this case in the 1930s) was not a product of rational consideration concerning the effects of the measures on a few indicators, but instead resulted from a power struggle. The devaluation did not take place at the time at which it was most necessary for improving the balance of payments. This would have been 1933, the only year between 1930 and 1939 that saw a deficit in the balance of payments (Klein 1975: 134). Instead, the investment interest reinforced the devaluation camp.

Financial and monetary policy resulted in an important unintended effect: growing state intervention in the economy. Indeed, the *purpose* of the consistent adherence to deflationary policy was to stop the trend toward increased state influence in economic matters. In Colijn's speech for 'Doctrina' and the 'Industrial Club' on 16 January 1935, titled 'What can we do and what must we avoid doing in order to increase the diminished wealth of our people', he himself turns against autonomous production limitations and price regulations as well as against 'state slavery' (cited by van der Ven 1952: 80).

The *result* of the deflationary policies and the delay of devaluation, however, was that the groups favouring regulation gained in strength through the support they received from the increasingly troubled capitalists, as well as from the labour movement. To retain sufficient support as free traders, the government was forced to make occasional concessions, to protect certain sectors, and even to stimulate production limits within cartels. The latter was to make sure that production and import quota would have the desired effect, i.e. higher profits.

In this manner, and against the will of the deflationists, an entire system of subsidies and state-funded employment developed, necessary to keep the destructive effects of the deflationary policies at bay. Even the trade and shipping capitalists – despite their principles – involved themselves in the fight over subsidies. Take the Society for the Defence of National Shipping Interests (Maatschappij ter Behartiging van Nationale Scheepvaartbelangen, Benas), which offered credit to the shipping industry, informally agreeing that their repayment was not required (Hirschfeld 1959: 44).

Another highly telling example is the credit request by Heldring on behalf of the Koninklijke Nederlandse Scheepvaart Maatschappij (Royal Dutch Shipping Company). Initially, this request seemed to be rejected because, among other reasons, Minister Verschuur feared that all shipping enterprises would ask for the same.

> Verschuur, or so I heard from van der Houven van Oordt, does not want to hear of subsidies. Not only not now, as seems to be Doornick's opinion *with a view to measures to lower wages and unemployment benefits* that the government wants to enforce in the Spring (Colijn as well recently confirmed this to me) and *that would be weakened by subsidies* (I disagree), but also not after.
>
> *(January 1934; Heldring 1970: 1060–1 [italics added])*

In this issue of subsidies for the shipping industry, we see how the struggle between group interests (fractions of capital) can go straight against the struggle between fractions of the bourgeoisie. Heldring, the free trader and deflationist, demands special governmental support to compensate for the disastrous results of

48 Ries Bode

the policies he proposed for his own interests in trade and shipping. And Verschuur, reformer of a protectionist orientation, provider of subsidies, resists specific measures in support of shipping. Charity begins at home!

The relation between deflation and the resistance to regulation was acknowledged by different sides. Vleeschhouwer saw this as well. In his eyes, protection would inevitably lead to 'socialization', because 'Internal freedom ... cannot be united with external protection in the long run' (Vleeschhouwer 1927: 196). And Hirschfeld argues with the benefit of hindsight that, had the government not held on to the Gold Standard for so long, it would not have been sucked so deeply into the swamp of government intervention (Hirschfeld 1946: 54). In contrast to England, the Netherlands saw its share of government spending in national income rise during the 1930s (Klein 1975: 145).

The attempt to adjust to the changed global market by upholding the Gold Standard was doomed to fail. Governmental intervention even developed faster than would have been the case with a floating guilder, without the possibility of this increasing governmental intervention leading to effective countercyclical policies. 'The countries of the gold bloc barred the road to an active economic policy, as long as they remained loyal to gold' (Keesing 1952: 308).

Because of this, it makes sense to delve a bit deeper into the riddle of the Pure Guilder (Dutch: *Gave Gulden*). In the development of Dutch economic policy making in the 1930s, the decision *not* to follow the devaluation of the English pound was strategic in nature. This decision necessitated a large number of protective measures intended as temporary. It meant, for example, the frequent use of quantitative import restrictions instead of import tariffs (Blaisse 1952: 143). These measures only partly compensated for the consequences of sticking to the Gold Standard in the face of the devaluation of the pound. In that light, it makes no difference that these measures, initially regarded to be temporary, became more systematic and permanent after 1933.

The main argument for protection remained safeguarding sufficient societal support to push through adjustments *while maintaining the Pure Guilder*. The increasing significance of industrial development in the Netherlands of course pushed up the price the deflationists had to pay to uphold the international value of the guilder. These costs mainly took the form of selective protection.

So, *based solely on the changes in trade policies from 1931*, it does not seem right to state that they 'indicate how Dutch industry appeared able to break the ancient tradition of the empire of the sea (meaning free trade), when this appeared necessary on the basis of temporary economic facts' (W.P.L.M. de Kort 1940, cited in Elshof 1973: 4). Again, the changes in trade policy were the price the deflationists paid for upholding the Gold Standard. Otherwise, according to de Kort's reasoning, one would have to conclude from the *reduction* in protectionist measures after the devaluation of the guilder that the industrialists were losing power again.

Likewise, one cannot consider the *more consistent adjustment policy* from 1933 onwards – after the failure of international attempts to agree multilateral tariff reductions – as a true turning point in the development of economic policy. After all, it was

Dutch bourgeoisie between the two world wars 49

precisely in 1933 that the decision was taken not to devalue the guilder – even though, as we have seen, that was the only year showing a balance-of-payments deficit in a decade.

It was hoped, however, that sticking to the Gold Standard would allow the Netherlands to profit from the monetary weakness of other countries and strengthen the country as a financial centre. 'We are not coin counterfeiters' – as Trip put it (Keesing 1952, part III: 279). Hirschfeld later wrote that: 'It was feared that the Netherlands' international reputation would suffer, were it to follow the English example' (Hirschfeld 1946: 53).

Blaisse, on the other hand, himself a representative of the Catholic industrialists, was more specific: 'The upholding of the Gold Standard also primarily benefitted specific interests of the Netherlands as a creditor nation' (Blaisse 1952: 310). His sketch of the interests that opposed one another in matters of monetary policy merits a longer citation.

> Multiple currents could be discerned within the deflationary camp. One small group trusted the automatic adjustments of costs and prices and defended the position that the government had to impede this process as little as possible. Year after year, the president of the Nederlandse Bank included in the institution's reports authoritative admonitions against artificial limitations, like wage rigidity, tax increases, and trade policy measures, which would inhibit or block necessary adjustments. The large Chambers of Commerce often spoke in the same spirit. The liberal group in the Second Chamber however, less orthodox in its doctrine, while sympathizing with this way of thinking, it had to consider the demands of practical politics to a larger degree. This often caused its parliamentary group, or its individual members, to be the first to demand supportive measures for agriculture, for Twente, the ports, or the shipping sectors ... Just as the advocates of adjustment policies were not, those who wanted to bridge the difference in level from the other side, namely by reducing the value of the currency, were not unified either. On the one hand, those in favour of devaluation were to be found in liberal and entrepreneurial circles, which expected that by abolishing price disparities, the economic balance would be restored by monetary means. They expected the government to subsequently retreat to a more modest position and leave the further healing to the societal forces of regeneration. They especially counted on the disappearance of the import restrictions – so vexatious for trade and shipping – and the agricultural crisis measures. On the other hand, one could find fervent defenders of devaluation among those fighting for economic reform, who regarded the upholding of the Gold Standard as a barrier for 'pump-priming' the domestic economic cycle and other more far reaching projects.
>
> *(Blaisse 1952: 142–3, 145)*

Translated into the terminology of this article, this means that, under the influence of the economic consequences of adjustment policy, a breach developed in the liberal camp with respect to monetary policy. During the five years after 1931, a monetary policy was introduced that could only benefit the money capitalists. Firstly, because – thanks to the strong guilder – the possibilities for foreign investment were enlarged. Secondly, because the resulting capital flight kept interest rates high in the Netherlands.

But deflationary policy was directly disadvantageous for trade and shipping capital, as well as for liberal agriculture and industry. Furthermore, protectionists and regulators also resisted. *The resistance from within the liberal camp was fuelled by particular group interests: resistance by 'fractions of capital'. The resistance of the protectionists and regulators, on the other hand, was underpinned by a comprehensive concept of control that differed fundamentally from the liberal concept and that thus constituted resistance by a 'fraction of the bourgeoisie'.*

As early as 1933, the public media (*De Telegraaf*)[11] had started a campaign in favour of devaluation. This resulted among other effects in the establishment of the Society for Stable Money Value (Vereniging voor Waardevast Geld) against deflation, led by the Rotterdam professors de Vries and Goudriaan (Heldring 1970: 1045). The initiative for this campaign came from Bronsink, who had a history in the shipping sector and a position as outside director of Hoogovens. The Association for Economic Policy, the trade and shipping capital behind the liberal party, had also become divided on this matter (Heldring 1970: 1143).

In sum, those interests that were directly hit distanced themselves from the orientation of money capital. In the years that followed, an increasing number of forms of cooperation developed between liberal and regulation-oriented segments of industrial capital. The Catholics, representatives of the latter, had resisted sticking to the Gold Standard for a long time. It was the reason behind Steenberghe's resignation as the Minister of Economic Affairs in 1935, only to return in 1937, after the devaluation (Hirschfeld 1959: 52ff; Heldring 1970: 1122). But Verschuur too was actually – according to his secretary-general – against adherence to the Gold Standard all along (Hirschfeld 1946: 87).

The essential turning point in Dutch economic policies was the abandonment of the Gold Standard. Only then did it become possible to conduct a countercyclical economic policy. That did not mean that the ideas of Keynes, which especially resonated with the CHU and the Catholic regulators (as well as with the Social Democrats), were adopted in every respect. For example, the concept of deficit financing was not accepted yet (Blaisse 1952: 145; Klein 1975: 127).

The fact that devaluation only took place in 1936 illustrates the persistence of the descendants of the patrician liberals, i.e. liberal money and commercial capital. Their influence had been felt less within political parties as such, but more in the background, in the contacts with small but decisive cliques within the CHU, the ARP, and the VB. The devaluation marked their political demise. Independent money capital and commercial and shipping capital, interlinked through family ties, was eclipsed. That it had been able to maintain so much influence for such a long time was due to its early rise, the international position of the Netherlands, and the weak labour movement in the Netherlands.

The deflationary and regulating road and the class struggle: controversies over social policy

The previous sub-section covered the controversies within the Dutch bourgeoisie regarding the solution to the crisis and its effects, without explicitly inquiring into the role of the labour movement. This approach is, of course, impossible when we turn to social policy, if only because the Social-Democratic part of the labour movement, from the moment that it tried to offer a comprehensive alternative to the crisis policy *based on the maintenance of capitalist relations of production* (see the Labour Plan [Plan van de Arbeid]of 1935 [Alberda 1935]), began to play an important role in the dynamics of the contradictions within the bourgeoisie. From that moment on, it became possible for parts of the bourgeoisie to design a programme incorporating solutions proposed by social democracy and integrate them into a comprehensive concept of control. Which roads in the field of social policy were open for the different parts of the Dutch bourgeoisie and which political forces propagated them?

Extreme deflationary policies had been implemented in earlier economic crises, as in 1920–23, which had aimed to unleash the spontaneous self-cleansing effect of capitalism. From 1929 onwards, the differences in opinion regarding this mode of crisis policy were growing; not only between the capitalists and organized labour (workers were, after all, the ones to bear most of the burden of deflation), but also among capitalists themselves.

In the period directly following WWI, integration of the demands of labour had come to the fore for the first time. After all, following the initial panic, during which all parts of the bourgeoisie were prepared to confront the workers' revolt by all means necessary, came the phase of accommodation. Even the liberals toyed with the idea of temporarily co-opting the still undefeated labour movement. In response to the 1918 election, Heldring wrote:

> I regret that the election results do not allow for a radical socialist government, which I would regard as a safety valve against the bolshevism that awaits us. A conservative government would nowadays have a provocative impact on the tense public sentiments.
>
> *(1970: 230)*

At a later stage, conservative old liberals would refrain from such considerations. It would be the Liberal Democrats (Vrijzinnig Democraten) who would become proponents of the integration of social democracy by encouraging its *participation in government*.

After the gravest threat had faded, participation in government by social democracy became too high a price to pay for parts of the liberal current – as became revealed in the drifting apart of the Union Liberals (Unie Liberalen) and the liberal left wing, the Liberal Democrats. The Union Liberals moved closer to the right-wing 'free liberals', the VB (Oud 1948–51, II: 3–4).

The circles of the Catholic industrial bourgeoisie and the Protestant petty bourgeoisie ('Kleine Luyden', 'little people') pursued a different form of integration that was an extension of their own emancipation struggle, which was directed against the hegemony of commercial, bank, and colonial capital. This struggle had promoted the incorporation of the religious parts of the working class into political, cultural, and other societal organizations; the confessional parties were, in turn, supported by such organizations, which were supposed to offer an answer to the class struggle to the extent that the influence of social democracy on the religious workers could be contained.[12] This specifically confessional form of integration made the confessional parties oppose the left liberal type of integration, which was based on social democratic participation in government, because this might affect their following among the workers (Oud 1948–51, II: 151–2).

The mass support for the Catholic emancipation movement explains the strength with which the industrial bourgeoisie could rise despite the weakness of the labour movement of Catholic origin, and with that the weakness of the labour movement as a whole. Accordingly, pillarization has always been treasured by right-wing politicians (Tichelman 1973: 10; Fennema 1976: 63).

This approach to mass social integration proposed in confessional circles also had a business aspect. Commercial capitalists have more scope for manoeuvre in the class struggle; they can repress labour unrest more fiercely, because they have less to fear from negative effects on labour productivity. After all, labour in this sector is predominantly unskilled, with easily replaceable employees. Colonial capital can stay aloof from social questions entirely: 'it only appears in the gentle form of the *consumer*; production and its secrets remain hidden far beyond the horizon, in the southern hemisphere' (Roland Holst 1971 [1931], I: 187).

The industrial bourgeoisie, however, had to find an answer to the class antagonisms with the workers. Because regardless of how mind-numbing labour in the emergent industry might have been, industrial entrepreneurs were faced with the dilemma that, on the one hand, skill and experience positively influenced labour productivity and, on the other, opportunities for more permanent forms of organization were larger among these skilled layers of the working class. Together these factors gave rise to a certain degree of 'irreplaceability'.

Of course, the industrial entrepreneurs also believed the answer had to be cheap, because of the often remarked weak state of industry in the Netherlands. So, the answer had to be realized *through the state*, meaning as much as possible at the expense of the other capital fractions, or with non-economic measures. The latter was the achievement of the corporative ideology, which preached the doctrine of harmony between classes to be based preferably on religious principles. No wonder that the weak Catholic industrial bourgeoisie developed a special interest in corporatism, as long as economic policy remained tailored to the interests of liberal money and commercial capital and the internationally competitive industrial sectors.

The first economically oriented corporatist ideologue was Professor Veraart from Nijmegen, who was supported – albeit temporarily – by the southern Catholic entrepreneurs. In his 1918 'Vraagstukken der economische bedrijfsorganisatie'

('Questions of economic business organization'), he attempted to show the viability of price agreements among industrialists and of collective labour agreements – both with compulsory clauses. In 1921, he pleaded in 'Beginselen der Economische Bedrijfsorganisatie' ('Principles of economic business organization') for a societal order based on a cartel and price agreement system, which would have to be established by the entrepreneurs themselves. In this vision, the state's only task was to guard against excessive 'greed of the economic branches', to prevent disproportionalities (van der Ven 1952: 26–7).

To popularize such ideas, so-called Catholic Days were organized by the Roman Catholic Central Council of Corporations, an organization of Catholic entrepreneurs, middle-class and farmer organizations, and trade unions. Here the arguments for public corporatist organizations and collective labour agreements were heard from the likes of van Spaendonck, Kortenhorst, Romme, and others (van der Ven 1952: 29). The entrepreneurial reaction, however, which aimed to roll back the gains of the workers after 1919, also drove the classes apart within the Catholic pillar. From this point on, the intensity with which corporatist ideas would be emphasized by especially Catholic politicians would vary with the extent to which the labour movement and the economic conjuncture were experienced as a threat. For example, in response to a report on socialization of the Social Democratic Labour Party drafted by the Wibaut commission shortly after WWI, a socialization commission named after Nolens was established by motion of the Second Chamber. This commission, however, only published her conclusions in 1927.

Concerning the political parties, a regulatory or ordo-liberal current also developed within traditionally liberal parties. Such a current developed within the CHU – traditionally the main representative of Rotterdam liberal shipping and trade capital – around the group of the 'Rotterdam professors'. These gentlemen, among whom Lieftinck, van Rhijn (who was secretary-general at the Ministry of Economic Affairs before the war, was active during the war in the Ministry of Agriculture, and after the war served as state secretary for Social Affairs[13]), and F. de Vries (who after the war, among other roles, was chairman of the Socio-Economic Advisory Council (Sociaal-Economische Raad), in which employees' and employers' organizations participated) led the current that during and after WWII crossed over to the Dutch People's Movement (Nederlandse Volksbeweging) and the Labour Party (Partij van de Arbeid) (Hoek 1970: 30, 124 ff.).

The writings of these CHU regulators were an obstacle for people like Colijn and Heldring, who wondered how such cuckoo eggs could have ever hatched in the seemingly reliable conservative-liberal CHU nest. As Heldring argued, citing the judgement offered by Colijn: 'the Christian-Historical party has fully outlived its role and, in his opinion, is further undermined by the Rotterdam professors, who are the most forceful apostles of regulation' (Heldring 1970: 1288).

In 1937 a report was published by a commission chaired by Lieftinck, addressed to the CHU leadership, entitled 'Vrijheid en gebondenheid in het bedrijfsleven' ('Freedom and restraint in the business world'). Among other observations, the report argued that the economic system, supported by free competition and the price mechanism as decisive regulators of economic life, is showing such deficiencies and has caused so much justified resistance, that it can no longer control the organization of economic life to the extent that it once did.

(cited in van der Ven 1952: 92)

Therefore, it argued, another socio-economic order had to be established that would obviate 'a comprehensive regulation of economic and social life by the government'. A minority report was appended that spoke out against regulation, making it 'obvious that indeed there was no possibility for compromise'.

Within the Roomsch-katholieke Staatspartij (Roman Catholic State Party; RKSP), the prime stronghold of the regulators, the few liberals (like Trip and Welter) were increasingly being pushed into the background. It was only because of his free trade views and his track record in the colonial banking sector that a man like Trip, despite his Catholicism, was acceptable to commercial and money capital as President of 'De Nederlandsche Bank' (Heldring 1970: 486).

In the ARP, relations were less clear, although here too a protectionist regulation current was present, personified by Diepenhorst.

These developments were all dominated by the growing cooperation between and, indeed, hegemony of, Catholic and liberal industrial interests. In this cooperative endeavour, which would develop further during and after the war, specific group interests once again had to be reconciled. The resulting fraction of the bourgeoisie succeeded in keeping the opposing group interests within the bounds of its conception of 'the' general interest. The common *victims* of this general interest after WWII would primarily turn out to be the working class and parts of the agricultural population.

Politically, the rapprochement between the industrial capital fractions was completed by the mutual convergence of the crisis response projects of the corporatist Catholics, the Social Democrats, and the reform-minded members of the CHU.

Conclusion

If the developments described above were to be traced into the 1940s, it would become clear that these years were marked by a further political crystallization in the same direction: a continuation of the trend that started in the 1930s. This trend can be described as the very slow impact on political relations of changing power relations at a societal scale among industrial capital, independent commercial and bank capital, and associated shipping capital. Industrial capital was primarily oriented towards the domestic market, the latter two were primarily internationally oriented, especially towards the Dutch East Indies.

Societal power relations were changing for three reasons. Firstly, because of the increasing importance of domestic industrial development; secondly, because of the development of global market relations in the 1930s (and corresponding changes in international politics); and thirdly, because a part of the old shipping, commercial,

Dutch bourgeoisie between the two world wars 55

and bank capital was increasingly reorienting towards domestic industrial development. The last point is especially true for the Rotterdam arm of the old liberal fraction of the bourgeoisie, a large part of which felt at home in the CHU.

Industrialization, corporatism, protectionism, and active *trade policy* are the keywords with which the fraction of the bourgeoisie oriented towards domestic industrial development characterized its comprehensive concept of control after WWII. Providing some clarity concerning its pre-war backgrounds is the purpose of this article.

Notes

1 This article was translated from the original by Pascal van Opzeeland. The original text was followed as closely as possible. Quotations from Dutch originals appear in English translation. For a better understanding by a non-Dutch audience, editorial explanations are given in these endnotes (editors' note).
2 *Stamokap* theory (Staatsmonopolistischer Kapitalismus, or State Monopoly Capitalism) had become, in the 1960s and 1970s, the dominant account of contemporary advanced capitalism within the leading communist parties in both Eastern and Western Europe. This approach is reviewed extensively in B. Jessop (1982), The capitalist state. Marxist theories and methods, Oxford: Martin Robertson (editors' note).
3 The Dutch 'stroming' is translated here as 'current'. Elsewhere in this text, the same word has been translated variously by current, tendency, grouping or fraction, depending on context (editors' note).
4 This steel works is located in IJmuiden, near the Amsterdam seaport.
5 Named after the founding brothers Clemens and August Brenninkmeijer.
6 A more elaborate presentation of this point is presented in Hirsch (1978 [1974]). This text illustrates parallels between Dutch and German work on the state at this time.
7 The Netherlands has a bicameral parliamentary system, with the Second Chamber serving as the primary political chamber, and the older First Chamber (informally, also called the Senate) as a *chamber de réflection*.
8 Johan Rudolph Thorbecke (1798–1872) was the founder of Dutch liberalism and the chief author of the liberal democratic Dutch constitution of 1848.
9 A region in the eastern province of Overijssel, with Enschede as the central city.
10 An important representative of French industrialists who was minister several times, including posts as minister of armaments, reconstruction, liberated areas, trade, finance, and labour.
11 *De Telegraaf* was, and remains so, the largest circulation popular newspaper with a clear non-denominational right-of-centre profile.
12 This compartmentalization of Dutch society into religious and philosophical groupings or 'pillars' has been described in the political science literature as 'pillarization' (Lijphart 1975; see Fennema 1976 for a critique).
13 Unlike the Secretary-General, who is the highest-ranking civil servant in a particular ministry, state secretaries are deputy ministers in government.

References

Albarda, J.W. (1935). *Plan van de arbeid: rapport van de commissie uit NVV en SDAP*. Amsterdam: De Arbeiderspers.
Baran, P.A. and Sweezy, P.M. (1966). *Monopoly capital. An essay on the American economic and social order*. Harmondsworth: Penguin.
Baruch, F. (1962). *Grote macht in klein land. Een beeld van het monopoliekapitaal en zijn invloed in Nederland, deel I en II*. Amsterdam: Uitgeverij Pegasus.

56 Ries Bode

Becker, F. and van Oenen, G.J. (1975). De economische ontwikkeling in het Interbellum. University of Amsterdam, unpublished manuscript.

Bettelheim, C. (1946). *L'économie allemande sous le nazisme. Un aspect de la décadence du capitalisme.* Paris: Marcel Rivière (new edition 1971: Paris: Maspero).

Blaisse, P.A. (1952). *De Nederlandse handelspolitiek in de Nederlandse volkshuishouding tussen de twee wereldoorlogen,* Part II (Ed. P.B. Kreukniet). Utrecht: Spectrum.

Bode, R. (1978). Schets van de ontwikkeling van het Nederlandse kapitalisme en zijn burgerij. Unpublished MA thesis. University of Amsterdam FSW-A (DOGIB).

Bosch, K.D. (1948). *De Nederlandse beleggingen in de Verenigde Staten.* Amsterdam: Elsevier.

Brugmans, I.J. (1976). *Paardenkracht en mensenmacht. Sociaal-economische geschiedenis van Nederland, 1795–1940.* Den Haag: Martinus Nijhoff.

Busch, K. (1974). *Die multinationale Konzerne. Zur Analyse der Weltmarktbewegung des Kapitals.* Frankfurt: Suhrkamp.

Centraal Bureau voor de Statistiek (1975). *75 Jaar statistiek van Nederland.* Den Haag: Staatsuitgeverij.

Chamber of Commerce Amsterdam (1936). *Memorial book,* part 1, ed. J.C. Westermann. Amsterdam: Kamer van Koophandel en Fabrieken.

Cogoy, M. (1973). Werttheorie und Staatsausgaben. In C. von Braumühl, C. Funken, M. Cogoy, and J. Hirsch (Eds), *Probleme einer materialistische Staatstheorie* (pp. 129–198). Frankfurt: Suhrkamp.

Daalder, H. (1966). The Netherlands opposition in a segmented society. In R.A. Dahl (Ed.), *Political oppositions in Western democracies* (pp. 188–236). New Haven, CT: Yale University Press.

Elshof, P. (1973). De strukturele veranderingen van de Nederlandse ekonomie tussen 1930 en 1950. Unpublished. University of Amsterdam DSW-A (DODO).

Fennema, M. (1975). *De multinationale ondernemingen en de nationale staat.* Amsterdam: Socialistiese Uitgeverij.

Fennema, M. (1976). Professor Lijphart en de Nederlandse politiek. *Acta Politica* 1: 54–78.

de Graaff, A. (1952). De industrie. In P.B. Kreukniet (Ed.), *De Nederlandse volkshuishouding tussen de twee wereldoorlogen,* vol. 8 (pp. 1–207). Utrecht: Spectrum.

Heldring, E. (1970). *Herinneringen dagboek van Ernst Heldring,* Parts I, II and III (Ed. J. de Vries). Utrecht: Het Nederlands Historisch Genootschap.

Hirsch, J. (1974). *Staatsapparat und Reproduktion des Kapitals.* Frankfurt: Suhrkamp.

Hirsch, J. (1978 [1974]). The state apparatus and social reproduction: Elements of theory of the bourgeois state. In J. Holloway and S. Picciott (Eds), *The state and capital. A German debate* (pp. 57–107). London: Edward Arnold.

Hirschfeld, H.M. (1946). *Actieve economische politiek in Nederland in de Jaren 1929–1934.* Amsterdam: Elsevier.

Hirschfeld, H.M. (1959). *Herinneringen uit de Jaren 1933–1939.* Amsterdam: Elsevier.

Hoek, J.S. (1970). *Politieke geschiedenis van Nederland: Oorlog en herstel.* Leiden: A.W. Sijthoff.

Holloway, J. and Picciotto, S. (1980). Capital, the state and European integration. In P. Zarembka (Ed.) *Research in political economy,* vol. 3 (pp. 123–154). Greenwich, CT: JAI Press.

Jessop, B. (1982). *The capitalist state: Marxist theories and methods.* Oxford: Martin Robertson.

de Jonge, J.A. (1976). *De industrialisatie in Nederland tussen 1850 en 1914.* Nijmegen: Socialistische Uitgeverij.

Keesing, F.A.G. (1952). De conjuncturele ontwikkeling van Nederland en de evolutie van de economische overheidspolitiek, 1918–1936. In P.B. Kreukniet (Ed.) *Nederlandse Volkshuishouding tussen de twee wereldoorlogen,* Part II and III. Utrecht: Spectrum.

Klein, P.W. (1975). Depression and policy in the thirties. *Acta Historiae Neerlandicae, Studies on the History of the Netherlands* 3: 123–159.

de Leeuw, A.S. (1975 [1936]). *Nederland in de wereldpolitiek van 1900 tot heden*. Nijmegen: SUN.

Lieftinck, P. (Ed.) (1938). *Het bedrijfsleven tijdens de regering van H.M. Koningin Wilhelmina 1898–1938*. Haarlem: Spaarnestad.

Lijphart, A. (1975). *The politics of accommodation: Pluralism and democracy in the Netherlands*, 2nd ed. Berkeley, CA: University of California Press.

Mandel, E. (1971). *The formation of the economic thought of Karl Marx, from 1843 to Capital*. London: NLB.

Mandel, E. (1972). *Late capitalism*. London: NLB.

Martin, J.S. (1950). *All honorable men*. Boston, MA: Little, Brown.

Marx, K. (1978). The class struggles in France, 1848–1850. In *Marx-Engels Collected Works*, vol. 10 (pp. 45–145). London: Lawrence & Wishart.

Oud, P.J. (1948–51). *Het jongste verleden, Parlementaire geschiedenis van Nederland 1918–1940, 1948–1951*, Parts II and III. Assen: Van Gorcum.

Plate, A. (1936). *Onze handelspolitiek*. Haarlem: De Erven F. Bohn.

van der Pijl, K. (1978). *Een Amerikaans plan voor Europa. Achtergronden van het ontstaan van de EEG*. Amsterdam: Socialistische Uitgeverij.

Rijkens, P. (1965). *Handel en wandel: nagelaten gedenkschriften, 1888–1965*. Rotterdam: Ad. Donker.

Roland Holst, H. (1971 [1932]). *Kapitaal en arbeid in Nederland, Parts I and II*. Nijmegen: SUN.

Smit, C. (1975). *Tien studiën betreffende Nederland in de eerste wereldoorlog*. Groningen: Tjeenk Willink.

Sohn-Rethel, A. (1975). *Grootkapitaal en fascisme. De Duitse industrie achter Hitler*. Amsterdam: van Gennep.

Teulings, A. (1975). *Philips. Geschiedenis en praktijk van een wereldconcern*. Amsterdam: van Gennep.

Tichelman, F. (1973). Nederland van handelskapitalisme tot industriestaat. *De Internationale* 1 (2): 8–13. www.marxists.org/nederlands/tichelman/1973/1973nederland.htm

Vandenbosch, A. (1959). *Dutch foreign policy since 1815. A study in small power politics*. Den Haag: Martinus Nijhoff.

van der Ven, F.J.H.M. (1952). *Economische en sociale opvattingen in Nederland in de Nederlandse Volkshuishouding tussen de twee wereldoorlogen, Deel I* (Ed. P.B. Kreukniet). Utrecht: Spectrum.

Veraart, J.A. (1918). *Vraagstukken der economische bedrijfsorganisatie*. Den Bosch: C.N. Teulings.

Veraart, J.A. (1921). *Beginselen der economische bedrijfsorganisatie*. Bussum: Uitgeverij Maatschappij;Brussels: De Standaard.

Vleeschhouwer, J.E. (1927). *Actieve handelspolitiek, feiten en uitkomsten*. Den Haag: Nederlandse Vereniging voor Vrijhandel.

2

CLASS FORMATION AT THE INTERNATIONAL LEVEL

Reflections on the political economy of Atlantic Unity (1979)

Kees van der Pijl

In Marxist theory, the international dimension of class formation has received rather limited attention. Although a socialist strategy linked to a struggle for national independence has often been rejected as inherently reactionary,[1] class and the process of class formation tend to be situated theoretically within the framework of the national state. It is my contention in this paper that the international dimensions of imperialist integration and rivalry should be considered as basic features of each national class configuration.[2] To illustrate my point, I will put forward some preliminary ideas on the process of class formation of the bourgeoisie at the international and, more particularly, the 'Atlantic' level.

Present-day Marxist theory has little to offer in this respect. Apart from the 'national' bias (but intimately related to it), the struggle between classes and their actual fractioning in the process of capital accumulation is either theorized in a historicist fashion or dissociated from the historical process altogether. Two main currents of Marxist thought seem to stand out.

First and foremost, Soviet Marxism. As it developed under the conditions of the building of socialism in a single, backward country against the odds of international reaction, dialectical materialism inevitably came to separate the day-to-day economic struggle of the working class, with its hardships and defeats, from the march of history which would somehow prevail. Hence, in its Soviet codification, Marxism came to be characterized by both economism and historicism. This can be seen in the theory of State Monopoly Capitalism. Here, the mediation of relationships between state and capital through international class alignments tends to be replaced by a notion of their immediate fusion, leaving little or no room for class struggles other than a final one aimed at taking over the state from the monopolies. Consequently, the unity of the bourgeoisie is generally taken for granted; if its international orientation changes, the explanation is to be found during the main struggle.[3]

At the other extreme, Louis Althusser and his followers posit the autonomy of non-economic factors in a three-tier conception of social formations, comprising economics, politics, and ideology. For them, the instances of the superstructure are active 'with their own essence and efficacy' (Althusser 1969: 100), being structurally similar, rather than structurally related, to the economic instance. Therefore, with Althusser as with Poulantzas, the position of classes in society acquires a positive quality. In the determination of these positions, technicism has to replace Marxism: for instance, in Poulantzas's analysis of the internationalization of capitalist relations and the national state (in Poulantzas 1975), it is the superior technology of labour processes in the orbit of American capital which makes for American take-overs in Europe, and eventually, for the effective domination of the American bourgeoisie within each national context. But, whatever the wealth of the resulting picture of classes and political orientations among them, the dynamics of interimperialist, or rather 'internal-imperialist' rivalry and integration again have to be relegated to the realm of the 'conjuncture'.

What is lacking in both strands of theory is an appreciation of the intrinsic relation between immediate production and class struggle, and social production and transformation in a broader, historical sense. For Marx, the analysis of capitalism has to overcome the self-evidence and apparent technicality of the mode of production by relating the immediate forms of production and exchange to the contradictory process of capitalism developing into socialism. In developing the productive forces, capital is engaged in a 'flight forward'. 'As the system of bourgeois economy has developed for us only by degrees', he writes in the *Grundrisse*, 'so too its negation, which is its ultimate result ... Everything that has a fixed form, such as the product etc., appears as merely a moment, a vanishing moment, in this movement. The direct production process itself here appears only as a moment' (Marx, *Grundrisse*: 712).

In order to capture these moments in historical materialist categories, i.e. to show that the contradictory nature of social relations is not metaphysical, but is rooted in the process of their material reproduction, Marx uses the method of rising from the summary to the concrete. In *Capital*, the labour process, the process of circulation of capital in its different functional forms and, finally, the profit distribution structure *comprising* the social formation are treated as if temporarily taken out of the real, living totality; but as moments of a process. To quote the *Grundrisse* again: 'all of these fixed suppositions themselves become fluid in the further course of development' (1973: 817). So do classes, which relate to 'places occupied in a historically determined system of social production'[4] but which similarly can be defined more closely at the consecutive levels of abstraction mentioned.

The internationalization of capital in the Atlantic area, to which we now turn, can be explained by analysing the ways capital has found to overcome the contradictions that are inherent in the capitalist process of production, circulation and distribution of profit. This will be looked at in the second part of this paper. In part III, I will go into the different political orientations of the bourgeoisie that accompanied the coming into existence of an integrated circuit of social capital in the Atlantic area. Here, the main problem will certainly be to avoid a reductionist explanation of politics, while still seeking to establish the structural connections that permit the use of the term *relative* autonomy where political and ideological developments are concerned.

It will be my contention that the attitudes among American and Western European bourgeoisies towards Atlantic unity can be traced in particular to the process of circulation of capital in its different functional forms. Circulating capital only gradually penetrated the existing international circuits of simple commodity and money circulation as capital, that is to say, as a social relation which expands by appropriating surplus value, directly or indirectly. Thus, following the internationalization of the circuit of commodity capital in the 19th century, the circuit of money capital internationalized through portfolio investment and investment bank operations in the period of classical imperialism. One step further, the internationalization of the circuit of productive capital takes the form of direct foreign investment by multinational manufacturing firms (cf. Palloix 1974: 109ff.).

In each context, capitals from both sides of the Atlantic were brought together into specific functional combinations. Eventually these would have dissolved into one integrated circuit of social capital, were it not for their being involved in 'certain relations ... between political alliances, between states, on the basis of the territorial division of the world, of the struggle for colonies', of the 'struggle for spheres of influence' which, as Lenin notes, 'develop parallel to and in connection with relations between capitalist associations ... based on the economic division of the world' (1917: 253).

The connection between the two has to be established by fixing elements of a dynamic whole, changing with the relationship of forces they operate upon. For instance, it is important to note that sections of the bourgeoisie, related to fractions of social capital, are distributed unevenly within different national states (in the sense of trade and transport being predominant in the Netherlands, banking in Switzerland, finance capital in Germany, etc.). Hence, not only will the pattern of internationalization from each country differ depending on the overall stage, but domestic class relations, too, will affect, and be affected by, internationalization in quite dissimilar ways. Moreover, as Palloix has pointed out, the role of the state and the structure of the state apparatus differ with each type of internationalization (Palloix 1974: 133ff.). Together with factors like geographical ones (including strategic position in a military sense), these differences mean that national foreign policy is autonomized relative to the tendency of capital and, necessarily, of its complementary political forms, to become international, to develop into an integrated circuit of social capital and an international capitalist class.

This autonomization is not identical to the separation of the political from the economic, as Althusser has it, but rather it is the form through which the process of integration develops. An example may illustrate this. In the early 1960s the American government proposed to the EEC the elimination of all tariffs on agricultural products and on products in which at least 80 percent of trade among capitalist countries was accounted for by exports of the USA and the EEC combined (assuming Britain's membership). The implementation of the latter proposal, in particular, would have led to the development of an integrated circuit of capital in the branches of Department I generally considered as a mark of national economic sovereignty (advanced machine tools, heavy equipment, including nuclear power plants, aerospace industry, etc., cf. Palloix 1974: 88). Added to an already integrated circuit of multinational capital in the more mobile branches of Department I (like oil and chemicals) as well as in consumer goods manufacturing, Atlantic unity would have acquired a very real meaning had not the proposals been blocked by the French veto on British membership and by objections of a protectionist nature on the part of EEC countries (Evans 1967: 7–9). However, the veto, as much as the other foreign policy positions that set France apart from the other Atlantic countries at the time (whether they concerned the military, colonial or Cold War fields and no matter how 'autonomously' they were being pursued), cannot be understood in isolation from the objective requirements, domestic compromises already made and other attributes of the rise of French productive capital to international dimensions. In this case, too, 'nationalist' policies with regard to particular capitals tend to improve the terms on which "national" capitals are integrated into the circuit of world capital rather than to resist that integration' (Clarke 1978: 62). The active role, this time of the French government with respect to current liberal arrangements, like the European Monetary System, is a clear confirmation of this function of the initial nationalism. On the other hand, the problems over EEC monetary compensation for agricultural products, which for a moment threatened to postpone the whole thing, testify to the still considerable weight of the French farm bloc twenty years after its political support was necessary for the reinforcement of French industrial capital (cf. below).

How then do sections of the bourgeoisie on both sides of the Atlantic align as classes, considering that their alignment develops through international politics, involving rivalry and conflict as well? With this question, I come to the actual thesis of this paper.

The bourgeoisie which sponsored imperialist expansion from its main European centres before World War I were associated either with productive capital in their respective countries, or with overseas operations through the international circuits of commodity and money capital or with both. As far as particular links with the United States were concerned, European money capital mainly came from the traditional colonial empires, like the British, French or the Dutch; owing to the wide range of overseas profit opportunities, the 19th century imperial structure did not foster the close integration of the circuits of money capital and domestic productive capital. Rather, the prevailing orientation of well-to-do imperialism was to look at domestic industry through the eyes of cosmopolitan liberalism, i.e., in rentier terms.

In countries like Germany, on the other hand, finance capital had developed to a far greater extent and money capital was less prone to internationalization as a separate circuit. These of course were only tendencies: in all European countries, the liberal section of the bourgeoisie, engaged in overseas operations, had to reckon with an industrial bourgeoisie which was more keenly aware of the need for industrial expansion and for handling the working class at home.

The aftermath of World War I witnessed the development of a similar differentiation among the American bourgeoisie, as American portfolio capital got linked up with productive capital in Europe, with German industrial cartels in particular. However, in the 'thirties, after American capital had gone through its epoch-making restructuring towards a mass consumption economy, the European engagement of US money capital was superseded by direct productive investments of the multinational form of finance capital – at least within the Atlantic context.

The Nazi economy, on the other hand, although fuelled in part by American money capital, and the involvement of US multinationals notwithstanding, embodied the impotence of German productive capital and the sections of the bourgeoisie associated with it to engage in this Atlantic circuit of social capital. Expressing the situation European industrial capital as a whole had got into because of the social irresponsibility of money capital and the depressed living standards, national socialism represented an extreme political variety of a more general trend towards the integration of industrial capital and labour along corporatist and authoritarian lines on the part of the European industrial bourgeoisie and hence was outlived by it.

Accordingly, American involvement in Europe from the 1930s on, and again after the Second World War, tended to fit into the pattern of an integrated, Atlantic circuit of social capital much more than did European involvement the other way around. Reproducing, in a number of respects, the former position of the British Empire and Sterling, the new Pax Americana brought together the liberal elements among the bourgeoisie on both sides of the Atlantic. However, this Atlantic unity could only materialize in a political sense if a number of specific conditions were met.

First, the accumulation pattern of capital in the Atlantic area would have to allow the appropriation of substantial shares of surplus value by the sections of the bourgeoisie most receptive towards Atlantic unity. On the American side, no specific fraction of capital needs to be mentioned, except maybe for finance capital's special relationship with European markets and qualified labour, suggesting a pattern of accumulation characterized by the expansion of productive capital. As for the European bourgeoisie, its liberal wing traditionally collected profits from the international circuits of money and commodity capital. In the context of the post-war Atlantic circuit of social capital, these profits take such various forms as commercial profit, dividends on American stock, interest payments and rent, etc. So, besides US industrial production, international trade would have to rise significantly, too. To complement this economic definition of the alignment of liberal sections of the European bourgeoisie with American capitalism, a second condition is to be found in a rise in living standards engendered by accelerated relative surplus value production 'made in USA', thus allowing the liberal bourgeoisie to govern without having to offer the working class anything but liberalism, i.e. free wage negotiations.

Finally, the expansion of production in the US and of trade with Western Europe would need to be complemented by a firm stand, in terms of both rhetoric and actual military measures, vis-à-vis those bastions of socialism which cannot be won over in the context of the second condition. Here, the output of full capacity industrial production in the US, the ideological allegiance of sections of the working classes involved and the cosmopolitanism-turned-anti-communism of the liberal bourgeoisie represent different moments of one and the same process of capital's flight forward in the era of the transition to socialism.

The problems arising with the above enumeration of conditions are obviously enormous, in particular if the tendency towards autonomization of interstate relations is taken into account. Still, on the basis of a number of statistical indicators in combination with an assessment of actual political developments, we can single out 1947–49 and 1961–65 as periods of enhanced Atlantic unity.[5] As we will see below, the New Deal in a number of respects paved the way for this kind of international 'activism' on the part of the United States: in terms of the domestic political coalition involved, the policies of Truman and Kennedy relied on earlier developments.

Alternating with such an activist configuration of Atlantic capitalism, conservatism on the part of the American bourgeoisie – reminiscent of the orientation of international money capital – has tended to leave Europe to the right-wing industrial bourgeoisies, stimulating regional arrangements in the absence of active American involvement, other than financial.

Americanism and Fordism

In the United States, the scarcity of labour power at the turn of the century and the capitalist response to it mark the beginnings of a new type of capitalist development. Threatening sustained accumulation while opening prospects for the marketing of consumer goods, the scarcity of labour power was combatted by the introduction of the assembly line in consumer goods manufacturing industry. Thus, mass production further subjected the workers to capital, allowing relatively high wages thanks to relative surplus value production at the same time.

In Europe, on the other hand, a large reserve army of labour kept wages and labour costs down; a similar counterstrategy of capital against the independence of artisan-like production would have seemed irrational and besides, would have run upon other obstacles. Unlike the highly secular, 'rootless' American demography and class structure, in Europe 'a heap of passive sedimentations produced by the phenomenon of the saturation and fossilization of civil-service personnel and intellectuals, of clergy and landowners, piratical commerce and the professional ... army' (Gramsci 1978: 281) resisted a parallel leap forward in terms of social organization of production.

The crisis of 1929 and the early 1930s marked the watershed between the old and the new structures of the capitalist system and, therefore, between the USA and Europe. To analyse these structures more concretely, we have to look at the changes that were brought about by the counterstrategies of capital in the sphere of circulation.

The new production techniques were a capitalist response to the combined challenge of a mass market for consumer goods and scarce labour power resisting subordination to capital in production. The old methods of work, however, were embedded in a comprehensive social structure dominated by rentier interests, banks 'feeding' on these interests and giant monopolies in heavy industry often dominated by the banks. In the USA as well as in Europe, such a power bloc and, in particular, the development of the iron and steel industry and associated industries like mining, railway material, shipbuilding and armaments had been dialectically related to imperialist expansion and war. If they had to be revolutionized for profit reasons, this whole structure of profit distribution would have to change, too.

When demand for steel products and especially for flat-rolled steel used by the automobile and food-canning industries expanded, the American iron and steel industry was confronted with 'unmanageable' qualified (skilled) workers. To remove this obstacle to progress, absolute surplus value production was initially stepped up, but only after the introduction of the continuous wide-strip rolling mill in the second half of the 1920s could the problems be overcome. In principle, the steel industry had become attached to the system of relative surplus value production and intensive accumulation.

However, the rapid introduction of the new equipment and the depreciation of existing machinery aggravated the hardships of the American iron and steel industry during the economic crisis that followed. In fact, the whole structure of rentier interests and investment banks connected with them fell apart, as speculation in railway and real-estate bonds had finally run up against the fact that the railway age was over. Profit rates of the iron and steel industry for decades fell back to below-average levels, and aggregate profits of financial conglomerates predominantly involved in railway investment and iron and steel production at the time (Morgan and Kuhn, Loeb & Co.) showed a comparable, though relative, decline (ECE 1953: 35; Perlo 1960: 165).

In the face of mass unemployment and threatened by an avalanche of closures and bankruptcies, American capitalism seemed unable to recover on its own. Accordingly, the hand of the state had to strengthen the invisible one considerably in order to guide the different component parts (banks, branches of industry) of the old production and profit distribution structure to their position within a restructured mass production economy (and to eliminate some of them altogether). It *could* do so (as capitalist interests favouring a consumer-oriented solution to the crisis were weak if compared to the Wall Street financiers and big industrial conglomerates that were being challenged), only because of the threatening impact of revolting farmers and industrial workers organizing on an unprecedented scale. This created Roosevelt's room for manoeuvre to devalue the dollar and to set up the legal and political framework for a more viable social order of capitalism.

After the first shock, key finance capitalists soon tuned in on the New Deal. Winthrop Aldrich, representative of the Rockefeller group, spoke out in favour of it, and the important mass-production industries supported New Deal trade policies even if they '(might) not agree with some of the other national policies'.[6]

In due course, however, the labour relations aspect of the New Deal was modified so as to better suit the class interests of big capital. In 1937 pressure was brought to bear on the Roosevelt administration to cut public spending for employment and thus quell working-class militancy. Within a year, industrial production fell back, unemployment rose and strike activity was reduced spectacularly from involving two million workers in 1937 to about 690 thousand in 1938. The mighty CIO [Congress of Industrial Organizations] drive, organizing millions of workers in the new mass production industries, did not bring about a social revolution, on the contrary. As Keynes, who provided the theoretical justification of the social transformation of capitalism pioneered in the New Deal, put it in the Concluding Notes of his *General Theory*: 'With the disappearance of (the rentier aspect of capitalism) much else in it besides will suffer a sea-change ... [But] the euthanasia of the rentier, of the functionless investor, will be nothing sudden ... will need no revolution' (Keynes 1970 [1936]: 376).

What remained was a lasting state intervention in industrial employment, agriculture and monetary affairs. Responding to the crisis in both labour relations and the credit system, the American state directly intervened in the relation between these two spheres, that is to say 'in the circulation of capital as far as it necessitated new class compromises that could not be realised by the capitalists themselves' (de Brunhoff 1976: 53). Called upon to manage a social order based on relative surplus value production in which real wages had become the main strategic variable, but which was also highly vulnerable because of its more intricate social division of labour, the state undertook to level off and postpone the consequences of non-valorization of value by what de Brunhoff calls 'pseudo-valorization' through inflation, and by anti-cyclical measures. Of these, the 1937 cuts were the first example in the history of the new capitalism (Kalecki 1972 [1943]: 424).

In 1929, the social nature of production had revolted against its indiscriminately being geared to private profit; in 1933 new forms of circulation were created by the state to shore up the accumulation conditions for monopoly capital. As regards the iron and steel industry, its absorption into a subordinate layer of social production, like many other features of the new state monopolistic structures supporting intensive accumulation, had to wait until the Second World War. During the war, the American state financed new plant and equipment on an unprecedented scale in the context of the war production effort. After the war, when the new plants were turned over to the major steel companies at prices that were symbolic at best, the iron and steel industry passed under the tutelage of the steel users through credit-and-delivery contracts, with only a few exceptions.

Accordingly, in the USA, a high value of labour power dialectically brought about mass production of consumer goods, upsetting the structure of profit distribution that had developed around railway financing and production. Eliminating the excessive power of Wall Street high finance, the New Deal introduced state intervention with respect to the circulation of money capital, hence, to the level of industrial activity and real wages; in the previous period this articulation had been left to the bankers and industrial capitalists themselves.

66   Kees van der Pijl

Through the Marshall Plan, the conditions for relative surplus value production and intensive accumulation were exported to Western Europe. One aspect of the Schuman Plan of May 1950 was the belated subjugation of the European iron and steel industry to the assembly industries. In the European Coal and Steel Community, the cartel-prone European iron and steel branch and the profit-distribution structure connected with it, hence the 'heap of passive sedimentations' (Gramsci) that underlay its support for fascism, were restructured so as to conform to the American model.

Still, even when the conditions for a mass market had been established, the EEC was not to become a mere imitation of the USA. Rather, it provided a context in which the 'old' and the 'new' class and profit structures were being reproduced in a contradictory fashion. On the one hand, the EEC has been an effective extension of a continuous mass market, originating in the USA. On the other hand, it has operated as a protectionist bloc in its own right, centring around a Franco-German axis seeking to preserve an exclusive sphere of influence in Western Europe and Africa.

As was indicated above, different fractions of the bourgeoisie have been associated with these contradictory tendencies. Their political pre-eminence has been closely related to American initiatives in the field of free trade and capital movements to create favourable conditions for the accumulation of capitals in their orbit.

Internationalization of capital and internationalization of the bourgeoisie

The pre-war Atlantic framework

Though the term 'isolationism' is of doubtful value when describing American foreign policy in the 1920s, it is a fact that at the time, American imperialism was not the vanguard of international reaction that it is today. This task was left to the bourgeoisie in Europe, if only because the rentier-oriented profit structure of railway capitalism did not require direct American intervention in European affairs: capitalists associated with this profit-distribution structure tended to evaluate economic activity and prospects for investment in rentier terms alone. Accordingly, a steady flow of American portfolio capital was bolstering the economic position of the old iron and steel industry in Europe. The same cartel profit rates that hampered the development of socially more viable assembled consumer goods production, were highly attractive to American speculators. Between 1924 and 1930, $1239 million worth of German bonds were sold to US citizens, the most important broker being the firm of Dillon, Read & Co, and the most important outcome in Germany itself the formation of the *Vereinigte Stahlwerke* (Kolko 1962: 718). The German ruling classes, the more so after Hitler's rise to power, were generally considered to be efficient protectors of such stationary American property.

On the other hand, to American capital engaged in mass production and seeking new places to settle in an effort to evade the growing combativeness of American workers, Hitler's try at a United Europe could only be of transient interest. Unlike cartelized national branches of industry, multinational firms like General Motors,

International Telephone & Telegraph and General Electric – and to a lesser extent, Standard Oil, NJ – (to name only the foremost direct investors in Germany before the war) in the long run needed a developed mass consumption market to complement their military production, and certainly they preferred free trade and free capital flows to war-prone fascist autarky with its forced reinvestment of profits and other nuisances.

Transcending the basically defensive rentier orientation, these preferences were fully consistent with the assertive, Wilsonian liberalism that pervaded the State Department under Roosevelt's Secretary of State Cordell Hull. 'Hull's freer trade pleas appealed to many groups besides the Southern Democrats' (Gardner 1964: 15). Indeed, his conception of free trade as a condition for peace corresponded closely to the requirements of internationally operating manufacturing firms.

The political activism that went with the thrust towards a more viable social order based on relative surplus value production was also formulated by Undersecretary of State Sumner Welles. Stressing the need for an international order composed of socially and politically stable regional associations, Welles heralded what under Kennedy was to be enacted as the 'Alliance for Progress' with regard to Latin America, urging American capital to seek association with indigenous capital rather than creating 'an empire within another sovereign state'. As far as Europe was concerned, Welles favoured a dismemberment of Germany into three parts so as to prevent future German aggression. If, as he hoped, 'the end of the war [would see] the lowering of customs barriers within Europe, and the creation of customs unions, the new German states should be afforded free opportunity to take part in such customs unions' (Welles 1945: 240–1, 353).

After Hitler had come to power, the fractions of German capital and of the German bourgeoisie that were favourable to American penetration and liberalism (like the Dresdner Bank groups, Thyssen and figures like Schacht and Goerdeler) lost their influence and for the moment, Atlantic arrangements had to be restricted to relations with Britain and France. From the Reciprocal Trade Agreements Act of 1934, through the Tripartite Monetary Agreement of '36 to the proclamation of the Atlantic Charter by Roosevelt and Churchill (the latter claiming 'due respect to existing obligations') in 1941, these arrangements increasingly reflected the rise of the USA as the most vital centre of capitalism that was associated with capitalism's need to overcome the structures of rentier imperialism in order to survive. Of course, Churchill and Eden proved to be uneasy allies in this process.

Behind all American activist thinking during the war – whether it pertained to creating stable social structures or stable international arrangements – loomed the need for markets. 'We will have a capital equipment industry nearly twice the size which would be needed domestically under the most fortuitous conditions of full employment and nearly equal to the task of supplying world needs', it was stated in a report of one of the several study groups that tackled the problem (quoted in Eakins 1969: 156). However, the American initiative to shape an open Atlantic economy in which the US output of means of production could enter as an element of an integrated circuit of capital could only be expected to succeed when capitalism was seriously challenged in Europe.

68 Kees van der Pijl

The Marshall Plan and Atlantic unity

To understand why two years had to pass before the USA could intervene to establish free trade and capital movements in Europe, one needs to look at the class relations in Europe immediately after the war. As the old production and profit distribution structure broke down with the collapse of fascism, both modernizing capitalist elements and the working classes were pressing their demands for change. In such a situation, only those groupings of the right that had cultivated a working-class base of their own – the Christian Democrats, in particular – could be trusted to handle the precarious give and take that was necessary to save capitalist production relations.

Of course, this was not merely a matter of capitalists' calculations. Metropolitan and colonial trade and shipping had declined during the war, as had those branches of industry, like textiles, that had developed in the context of empire. Accordingly, the European liberal parties and liberal tendencies, who, besides drawing their strength from rentier quarters, depended strongly (though not exclusively) on class fractions involved in the activities mentioned, were in a weak position immediately after the war. Having developed no working relationship with the working class beyond cash payment, they had to leave the task of reconstruction to the class fractions which had developed a corporatist relation between capital and labour. The Resistance had in several countries already created the political framework for cooperation between Christian Democrats and Communists, and these parties formed the basis of the post-war coalitions that sprang up on the continent with programs of national industrial reconstruction. The Social Democrats provided a surrogate for both, depending on the specific national political configuration; in France, the Gaullists rallied behind the popular general, who qualified as the 'Republican monarch' that his comrade-in-arms Debré and the banker, Monick, of the Banque de Paris et des Pays-Bas (predominant in terms of 'modern' industrial investment in France) had declared to be necessary for post-war France (Claude 1968: 55).

Hence, in 1946–47, though they were actively seeking and obtaining loans and credits from the Americans, European ruling coalitions were orientated towards national reconstruction and were not very receptive to American penetration. In the words of the Kolkos:

> Western Europe's recovery was a matter of time. Ironically, this rehabilitation, especially in France and in the lowlands, was not only largely internally generated but also proceeding in a distinctive, self-contained manner that diminished the United States' role and posed a major danger to America's plans for a reformed world capitalism.
>
> *(Kolko and Kolko 1972: 163)*

Confronted with the threat of an independent recovery with a protectionist bent and Communist participation, the Truman administration launched the Marshall

Plan. Developments in both the USA and Europe had made the need to secure the labour reserves and markets of Western Europe for the benefit of American capital acute. On both sides of the Atlantic, class relations were upset by the threat of impending crisis.

In the US, the policies of the Truman government reflected the weaker basis for activism as compared to the New Deal period. Measures that were proposed in the fields of domestic reform and foreign involvement had to be inserted in a Cold War context to have them enacted, as the American upper and middle classes were frightened both by the increased strike activity that reminded them of the labour radicalism of the 'thirties, and by the interplay of worldwide social upheaval and the expansion of a Soviet sphere of influence.

Owing to cheap plants in basic industries (cf. above) and to pent-up demand for consumer goods, the new industrial system in the US had easily adapted to peace-time conditions, and the rise in living standards seemed to make a Red Scare irrelevant. Still, anti-labour sentiment was strong, and in 1946, a Republican majority in Congress was elected on an anti-labour, anti-taxation platform. This resulted, among other things, in the promulgation of the highly restrictive Taft-Hartley act. Through this measure, with its provisions against real or alleged communist union leaders, the remaining political sting was to be taken out of working-class organizations.

As far as Western Europe was concerned, the adoption of a mass-market, consumer-oriented capitalist economy seemed to be the only answer to the severe crisis at the time. To stem the upsurge of popular discontent and Communist electoral successes, a dramatic initiative on the part of the Free World was mandatory. Indeed, the integrationist bourgeois leadership that had worked with the Communists up to that time was losing control of the Communists as the Communists themselves lost control of the working masses who had voted for them, but who now demanded solutions to the food shortages and rising costs of living. Marshall Aid provided the solution.

A free trade and payments offensive, coinciding with a violent attack on militant working-class strongpoints in trade unions and the state and an offensive posture vis- à-vis the Soviet Union, the Marshall Plan was instrumental in bringing European reconstruction along national lines to a standstill. The devaluations, the dumping of agricultural surpluses, the installation of industrial equipment which would be efficient only if trade was expanded dramatically (like the wide-strip mills in the steel industry) as well as the loss of communist support tore apart the class basis of the governments of national unity where they had existed. Aside from the Marshall Plan, the position of the national, protectionist industrial bourgeoisies was further undermined by loss of colonial monopolies, because the colonial market and a raw material reservoir of their own had been crucial considerations in most reconstruction plans, national as well as 'European' (often British-sponsored plans for joint exploitation of the colonies).

On the other hand, although it eliminated many a small rentier, the absorption of the former colonial empires into a wider 'free world' under American hegemony and protection offered an opportunity for colonial capital either to repatriate to the metropolitan areas or to resettle in comparable tropical areas. In

70 Kees van der Pijl

the case of the French Banque de l'Indochine, for instance, its assets in 1931 were still concentrated between 80 and 90% in South East Asia; in 1953, it had redistributed its investments towards Western Europe (32%), the Western Hemisphere (26%) and Africa (27%) with only 18% left in Indo-China. In the process, however, the bank had to associate itself with *Schneider/Union européenne*.

It could be expected that representatives of these groups would favour free trade and capital movements more than other fractions of capital, and they did. Edmond Giscard d'Estaing, prominent banker in the Indochine group, was president of the French section of the European League for Economic Cooperation (ELEC), the highly influential liberal wing of the European Movement; his son Valéry, married to the granddaughter of E. Schneider, likewise has been a consistent champion of liberalism.

Meanwhile, on the economic plane, these same interests were the main beneficiaries of the Marshall Plan as far as private capital was concerned (the greater part of the Marshall funds was channelled into the public sector, especially for power-generating equipment, and further consisted of payments for agricultural surpluses and subsidies for productivity programmes). In France, Schneider, Simca (at the time, associated with Ford) and SOLLAC (the wide-strip mill of Lorraine steel capital, associated with the Morgan group as well as with the banks and industrial firms later to regroup into the Suez alliance) together got almost five times the amount that was received, as an additional credit, by USINOR, the wide-strip mill of Northern steel, which was associated with the Banque de Paris et des Pays-Bas and, hence, with the more national approach.

Of course, a comprehensive account of the economic and political effects of the Marshall Plan cannot be given here. But the pattern was very much alike in all countries involved. In the Netherlands, Hoogovens iron and steel works got the bulk of the dollar grants to private industry, again to build a wide-strip mill. But not only the industrial bulwarks of the liberal bourgeoisie of colonial origin (Hoogovens was associated with Royal Dutch/Shell and with the foremost colonial and shipping bank, NHM – today's Algemene Bank Nederland) were reinforced. Also, the liberals returned to the cabinet in 1948. It was the new liberal foreign minister Stikker (of Heineken and the NHM) who in the OEEC [Organization of European Economic Cooperation] proposed to liberalize intra-European trade a few days after Schuman had made public his coal and steel plan. In Italy, an orthodox banker, Einaudi, was installed by Prime Minister de Gasperi to conduct a deflationary policy to the detriment of industrial employment.

But nowhere was the connection between active American involvement and liberalism as clear as in Western Germany. To quote the Kolkos again,

> [i]n April 1948, shortly before the monetary reform, the Christian Democrat laissez faire economist Ludwig Erhard replaced the Social Democrat Viktor Agartz as chairman of the Bizonal Economic Council … With the council safely in conservative hands, the occupation greatly expanded its powers when it introduced the new currency, making it an incipient finance ministry … [The currency reform]

wiped out the small savers ... and while prices and profits skyrocketed, real wages fell sharply and unemployment nearly doubled by December 1948.

(Kolko and Kolko 1972: 433–4)

For the European working class, the liberalization that followed the launching of the Marshall Plan certainly did not as yet mean an ability to improve their position by free wage negotiations, as the overall political objective of the Plan was to cut the working class down to size. Still, the other elements of liberal economic policy, like free trade and convertibility and the predominant orientation in state intervention towards monetary instruments, were all there. Events in the years to follow would demonstrate that their persistence indeed depended on activist policies on the part of the USA.

American conservatism and the foundation of the EEC

The aftermath of the Korean War was to show that in the United States, an isolationist turn in foreign policy was still possible. During the early phase of the Marshall Plan, activism and its proponents from mass market industry and trade like Hoffman and Clayton had held the reigns. The interests associated with American portfolio investments in German heavy industry (Dillon, Read & Co., the Schröder Bank) as well as Standard Oil and other Rockefeller firms and banks, had supported the Marshall Plan, mainly from a Cold War point of view. Their representatives, like Forrestal, Draper and McCloy, held positions in the defence branch and in the US/Bizonal occupation authorities in Germany. With the outbreak of the Korean War and the establishment of the European Coal and Steel Community, their influence had already grown significantly. But only in the Eisenhower government did this tendency gain the upper hand through Nixon and J.F. Dulles.

Internationally, the Eisenhower administration, after having cut back the budget for foreign aid by 1 billion dollars, concentrated on improving the position of American oil companies in the Middle East (the Mossadeq episode, Lebanon), rather than promote industrial exports and cultivate support for free trade among the ruling circles in Western Europe. In this period, the Germans took over the job. Instead of relying solely on US guardianship, Western Germany was to be rearmed, and heavy pressure was brought to bear on the states involved to have the European Defence Community ratified in the respective parliaments.

Accordingly, the stress on the need for European integration had undergone a significant change of content. Before, economic integration in the sense of liberalization had been a constant American concern, but political unification had been looked at rather distrustfully. Even in 1949–50, references to political unification in Hoffman's and other Marshall Plan officials' speeches were being censored by the State Department, and Acheson in particular was not at all enthusiastic for European political integration, as he 'tended ... to look at things in the way the British did, and to stress an Atlantic rather than a European approach' (Beloff 1963: 55, 65–6).

72 Kees van der Pijl

But in 1952, Senator Tom Connally, in a report on Western Europe, saw European integration in more positive, if isolationist, terms. Integration should serve, in his opinion,

> to see Europe strong enough eventually to stand on her own feet. To permit integration in the military and economic fields to become effective, there must be ... some kind of political federation which should of course be shaped by the Europeans themselves.
>
> *(quoted in Beloff 1963: 96)*

Moreover, according to the same source, in the economic field the American government had already become less interested in working at Atlantic arrangements by the last year of the Truman administration.

In this context, Dulles' threat of an 'agonizing reappraisal' of American support if the EDC [European Defence Community] failed to be ratified contrasted sharply with the conception that had been behind the Berlin airlift – and that would be behind Kennedy's appearance at the Berlin Wall. It prompted the European states almost by default to take an aggressive stand on their own, meant to be directed against the communist East, but because of the specific class configuration at the time, stimulating a last try at empire instead. With Suez, interimperialist strife reached a high point.

As far as American class relations were concerned, the cutbacks in foreign aid had had their counterpart in reduced domestic spending. With the Republican government, Hoover seemed to step back on the stage and with him, laissez-faire economics. Having been elected with strong conservative and Southern middle class support, the abandoning of economic controls had been one of the first measures of Eisenhower in 1953. Likewise, government enterprises were sold or closed down, almost up to the sale of the Tennessee Valley Authority which Eisenhower personally favoured but ruled out as 'going too far' (Degler 1968: 87). Labour was handled by economic policy much more than by the carrot-and-stick policies of Truman's and McCarthy's days. The cutback in state expenditure from 1953 onwards, supervised by the Secretary of the Treasury, Humphrey, increased unemployment. Strike activity fell back from 59 million workdays in 1952 to an average of about 25 million until 1959.

In Europe, on the other hand, the relative disengagement of the USA from its affairs provoked a resurgence of the right wing of Western European politics as much as the Marshall Plan had stimulated its orientation towards a mass-market economic and social order.

Thus, the Messina Conference of 1955, which laid the foundations for the EEC, was characterized by what Spaak in his Memoirs calls 'a certain degree of confusion' (Spaak 1971: 228–9). On the one hand, its final resolution still reflected the impact of the Marshall Plan where it spoke of agreement on 'the establishment of a European common market free from tariff barriers and all quantitative restrictions on trade'. On the other hand, mention was made of joint sectoral plans, obviously meant to be extensions of the much more cartel-like ECSC structures.

The EEC as it was prepared and established between 1955 and 1958 was in fact a complicated class compromise in which the requirements of the common market for industrial goods had to be accommodated to the demands of the existing class supports of the right-wing bloc from which the industrial bourgeoisie eventually emerged as the dominant political force in the first four years of the EEC's existence (up to 1962). The Common Market alleviated the scarcity of labour power in West German industry and facilitated its further expansion in new markets, and it has often been noted that the Rome Treaty amounted to a swap of the German agrarian market for the French industrial one. The price to be paid by both German industrial capital and French wheat merchants, however, was protection. This was to take the form of the common external tariff and agrarian price supports, respectively, because in West Germany, farmers were an important factor in the conservative class alliance behind the ruling Christian Democrats, while in France the archaic type of accumulation, prevailing throughout the 1950s, had favoured 'a strong presence of the small bourgeoisie on the political scene within a class alliance held together by the common fear of the ascending proletariat' (Rehfeldt 1976: 12). Here, the disentanglement from the Algerian struggle complicated the situation still further. It provided the dramatic background against which de Gaulle could introduce an authoritarian regime meant to make the rate of exploitation of French workers compensate for colonial revenue, while enhancing the competitive power of French industry.

The establishment of the EEC worked to synchronize class relations in the countries involved in much the same way as the Marshall Plan had done. In all countries, the need to keep the working class under control, while securing the hegemony of mass-market, large-scale industrial capital, brought the early post-war coalitions – of course, minus the communists – to the fore again.

Hence, the EEC laid the foundations for a free market economy based on relative surplus value production and intensive accumulation, but again, in the absence of activist American involvement, the 'precarious give and take' in terms of class relations had to be entrusted to the integrationist sections of the industrial bourgeoisie in Western Europe. The Atlantic bourgeoisie once more had to wait for American activism in order to gain power. In 1958, only the British championed liberal Atlantic arrangements, but the favourable response to their Free Trade Area proposals on the part of some liberals like Erhard was disapproved of by American and continental European ruling coalitions alike (cf. Beloff 1963: 132).

Concluding remarks

What has been presented in the foregoing analysis cannot be more than a tentative sketch. Rather than concluding, therefore, I will briefly go into three questions that have remained unanswered, but which are relevant to further discussion.

The first question has already been touched upon in the introduction. It concerns the role of NATO, and military strategy in American activism. Here the Atlantic offensive of the Kennedy administration can be taken as an example. In this

74 Kees van der Pijl

case, too, the need to revitalise the domestic economy was at the root of the offensive international stand. In the words of the economist, Walter Heller: 'The nation's lagging growth rate and frequent recessions had been the prime campaign issues in the 1960 election ... The need to "get the country moving again" remained at the centre of the Kennedy Administration's concern after it took office' (Heller 1968).

Internationally, an attack on the protectionism of the EEC was mandatory not only to find markets for increased production: 'A lowering of the [EEC] common external tariff should reduce the incentive for American firms to establish branches in Europe and thus help stanch the outward flow of capital from the United States' (Evans 1967: 5–6).

American conservatism in the preceding period, however, not only provoked EEC protectionism. The continentalist bourgeoisies of Europe for obvious reasons had also developed a desire to organize their military potential on a regional basis. In particular, ideas of a European nuclear force were circulating and being championed, among others by the German defence minister, Strauss. The French demanded the establishment of a joint nuclear directorate within NATO.

The Kennedy administration actively sought to counteract these tendencies. Skilfully using the proposals for a multilateral nuclear force it had inherited from the Eisenhower government, it tried to reintegrate its European allies in NATO. The Nassau agreement of 1962 with the Macmillan government was the first, if comparatively easy, success in this respect.

Hence, when in the EEC countries the Europeanist ruling coalitions were being replaced by a liberal tendency in the course of 1962–63, the renewed allegiance to NATO played its role alongside the Atlantic free trade conjuncture and economic liberalism.[7] Only France became increasingly isolated, eventually suspending its participation in both the EEC and NATO during 1965–66. Still, even here, Atlantic liberalism made itself felt as from 1962 to 1966, when he was replaced by Debré, Giscard d'Estaing held the important post of minister of finance.

The second question relates to the periodization from the mid-sixties on. How did the overall balance of forces between the imperialist powers develop; what are the limits of American supremacy? It seems to me that the Kennedy episode already revealed the problem of capital moving to Europe and the political consequences of this trend for the balance of forces in the Atlantic area and the world. This problem was aggravated from 1966 onwards.

Domestically, the Kennedy offensive had been based on a careful 'policy mix' of increased government spending (social and foreign aid, military expenditure) and a policy of easy money, to facilitate credit for private industrial expansion. However, in December 1965 the Federal Reserve, in order to stem inflation and defend the value of the dollar, raised the rate of interest despite the opposition of the government (which had become Johnson's, in the meantime) (de Brunhoff 1976: 72ff.). When the President persisted in applying the economic programmes inherited from the Kennedy platform even to the point of introducing a ban on private direct investment of American capital in Europe, the conflict between finance capital and the Democratic government became an aspect of the presidential elections of 1968 that brought Nixon to power (Davidson and Weil 1970: 63).

At first, Nixon's economic policy consisted of the expected cutbacks in state expenditure and related monetary measures. But from 1971 onwards, his conservatism took on a more narrow and aggressive quality. Confronted with the decline of American economic hegemony, Nixon tried to recapture a competitive position for American capital by his famous dollar coup in the summer of that year. This blunt abandoning of accepted rules of conduct (and of International Monetary Fund and General Agreement on Tariffs and Trade obligations), however, was branded as dangerous and isolationist by the representatives of American finance capital and European liberals (the former deserting the Nixon government in protest), and actually provoked the formation of the Trilateral Commission with its stress on internationalism and free trade and capital movements (Frieden 1977).

Yet, even before the Trilateral presidential candidate, Jimmy Carter, was elected, a liberal, Atlanticist tendency took over in France and Germany in 1974. Today, for the first time since 1945, class formation in the USA seems to be reflecting strategies of international capital originating from a European context rather than vice versa, as can be seen in the fight over Carter's energy program. The proposed European Monetary System likewise seems to indicate that international capital has found its champion in the liberal, free market bourgeoisie of Western Europe and is seeking to make the Americans respond to the liberal call from Europe rather than the other way round. Of course, further research and analysis are mandatory as to the real nature of these developments.

The last question to be looked at briefly relates to working-class strategy. As the reader may have concluded already, the understanding of the position and role of the working class in the international class configuration as analysed in this paper poses a very difficult problem. On the one hand, Atlantic liberalism affects the workers in the countries involved in a variety of ways, even including the loss of union freedom to negotiate wages and working conditions, which was supposed to be a characteristic of corporatist or 'Fordist' strategies of European capital. On the other hand, right-wing governments of the latter inspiration have sometimes introduced free wage negotiations, contrary to the schema suggested in the introduction.

At the ideological level, the picture is also rather contradictory. Certainly, activism as an offensive posture of international capitalism has inspired not only the bourgeoisie with new confidence in the viability of the mode of production. The benefits of enhanced intensive accumulation and relative surplus value production have also tended to foster reformist tendencies among the working class. 'The reformist ideology', Claudin writes, 'secreted organically by the system's capacity to develop the productive forces, holds a place of honour among capitalism's moral as well as political justifications' (Claudin 1975 [1970]: 100). In particular, '[r]eformism is ... nourished by structural transformations in capitalism that relate to the development of the productive forces' (60). But developments in the communist movement have been influenced less by the modalities of Atlantic unity than by those of Soviet policy, except for the strategy of the American Communist Party following the New Deal (cf. Weinstein and Eakins 1970: 3) and perhaps 'Eurocommunism'.

76 Kees van der Pijl

The basic complication, however, lies in the fact that the political strength of the working class in Atlantic capitalism has varied from state to state, due to differences in the size of the reserve army of labour, the relative weight of capitalist industry in each social formation and the traditions, intensity and course of class struggle in general.

There remains, therefore, a typically national aspect to the position of the working class that cannot be denounced as reactionary or backward just because capital internationalizes more easily than a working-class district. On the contrary, vis-à-vis a bourgeoisie which is fractioned along international lines, pursuing mutually contradictory class strategies in the process of internationalization of capital, the working class indeed might find the national state to be the only context of power within which it can unite effectively against a divided ruling class.

It seems to me that moderate plans for reform with a socialist potential, like the Advanced Democracy of the French Communist Party, or the Alternative Economic Strategy in Britain, should be discussed from this angle.

Note

This paper is a revised version of my contribution to the CSE Annual Conference at Bradford, July 1978. It develops the argument of my book, *An American Plan for Europe* (in Dutch, Amsterdam 1978) which is based on research in progress at the Department of International Relations, University of Amsterdam. Many thanks to Simon Clarke for his assistance in preparing the final version of this paper.

Notes

1 Cf. for example Nairn's *The Left against Europe* (1973) or, from quite another angle, Picciotto and Radice (1973).
2 A recent Dutch study on the bourgeois state argued that 'interimperialist antagonisms as well as the domestic fractioning of the bourgeoisie find their political expression in the "national" power bloc; accordingly, there will be connecting links between the antagonisms occurring within different "national" power blocs' (Stuurman 1978: 352, my translation).
3 I am referring specifically to the French Communist Party's version of the theory, cf. Collectif PCF 1971. A striking example of an international reorientation being analysed as an outcome of national class struggle (May 1968) is in vol. II, p. 183. It should be stressed, however, that there are many varieties of the theory of State Monopoly Capitalism, some of which are more sophisticated than others. The work of Herzog in France and theories developed in the German Democratic Republic are examples of this, cf. Wirth 1972.
4 'Classes are large groups of people differing from each other by the place they occupy in a historically determined system of social production, by their relation (in most cases fixed and formulated in law) to the means of production, by their role in the social organization of labour, and, consequently, by the dimensions of the share of social wealth of which they dispose and the mode of acquiring it. Classes are groups of people one of which can appropriate the labour of another owing to the different places they occupy in a definite system of social economy' (Lenin 1919: 421).
5 To mention only two such indicators: Menshikov (1975: 43) found three periods in which the increase of production in the USA was based chiefly on the growth of

Class formation at the international level **77**

investment in fixed capital: 1947–48, 1953–57 and 1960–65. The average annual growth of production for the second period, however, was only 2.2% for the other two, 5.9% and 4.9% respectively. Secondly, according to a recent Brookings Institution study by B. M. Blechman and S.S. Kaplan, *Force Without War, US Armed Forces as a Political Instrument*, American armed interventions were most numerous in two periods: 1946–48 (on average, 8 a year), and 1960–65 (15 a year).

6 Statement by an official of General Motors Export Company, quoted in Gardner 1964: 25. On the interests supporting Roosevelt, cf. Schwarz 1969.

7 In Germany, the conservative triangle of Adenauer-Brentano-Strauss (the latter by means of the '*Spiegel* affair') was replaced by the Atlantic combination Erhard-Schroder-Hassel. In the SPD, there was the rise of Willy Brandt, who personified the break-away of his party from the neutralist stance of Schumacher's days, and who as mayor symbolically stood by when Kennedy pronounced his citizenship of West Berlin at the Wall. In the Netherlands, the reactionary government of the Catholic and wartime collaborator De Quay was replaced by a government in which the liberal tendency was considerably reinforced. Also in 1963, the first centre-left government of Italy was sworn in as part of a liberal solution to contradictions arising out of the exports boom, etc. For the backgrounds of the Macmillan government in these terms, cf. Overbeek 1978, a revised version of which will appear in *Capital & Class* 10 (see Chapter 3).

References

Althusser, L. (1969). *For Marx*. London: NLB.

Beloff, M. (1963). *The United States and the unity of Europe*. Washington, DC: Brookings Institute.

de Brunhoff, S. (1976). *Etat et capital. Recherches sur la politique économique*. Paris: Maspero.

Clarke, S. (1978). Capital, fractions of capital and the state. 'Neo-Marxist' analyses of the South African state. *Capital & Class* 5: 32–77.

Claude, H. (1968). *Histoire, réalité et destin d'un monopole: la banque de Paris et des Pays-Bas et son groupe (1872–1968)*. Paris: Editions sociales.

Claudin, F. (1975 [1970]). *The communist movement. From Comintern to Cominform*. Harmondsworth: Penguin.

Collectif PCF (1971). *Traité marxiste de l'économie politique. Le capitalisme monopoliste d'État, 2 volumes*. Paris: Editions sociales.

Davidson, I. and Weil, G. (1970). *The gold war*. London: Secker & Warburg.

Degler, C.N. (1968). *Affluence and anxiety, 1945–present*. Glenview, IL: Free Press.

Eakins, D.W. (1969). Business planners and America's post-war expansion. In D. Horowitz (Ed.), *Corporations and the cold war* (pp. 143–179). New York: Monthly Review Press.

ECE (1953). *The European steel industry and the wide-strip mill*. Geneva: ECE.

Evans, J.W. (1967). *US trade policy. New legislation for the next round*. New York: Harper and Row.

Frieden, J. (1977). The Trilateral Commission. Economics and politics in the 1970s. *Monthly Review* 29(7): 1–18.

Gardner, L.C. (1964). *Economic aspects of New Deal diplomacy*. Madison, WI: University of Wisconsin Press.

Gramsci, A. (1978). Americanism and Fordism. In *Prison Notebooks* (pp. 277–318). London: Lawrence & Wishart.

Heller, W.W. (1968). Preface. In *Perspectives on economic growth*. New York: Random House.

Kalecki, M. (1972 [1943]). Political aspects of full employment. In E.K. Hunt and J.G. Schwartz (Eds), *A critique of economic theory. Selected readings* (pp. 420–430). Harmondsworth: Penguin.

78 Kees van der Pijl

Keynes, J.M. (1970 [1936]). *The general theory of employment, interest and money*. London: Macmillan.

Kolko, G. (1962). American business and Germany, 1930–1941. *Western Political Quarterly* 15 (4): 713–728.

Kolko, G. and Kolko, J. (1972). *The limits of power. The world and United States foreign policy, 1945–1954*. New York: Kren.

Lenin, V.I. (1917). Imperialism: The highest stage of capitalism. In *Collected works*, Vol. 22 (pp. 185–304). Moscow: Progress.

Lenin, V.I. (1919). A great beginning. Heroism of the workers in the rear. 'Communist subbotniks'. In *Collected Works*, Vol. 29 (pp. 409–434). Moscow: Progress.

Marx, K. (1973 [1937]). *Grundrisse*, transl. M. Nicolaus. Harmondsworth: Penguin.

Menshikov, S. (1975). *The economic cycle. Post-war developments*. Moscow: Progress.

Nairn, T. (1973). *The left against Europe*. Harmondsworth: Penguin.

Overbeek, H.W. (1978). Finance capital and crisis in Britain. Paper presented at CSE Annual Conference, Bradford, UK (a revised version is reprinted as Chapter 3 in this volume).

Palloix, Chr. (1974). *Le processus d'internationalisation dans la sidérurgie et les industries mécaniques et électriques*. Grenoble: Institut de recherche économique sur la production et le développement.

Perlo, V. (1960). *Das Reich der Hochfinanz*. Berlin: Dietz Verlag.

Picciotto, S. and Radice, H. (1973). Capital and the state in the world economy. *Kapitalistate* 1: 56–68.

Poulantzas, N. (1975). *Classes in contemporary capitalism*. London: NLB.

Rehfeldt, U. (1976). American investment in France and Gaullist policy of national independence. Paper presented to the European Consortium for Political Research Conference, Louvain la-Neuve.

Schwarz, J. (Ed.). (1969). *1933: Roosevelt's decision. The United States leaves the Gold Standard*. New York: Chelsea House.

Spaak, P.-H. (1971). *The continuing battle. Memoirs of a European, 1936–66*. London: Orion.

Stuurman, S. (1978). *Kapitalisme en burgerlijke staat*. Amsterdam: SUA.

Weinstein, J. and Eakins, D.W. (Eds) (1970). *For a new America*. New York: Random House.

Welles, S. (1945). *The time for decision*. Cleveland, OH: Harper & Bros.

Wirth, M. (1972). *Kapitalismustheorie in der DDR*. Frankfurt: Suhrkamp.

3

FINANCE CAPITAL AND THE CRISIS IN BRITAIN (1980)

Henk Overbeek

Introduction

In this contribution,[1] I will analyse the development of the crisis in Britain over the last few decades. In other studies of this subject, a number of factors have received ample attention: the changing role of the state in the economy, the falling rate of profit, the problem of the nationalities making up the British state, the development of the world economic system are but a few of these factors. What is missing in most approaches, however, is discussion of one problem: the structure of power relations among individual capitals in Britain and the way in which this structure influences and is influenced by events on the political and international planes. I hope that this article can contribute something to stimulating research in this field.

In all major capitalist countries, a tendency can be observed whereby the centre of gravity of the process of extraction of surplus value shifts to ever higher levels of manufacturing. In this way basic industries, and in general industries with a low organic composition of capital, tend to become dominated by, and more and more attuned to, the interests and needs of industries manufacturing final consumer goods and sophisticated means of production. This development has important implications for social relations and political orientations. In these new industries, the production of relative surplus value reaches enormous heights and thus creates room for concessions to the working class. The conditions of production in these industries (continuous production, a high proportion of skilled labour, a high organic composition) require above all the continuity of the production process and thus a reasonable measure of social harmony.

These are also the industries most prone to internationalization of production and sales, and are thus particularly interested in market enlargement through international free trade.

80 Henk Overbeek

These needs differ at least quantitatively from the needs of older industries working under less advanced conditions. There, the reliance on the home market is much heavier, and room for concessions to the working class is much smaller.

In the United States, this development took place in the late '20s and in the '30s of the New Deal. The basis for this development in the States was formed by the shortage of cheap labour, which led to an early emphasis on the application of labour-saving innovations. In Europe, where labour was plentiful and cheap, the need for labour-saving techniques was much less pressing. Here it was only after World War Two, and strongly influenced by American intervention through the Marshall Plan, that this shift in the economy was performed. Britain, we would say, experienced a first taste of this during the '30s, but the further unfolding of this tendency was inhibited and slowed down considerably during the first ten years or so after 1945.

During the twenties, the prevalent coalition of interests was that between banking capital on the one hand, and colonial and mining capital on the other. Coal and steel capital belonged to the same coalition, but this position was partly forced upon it by the deflationary policies imposed by the other two. Of this dominant coalition, only the coal and steel capitalists directly confronted the British working class, as the other two fractions depended for their expansion on the exploitation of workers and peasants elsewhere in the world. Politically, this coalition remained a dominant force until well into the nineteen fifties. Economically, a new fraction of British capital, born during the domestic boom of the nineteen thirties, became the most advanced appropriator of surplus value: modern industry, and especially mass consumer goods industry. Unimpeded accumulation for this fraction required completely different labour relations, which were drawn up during the thirties (the Macmillan Report) and put into practice under the guidance of the Labour and Tory governments of the late forties and early fifties and under pressure from the unions.

By the late fifties there was a reorientation of British foreign policy, away from continued dependence on the Commonwealth and towards better relations with the expanding markets in Western Europe, resulting finally in the British application for European Economic Community (EEC) membership in 1961. This application, however, was turned down, presenting British capital with a distressing situation.

During the sixties, the position of British capital deteriorated fast. Growing foreign competition, the growing costs of the 'welfare state', and the effects of the third technological revolution, in addition to the decline of the [British] Empire and the loss of export markets led to a situation in which something drastic had to be done to re-establish profitability for British capital. The Wilson government abandoned full employment as its number one priority and the pound was devalued. The largest British corporations and those parts of the City that had become closely related to those corporations did not wait for British membership of the EEC, and invested heavily in Western Europe.

In this situation, the final entry into the EEC in 1973 could mean only one thing: even further deterioration of the competitive position of British capital, notwithstanding an enormous wave of centralization of capital. British finance capital (which term we shall define in the following section) was presented with almost insurmountable problems.

Fractions of capital, finance capital, and financial groups

In trying to define 'finance capital', it may be useful to consider some widely shared misconceptions first. The first problem is the question of whether or not money capital can exist independently of productive capital. In my view this can only be the case when money capital relates to non-capitalist spheres of production. Profits made in the financial sector of the economy are nothing but a redistribution of the surplus product created in the productive sector, within or outside the country under consideration. Capital is a social relation. This implies that capital in the money form must be exchanged against labour to be capital at all.

So, money capital cannot exist independently of productive spheres. Under fully developed capitalist conditions of production and exchange we can therefore maintain that there is no such thing as an independent circuit of money capital. This is an important point to make as it directly affects our analysis of the position of the City of London, both in Britain and in the world economy at large. The consequence of this is that a definition of finance capital simply in terms of the integration of the circuits of money capital and productive capital is a platitude. The crucial question is the particular historic form of this integration. This is the point of Lenin's critique of Hilferding's definition of finance capital, namely that he failed to link the concept of finance capital to the outstanding features of capitalist development in the period of the genesis of finance capital: concentration and centralization of capital.

What, then, is the relation between these phenomena? Centralization of capital, although being a general tendency of capitalist production, is particularly employed by capitalists as one of the means to counteract any tendency of the rate of profit to fall (Marx, *Capital*, Vol. 3, Part III).

The available data on the centralization of capital in Britain confirm that centralization accelerates in periods of capitalist stagnation (Aaronovitch and Sawyer 1975: 124), around 1920, around 1930, and again from 1955 onward. At the same time, however, the involvement of financial institutions in this process increases. Many companies were not able to repay their loans in time, thus giving banks a vested interest in the well-being of the companies concerned.

In other cases, whole branches of industry will need thorough reorganization, often leading to the formation of oligopolies or cartels. In this process of restructuring and socialization the production of surplus value and the relative importance of different branches of production changes, and with it the established structure of relations between and among different capitals. Financial companies play an important part in this process, both by providing finance and by selling their expertise.

Thus, while both centralization and the increase in the number of links between individual capitals are general phenomena of the capitalist mode of production, economic crisis has a stimulating effect: centralization accelerates, and individual capitals increase or shift their relations with each other.

A further question is whether finance capital necessarily entails the domination of banking capital over industrial capital, as is often assumed. The argument, going back to Hilferding and Lenin, rests upon Marx's treatment in *Capital* of the money form of capital as the form social capital assumes, as it is most easily transferred to those branches where profits are highest. 'Money capital' as a form of capital in the abstract, however, must be clearly distinguished from 'banking capital' or 'finance capital', which refers to the institutional framework in which capital appears in the real world. The same distinction should be made, of course, between 'productive capital' and 'industrial capital'. This suggests that banks (and other purely financial institutions) do not necessarily form the centres of power.

A last problem I would like to address here is the 'nationality' of finance capital. The work of Hilferding and Lenin was based on data from the United States and, primarily, from Germany. In Germany, however, capitalist industry was built up under the auspices of the state, which directly intervened in the accumulation process while effectively shutting off the national economy from foreign competition. Consequently, finance capital assumed a strong nationally organized form, while this was not the case in other countries. Thus, we would disagree with Bukharin when he states that the tendency toward 'nationalization' of the economy is always stronger than the tendency toward 'internationalization', and that the formation of 'state capitalist trusts' is a general law of capitalist development.

Considering the elements mentioned above, I would propose the following working definition of finance capital: by finance capital we mean the integration of the circuits of money capital, productive capital, and commodity capital under the conditions of monopolization and internationalization of capital by means of a series of links and relationships between individual capitals.

The integration of these circuits takes on a durable structural character that is expressed in a network of relations between individual capitals, into which state organs are incorporated to the extent that state intervention in the economy is developed. These relations can be of the following nature:

1. financial (share ownership; long-term credits and bonds; short credits);
2. services (advising on mergers and take-overs; managing investment portfolios for other firms);
3. institutional (interlocking directorships);
4. informal (informal arrangements; familial ties).

In some measure, all these relations will develop, but due to specific historical and legal conditions in different countries, different types of relations have been particularly prominent. Thus, in Germany and the United States the financial and institutional relations have historically been prominent, while in Britain relations of the second and fourth type have long been the most important ones.

In its developed form, finance capital is divided into financial groups. These are groups of companies tightly connected to each other, with a clear focal point (usually a bank) from which the group strategy (investment decisions in the first place) is handed down to all lower levels concerned. Spectacular examples of these financial groups are found in the United States: the Rockefeller group with its centre in the Chase Manhattan Bank, the Morgan imperium, the Mellon and Dupont groups, and so on. In Britain, however, it is almost impossible to distinguish financial groups in this sense: the network of relations in Britain has had a rather amorphous character until recently.

The explanation of this fact must be sought in several factors. First of all, finance capital was very late to develop in Britain. Prior to World War I there was hardly any centralization of capital. British industry enjoyed a near monopoly on the world market until around 1880. No tariffs were imposed on foreign trade, which meant the absence of an important stimulus to the formation of cartels and trusts (Aaronovitch 1961: 38). In other countries (United States, Germany, Japan) large-scale modern industry was set up in the last quarter of the nineteenth century either with strong backing by the state or on the basis of a huge domestic market, while in Britain small-scale structures and attitudes lingered on.

Second, British banking was directed mainly at foreign operations. British industry realized surplus profits on the world market and consequently generated no demand for long-term finance, while at the same time (of course partly as a result of this) British banking made greater profits in financing foreign trade and handling portfolio investments abroad than it did in its domestic operations (Aaronovitch 1961: 39–40).

Third, as a result of its very early international orientation, there have always existed important relations between American and British capital, as a large part of the capital exported out of Britain during the nineteenth century went to the United States. As a consequence, it is possible that the structure of relationships between British companies is obscured by relations between British and American companies. Although we have not been able so far to do so, we feel that a thorough and systematic analysis of these relations would reveal a much clearer picture.[2]

A last reason is that systematic information about relations between companies is available only on interlocking directorships. Thus, although being aware of its limited analytical value in the case of Britain, we must rely on these data if we want to say anything at all about the development of finance capital in this country. It would be much more satisfactory to consider interconnections between capitals within related circuits of capital, but such data are not available.

Having established what we understand by finance capital and financial groups, we can now proceed to analyse the forms in which finance capital took shape in Britain and the way in which its development partly shaped the severe crisis of British capitalism in the nineteen seventies.

Transition between the wars

Up to the First World War, the British economy was dominated by two large groupings of capital. The larger part of the financial world (merchant banks and London clearing banks in particular), linked to colonial capital, accounted for the bulk of Britain's foreign earnings and thus for the role of the City as the financial centre of the world. The second group of capitals that accounted for Britain's supremacy during the larger part of the nineteenth century consisted of the coal, steel, textile, and railway industries. The 1920s are characterized primarily by the decline of these industries and the failure of attempts to reverse this process, not-withstanding the continuing prominence of this group well into the thirties in the political field. The twenties are further characterized by the steady rise in economic weight of the 'new industries' producing mass consumer goods. It is the developing balance of power of these three groups that make up the theme of this section.

The first signs of monopolization in the British economy of any importance date back to around 1895. It was, however, as a result of the depression following the post-war boom in 1919–20, and as a result of the activities of the state intended to counter this depression by means of forced amalgamations in some basic industries, that the concentration and centralization of capital gained any real momentum. However, this first merger movement did not dramatically alter the structure of relations between capitals that had developed before 1914. The integration of the circuits of different forms of capital had until then been restricted to a loose fusion of internationally operating banking capital on the one hand and colonial capital on the other. The depression of the early twenties added to this network the coal and railway companies which were particularly hit by that depression.

As a consequence of their financial stakes in the industries mentioned, several banks now acquired formal links in the form of interlocking directorships, by placing their directors on the boards of those companies so heavily in their debt (Stanworth and Giddens 1975: 12).

This development was forced upon the companies concerned by necessity, and did not point to the constitution of clear-cut financial conglomerates, in which a single overall strategy was adopted. This is brought out most clearly by the debate caused by the government's decision to return to the Gold Standard at the pre-war parity in 1925. The City strongly supported the return, which was necessary for the maintenance of its leading role in international finance, in which American capital was making headway rapidly as a consequence of the outcome of World War I.

The Federation of British Industry on the other hand was in large majority opposed to this step which would entail a revaluation of 10%, and instead advocated a policy directed at protection of the Commonwealth markets (Winch 1972: 128). The City held the upper hand in this clash and at its insistence a policy of deflation was followed, which for many branches of industry meant the necessity to turn to the production of absolute surplus value to maintain the rate of profit. In the branches that had dominated British exports since the nineteenth century (coal, textiles, steel) this necessity was especially urgent.

The result of this policy was a period of violent class struggle in Britain. Money wages declined by 38% in the period 1920–24, and unemployment never sank below 10% of the workforce during the twenties (Glyn/Sutcliffe 1972: 26). The General Strike of 1926 represented at the same time the climax and the end of this intensified class struggle: in losing the General Strike, the working class lost the initiative it had still held in 1920. The defeat of the workers' movement removed the obstacles to the fulfilment of the requirements of the return to the Gold Standard by making possible mass redundancies and wage cuts.

During the 1930s, the British working class gradually regained some of its strength but now on the reformist basis of collaborating with capital. This process started in 1928, when the Trade Unions Congress leadership met with a group of entrepreneurs from the new modern industries, headed by Sir Alfred Mond, chairman of ICI (Imperial Chemical Industries). These contacts finally culminated in the Macmillan Report of 1931, in which the Trade Unions Congress accepted adaptation of the wages to the economic situation. As a result of this 'social contract avant la lettre', real wages (for those who had work, of course) remained unchanged during the years 1932–37, while they actually increased between 1929 and 1932 by 7.8% (Glyn/Sutcliffe 1972: 32–4).

This stability of real wages during the Depression, in such contrast with developments elsewhere in the imperialist countries, was made possible by the sharp decline of agricultural prices on the world market (Dobb 1973: 335). The traditional British dependence upon import of these goods and the gradual constitution of a Sterling bloc further contributed to the comparatively slight impact of the crisis in Britain: 'manufacturing production (1913 = 100) in the USA fell from 112.7 in 1929 to 58.4 in 1932; in Germany from 108 to 64.4, but in Britain merely from 109 to 90' (Hobsbawm 1975: 184).

During the twenties, those branches of industry which had an interest in the production of relative surplus value had been small and without much influence, although they were among the fastest growing (e.g. chemicals, motorcars, electrical appliances). During the thirties, however, they profited greatly from the peculiar situation then existing. Due to their conditions of accumulation – large scale of production, high organic composition of capital, semi-continuous production, a need for relatively few but highly skilled personnel – they became the principal proponents of a conciliatory policy toward the working class.

So, on the one hand, new industries flourished as never before; there was an enormous expansion of employment in several branches producing consumer goods, Britain became the second largest car-producing nation, wages were rising first and constant later, and there was considerable social peace. This sector was characterized by monopolization on the national level, rather than cartelization. It is clear that American direct investments in Britain, concentrated as they were in the modem and expansive sectors, heavily stimulated monopolistic tendencies in these branches of production.

On the other hand, however, there was stagnation in older industrial branches and regions, enormous unemployment (up to 45% at times in coal and steel), cartels were formed at the instigation of the government, and there was a general resistance to technological innovation. An example of this was the attempt in 1936 by William Firth to introduce a continuous wide-strip mill for manufacturing sheet steel (used in the production of motorcars for example). He was only granted permission by the Steel Federation to go ahead (in 1939) after having accepted a supervisory board manned by his principal competitors and the Bank of England (Burn 1961: 54–5).

On the international scene, Britain had been moving ever since the First World War towards stronger and stronger protectionism in reaction to the deteriorating competitive position of British capital on the world market. In 1931, Britain left the Gold Standard and Sterling was devalued by 20%. During the Commonwealth Conference in Ottawa in 1932, the system of imperial preferences was set up. The result was that the share of Commonwealth countries in British foreign trade increased rapidly. These protectionist measures completed the groundwork for the post-war developments. To summarize the most important aspects of the interwar years: during the nineteen twenties, economic policy in Britain was dictated by a powerful coalition of internationally operating banking capital and colonial capital, mostly engaged in extractive industries. The specific interests (be it real or perceived) of these groups required the return to the Gold Standard at the pre-World War I parity. The heaviest burden of this policy was carried by the old export-oriented industries (coal, steel, textiles) which, in order to cut their prices, had to revert to an increase of absolute surplus value because resources which could have been used for labour-saving innovation had dried up in the depression of the early twenties. Thus, out of necessity as much as out of disposition, capitalists in these sectors of the economy increasingly turned to restrictive practices and to cartelization. The state often had to come in to enforce the cooperation of all capitalists concerned, as is often the case when all are convinced of the desirability of limiting production but no one wants to be the first. The weakness of these groups, which had become especially clear during the thirties, found its counterpart in the growing strength of the 'new industries'. Born in the twenties, these branches profited greatly from the conditions in the years after the Great Crash. Insulation from foreign competition coupled to a rather stable effective demand made for rapid accumulation in these branches.

The encapsulation of the Empire was important not only in this respect, but also in that it gave banking capital enough breathing space not to come into conflict with modern industry which could still finance its expansion out of its earnings. The conflict could easily have occurred in this period, were it not for the collapse of the Gold Standard in 1931. It was now postponed, as we will argue, until after World War II.

The most serious friction between different groups of capital in these years occurred between the new manufacturing industries (the motorcar industry in particular) and the old basic industries (steel). The cartelization in Department I and the ensuing high coal and steel prices were a continuing source of conflict, which would only be resolved in favour of the manufacturing industries after the war. The same cartelization, which during the thirties was still an obstacle to the even more rapid development of modem industry, would after the war prove to be very helpful in restructuring these branches according to the needs of the mass-production industries.

Restructuring by the state: the post-war Labour government

In the previous section, we argued that as the war came, the balance of power between different groups of capital had shifted to such an extent that a radically different structure in the economy would be needed to accommodate the requirements of the newly emerged and increasingly powerful groups of modem industrial corporations. It would be up to the post-war Labour government to effect this restructuring. In this section, we will argue that the government did not nearly succeed in this task because of:

- the seemingly favourable competitive position on the world market of British capital in general in the years immediately following the war;
- the continued strength (at least with respect to the formulation of economic and foreign policy) of colonial interests (both banks and extractive industries);
- the commitment of the government to full employment.

In Britain, the war did not in itself create totally different social, economic, and political conditions, as it had done on the continent. First, established interests in Britain never lost control of politics. The important political parties and their leadership were not, as in Europe, corrupted by collaboration with occupying German forces. Second, working-class organizations were not crushed and/or forced to operate underground. The war, and the national effort to win it, greatly strengthened reformism, while in Europe the revolutionary forces in the working class were greatly strengthened in the resistance movements. Third, on the purely economic front, the productive potential underwent no spectacular expansion, as it had done during the First World War. The ruling class in this way hoped to avoid a deep recession such as had followed the post-war boom in 1920–21. Rather than expand and rationalize basic industries, the necessary raw materials and finished products were imported, if possible from the Commonwealth, if not, from the USA.

On account of all these factors together, Britain came out of the war with a productive potential that was heavily dated, if not altogether obsolete, in the basic industries: coal and steel. There was, however, no immediate necessity for the coal and steel capitalists to restructure their industries, as their European and Japanese competitors were temporarily unable to penetrate into the protected markets of the British Commonwealth and, even more important, world demand far outstripped world production. Under these conditions, capital operating on less than average productivity can still produce quite profitably. Thus, conditions were rather adverse for a new wave of rapid accumulation of capital on a new technological basis.

The Labour government, elected by a landslide in 1945 by an electorate bent on avoiding the return of massive unemployment, proved unable to alter this situation.

There were more than enough plans, but no Plan. All programmes meant to assist in the restructuring of important branches of industry, were left to committees and councils made up of the capitalists concerned with their implementation. These were interested in restriction rather than in restructuring their hopelessly unproductive industries, certainly when compared to the same branches in the United States (see Brady 1950: 205–11).

Labour's economic policy had two main aims: the restructuring of capital and, on the insistence of the trade union movement, the maintenance of full employment. A consequence of this last policy aim was that many unprofitable firms were kept alive through state subsidies and price regulation. The policies of Labour were thus internally contradictory. The maintenance of full employment in obsolete sectors does not go well with an effort to restructure and rationalize industry.

Another factor explaining the slow rate of growth, i.e. in comparison with other imperialist countries, was the successful resistance of the Bank of England to Dalton's cheap money policy. On the continent rapid expansion of credit facilities contributed greatly to economic recovery. However, in Britain the City, in yet another attempt to recapture a prominent place in world finance, exported capital and channelled investment into extractive industries in order to relieve the dollar shortage and, if possible, avoid a devaluation of the pound (Aaronovitch 1955: 69–71, 108–9, 113). This attempt failed in 1949, but the adverse effects of this policy for those industries primarily producing for the home market was nevertheless considerable.

The most important structural change in this period is that manifested by the nationalization of steel. At the end of the war steel companies played a pivotal role in groups of industrial capitals, more than half of the interlocking directorships among industrial companies involving steel companies (Stanworth and Giddens 1975: 15–18). When the Labour plans to nationalize steel came up, it is therefore no wonder that resistance was much heavier than in the earlier nationalizations of the coal mines and of the Bank of England. A further reason for the resistance against the nationalization of steel must be sought in the profitability of the industry, which it owed to the situation on the world market, where demand outstripped production, major competitors were temporarily out of business, and the dollar shortage limited American competitive power. Nationalization of such a profitable industry, it was feared by large sections of the bourgeoisie, would widen the horizon for the possible nationalization of other profitable industries, such as banking. It is our contention here that the nationalization of the steel industry in 1949 should be seen as the subordination of steel capital to the interests of its most important customers, the modern mass consumer goods industry, as the European Coal and Steel Community served the same purpose on the Continent (Bode 1975; van der Pijl 1978a).

Several developments concerning British steel supply supporting evidence for this hypothesis: when the final legislation was presented, some exceptions were made. Two vertically integrated companies (Ford, and Vickers, owners of English Steel and Darlington Forge) were explicitly left out of the Nationalisation Act. The recommendation of Paul Hoffman, Marshall Aid administrator and director of

Finance capital and the crisis in Britain **89**

Studebaker, carried a heavy weight: he threatened to cut off all aid to the British steel industry (most of which was going to the Steel Company of Wales, owners of the first continuous wide-strip rolling mill producing sheet steel for motorcar production) if the act were passed in its original form (Brady 1950: 189, 217, 220). This subordination is further indicated by the fact that at least one group of steel consumers, the motorcar manufacturers, had been complaining ever since 1934 about the high steel prices, and they did not seem too worried about the danger of creeping socialism, but rather welcomed the proposed nationalization (Brady 1950: 196, Burn 1961: 65, 68ff.).

Thus, a new era with radically altered relations of power between different branches of production and different groups of capital was clearly in the making. The 1950s and early 1960s would bring the decisive change-about, first in the economic field, and then on the political plane.

From global power to rejected EEC member

Notwithstanding the enormous sacrifices the country had had to make during the war, Britain seemed to resume its place as one of the leading world powers after the defeat of the Third Reich. The 'special relation' with the United States and the continued existence of the system of imperial preferences helped maintain this position.

It was on this basis that Churchill formulated the priorities of British foreign policy in his three-circle theory: British ties with the Commonwealth came first, the Anglo-American axis came second, and Western Europe only figured as the third area of interest. This policy, to which Britain would cling for almost twenty years, particularly served the interests of two prominent sections of British capital, namely banking capital (at least that part of banking capital with very extensive colonial and American interests), and the colonial monopolies and mining interests. The predominance of these interests in this period is illustrated in the work of Aaronovitch (1955, 1961).

However, the contradictory nature of this basis for British foreign policy showed itself almost immediately. Both pillars were undermined, by objective developments and by each other. The maintenance of the Empire, with its preferential treatment and the inconvertibility of Sterling, was a policy aim which fully contradicted US foreign policy after the war and stood in opposition to the interests of American capital. The United States tried to enforce the 'Open Door' through such US-dominated institutions as the International Monetary Fund and the General Agreement on Tariffs and Trade.

The successful penetration of American capital in the Empire foreshadowed the untenability of the British aims. The devaluation and return to full convertibility in 1949 should have made this clear right then, even though at that time the Commonwealth still represented the most important domain for the foreign expansion of British capital.

Given the predominance of this general foreign policy orientation, it should not be surprising that when the French minister Schuman announced the plan for a pooling of the European coal and steel sectors – intended as a first step toward further economic integration – British reactions were generally negative (Anouil 1960: 56–64). The Labour Party and the Trade Union Movement were mostly opposed to the scheme for fear that their priority of full employment would not stand up to the rationalizations foreseen in the Schuman plan. The meeting ground for all opponents of joining the European Coal and Steel Community was the intense dislike of the idea of supra-nationality, although they were led to this position by diverging motives. The same reasons still applied when in 1956 and 1957 the founding of the EEC was prepared. In 1958, the Federation of British Industries declared itself against membership of the EEC for what would prove to be the last time.

After 1955 the shift from the predominance of basic and extractive industries to the predominance of mass consumer goods industries, to which we alluded in the introduction, picked up pace again. These newly dominant industries, however, found in the Commonwealth a market with little and stagnating buying power and growing competition from American capital. In contrast, the markets of the EEC were expanding rapidly, and the growing importance of these markets for British exports has been documented by many authors.

The Suez disaster and the decolonization of the years following 1956 made it clear that the decline of Britain as a world power, which had been in the stars for decades in the economic field, could in the end not be resisted by political and military means alone. The role of liquidator of the Empire fell to a man well equipped for the job: Harold Macmillan, who became Prime Minister in 1958. It would take three more years, however, before the bridge was crossed and an application for EEC membership was filed. During these three years, there was a delicate balance in foreign policy between the old orientation towards maintenance of the Empire and the special relation with the United States, and a new orientation aiming at the creation of the largest possible area of free trade. For the time being, the balance was found in the creation of the European Free Trade Association. However, given its limited scope and given the failure of the attempt to make the EEC a member of the Association, this balance was bound to tip before long.

Accordingly, in 1961 the Tory government of Harold Macmillan filed for EEC membership.[3] By that time, however, General de Gaulle had come to power in France, and his government vetoed Britain's accession to the Common Market in 1963, mostly on the ground that Britain would prove to be an American 'Trojan horse'. If we want to assess the failure of this application correctly, we must go into the relations between American and British capital a bit further now.

American investment in the UK itself dates back to the middle of the nineteenth century (van Moock 1977: 7). These investments were to a large extent direct investments in manufacturing industry, and not in basic industries (10, 17). The market for the kind of goods produced by American firms in Britain had expanded during the decade prior to World War Two, thus stimulating American investment even more.

Between 1943 and 1950, American direct private investment in the UK increased from 519 million dollars to 847 million dollars, while in the same period total direct

American investment in all of Europe declined from 2025 million dollars to 1720 million dollars. The British share of American direct investment in Europe thus increased from approximately 25% to almost half (van Moock 1977: 27). This enormous share was maintained until 1960. During the sixties, the proportion of American capital in Europe which was invested in Britain declined to 32.4% in 1971.

We can see that the relative decline of Britain – i.e. the slow growth of the modern sectors – during the sixties was reflected in, and reinforced by, a slowing down of American direct investment in Britain. Nevertheless, American business in Britain grew much faster than British business and was heavily export-oriented. Continuation of this trend, it is estimated, will in 1980 lead to a situation in which 25% of British exports are in reality exports by American capital in Britain (Poulantzas 1976: 64).

Thus, in the course of a few decades, two groups of fast-growing, heavily monopolized capitals had sprung up which by the sixties urgently needed enlarged markets for their continued expansion. This enlargement could only be found in unimpeded access to the markets of the EEC, if possible without losing ground, in the traditional British export markets, but if necessary by acceding to an outwardly protectionist common market. As we have seen, under Eden and Churchill, Conservative governments of the 1950s remained committed to the old imperial policies for a considerable time after the material basis for that policy had been radically eroded. This policy led to continuous friction with the United States in the fields of international monetary arrangements, accessibility of the Empire to American capital, the conduct of the Cold War, and the final dissolution of the British role 'East of Suez'.

It was only after the Macmillan government had eliminated most obstacles to better Anglo-American relations, and after the victory of Kennedy in the 1960 elections with his more activist European policy (van der Pijl 1978b: 18), that the US gave up its earlier opposition to British membership of the EEC. The US remained firm on one point, however – a logical consequence of its preference for global free trade arrangements of the Kennedy-round type – and insisted that the Commonwealth would not be incorporated into the EEC system of preferences (Beloff 1963: 101, 106–7). Beloff sums up the American position as follows:

> By the spring of 1962, then, it might be said that the United States objective in economic policy was to bring the whole of the non-Soviet world under the same regime of generally freer trade and payments, but within this world it saw an emergent grouping of two major centres of power – the United States and an integrated Western Europe including Britain.
>
> *(113–4)*

Ironically enough, it was precisely this improvement in Anglo-American relations – highlighted by the Nassau agreements on military-nuclear cooperation – which supplied General de Gaulle with a strong reason to veto the introduction of an American Trojan horse into his 'Europe des Patries' in 1963.

Wilson's attempt to cure Britain

The failure of the attempt to join the Common Market added one more to the already impressive list of factors accounting for the slow rate of accumulation and the falling rate of profit in Britain, at least in comparison with the other major capitalist economies. In the middle of the sixties the crisis in the British economy was intensified by a downturn in all of the capitalist world. The problems British industry was facing (a strong labour movement, lagging productivity, stagnant export markets, political prominence of colonial and financial interests, an enormous export of capital, and falling profits at home) were now joined by a sharp surge of foreign competition.

Under the influence of all these concurring developments, there was an enormous increase in the centralization of capital. This process had already accelerated during the second half of the 1950s, accompanying the restructuring of capital that took place during this period. The branches in which merger activity was particularly prominent were electrical engineering, textiles, drinks, chemicals, and vehicles (Aaronovitch and Sawyer 1975: 125).

The merger movement was also more intense in the UK than in the EEC: between 1958 and 1962 there were 3384 mergers in the UK against 1000 in the EEC (Jalée 1970: 116). But the difference became especially striking in the wake of the 1966/7 recession: in 1967, there were 1068 mergers in the UK, as against 12 in the Federal Republic, 8 in France, 5 in the Netherlands, and 5 in Switzerland (Stanworth and Giddens 1975: 26n).

During 1967 and 1968 10 percent of all industrial, commercial, and financial assets changed owners, while a fourth of all companies worth more than $10 million were taken over (Spiegelberg 1973: 167). The government played an active part in some of these mergers (notably in the aircraft, shipping, and cotton industry), while in most other cases it stood by passively: between 1965 and 1975 only 33 of the approximately 1000 mergers qualifying for scrutiny by the Monopolies Commission were actually looked into (van Iersel 1976: 143ff.).

The result of this high mobility of capital was that the number of interlocking directorships between financial institutions and the top 50 industrial companies increased from 69 in 1946 to 88 in 1960, and to 94 in 1970. Financial institutions, and particularly the merchant banks, moved closer and closer to the centre of the network (Stanworth and Giddens 1975, passim).

To curb the threat of crisis, to the existence of which this wave of centralization testified, three forms of action are available to the state: a direct redistribution of income, indirect support of profit, and undermining the strength of the working class (Glyn and Sutcliffe 1972: 157). The Wilson government of 1964–70 was active on all these fronts. Through a wage freeze, tax cuts, a general incomes policy, and several nationalizations, Wilson tried to redistribute income in favour of profit.[4] He largely failed in this respect because working-class action successfully withstood the measures directly affecting its income position, and in this way the prospects for a restoration of profitability were worsened.

Devaluation and entry into the Common Market are mentioned by Glyn and Sutcliffe as two indirect supports for profits. However, entry into the EEC was once again blocked by the intransigence of de Gaulle, and devaluation failed to do its job, because Labour's policy aims in monetary affairs were contradictory. On the one hand, there were strong pressures on the government to defend the position of Sterling, which required maintaining an equilibrium in the balance of payments and deflationary measures. This was the road Wilson initially travelled. The effort to step up production and raise exports conflicted with this aim, as it demanded inflationary policies and a devaluation of the pound (Mandel 1974b: 33). When the Wilson government decided to follow the latter road in 1967, it was too late to have much impact, and it ran into opposition in the City to a devaluation of the pound (Westergaard and Resler 1974: 240).

The Wilson government was successful in one respect: although it did not succeed in its attempt to introduce anti-strike legislation, it succeeded where the preceding Conservative governments had not dared to go. It abandoned full employment as a number one priority. Some would even go so far as to say that unemployment was introduced as a deliberate policy (Glyn and Sutcliffe 1972: 177–80). This, of course, was a success for capital only a Labour government could possibly attain without endangering the foundations of the rule of capital:

> Between 1964 and 1970 the Labour government tried to serve two masters. It would not challenge capitalism, so it tried to support it; but it could not make its policy acceptable to the trade unions on whom it depended. Such contradictions are bound to beset a working class party in power, if it does not oppose capitalism, but tries instead to make it run more efficiently and more humanely.
>
> *(213)*

... and Heath's failure to finish the job

Whatever can be said about the Heath government coming to power in 1970, it is not that it tried to make capitalism run more humanely. On the contrary, Heath, true to his election pledge, tried it the hard way. His policy of confronting the working-class organizations was reminiscent of Nixon's New Economic Policy in many respects. But in foreign affairs, Heath followed the course initiated in the sixties (in which he himself had played an important part as negotiator for the Macmillan government) of joining the EEC. In this respect, the path followed was clearly in the interest of the now dominant sections of British industrial capital, aimed as it was at safeguarding British access to the largest and fastest-growing market for durable goods, the Common Market.

One obstacle to British entry had been provided by General de Gaulle, and behind him certain groups in French capital, who had feared an American Trojan horse. After 1968, however, a different attitude in France toward penetration by American capital (American investment in France came to be actually stimulated under Giscard) and a different conception of the EEC gradually came to the fore.

94 Henk Overbeek

In this new orientation, Britain was seen to be a possible counterweight to growing West German power in Western Europe.

The major domestic obstacle to British entry into the EEC had been the fact that all through the fifties and sixties, British foreign policy was either dominated or seriously constrained in its flexibility (which could have led to overcoming de Gaulle's obstinate posture) by a coalition of two groups of capitals: banking capital (the City) and colonial and mining capital. In this paper, we have been arguing that this coalition of interests came under increasing stress as the centre of gravity of surplus value production shifted toward advanced industrial capital. This shift was accompanied by the slow but steady growth of a network of relations between industrial and financial capital. An important turning point was reached around 1970, a significant sign of this was the floating of Sterling. As late as 1969, the Wilson government was compelled to protect the pound against devaluation, but in 1970 the pound was floated without major opposition in the City.

A survey of City opinion, conducted by the *Banker*, confirms the turnabout in the outlook of the City. Of those interviewed, 55% were of the opinion that the City suffered little or nothing at all from the fall of Sterling, while a full 73% thought that their own sector of the City had hardly suffered from it. Sixty-six percent was in favour of maintaining a floating exchange rate, 23 percent even favoured an exchange rate below the market price, and only 11 percent would favour support by the state for the position of sterling (*Banker*, January 1978). This must partly be explained by pointing out that the activities of the City were more and more directed at the very lucrative Euro-dollar market.[5]

Heath's domestic policies, we feel, must be understood in terms of their effects on British industry which entry into the EEC would prove to have. Those industries that had not waited for British entry (which became effective in 1973) and had invested in production facilities on the continent have certainly welcomed the move, since it greatly enlarged their freedom of movement. However, those industrial capitals producing for the home market could expect the move into Europe to cause greatly intensified competition. Only an enormous improvement of their competitive power could ensure a chance for survival.

Improving the competitive power of domestic capital required first of all a sharp attack on the strength of the working class. We have already suggested that productivity in the UK lagged far behind productivity in comparable branches of the other major imperialist economies. One of the most important reasons for this had been the defensive strength of the working-class organizations. Thus, only an intensification of the policy of undermining this strength, begun in 1965 by the Wilson government, could hold the promise of success. The strength of the British working class did not find its expression primarily in high wages: 'until 1972 wage rates grew at a slower pace in Britain than in the Common Market or Japan, [but] ... wage costs per unit of output ... rose disproportionally in the UK' (Barnett 1973: 27). It is the fact that the working class was able to defend full employment until around 1966 which can partly be held responsible for this growing productivity gap between Britain and the rest of the imperialist world. It was therefore no big surprise that the first successful large-scale attack on the working class came in the form of abandoning full employment and the introduction of deflationary measures in the late sixties.

A second classical response to crisis is a reduction of the value of labour power, both in the form of an attack on real wages and in the form of cuts in social expenditure. We have suggested that this course of action, as a rule, is subject to the condition that it does not lead to serious disturbances in the relation between capital and labour. The instrumentality of a Labour government is very clear in this respect.

Intensification of the internationalization of capital (it could also be called internationalized blackmail) is the course of action by far preferred by capital. An example of this strategy is provided by Ford Europe: it is shifting more and more of its production to plants in Belgium and Germany and is now the largest car importer of Britain (*Economist*, 11 February 1978: 114).

However forceful the attack on the working class was during these years, and however successful in reducing its standard of living, it failed in its overriding purpose: that of restoring profitability to industry in Britain and thus convincing British capital to resume investment inside Britain. The enormous flight of capital from Britain in the early seventies in the form of speculative investment in real estate on the continent was the most spectacular expression of this fact.

The future of the British state and of British capital seems increasingly dim. The present situation, in our opinion, which is shared by Nairn (1979), precludes any possibility of a successful moderate solution. The final choice more and more seems to become the one between an authoritarian regime of the right and a social revolution from the left. In both cases, it is uncertain whether the British state can survive in its present, multinational form.

British finance capital now

We have argued that the loss of empire, non-entry into the EEC in the sixties, stagnation and crisis in the sixties and seventies, and finally the aftermath of entry into the EEC in 1973, all accompanied by a merger movement of staggering proportions, have led to enormous changes in the structure of relations between British capitals.

Let us now take a closer look, by way of conclusion, at the structure of British finance capital as it emerged in the mid-seventies. Interlocking directorships are of course only one form of structuring the relations between and among financial and industrial companies. Financial relations, it is sometimes argued, are far more important than directorial links. However, as we indicated in the introduction, information on financial links between companies is, for British capital, not readily and systematically available. Information regarding interlocking directorships is. The Stock Exchange Official Yearbook (1972, 1976) contains the names of the directors of all companies quoted on the London Stock Exchange, and so the construction of the network of interlocks is a tedious but simple affair. This is one reason why most researchers on British finance capital have largely concentrated on analysing these institutional relations.[6] In other countries, and particularly in the United States, information on financial links is more readily available and has been used extensively in the analysis of finance capital. The works of Victor Perlo and S. Menshikov are well-known examples.[7] But lack of better information is not the only justification for concentrating on interlocking directorships. After reviewing the available information on financial ties in Scottish industry and finance, Scott concludes that 'those connections which are regarded as most important in this respect [i.e. strategic control] will be those which are reinforced through directorial links' (Scott 1978: 7). Thus, until systematic information on other relations becomes available, we feel it is justified to concentrate on analysing interlocking directorates.

As we argued in the first section of this contribution, the network of relations in finance capital will change considerably in density and/or in structure when the continued accumulation of capital comes under pressure. Thus, we might expect that the very severe crisis of the years 1973–75 caused important changes in the network in Britain.

A survey of interlocking directorships among 26 large industrial corporations, four clearing banks, nine large insurance companies, and twelve of the most important merchant banks for the years 1972 and 1976 confirms this expectation. The most telling findings were:

- the total number of links increased by almost 15% from 112 to 128;
- the City, as a sub-system, has not become more tightly knit under the impact of crisis;
- the relations between financial and industrial companies increased by approximately 10 percent, from 57 to 63;
- the clearing banks and S.G. Warburg account for the bulk of this increase, while the importance of the insurance companies in the network diminished slightly;
- even more striking is the growth of the number of interlocks among industrial companies themselves from 17 to 27, or almost 60%;
- these changes are reiterated if we look at the centrality of firms, measured by the number of interlocks with other companies: one can say that industrial companies become far more central, especially when compared to insurance companies;
- on the basis of the above, we would conclude that to an increasing extent the axis of clearing banks–industrial companies is becoming the most important one.

As far as the general structure of relations among individual capitals is concerned, we can conclude that the connectedness has reached a point where we might speak of a qualitative break: finance capital as the integration of the different circuits of capital has come of age in Britain, along with the belated advent of a true stage of monopoly capital. If our observation in the first section of this article, where we indicated that formation of financial groups is the logical extension of this process, is correct, then a further test seems called for.

On the basis of the data I gathered, I came to the conclusion that by 1976 two large financial groups are in the making. I reached this tentative conclusion, which will serve as a guide to further research, by considering several sub-networks: the network of clearing banks and industrial companies, the network of companies with five or more links to other companies, and the network formed by multiple links (links between companies made up of more than one shared director).

The clearest group was that centred around the Midland Bank. It consists of the following companies: Midland, Montagu, Shell, BICC, Dunlop, Imperial Group, Unilever, Rothmans, Rank Organisation, Eagle Star, General Accident, and Prudential. The density of this group (the ratio between the actual and the possible number of links) is $27/11.6 = 40.9\%$. Were we to subtract the insurance companies, considered by Aaronovitch as coalitions of interest rather than as independently operating capitals, the density would increase to exactly fifty percent, or 5 times the density of the whole 1976 network (Aaronovitch 1961: 89–90).

The second large grouping is of much looser composition, and seems to be centred around two financial companies, Lloyds and S.G. Warburg. The other companies making up this group are: BP, ICI, British Leyland, British-American Tobacco, Hawker Siddely, Plessey, ICL, Guest, Keen & Nettlefolds, General Electric, Vickers, Reed International, Tate & Lyle, and Morgan Grenfell. The density of this group is 24.8% or 2.5 times the density of the whole network. Similar results were not found in the analysis of the network of 1972.

It would thus appear that British finance capital has finally entered the stage in which capitalist interests crystallize into true financial groups in which financiers of a type which is relatively new for Britain command the economy. It will be the task of political economists to closely follow the development of these groups in the future since knowledge thereof can teach us a lot about the possibilities and impossibilities of alternative working-class strategies.

Notes

1 This contribution is based on my paper 'Finance capital and crisis in Britain', presented at the CSE Annual Conference at Bradford, July 1978. I am grateful to the following people for their valuable comments on earlier drafts: C. Buijink, A. Maas, R. van Moock, E. Schrama, R. Bode, L. van Eerden, W. Gooijer, H. Post, K. van der Pijl, J. Rodenburg, D. Hellema, and P. van den Tempel. I profited much from the discussion about my paper at the CSE Conference. To Meindert Fennema I owe a special debt for his stimulating remarks, which greatly helped me to clarify many obscure points in earlier versions. A last and very heavy debt is owed to the editorial committee of *Capital & Class*. The comments I received on an earlier version of this article were most helpful, especially those of Simon Clarke. Nevertheless, all errors and faulty arguments are wholly my responsibility.

2 A first try to clarify this, on the basis of information contained in *Who Owns Whom* (1973), yielded promising results. It appeared that British banks are almost all related along several lines to American banks, and that these relations were almost exclusive in the sense that no major British bank entertained ties with more than one major American bank.

3 According to Nairn (1972: 17–22) this attempt was half-hearted. I do not agree with this interpretation, and find support in Camps (1964: 501), who speaks of de Gaulle's genuine surprise that the British really meant business.

4 An indication of how nationalization can contribute to this policy aim can be found in the following: 'The private steel sector in the U.K. now accounts for something like 15% of crude steel production and (having purchased billet from BSC [British Steel Corporation] and elsewhere and rolled it), about one third of the output of steel products. Mostly at a profit' (*Economist*, 25 March 1978: 97). At a profit, not necessarily because of the inherently more efficient production in the private sector, as the *Economist* suggests, but probably because of the 'state handouts that have gone to BSC', enabling nationalized steel to sell unprofitably to private steelmakers and leaving it to them to appropriate the surplus value actually created in the public sector.

5 Foremost in the Eurobond business is S.G. Warburg, affiliated to the New York banking house of Kuhn Loeb (dominated by the Warburg family) and associated with the Banque de Paris et des Pays Bas (see Spiegelberg 1973: 77, 94, 97; Mandel 1974a: 414).

6 Some studies in this field are: Aaronovitch 1955, 1961; Barratt Brown 1974; Stanworth and Giddens 1975; *Economist*, 11 June 1977: 132.

7 For a good overview of the analysis of interlocking directorships and related topics in different countries, see Fennema and Schijf 1978. An English-language version of this article was presented at the Planning Session of the European Consortium for Political Research in Grenoble, April 1978.

References

Aaronovitch, S. (1955). *Monopoly. A study of British monopoly capitalism*. London: Lawrence & Wishart.

Aaronovitch, S. (1961). *The ruling class. A study of British finance capital*. London: Lawrence & Wishart.

Aaronovitch, S. and Sawyer, M.C. (1975). *Big business. Theoretical and empirical aspects of concentration and mergers in the United Kingdom*. London: Macmillan.

Anouil, G. (1960). *La Grande Bretagne et la Communauté Européenne du Charbon et de l'Acier*. Issoudon: Impr. Laboureur.

Barnett, A. (1973). Class struggle and the Heath Government. *New Left Review* 77: 3–41.

Barratt Brown, M. (1974). The controllers of British industry. In J. Urry and J. Wakeford (Eds), *Power in Britain* (pp. 73–116). London: Heinemann.

Beloff, M. (1963). *The United States and the unity of Europe*. Washington, DC: Brookings Institute.

Bode, R. (1975). *De lotgevallen van een sektor*. Amsterdam: University of Amsterdam, unpublished manuscript.

Brady, R.A. (1950). *Crisis in Britain. Plans and achievements of the Labour Government*. Cambridge: Cambridge University Press.

Burn, D. (1961). *The steel industry, 1939–1959. A study in competition and planning*. Cambridge: Cambridge University Press.

Camps, M. (1964). *Britain and the European Community 1955–1963*. London: Princeton University Press.

Dobb, M. (1973). *Studies in the development of capitalism*. London: Routledge.

Fennema, M. and Schijf, H. (1978). De analyse van dubbelfuncties: theorie en methode. *Cahiers voor de politieke en sociale wetenschappen* 1(3): 11–59.

Glyn, A. and Sutcliffe, R. (1972). *British capitalism. Workers and the profit squeeze*. Harmondsworth: Penguin.

Hobsbawm, E.J. (1975). *Industry and empire*. Harmondsworth: Penguin.

van Iersel, J.P. (1976). Europe's fusiecontrole nog niet in zicht. *Nieuw Europa* 3: 138–150.

Jalée, P. (1970). *L'Impérialisme en 1970*. Paris: Maspero.

Mandel, E. (1974a). *Marxist economic theory*. London: Merlin.

Mandel, E. (1974b). *Decline of the dollar. A Marxist view of the monetary crisis*. New York: Pathfinder Press.

Marx, K. (1974). *Das Kapital, Band 3*. Berlin: Dietz Verlag.

van Moock, R. (1977). *US investeringen en US 'hulp' in het Verenigd Koninkrijk*. Amsterdam: University of Amsterdam, unpublished manuscript.

Nairn, T. (1972). The left against Europe? *New Left Review* 75: 5–120.

Nairn, T. (1979). The future of Britain's crisis. *New Left Review* 113–114: 43–70.

van der Pijl, K. (1978a). *Een Amerikaans plan voor Europa. Achtergronden van het ontstaan van de EEG*. Amsterdam: Socialistische Uitgeverij.

van der Pijl, K. (1978b). Class formation at the international level. Paper for the CSE Annual Conference, Bradford (Chapter 2 in this volume).

Poulantzas, N. (1976). *Klassen in het huidige kapitalisme: De internationalisatie van de kapitalistische verhoudingen en de nationale staat*. Nijmegen: SUN.

Scott, J. (1978). The intercorporate configuration. Substructure and superstructure. Paper for the ECPR planning session, Grenoble, April.

Spiegelberg, R. (1973). *The City. Power without accountability*. London: Blond and Briggs.

Stanworth, P. and Giddens, A. (1975). The modern corporate economy. Interlocking directorships in Britain 1906–1970. *Sociological Review* 23(1): 5–28.

Stock Exchange (1972). *Stock Exchange Official Yearbook*. London: Skinner and Co.

Stock Exchange (1976). *Stock Exchange Official Yearbook*. London: Skinner and Co.

Westergaard, J. and Resler, H. (1974). *Class in capitalist society. A study of contemporary Britain*. London: Heinemann.

Winch, D. (1972). *Economics and policy. A historical survey*. London: Fontana.

4

THE INTERNATIONAL CORPORATE ELITE (1984)

Meindert Fennema

Even though the study of interlocking directorates is basically a study of *inter*corporate power which cannot be based on theories and evidence of *intra*-corporate power, the structure of the corporation is important for the position of the directors, especially for their position as *interlocking* directors.[1] If, for example, the internal function of the board of directors is regarded as insignificant, the function of interlocking directorates will also be considered of minor importance.[2] In the opening section, the development of the decision-making structure of the large corporation and the main functions of different boards will be sketched. Furthermore, an international survey is necessary to compare national differences and to assign an identical meaning to corresponding positions. Since it is well known that formally similar positions may differ in content from one company to another within the same country, it is obvious that the idiosyncratic differences in companies from different nations will be even greater. For this reason, the goal of the opening section is very modest: only some major distinctions will be made to enable us to select the most important positions for discussion in the next section and to construct a simple typology of interlocking directorates according to the character of the position held in each of a pair of interlocked firms in subsequent sections.

The organization of the supervising and executive function in different countries

The separation of ownership and control was accompanied by important changes in the organizational structure of the large firms. Such changes first appeared in the American railroad companies. The size of these companies was very large indeed and most of them expanded rapidly in the second half of the nineteenth century. In an early railroad company, the key decisions were usually made by the so-called general manager, who acted in close consultation with the representatives of the large investors. After the Civil War, the railroad *system*, rather than the individual railroad, became the dominant operating organization, and a more explicit overall structure was needed. A central office was created to guide and coordinate the separate operating units. This central office was run by the heads of the functional departments responsible for transportation, sales, finance, etc. Thus, an executive committee was formed out of the functional specialists.

Consultation with the representatives of the large investors also needed a more formal arrangement. Thus, a board of directors was formed, consisting of the (most important) members of the executive committee and the representatives of the (most important) investors, who in the emerging joint-stock companies were the large stockholders. Here, key decisions could be discussed and long-term objectives determined.

In the nineteenth-century stock company, stockholders were still regarded as co-owners of the firm. In the twentieth century, the stockholders gradually came to be regarded as mere shareowners. Legally, it is the corporation that owns the assets and not the stockholders. The stock company is a legal entity endowed with property rights. Although shareholders have lost these property rights, they have the right to participate in the decision-making process of that legal entity by voting in the meeting of shareholders, which includes in many countries the right to vote for the nomination of the board of directors. In legal terms, the shareholder has lost juridical ownership, but, at least formally, she or he still has economic ownership (Valkhoff 1941: 34). Besides, the shareholders own their *shares*, which provides them with a claim on the remunerations of the company. In other words, *usus* and *usus fructus* have been separated. Share ownership has become revenue claim (*usus fructus*) and is only indirectly related to *usus* because it provides the owner with a right to participate in the decision-making process. This right has become dissociated from individuals and can only be exercised collectively. Therefore, the stock company was seen by Marx (1976) as the abolition of private ownership of capital and the introduction of *social* capital. A similar idea was expressed by Keynes when he wrote in 1926 about

> the trend of joint stock institutions, when they have reached a certain age and size, to approximate to the status of public corporations rather than that of individualistic private enterprise. One of the most interesting and unnoticed developments of recent decades has been the tendency of big enterprise to socialise itself.
>
> *(Keynes 1972 [1926]: 289)*

And Berle puts it another way: 'the capital is there, and so is capitalism; the waning factor is the capitalist' (Berle 1954: 39).

The central question in this section is the relation between two pivotal institutions of the 'socialized' stock company: the general meeting of shareholders and the board of directors. Formally, the highest authority of a joint-stock company is vested in the general meeting of shareholders. Individually, the shareholders have no possibility of exercising the economic property rights, as Valkhoff called it; only in the general meeting of shareholders can these rights be exercised. And even then, most of these rights can only be exercised *indirectly*, through the nomination of directors. *Throughout the history of the joint-stock company there has been a continuous trend towards domination of the board of directors over the meeting of shareholders.* The dominant position of the board of directors was legally acknowledged in the Netherlands when in 1971 the co-optation of the board was legalized, leaving the meeting of shareholders with a qualified veto power. Before 1971, however, the shareholders had been deprived of their economic property rights through the device of *priority shares*, which gave their holders (in many cases the board directors) the right to nominate the directors.

In other countries no such legal devices are available, but there are other methods of controlling the meeting of shareholders. In particular, *voting by proxy*, which enables certain persons to vote on behalf of the (small) shareholders, is used both in the United States and in Germany. In the United States, however, the proxy committee is generally controlled by the board of directors, while in Germany the banks exercise the voting rights for the shares belonging to their clients. Other devices to eliminate the control of the shareholders are the fiduciary institutions which hold shares in trust for their owners, and investment companies, which hold blocks of shares, while issuing their own shares to the public. In practice, the difference between fiduciary institutions, investment companies and other financial institutions is of little significance with respect to the problem of control (see Scott 1979). But who controls these financial institutions? The answer lies in the mutualization of control by crossing the holdings. It reinforces the group in control through interlocking directorates and 'a self-perpetuating board of directors' (Perlo 1957: 82).

Rather than representing the shareholders, the board of directors has come to represent the stock company. Through the board of directors arose the possibility of institutionalizing consultation with large stockholders. The consultations with important suppliers of raw materials, with important clients and with those who controlled financial resources could also be institutionalized by inviting their representatives on the board. And it was again the American railroad companies who were the first to develop an intricate network of intercorporate relations through interlocking directorates. This led to the investigations of the Interstate Commerce Commission, published in 1908 under the title *Intercorporate relationships of railways in the United States.*

Although it can be said that the board of directors as a whole represents the corporation towards third parties, this is not true for the individual director. Many directors represent large blocks of shares that are owned by cohesive groups of individuals such as families, or by institutional investors. Others represent their 'own' companies, which may have specific commercial interests to be defended.

This duality of the board of directors always exists. *On the one hand, the board has to supervise the executive officers on behalf of the financial interests represented on the board, and on the other hand it has to act as a unified body representing the company.* The duality can explode into a proxy fight over the nomination of directors. In continental European firms this duality has been solved by a two-board system. In this system there is an executive board representing the company as a legal entity towards third parties and a supervisory board representing the (large) shareholders. The supervisory board meets three to six times a year. Members of the executive board cannot be on the supervisory board.

In fact, the situation in continental Europe is even more complicated because there are both a 'German' and a 'Latin' version of the two-board system. In Germany and in the Netherlands the supervisory board (*Aufsichtsrat* and *Raad van Commissarissen*) tends to become involved in executive functions as soon as important decisions are to be taken. This is the case when the articles of association require that certain basic decisions only be taken with the consent of the supervisory board. In emergency cases, the supervisory board can even nominate one of its members to take over the management of the company (*Delegationsrat* in Germany and *Gedelegeerd Commissaris* in the Netherlands). Finally, the supervisory board nominates the members of the executive board (see de Boer 1957: 141). In the German two-board system, the supervisory board is often in control of the corporation, although the situation varies from company to company and depends heavily on the specific structure and history of the corporation. Sometimes the supervisory board is controlled by the executive board rather than the other way around.

The Latin variant of the two-board system can be considered the purest form of separation of the executive and supervising function. The supervisory board has in fact only an auditing function as indicated by its name: *commissaires aux comptes* in France and Belgium; *syndaci* in Italy.

A portion of the membership of these boards must be chosen from a national list of certified accountants;[3] the others can be chosen freely at the meeting of shareholders. The supervisory board in the Latin variant is by no means comparable to the German *Aufsichtsrat*, if only because this board does not nominate the members of the executive board and is not able to interfere with policy making. Subsequently, in the Latin variant of the two-board system the position of the meeting of shareholders is stronger than in the German variant. We find the Latin variant in Belgium, France and Italy. In France, however, the German variant has been optional since 1966.

In the Anglo-Saxon structure both the supervisory *and* the executive functions are entrusted to the board of directors, which meets more frequently than the supervisory board in the continental European system, normally once a month. However, in this one-board system a separation can be made between *inside* and *outside* directors. The inside directors are employed by the company and often form an executive committee, which has some resemblance to the executive board in the two-board system. The outside directors have a more supervisory function, representing large shareholders and other financial interests (see Frommel and Thompson 1975). But again, in many instances the inside directors may well dominate the outside directors on the board, in which case the outside directors become representatives *towards* third parties rather than *of* third parties.

104 Meindert Fennema

To summarize our survey so far, there are always two functions to be performed by the top organs of a joint-stock company:

1. the supervising function related to the representation of the (large) shareholders and other financial interests; and
2. the executive function related to the management of the firm and to the representation of the firm towards third parties.

In continental Europe these two functions are performed by two separate boards, while in the United States, the United Kingdom and Sweden these functions are performed by one board, within which a separation can be made between inside and outside directors.

Selection of the international corporate elite

From the two-board corporations, members of both boards were selected. From the one-board corporations, all members of the board of directors were selected. Members of the executive committee in the one-board corporations who were not on the board of directors were also selected, as were the highest officers in the two-board corporations who were not members of either of the two boards. This was done to determine whether or not interlocking directorates between the corporations in the sample are also carried by officers outside the board of directors.

Members of advisory boards or committees were selected as a special category. These boards have no formal authority in the company. Most of them have been set up by banks to satisfy the need for (international) consultation. Such is the case, for example, with the international advisory boards of Chase Manhattan and Chemical Bank (New York) and the European advisory boards of AMRO and Midland Bank. These latter boards were created to coordinate the activities of the European Banks International Company.

In toto, 6054 persons and 6523 positions were selected for 1970, i.e. a mean of nearly 37 positions per firm. Of the persons, only 372 had a position in two or more firms in the sample. Only six were not a member of the board of directors in a one-board corporation or of the supervisory board or the executive board in a two-board corporation. From this it can be concluded that *very few officers outside the board of directors carry interlocks between the very large firms and that the term interlocking directorate remains an appropriate term for the interlocks investigated here.*

We regarded the 372 persons who carry the international network as the international corporate elite. In the remainder of this chapter we will present some network characteristics of both the international corporate elite and the interlocks they carry (see below).

Network characteristics of the international corporate elite

In the first section, we said that the analysis presented in this book would be structural and institutional: *structural*, because the members of the elite are only considered in relation to each other, and *institutional*, because the firms are regarded as the main actors, while the members of the elite are regarded as channels of communication and control between these firms.

Does it not seem illogical, then, to start with a description of the characteristics of individual members of the elite? Indeed, the categorization of individuals according to specific variables seems neither structural nor institutional. The objection is partly warranted. To make a distinction between members of the corporate elite who are finance capitalists and those who are not, between those who carry many interlocks and those who carry few, is certainly not an institutional approach. But it is structural in so far as the variables used in this section are *network* variables: individuals are distinguished according to the positions they have in the network of interlocking directorates.

The finance capitalists

If the theory of finance capital is correct, the interlocking directorates of the sample are predominantly carried by persons who have a position in at least one bank and at least one industrial company. These persons are called after Zeitlin (1976) finance capitalists. Of the 372 persons who carry at least one interlocking directorate, 262 are finance capitalists in this sense. Only three persons exclusively carry interlocks between banks. These three (L. Medugno, F. Persegani and U. Tabanelli) carry interlocks between Banco di Roma, Credito Italiano and Banca Commerciale Italiana, three out of four Italian banks in the sample. They constitute an exceptional case, also because Persegani and Tabanelli are both members of the board of auditors (*Collegio Sindacale*) of Credito Italiano and of Banco di Roma (see the first section).[4] The remaining 107 persons in the sample have only functions in industrial corporations. This does not imply that they are not affiliated with financial institutions. They may be affiliated with financial institutions other than banks, such as insurance companies or pension funds, or they may be affiliated with banks that are not included in the sample. This is particularly serious for those who are directors of Belgian or Swedish industrials, because the sample includes no banks from these countries. As a consequence, three members of the Swedish Wallenberg family, the late Jacob, Marcus and Marcus junior, are counted as non-finance capitalists, although it is well known that the centre of their financial empire is the Enskilda Bank (Hermansson 1971: 238ff.). If we exclude all those affiliated with Belgian and Swedish industrials, the number of persons with only industrial affiliations drops to 95. Thus, roughly three quarters of the interlocking directors in the sample can be defined as finance capitalists, while only a quarter cannot. If we compare this with previous research, the number of finance capitalists in the sample is high. In the network of 86 Dutch firms in 1969 there were 248 interlocking directors. Of these, 140 were finance capitalists, 55 carried only interlocks between financial firms and 53 carried only interlocks between non-financial firms (Helmers et al. 1975: 22).

These results are in accordance with those of Soref (1980), who has done extensive research on the finance capitalists in the United States. Studying 196

106 Meindert Fennema

directors of a much larger sample of firms, Soref found that 62 of these were finance capitalists. The finance capitalists were found to be significantly more affiliated with the larger companies.[5] Another conclusion from Soref's study can also be confirmed. Soref found that finance capitalists have significantly more directorships than non-finance capitalists in the United States. Of the 95 non-finance capitalists studied here, only 7 have more than 2 directorships and only 1 has more than 3 (F.H. Ulrich). Of the 262 finance capitalists 62 have more than 2 directorships and 18 of these have more than three directorships. Thus, while less than 10 percent of the non-finance capitalists has more than two directorships, 24 percent of the finance capitalists has more than two directorships. Finally, we want to know whether the international interlocks are also predominantly carried by finance capitalists. Of the 113 international interlocks (i.e. an interlocking directorate between two firms of different nationalities), 97 are carried by finance capitalists, while 16 are carried by non-finance capitalists. The finance capitalists, being three quarters of the international corporate elite, carry 86 percent of the international interlocks (Table 4.1).[6]

But do finance capitalists carry *significantly* more international interlocks? This question can only be answered by calculating the possibility that a random distribution of all interlocks would result in a distribution in which at least 97 of the international interlocks were carried by finance capitalists. According to a hyper-geometrical distribution this possibility is less than 4 percent. Of the interlocks carried by finance capitalists, 20 percent is international, while of those not carried by finance capitalists only 13 percent is international.

The big linkers

In the former paragraph it was mentioned that the finance capitalists hold more directorships than the non-finance capitalists. In this paragraph the total distribution of positions will be discussed and compared with the results from previous research. The theoretical relevance of the distribution of positions lies in the fact that persons who hold a large number of directorships carry an even larger number of interlocks. A person holding directorships in n firms carries $n(n-1)/2$ interlocks. These n firms form a completely connected subgraph.[7] And since all interlocks are carried by one person, it is called a person clique (see Figure 4.1a).

TABLE 4.1 Distribution of international interlocks

		Interlock carried by a financial capitalist		
		Yes	*No*	*Total*
International interlock	Yes (row pct)	97 (85.8%)	16 (14.2%)	113 (16.8%)
	No (row pct)	383 (78.5%)	105 (21.5%)	488 (81.2%)
	Total	480 (79.9%)	121 (20.1%)	601 (100%)

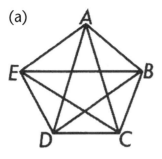 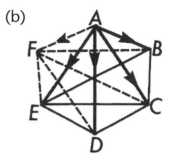

FIGURE 4.1 Different types of interlock

Now, *if* the person carrying n(n-1)/2 interlocks is an executive of, let us say, firm A, then all interlocks between other firms and firm A are called *primary*, while the interlocks among the other firms are called *secondary*. When *n* increases, the number of secondary interlocks increases more rapidly than the number of primary interlocks. The number of primary interlocks is n-1, while the number of secondary interlocks is (n-1)(n-2)/2, increasing quadratically with n. If, for example, n goes from five to six, then the number of primary interlocks increases by one, while the number of secondary interlocks increases by four (see Figure 4.1b). Since it has been argued that secondary interlocks are less likely to be control lines, we can conclude that large person-cliques increase the potential for communication more than the potential for control.

In Table 4.2 the distribution of directorships of directors over the members of the corporate elite is given, and the number of interlocks is calculated per person and in total. As can be seen from Table 4.2, half of all interlocks (300) are carried by a person who holds only two directorships. Nearly a quarter of all interlocks are carried by a person holding four or more directorships, even though these 19 persons

TABLE 4.2 Distribution of directorships among the international corporate elite

Number of persons	Number of directorships	Number of interlocks Per person [n(n-1)/2]	Total
1	7	21	21
1	6	15	15
1	5	10	10
16	4	6	96
53	3	3	159
300	2	1	300
5682	1	0	0
6054			601

108 Meindert Fennema

constitute only 5 percent of all multiple directors. We will call these 19 persons the *big linkers*. Their contribution to the network will be analysed in this section.

Is the proportion of big linkers in the international network high or low when compared to the different national networks? To answer this question, we must compare the distribution of positions over the corporate elite in different nations with the distribution of positions over the international corporate elite. Zijlstra (1979) has summarized the different national studies for this aspect, making the task of comparing their results with ours on the international level much easier (see Table 4.3). The proportion of big linkers (fourth row in Table 4.3) is much smaller in the international network than in the national networks. This is also true when the big linkers are considered not in proportion to all directors (fifth row in Table 4.3), but in proportion to the total number of multiple directors. In the latter comparison the big linkers constitute 5 percent of the multiple directors in the international network, whereas they constitute between 11 and 24 percent in the national networks.

Although the figures from Table 4.3 are not comparable in all respects, since the number of firms and the selection criteria for the directors vary in the different samples, some general conclusions can safely be drawn. First, in the international sample of 1970 the percentage of selected persons who do not carry an interlock is higher than in any of the national networks presented in the table. It is even higher than that of the Scottish selection, which is exceptionally high in relation to the truly national samples. Second, among the multiple directors, the number of

TABLE 4.3 Distribution of positions over the populations of persons in interlock networks

	Networks of financial and industrial corporations											
	USA		USA		Belgium		Scotland		Nether-lands		International network	
Posi-tions held by one person	1935		1965		1975		1973		1972		1970	
	N	%	N	%	N	%	N	%	N	%	N	%
1	2234	82	2602	82	48202	73	1178	90	690	78	5682	93
2	303	11	372	12	9706	15	79	6	102	12	300	5
3	102	123	3453	5	3453	5	31	2	44	5	53	0.9
>3	83	3	67	2	4687	7	28	2	45	5	19	0.3
	2722	100	3165	100	66048	100	1316	100	882	100	6054	100

Source: Adapted from Zijlstra 1979; USA 1935: Dooley (1969)/US National Resources Committee (1939); USA 1965: Dooley (1969); Belgium: Vessière (1978); Scotland: Scott (1978); Netherlands: Mokken and Stokman (1974)

persons who carry just one interlock is exceptionally high as well. While in all national networks the percentage of persons carrying just one interlock is between 55 and 65 percent, for the international network in 1970 this percentage is 80. Conversely, the number of big linkers is smaller in the international network than in different national networks. Consequently, the number of large person-cliques is smaller in the international network than in the national networks previously studied.

Since the big linkers preponderantly carry weak ties, we assume that they carry the system of business communication rather than the specific control and domination network. Their position in many different firms can provide them with information from many different sources and, since they are often grand old men, their prestige in the business world is such that they may well represent large parts of the business world. As Barratt Brown aptly stated, they are 'trying to supply some order and coordination in place and anarchy' (Barratt Brown 1973: 103). This is especially true for those big linkers who are not tied to one firm, i.e. who have no executive position in any of the firms in which they are directors. Such big linkers are called *network specialists*, even though they are often former presidents of large firms. Of the 19 big linkers, 12 are network specialists. Ten out of the 12, however, are outside chairmen of the board of directors, a position which is often given to the former president of the corporation.

Do the big linkers play an important role in linking firms of different nationalities together? At first sight, it does not particularly appear so. Of the 142 arcs carried by the big linkers, 36 are international arcs (25.4 percent). In the Western network as a whole, the number of interlocks is 570, of which 129 are between firms of different nationalities (22.6 percent). The 19 big linkers induce a network between 50 firms in the sample. Forty-two comprise one component with 130 interlocks. (For the definitions of the graph-theoretical concepts used here, the reader is referred to the fifth section.) Two other components are 4-cliques (US General Electric, Chrysler Chemical Bank, Procter & Gamble, British Insulated Callender's Cables, Mobil Oil, IBM, First National City Bank). In the large component, we find firms from nine different countries. Apart from Belgium and Luxembourg, all Western countries are represented. In other words, less than 5 percent of all directors in the network link 30 percent of the firms in the network in such a way that firms from all Western countries are interlocked. Conversely, if the big linkers are deleted, the remaining directors carry a network that is much more fragmented along national lines.[8] The big linkers have indeed a high potential for international communication.

Types of interlocking directorates

In the foregoing section, we distinguished several types of interlocking directors. By doing so, we were able to trace some elementary characteristics of the structure of the international corporate elite. While it remained a personalistic approach, by the end of the section, it became clear that both the personal attribute of holding

110 Meindert Fennema

directorships and its distribution have a direct influence upon the structure of the network. In this section we will focus completely on the structural and institutional aspects of the study. The lines between firms will now be distinguished according to the types of interlocks that constitute these links. The present section considers multiple interlocks and then proceeds to distinguish interlocks according to the positions of the multiple director.

Multiple interlocks

A simple method of distinguishing between different types of interlocking directorates is to look at their multiplicity. The normal interlocking directorate is carried by one person, who has a position in both corporations. There may, however, be more persons having positions in both corporations. If this is the case, we speak of a multiple interlock or of a *line with a multiplicity equal to the number of persons who have a position in both corporations.* [9] This multiplicity is an indication of the intensity of the line between two corporations. In the first section, it was assumed that two corporations are the more tightly linked, the higher the multiplicity of the line between them. Thus, by eliminating the lines with multiplicity 1, one can assume to have eliminated the less important interlocks from the network. The first to do this were Sonquist and Koenig (1975). We will use a more refined method than theirs of stepwise elimination of multiple interlocks. This procedure, which has been used by Stokman (1977), first eliminates the lines with multiplicity 1, then the lines with multiplicity 2 and so on. In this way we obtain a series of nested networks. In the international network between 176 large firms in 1970 there are 601 interlocks of which 281 are single. The multiplicity of the lines is given in Table 4.4.

Weak, strong and tight ties

As we suggested in the opening section and elaborated throughout this section, the positions held by a multiple director are of great importance to the significance of the interlock that is carried by this multiple director. From the different positions discussed in the first section, five different categories of positions have been constructed: three

TABLE 4.4 Lines in the network according to their multiplicity

Multiplicity	Number of links
1	281
2	78
3	26
4	12
5	4
6	3
	Total: 404

outside positions (member of the advisory board, outside director and chairman of the board of directors) and two inside positions (inside director and president).

Members of the supervisory board in a two-board corporation have been placed in the category 'outside director'; members of the executive board in a two-board corporation have been placed in the category 'inside director'. Non-director executives have not been assigned a separate category since only six of these carry an interlock. These six have been lumped into the category 'inside director' (see Figure 4.2).

Now the total number of interlocks is 601. Nearly half of these (273, or 45.4 percent) is carried by a person who is outside director in both firms. And if one looks at the interlocks carried by a person who has an outside *position* in both companies, the numbers rises to 408 (67.7 percent).

Furthermore, 93 interlocks (15 percent) are carried by the president of one of the companies, and if one adds those who are inside director in at least one of the interlocked companies, the number increases to 193 (32 percent). Of these 193

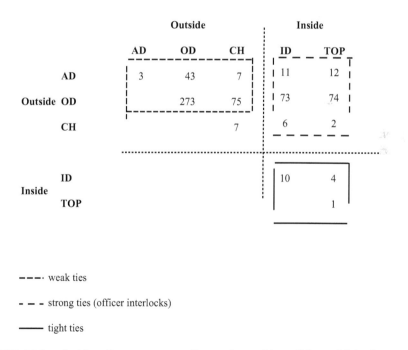

FIGURE 4.2 Interlocking directorates according to the position of the multiple directors

Note: AD: member of advisory board or committee; OD: outside director in a one-board corporation; member of supervisory board in a two-board corporation; CH: chairman of the board of directors in a one-board corporation; chairman of the supervisory board in a two-board corporation; ID: inside director in a one-board corporation; member of the executive board in a two-board corporation; TOP: president managing director in a one-board corporation; chairman of the executive board in a two-board corporation interlocks, 178 are carried by a person who is inside director or president in one company and outside director in the other. In 15 cases, however, the interlocking director has an executive position in both companies. Such an interlock is rare (2.5 percent of all interlocks) and indicates a concern relation between the interlocked corporations, although there is no a priori argument that the two corporations are hierarchically linked. Such interlocking directorates we will call *tight ties*. The remaining 178 interlocks carried by an inside director or a president do indeed indicate a dominance relation between the interlocked firms. If we assume the inside director or president to represent his own firm A in the board of the firm B in which he has an outside position, the hierarchy line runs from A to B and the interlock between A and B can be given a direction. I will call such directed interlocks *strong ties*. Finally, the 1408 interlocks carried by persons who have an outside position in both firms do not indicate a hierarchical line between the two interlocked companies, nor do they necessarily indicate a close relationship between the interlocked firms. I will call them *weak ties*. Two types of weak ties will be distinguished. The first is the secondary interlock, which is created when a person is an inside director in firm A and an outside director in firm B and firm C. Between B and C there exists a secondary interlock (see also Figure 4.1b). But not all weak ties are secondary interlocks. If a person has no inside position in any firm but is an outside director in more than one firm, he carries one or more weak ties that are not secondary interlocks.

It is possible to calculate the number of weak ties in the international network. As can be seen from Figure 4.2, this number is 1408, while the number of strong ties is 178. The proportion of weak ties in the network is roughly two thirds, while the proportion of strong ties is roughly one third. From Table 4.2 it is possible to calculate the maximum number of secondary interlocks in the network. To carry a secondary interlock a person must have in at least three firms a directorship. Fifty-three persons have directorships in three firms. These 53 persons carry a maximum of 53 secondary interlocks. The remaining 19 persons may carry more secondary interlocks. Sixteen of them have directorships in four firms and thus carry a maximum of 48 secondary interlocks. One person has directorships in five firms, carrying a maximum of six secondary interlocks. Another has directorships in six firms, carrying a maximum of ten secondary interlocks; and yet another has directorships in seven firms, carrying a maximum of 15 secondary interlocks. The maximum number of secondary interlocks in the international network is 132. This means that at least 276 weak ties must be carried by persons who have no executive (inside) position in any of the firms in our sample. Such a person may either have an executive position in a firm outside the sample or no executive position at all. If the person has no executive position in a corporation, it is likely that he has been invited to sit on the boards of several corporations for specific expertise or contacts he has outside the business system. The weak ties he carries are then typically the unintended result of these independent corporation decisions. This may even be the case if the person is the president of a smaller firm and is invited for similar reasons to be on the board of several large ones. Although these weak ties generally do not indicate control or domination relations, they form an integral part of the business system and should not be neglected in the analysis.

If the network of strong ties is a network of control and domination, it can be assumed that the direction of control or domination is from the firm in which an executive position is held to the firm in which the outside position is held. If the network is regarded as an information network, then the information may go from the firm in which the outside position is held to the firm in which an executive position is held.[10] Warner and Unwalla (1967) called the strong ties *officer interlocks*. Among the 1131 United States firms they investigated, 1552 officer interlocks were found, 27.2 percent of the total number of interlocking directorates between these firms. This proportion is remarkably close to the proportion of strong ties in the international network (29 percent). The different types of interlocks (weak, strong and tight ties) define different partial networks. The network containing only weak ties can be interpreted as a communication network, cementing the (international) business system. The network containing only strong ties (officer interlocks) can be conceived as a dominance network, which, at the higher levels of multiplicity, may indicate financial groups. Finally, the network containing only tight ties may indicate the existence of economic concerns formed by two or more firms.

Summary

Although the book from which this article, where it appeared as Chapter 4, is drawn does not discuss the internal organization of corporations, it is necessary to compare the division of authority among the top committees of the corporations in different countries. In all corporations there exists a duality in the supervising function, associated with external control, and the executive function, associated with internal control. In the two-board corporations this duality has been 'solved' by the creation of a supervisory board and an executive board. This two-board system is dominant in continental Europe. Within the two-board system, there are 'German' and 'Latin' variants. The one-board system is found in Anglo-Saxon countries. The duality of supervisory and executive functions is here reflected in the distinction between outside and inside directors.

The first important finding of this empirical study is that *executives who are not members of executive boards or boards of directors carry hardly any interlocks between the 176 firms of the sample.*

Of the 601 interlocks between these firms, 68 percent is carried by a person who has an outside function in both interlocked firms (*weak ties*), 29 percent is carried by a person who is an executive in one firm and outside director in the other (*strong ties* or *officer interlocks*), while less than 3 percent is carried by an inside director in both companies (*tight ties*). In the fourth section, we suggested a possible interpretation of these three types of interlocks, according to which the networks of weak, strong and tight ties can be fruitfully analysed. Another difference between interlocks is based on the *network* characteristics of the carrier of the interlock. Thus, a distinction was made between persons affiliated with at least one

114 Meindert Fennema

bank and persons affiliated only with industrial firms. The former we called *finance capitalists*. Interlocks carried by a finance capitalist have a different meaning from those carried by a non-finance capitalist. As expected from the theory of finance capital, the proportion of finance capitalists in the network is higher than that in the national networks in the Netherlands and the United States, where previous research has been done. Accordingly, it was found that the finance capitalists carry significantly more international interlocks.

A second relevant network characteristic is the amount of interlocks carried by one person. Those who carry six or more interlocks in the network are the big linkers. The number of big linkers in the network, 19, is much lower than the number of big linkers found in previous research on national networks. This can be explained by the fact that a restricted number of firms is included for each country in the sample. But even though the number of big linkers in our sample is relatively low compared to the number of big linkers in previous studies of interlocking directorates in the Netherlands and the United States, their role in the international network seems important. They link the different national (sub-)networks together in an international network of communication.

Finally, a distinction was made according to the multiplicity of the lines in the network, defined as the number of interlocks between two firms. The higher the multiplicity of a line, the more intense the relation between the firms connected by that line.

Postscript

In a follow-up study, Heemskerk et al. (2016) presented a longitudinal comparison of the international corporate network, starting from the 1976 network. My 1981 book had already demonstrated that the big linkers had become more prominent between 1970 and 1976.

As Table 4.5 illustrates, the number of big linkers had declined from 23 in 1976 to 18 in 1996. Following the corporate governance reforms of the late 1990s, this number dropped further to only five in 2006. These five elite members nonetheless carried 20 percent of the network in 2006 and 12 percent in 2013. While big linkers were becoming an anomaly, single linkers – corporate elite members with only two positions among firms in the sample – increasingly carried the entire network. In 2006, they already accounted for about half of all ties and they contributed the majority of the network ties by 2013 (57 percent).

This development may have far-reaching consequences. The network no longer depends on a small core of big linkers but is based on a growing number of single linkers. This is equally true for the subset of transnational ties. In 1976, the big linkers together supplied 48 percent of all transnational interlocks. By 2013, this had dropped to 13 percent. The single linkers, on the other hand, increased their share of transnational interlocking activities from 33 to 44 percent. Consequently, the ensuing corporate network is less hierarchical and centralized than it used to be; it is less dominated by a small number of big linkers and thus more diffuse.

TABLE 4.5 Distribution of interlocks over directors

	1976	1996	2006	2013	Δ % 76-96	Δ % 96-06	Δ% 06-13
Directors with:							
Four or more positions (big linkers)	23	18	5	5	-21.74	-72.22	0.00
number of interlocks	175	124	64	30	-29.14	-48.39	-53.13
share of all interlocks	31%	26%	20%	12%	-16.08	-24.34	-41.04
Three Positions	45	48	35	28	6.67	-27.08	-20.00
number of interlocks	135	144	105	82	6.67	-27.08	-21.90
share of all interlocks	24%	30.5%	33%	32%	26.33	6.88	-1.77
Two Positions (single linkers)							
number of interlocks	249	204	153	146	-18.07	-25.00	-4.58
share of all interlocks	45%	43.2%	48%	57%	-2.97	9.94	20.03

Source: Heemskerk et al. (2016)

The fragmentation of national corporate elites stands in contrast with the remarkable robustness of the transnational network even without an increase in the number of transnational interlocks. While the national networks have thinned out, the processes of transnationalization have continued. The increase in global trade, foreign direct investments and capital flows produced transnational interlocks, particularly in Europe. Beyond the national, the network has become increasingly transnational in its orientation. More corporate elite members are engaging in cross-border board interlocks.

Strikingly, in 2013 nine tenths of the transnational interlocks occurred among firms based in Europe or the USA, thus lending further credence to van der Pijl's (1984) thesis that the global corporate elite is centred in the North Atlantic region (Burris and Staples 2012; Carroll et al. 2010).

Our results show that, as a group, the corporate elite has become less densely connected but more international in character. Thus, even though the absolute number of transnational board interlocks has somewhat dropped, we may conclude that the transnational network has become more important in relative terms.

Notes

1 Editors' note: as this is chapter 4 of Fennema's book, *International networks of banks and industry* (The Hague: Martinus Nijhoff), we have removed cross-references to other chapters.
2 For a defence of this position, see Gordon (1966 [1945]) and more recently Mace (1971).
3 The *commissaires aux comptes* and the *syndaci* are not comparable to the accountants in the Netherlands and Germany and the auditors in the Anglo-Saxon countries. The latter cannot be regarded as part of the company; they represent the public interest rather than the shareholders.
4 Medugno is a director of Banca Commerciale Italiana and of Banco di Roma.
5 It is not true, as Soref maintains, that his study is the first systematic study on finance capitalists. The Dutch study of Helmers et al. in 1970 was the first (1975).
6 Two international interlocks are carried by two non-finance capitalists affiliated with a Belgian and a Swedish firm. If we regard them as finance capitalists, the percentage increases to 84.
7 A completely connected subgraph is defined as a collection of firms, in which each firm is adjacent to all other firms in the collection.
8 The network without big linkers has been compared with the network as a whole. At multiplicity level >1 very little seems to have changed. Rather than the large component *Morgan 127*, we now find a large component *Chemical Bank 119*. At multiplicity level >2, however, an important change has taken place: the core component *Dresdner Bank 58* has split into two components, *Dresdner 15* (only German firms) and *Morgan 33* (American, Canadian, Dutch and British firms). And, at multiplicity level >3, *Morgan 33* has split into four strictly national components. Elimination of the big linkers does indeed cause a fragmentation of the network along national lines.
9 A line is defined as a direct relation between two firms regardless of how many interlocks exist between them. The multiplicity of a line is equal to the number of interlocks between two firms.
10 A control or dominance network is necessarily a network of information as well. But the reverse is not true.

References

Barratt Brown, M. (1973). The controllers of British industry. In J. Urry and J. Wakeford (Eds), *Power in Britain* (pp. 73–116). London: Heinemann.

BerleA.A. (1954). *The 20th century capitalist revolution.* New York: Harcourt Brace.

de Boer, H. (1957). *De commissarisfunctie.* Amsterdam: De Bussy.

Burris, V. and Staples, C.L. (2012). In search of a transnational capitalist class: Alternative methods for comparing director interlocks within and between nations and regions. *International Journal of Comparative Sociology* 53(4): 323–342.

Carroll, W.K., Fennema, M. and Heemskerk, E.M. (2010). Constituting corporate Europe. A study of elite social organization. *Antipode* 42(4): 811–843.

Dooley, P.C. (1969). The interlocking directorate. *American Economic Review* 59: 314–323.

Frommel, S.N. and Thompson, J.H. (1975). *Company law in Europe.* Deventer: Kluwer.

Gordon, R.A. (1966 [1945]). *Business leadership in the large corporation.* Berkeley, CA: University of California Press.

Heemskerk, E., Fennema, M. and Carroll, W.K. (2016). The global corporate elite after the financial crisis: Evidence from the transnational network of interlocking directorates. *Global Networks* 16(1): 68–88.

Helmers, H.M., Mokken, R.J., Plijter, R.J. and Stokman, F.N. (1975). *Graven naar Macht. Op zoek naar de kern van de Nederlandse economie.* Amsterdam: Van Gennep.

Hermansson, C.-H. (1971). *Monopol och Storfinanz de 15 familjerna.* Stockholm: Rabén & Sjögren.

Interstate Commerce Commission (1908). *Intercorporate relationships of railways in the United States.* Washington, DC: United States Government Printing Office.

Keynes, J.M. (1972 [1926]). The end of laisser-faire. In *Collected Writings, Vol. IX* (pp. 272–294). London: Macmillan.

Mace, J.L. (1971). *Directors. Myth and reality.* Boston, MA: Harvard Graduate School of Business Administration.

Marx, K. (1976). *Capital, Volume III.* London: Lawrence & Wishart.

Mokken, R.J. and Stokman, F.N. (1974). Interlocking directorates between banks and institutions in the Netherlands in 1969. Paper presented at the Joint Sessions of the European Consortium for Political Research, Strasbourg.

Perlo, V. (1957). *The empire of high finance.* New York: International Publishers.

van der Pijl, K. (1984). *The making of an Atlantic ruling class.* London: NLB.

Scott, J. (1978). The intercorporate configuration. Substructure and superstructure. Paper presented at the Joint Sessions of the European Consortium for Political Research, Grenoble.

Scott, J. (1979). *Corporations, classes and capitalism.* London: Hutchinson.

Sonquist, J.A. and Koenig, T. (1975). Interlocking directorates in the top U.S. corporations. A graph theory approach. *Insurgent Sociologist* 5(3): 196–229.

Soref, M. (1980). The finance capitalists. In M. Zeitlin (Ed.), *Classes, class conflict, and the state* (pp. 62–82). Boston, MA: Little, Brown.

Stokman, F.N. (1977). *Roll calls and sponsorship. A methodological analysis of Third World group formation in the United Nations.* Leiden: A.W. Sijthoff.

US National Resources Committee (1939). *The structure of the American economy.* Washington, DC: US Government Printing Office.

Valkhoff, J. (1941). De eigendom in de moderne maatschappij. *Handelingen van de Nederlandsche Sociologische Vereeniging* 9(March): 21–41.

Vessière, M. (1978). La structure des cumuls dans le champ politique et dans le champ économique en Belgique. Paper prepared for the Joint Sessions of the European Consortium for Political Research, Grenoble, April.

118 Meindert Fennema

Warner, W.L. and Unwalla, D.B. (1967). The system of interlocking directorates. In W.L. Warner, D.B. Unwalla and J.H. Trimm (Eds), *The emergent American society, Vol I. Large scale organizations* (pp. 121–257). New Haven, CT: Yale University Press.

Zeitlin, M. (1976). On class theory of the large corporation. Response to Allen. *American Journal of Sociology* 81: 894–903.

Zijlstra, G.J. (1979). The organization of organizations. Interlocking directorates and their analysis. Paper prepared for Joint Sessions of European Consortium of Political Research, Brussels, April.

5

TRANSNATIONAL CLASS AGENCY AND EUROPEAN GOVERNANCE

The case of the European Round Table of Industrialists (2000)

Bastiaan van Apeldoorn

This article analyses the political and ideological agency of an emergent European transnational capitalist class in the socioeconomic governance of the European Union (EU) by examining the case of the European Round Table of Industrialists (ERT). It seeks to show that the ERT – as an elite forum mediating the interests and power of the most transnationalized segments of European capital – has played a significant role in shaping European governance in as much as it has successfully articulated and promoted ideas and concepts that have at critical times set the political agenda and, beyond, have helped to shape the discourse within which European policy making is embedded. Here, the increasingly neoliberal orientation of the ERT reflects, and at the same time is a constitutive element within, the construction of a new European order in which governance is geared to serve the interests of a globalizing transnational capitalist elite, and hence the exigencies of global 'competitiveness'. Although in recent years some detailed work has been done on the role of the ERT in the internal market programme, there has as yet been little attention paid to (and thus interpretation of) the *content* of the ideas promoted by the ERT and hence to the ideological power that this forum of transnational capitalists exercises.[1]

The article is divided into four main parts. The first briefly elaborates the theoretical framework that informs my analysis. Drawing upon what has come to be labelled the 'neo-Gramscian school' in International Relations, I will advance a historical materialist understanding of the dynamics of European integration, emphasizing in particular the role of *transnational* social forces – as engendered by the capitalist production process – in the political and ideological struggles over European order.[2] The second part introduces the case of the European Round Table. I will claim that the ERT is neither a simple business lobby nor a corporatist interest association, but must rather be interpreted as having developed into an elite platform for an emergent European transnational capitalist class from which it can

120 Bastiaan van Apeldoorn

formulate a common strategy and – on the basis of that strategy – seek to shape European socioeconomic governance through its privileged access to the European institutions. It is this latter role of the ERT that will be the focus of the final two parts. As such, the third presents an analysis of the evolution of the ERT's strategic project and the initiating role the Round Table played in the relaunching of the integration process from Europe 1992 to Maastricht. Following this, the fourth part will analyse the ideological orientation and strategic outlook of today's Round Table and its current role in shaping what I will call the neoliberal discourse of *competitiveness* which, I argue, increasingly underpins European governance.

Transnationalization, capitalist class strategy and European governance

In its focus on the strategic role of a transnational capitalist class in shaping European socioeconomic governance the following analysis goes beyond the established approaches to the study of European integration – in particular, the still dominant rival perspectives of intergovernmentalism versus supranationalism – in several respects.[3] First, conventional integration theories tend to focus largely on the institutional *form* of the integration process, thus ignoring the question of its socioeconomic *content*, or the 'social purpose' underlying European order.[4] Whereas intergovernmentalists and supranationalists quarrel over the relative power of, respectively, national and supranational public authorities in the decision-making process, a focus on the social purpose of European integration calls for an understanding of the *social* power underpinning public power and thus for an analysis of the underlying social forces.

Second, established integration theories tend to suffer from a narrow rationalism that disables them from acknowledging the power of ideas and ideological practices in the construction of European order and in defining its social purpose.[5] There, however, our analysis cannot stop as we have to examine how, by whom and for what purpose that discourse has been constructed. From a Gramscian perspective it is emphasized that ideas must be located in social practice and thus cannot be separated from the (social) structures in which actors are located and which shape their agency. Ideas are produced by human agency in the context of social power relations and are, as such, bound up with the strategic action of social actors.

Third, whereas in intergovernmentalist accounts the transnational level is ignored altogether, supranationalist approaches do explicitly acknowledge the role of trans-national actors but tend to see that role as subservient to the alleged functional logic of the integration process and/or the supranational leadership of the European Commission (EC), thus denying the autonomy of these actors.[6] The point of departure for the present analysis is that the social forces underpinning European order are not necessarily internal to the EU or its member states but must rather be located within a global political economy in which capitalist production and finance are undergoing a sustained transnationalization and globalization, reflected inter alia in the increasing dominance of the transnational corporation (TNC) as an actor in the world economy and the concomitant growing structural power of transnational capital.[7] This transnationalization of global capitalism can be argued to engender a transnationalization of social forces, in particular, those forces bound up with transnationalizing and globalizing capital. In what, following the pioneering work of Kees van der Pijl and others, can be conceptualized as a process of transnational class formation, we witness the rise of transnational capitalist elites as key actors in global politics.[8]

In its focus on class agency, this article also aims to contribute to a research agenda that reclaims the centrality of class agency in the study of political economy. The class-theoretical premise underlying this agenda is that the class domination by which capitalist societies are characterized cannot be understood from a structuralist perspective that merely focuses on the structural domination of capital over labour, but rather that the reproduction of this power of capital – and of the capitalist class – has to be explained also in terms of collective human agency within concrete social power struggles taking place on the structural terrain of the accumulation process. As Leslie Sklair puts it, '[capitalist] class hegemony does not simply happen as if by magic. The capitalist class expends much time, energy and resources to make it happen and to ensure that it keeps on happening.'[9]

The transnational capitalist class engendered by the globalization of capitalist accumulation is not conceived here as a unitary actor. In fact, significant differences in ideological and strategic orientations may exist within the ranks of this class – differences related to structural (but not fixed) divisions within capital.[10] The important point for the purpose of this article which focuses on the role of transnational class strategy in European governance, is that through the *political* organization of capitalist class elites these differences can be (temporarily) transcended and a unity of purpose and direction achieved, a unity that may then be elevated to a higher plane, that is, constituting an appeal across different groups and classes (and class fractions), thus entering into the struggle for – to use a Gramscian term – hegemony.[11] In this process of capitalist class formation, transnational elite groups and their (informal) organizations are seen as playing a key role.[12] This article interprets the ERT as one such organization with respect to the process of transnational class formation in Europe.

The political agency of the ERT must be located, however, within a wider configuration of social forces dominated and cemented by a globalizing transnational elite consisting primarily of the top managers and owners of transnational capital, but also of politicians and civil servants occupying key positions in transnationalizing state structures. In the emergent transnational state-society complex of the EU we may thus start to discern the contours of a transnational power bloc at the apex of which we find a transnational capitalist class elite allying with the more outward-looking elements of 'EU government', the European Commission in particular. As the case of the ERT will show, parallel to the relaunching of the integration process – and marking a sharp contrast with the relatively antagonistic relations of the 1970s – the mid-1980s and 1990s witnessed the development of what has been described as a 'partnership' between big business and the Commission. The other side of the coin of this partnership was and is the extreme weakness of organized labour within the

122 Bastiaan van Apeldoorn

Euro-polity, where it can make for much less of a counterveiling force than at the national level where capital is to some degree 'locked into' (neo)corporatist structures.[13]

The strategic alliance between the corporate executives of Europe's leading TNCs and the political executives of the Commission that emerges from our analysis of the ERT can be seen as indicative of the growing power of transnational capital and is further facilitated both by the position of the Commission within the overall structure of EU governance as well as the nature of the EU polity in general. With regard to the first point, although the Commission has the right of initiative (and can thus to an important degree shape the EU agenda), the fact that its policy making is dependent upon the decision-making power of the Council of Ministers, and hence upon the veto power of individual member states, means that it is often crucial for the Commission to enlist the support of powerful social groups. With regard to the second point, the undemocratic nature of the EU polity in general – including its underdeveloped system of political parties and lack of other institutions, such as strong organized interest groups, that can generate not just legitimacy but indeed also the demand for legitimacy and (democratic) accountability – makes it easier for the Commission to rely rather exclusively on 'business advice' without needing to legitimate this. Indeed, one could argue that the democratic deficit of the EU, on the one hand, and the increasing dominance of social forces bound up with transnational capital and its largely neoliberal project, on the other, are two sides of the same coin in as much as the former can be seen as reflecting a wider phenomenon that Stephen Gill calls the 'new constitutionalism'. This he defines as 'the politico-legal dimension of the wider discourse of disciplinary neoliberalism' seeking 'to separate economic policies from broad political accountability in order to make governments more responsive to the discipline of market forces and correspondingly less responsive to popular-democratic forces and processes'.[14] It is within this context that we must place our analysis of the ERT and its role in European governance.

The ERT: an elite platform for Europe's transnational capitalist class

> I would consider the Round Table to be more than a lobby group as it helps to shape policies. The Round Table's relationship with Brussels is one of strong co-operation. It is a dialogue which often begins at a very early stage in the development of policies and directives.
>
> *(Wisse Dekker, former Chairman of the ERT)*[15]

The ERT is not a lobby, but rather a group of European citizens who express their opinions on the best ways to make Europe and European companies competitive on a world-wide basis to politicians, governments, the Commission, and other institutions.

> *(Jérôme Monod, former Chairman of the ERT)*[16]

The ERT is partially a lobby, but not for the interests of individual sectors, but for the competitiveness of Europe. As this is a fundamental concern, which the European public authorities share with us, we are also a privileged partner in the dialogue about these concerns.

(Helmut Maucher, current Chairman of the ERT)[17]

When integration was at a low point in the early 1980s and growing global (mainly Japanese and US) competition threatened the position of large sections of European industry, leading members of Europe's business community began to perceive the need for a European-level political initiative that was lacking from Europe's politicians. As Europe's official employers' organization, UNICE, was deemed to be ineffective, it was at the initiative of Pehr Gyllenhammar, the cosmopolitan chief executive officer (CEO) of Volvo, and with the support of Etienne Davignon, the European Commissioner who had been instrumental in creating the new *rapprochement* between big business and the Commission in the preceding years, that 17 industrialists of major European companies came together in 1983 to found the Round Table of European Industrialists (later ERT).[18] The self-proclaimed aim of the new organization was 'to revitalise European industry and make it competitive again, and to speed up the process of unification of the European market',[19] two goals that became part of a single strategy in which 'Europeanization' was seen as the answer to European industry's lack of global competitiveness.

Today, the ERT consists of 45 CEOs and chairmen of Europe's most transnational and biggest industrial corporations, with almost all EU countries as well as most industrial sectors 'represented' (see Table 5.1 for current membership).[20] The membership of the ERT is personal (rather than corporate), but is at the same time dependent on the member's continued position as the CEO or chairman of his company. As a senior official[21] of the ERT explained:

we insist that it is the chief decision maker who is the member, for the simple reason that eventually these great men, when they have decided something around the table, have to go home and *put their mouth and their money to the policies.* [22]

Looking, then, at the capital behind the private 'European citizens' (remember Monod's observation above), we find that 36 companies of the current 45 members appear on the *Financial Times'* Europe 500 (which ranks Europe's companies by market capitalization and therefore excludes companies that are not publicly quoted) and 20 are amongst the top 100.[23] On a global level, *Fortune's* Global 500, which ranks companies by total sales, lists 27 companies of ERT members.[24] We are thus dealing here with a group of Europe's largest non-financial enterprises. As such, the ERT membership makes up a substantial part of Europe's corporate elite, the internal coherence of which is established and maintained through a process of networking, inter alia through organizations like the ERT.[25]

TABLE 5.1 Members of the ERT and their companies, May 1999

Name	Company	Country	Sector
Americo Amorim	Amorim Group	Portugal	cork products
Percy Barnevik	Investor AB	Sweden	holding company
Jean-Louis Beffa	Saint-Gobain	France	building materials
Peter Bonfield	British Telecom	UK	telecoms
Cor Boonstra	Philips	Netherlands	electronics
Antony Burgmans	Unilever	Netherlands/UK	agro-alimentary
Bertrand Collomb	Lafarge	France	building materials
François Cornélis	Petrona	Belgium	oil
Alfonso Cortina	Repsol	Spain	oil
Gerhard Cromme (Vice-Chair)	ThyssenKrupp	Germany	mechanical engineering
Dimitris Daskalopoulos	Delta Dairy	Greece	agro-alimentary
Etienne Davignon	Société Générale de Belgique	Belgium	holding company
Carlo De Benedetti	Cofide-Cir Group	Italy	holding company
Thierry Desmarest	Total	France	oil
Jean-René Fourtou	Rhône-Poulenc	France	chemicals
Paulo Fresco	FIAT	Italy	motor vehicles
José Antonio Garrido	Iberdrola	Spain	utilities
Fritz Gerber	Hoffmann-La Roche	Switzerland	chemicals
Ulrich Hartmann	Veba	Germany	utilities
Daniel Janssen	Solvay	Belgium	chemicals
Alain Joly	Air Liquide	France	chemicals
Jak Kahmi	Profilo Group	Turkey	electronics
David Lees	GKN	UK	engineering
André Leysen (Vice-Chair)	Gevaert	Belgium	holding
Flemming Lindeløv	Carlsberg	Denmark	agro-alimentary
Helmut Maucher (Chair)	Nestlé	Switzerland (Germany)	agro-alimentary
Charles Miller Smith	ICI	UK	chemicals
Jérôme Monod	Suez Lyonnaise des Eaux	France	utilities
Mark Moody-Stuart	Shell	Netherlands/UK (UK)	oil
Egil Myklebust	Norsk Hydro	Norway	oil
Jorma éllila	Nokia	Finland	electronics

Name	Company	Country	Sector
Lars Ramqvist	Ericsson	Sweden	electronics
Frank Riboud	Danone	France	agro-alimentary
Nigel Rudd	Pilkington	UK	building materials
Richard Schenz	OMV	Austria	oil and gas
Manfred Schneider	Bayer	Germany	chemicals
Jürgen Schrempp	Daimler-Chrysler	Germany	motor vehicles
Louis Schweitzer	Renault	France	motor vehicles
George Simpson	Gen. Electric Company	UK	electronics
Michael Smurfit	Jefferson Smurfit	Ireland	forestry and paper
Peter Sutherland	BP Amoco	UK (Ireland)	oil
Morris Tabaksblat	Reed Elsevier	UK/Netherlands (Netherlands)	publishing
Marco Tronchetti	Provera Pirelli	Italy	rubber products
Cees van Lede	Akzo-Nobel	Netherlands	chemicals
Heinrich von Pierer	Siemens	Germany	electronics
Mark Wössner	Bertelsmann	Germany	media

Source: names of members and companies: ERT website (www.ert.be); country and sector: own research

Note: if the nationality of the member differs from that of his company, the former is given in parentheses

Although but one of many European business groups, the ERT occupies a unique place within the EU's evolving landscape of 'transnational pluralism'.[26] The agency of the ERT falls neither under the logic of pluralist lobbying nor that of corporatist interest intermediation,[27] but should instead be interpreted as the elite organization of an emergent European transnational capitalist class, articulating and defending the long-term interests of this class.[28] As such, the ERT must also be distinguished from the kind of 'functional' interest groups that early integration theorists expected to be instrumental to the functional logic of the integration process, and in which category we would, for instance, find UNICE. Whereas UNICE is the official European federation of national employers' associations and as such has a public and formal ('corporatist') role to play vis-à-vis the Commission and as a 'social partner' in the dialogue with the European Trade Union Federation (ETUC), ERT is not an interest association at all. In contrast to corporatist organizations, the ERT has no members either to represent or to discipline. Rather, the ERT *is* its members. As Vice-Chairman of the ERT, Gerhard Cromme, who formerly also had a leading position within UNICE, puts it:

> The European Round Table is a forum in which European business leaders meet ... we are not an association, we are not an interest group ... and we also do not engage in lobbying in that sense but leave that to the relevant institutions ... UNICE is an association of interest representation whereas ERT is not ... [but is] a private gathering of people who discuss themes and then try to arrive at a common opinion.[29]

As many ERT members and associates emphasize, these organizational characteristics of the ERT – a private and relatively small club of the heads of Europe's largest corporations – give the ERT a number of advantages over formal associations.[30] First, compared to big cross-sectoral associations representing several 'constituencies', the Round Table has less diverging interests to balance and can act with relative speed and flexibility. Moreover, unlike UNICE which, as the official voice of business, has to respond to the details of all proposed EU regulation, the ERT is free to 'set the political highlights' according to its preferences.[31]

Second, the fact that the members themselves *are* the Round Table *and* that these members control Europe's biggest companies gives the ERT a power that at least in its immediacy cannot be matched by any interest group where power is mediated through a bureaucracy of representation. In consequence, according to another prominent ERT member, who also had a leadership position within UNICE, the Round Table 'tends to be taken more seriously', precisely 'because it is the big industrial leaders [themselves] who go and talk with the Commissioners'.[32] The ERT's privileged political access is also underlined by Peter Sutherland, now ERT member, but also a prominent former Commissioner (for competition) under the first Delors Presidency, who said in an interview:

> I think that the importance of the ERT is not merely in the fact that it coordinates and creates a cohesive approach amongst major industries in Europe but because the persons who are members of it have to be at the highest level of companies and virtually all of them have unimpeded access to government leaders because of the position of their companies ... That is exactly what makes it different [from other organizations] – the fact that it is at head of company level, and only the biggest companies in each country of the European Union are members of it. So, by definition, each member of the ERT has access at the highest level to government.[33]

Third, the ERT's elite character allows it to play a more strategic and proactive role, one that transcends lobbying or interest representation in a more restricted sense. The ERT does more than defend relatively clear-cut (narrow) corporate interests: it rather seeks to define the *general class* interests of transnational (industrial) capital, that is, to formulate a relatively long-term and forward-looking strategy oriented towards the shaping of European socioeconomic governance.[34] As former ERT vice chairman, David Simon, explained, precisely because it brings together around

Transnational class agency, European governance **127**

45 bosses who run businesses, they [the ERT members] will tend to take a more strategic view than an association ... because, after all, that's what they're responsible for, they're responsible for direction and strategy. [The ERT thus] tries to concentrate on strategy and direction for the economy at large.[35]

The political agency of the ERT

Although occasionally also engaging in more conventional lobbying activities, ERT's agency normally transcends that level in as much as it seeks to set the political agenda and, beyond that, to shape the discourse in which European decision making is embedded.[36] Such an exercise of *ideological* power is what distinguishes the ERT most clearly from more traditional business lobbies. The ERT communicates its ideas in different ways. It regularly publishes reports on either specific themes or of a more comprehensive nature, and frequently sends letters and communiqués to individual politicians or to collective bodies such as the European Council. But, as Keith Richardson, ERT's former Secretary General, points out, 'the most influential mode of all is perhaps still face-to-face communication' between the CEOs of the ERT and Europe's leading politicians and policy makers.[37] At the intergovernmental level, the ERT operates mainly through its individual members. In this respect it is significant that the ERT consciously recruits from all member states. Furthermore, in conjunction with its six-monthly plenary session, the ERT also always meets (usually around a dinner) with several prominent members (normally including the prime minister) of the government then taking over the Council presidency on the eve of the Council summit. At the supranational level, this transnational elite interaction is probably even stronger. A Round Table delegation generally meets the Commission president about twice a year rather formally.[38] In addition, ERT members often have more ad hoc meetings with various Commissioners. This direct personal access to the Commission is probably facilitated by the fact that the Round Table has always had one or two former Commissioners amongst its membership, most notably Etienne Davignon from 1986 onwards and, more recently, Peter Sutherland, who joined as chairman of BP (while also serving as the chair of the European arm of Wall Street's quintessential investment bank, Goldman Sachs).[39] At the national level, former ERT Vice Chairman, David Simon, recently made the reverse step, that is, from business (and membership of the ERT) to government, by becoming a minister for trade and competitiveness in Europe in the new UK Labour government, making him, in the words of one senior ERT associate, 'a very useful contact'.[40]

In sum, what we see developing around the ERT is a transnational elite network that ties together the elite of European business with key policy makers and politicians at both the national and supranational levels of the European polity. In the remainder of this article I will examine how the ERT has used this position to shape European socioeconomic governance.

The ERT's evolving strategic project and the relaunching of Europe

The relaunching of European integration with the internal market programme has been interpreted by intergovernmentalists as the result of a convergence of national

128 Bastiaan van Apeldoorn

policy preferences enabling successful intergovernmental bargaining and by supranationalists as driven by the policy entrepreneurship of the Commission, operating in alliance with transnational business (but the latter playing a merely supportive role) and responding to Europe's perceived economic decline after the end of the 'golden age'.[41] I maintain that, if we want to understand the socioeconomic *content* of the relaunched integration process, we have to understand it as the outcome of political struggle, not so much between states but between social forces (who may be 'represented' by a variety of actors) developing strategies and engaging in a struggle over European order at all levels of Europe's polity.[42] As indicated, the most dominant of these social forces increasingly operate within a transnational setting, in particular, an emergent transnational capitalist class.

Taking the relaunching of Europe from the mid-1980s onwards as the historical context I claim that one can identify three rival projects within the subsequent transnational struggle over Europe's social purpose.[43] In the *neoliberal project* – which first found ideological expression in the early 1980s in the 'Eurosclerosis' discourse – the relaunching of the integration process was conceived as an opportunity to further open up the European region to the globalizing world economy and, moreover, to accelerate the deregulation and privatization of the European economies, thus liberating the 'beneficial' forces of the market from the fetters of government intervention and other 'rigidifying' institutions impeding the necessary adjustments to a changing global environment. The benefits of the internal market project were thus seen as principally deriving from the freer market it would create, emphasizing its deregulatory effects and expected efficiency gains.

Advocates of the *neomercantilist project* in contrast blamed Europe's loss of international competitiveness less on labour market rigidity, trade union power or the welfare state, and more on the fragmentation of the European market, insufficient economies of scale and the perceived technology gap vis-à-vis the USA and Japan, all in a context of intensifying global competition. This project thus constituted a more defensive regionalization strategy in which the internal market was conceived as the creation of a European 'home market' in which (would-be) 'European champions' would be able – thanks to the larger economies of scale – successfully to confront the growing non-European competition.

Such a regeneration of European industry was to be further promoted by an active pan-European industrial policy, in particular in the area of new technologies, of which a protectionist European trade policy was often advocated as a (temporarily) necessary complement.[44]

The *social democratic project*, finally, sought to re-embed the new European market in a supranational framework of social regulation and thus protect and consolidate the so-called 'European social model'. This project developed within the context of the initial success of the internal market programme as social democrats came to see European federalism as the answer to the dilemmas of the European left in an era of globalization and was advocated most prominently by Jacques Delors, who as President of the Commission sought to move the integration process beyond market integration and towards state building, hence promoting his vision of an 'organized capitalism'.[45]

Neoliberalism and neomercantilism can be interpreted as contending strategies on the part of rival groups or 'fractions' within the ranks of Europe's emergent transnational capitalist class. Throughout the 1980s and into the 1990s the main dividing line within this transnational elite was between, on the one hand, a 'globalist' fraction consisting of Europe's most globalized firms (including global financial institutions) and, on the other hand, a 'Europeanist' fraction made up of large industrial enterprises primarily serving the European market and competing against the often cheaper imports from outside Europe.[46] The perspective of the former has tended towards neoliberalism, whereas the latter came to promote neomercantilism. Although they aspired to become more global, in the 1980s many of Europe's large industrial firms were still more *regional* TNCs. The ERT in this period was also dominated by this 'Europeanist' fraction and its strategic orientation thus tended towards a defensive regionalism, the heart of which was the promotion of a big (and if necessary protected) European home market.[47]

From Europe '92 to Maastricht

ERT's campaign for a completion of the internal market was launched right after its founding in 1983 with a memorandum to Commissioner Davignon in which the Round Table stated that

> Europe remains a group of separated national markets [which] prevents many firms from reaching the scale necessary to resist pressure from non-European competitors. The European market must serve as a unified "home" base necessary to allow European firms to develop as powerful competitors in world markets.[48]

Although plans for the completion of the internal market had been circulating within the EC for years, concrete progress was not made and it was in this respect that the pro-European offensive on the part of the Round Table had a very significant impact.[49] Indeed, ERT members were among the first within Europe's elite to publicly propose a *European* solution – in contrast to the then dominant *national* (champion) industrial strategies – to Europe's economic woes. Whereas up to the mid-1980s 'Europessimism' was still pervasive, the ERT warned in a 1985 report against the danger of the idea of Europe's decline 'being etched permanently into a new European consciousness' and concluded that 'Europe is not locked into decline – the exit doors are wide open. It remains only to go through them.'[50]

The basis of ERT's agenda-setting role with regard to what came to be the Europe 1992 programme had been a plan presented in late 1984 and early 1985 by the then CEO of Philips, and founding member and later chairman of the Round Table, Wisse Dekker, which laid out a detailed programme for the creation of a 'European Community Home Market' by 1990. Dekker's 'agenda for action' – which was quickly

130 Bastiaan van Apeldoorn

adopted by the whole Round Table – has been said by many to have directly inspired the Commission White Paper of June 1985.[51] Indeed, the critical role the ERT played in this respect has been acknowledged by several of the actors involved. Former Commissioner Peter Sutherland, for instance, has stated:

> I believe that it [the ERT] did play a significant role in the development of the 1992 programme. In fact one can argue that the whole completion of the internal market project was initiated not by governments but by the Round Table, and by members of it, Dekker in particular, and Philips playing a significant role and some others ... And I think it played a fairly consistent role subsequently in dialoguing with the Commission on practical steps to implement market liberalization.[52]

Although the ERT was thus instrumental in relaunching the European project by rallying around the idea of a unified European market, the internal market that was created on the basis of the White Paper did not turn out to be the kind of home market that many of the early Round Table members (of the 'Europeanist' fraction) had envisaged, that is, a relatively protected market in which Euro-champions could prosper in order to confront the global competition. The internal market did favour the creation of further economies of scale and did make the European market a home market more comparable to that of the USA and Japan. In the end, however, the internal market programme was hardly supported by the kind of 'flanking' policies that the neomercantilists had advocated. Responding to the demands of, among others, (members of) the ERT, the Commission did launch intra-European cooperation programmes in research and development, such as ESPRIT, and also later started to promote the development of trans-European infrastructure networks. Such policies, however, fell far short of any neomercantilist industrial *relance*. The fears of a protectionist Europe also turned out to be unfounded. Although those sectors of European industry – in particular, cars and electronics – that lobbied the hardest for protectionist measures[53] had their demands partially met, these limited protectionist policies have since gradually been ended, accelerating the integration of the EU into the global economy.[54]

In the transnational struggle over Europe's relaunching, neoliberal social forces can thus be seen gradually to have gained the upper hand over those that had favoured a neomercantilist interpretation of the internal market. This struggle had also been fought out within the ranks of Europe's transnational business elite, as united within the ERT, in which the 'Europeanist' fraction slowly lost its dominant position and moreover itself gradually abandoned its earlier neomercantilist perspective.[55] Not only did many globalist companies join the Round Table, but also the older ERT companies that were formerly still more oriented towards and dependent upon the European market became more global themselves.[56] This shifting balance of power between the globalist and 'Europeanist' camps must, however, also be seen in the context of the rising dominance of neoliberal ideology within the European political economy and the appeal neoliberalism gained as an alternative strategy after the political failure of the neomercantilist project. Concomitant, then, to the changing composition of its membership, the ideological and strategic orientation of the ERT gradually shifted away from a protective Europeanism and towards a neoliberal globalism. The broadening of ERT's membership with the addition of many prominent exponents of the globalist fraction (such as the heads of global giants like Unilever, Shell, BP and La Roche) also allowed the Round Table to develop more into an elite forum for the *whole* of an emergent European transnational capitalist class. The ERT of the 1990s thus became a forum within which this class came to redefine its interests along neoliberal lines and from which it has sought to shape European governance accordingly.

A first testimony to the ERT's shift away from its earlier protective regionalist orientation can be found in its September 1991 report *Reshaping Europe* – even if this still also contained many elements that revealed an as yet uneasy compromise between globalists and 'Europeanists' – in which it presented its blueprint for the post-1989 European order in the run-up to the Treaty of Maastricht.[57] In the report the ERT called for both a widening and a deepening (and in this sense still going beyond a neoliberal conception) of the European integration process, with a monetary union singled out as the most important next step. However, support for the single currency was not equally strong amongst all members.[58] The French and Italian members were strongly in favour, whereas most Germans and British were still only lukewarm. *Reshaping Europe* – reflecting part of the old neomercantilist agenda, albeit in recast form – furthermore advocated an 'effective industrial policy', giving 'top priority' to the so-called TENs.

In contrast to the 1992 project, the ERT's direct involvement in the Maastricht process was limited in as much as the initiative seemed to have been taken over again by Europe's politicians, no longer needing business interests to prod them along the path of deepening integration. Indeed, one can argue that Maastricht was partly the result of a kind of 'spillover' from the success of Europe 1992 and the temporary 'Europhoria' to which it had led.[59] In as much, then, as the ERT had played an initiating role with regard to the internal market programme one can argue, by that very fact, that it also helped to set the stage and create the preconditions for the second phase of Europe's 'relaunch'. Moreover, when we analyse the (socioeconomic) content of the Maastricht treaty, we encounter several of the ideas that the ERT, or at least part of the ERT membership, had been pushing for years, in particular, the idea of a monetary union as a necessary complement to the internal market, as well as an enhanced European role in infrastructure and R&D. Moreover, other parts of the treaty, most notably the social protocol, were not only testimony to the efforts of social democratic forces to put this on the agenda, but as much, if not more, to the role of transnational capital, represented inter alia by the ERT, in watering it down and seeing to it that this minimal programme would only be minimally implemented.[60] There is no doubt that the ERT made quite extensive use of its high-level contacts to promote its agenda. Delors got an advance copy of the *Reshaping Europe* report[61] and there were several

132 Bastiaan van Apeldoorn

consultations between the ERT and important Commissioners like Frans Andriessen, Ray MacSharry, Sir Leon Brittan and Delors himself, that is, with people 'to which we [the ERT] could explain our views on the Maastricht process'.[62] At the national level there were similar consultations between individual members of the ERT and key policy makers of the respective national governments.[63]

With regard to Economic and Monetary Union (EMU) it has to be pointed out that, as a strong consensus was lacking, the ERT could not push so strongly for EMU as some members would have liked. However, these members did organize themselves in a separate organization called the Association for Monetary Union of Europe (AMUE). Amongst the core membership of AMUE we find many ERT companies such as Fiat, Philips, Siemens and Total, whereas prominent (former) ERT members, such as former Vice Chairman André Leysen, Giovanni Agnelli (Fiat) and Etienne Davignon, are long-serving members of AMUE's governing board.[64] From the start, the industrialists of AMUE had close contacts with the Commission, and in particular with Delors, in their efforts to promote monetary integration. At a joint press conference of a delegation of AMUE (consisting of the CEOs of Fiat, Philips, Solvay and Total) and Delors, the latter expressed his appreciation of the 'very important' support of AMUE and stated that 'company managers not only follow us, but often precede us'.[65] Already in April 1988 – two months before the Delors Committee, which subsequently prepared the way for EMU, was set up – AMUE presented a detailed blueprint for monetary union and in the following years published annual surveys indicating wide business support across Europe.[66] On the eve of the Hanover summit, at which the Delors Committee was created, AMUE sent a communiqué to the government leaders expressing their support for the creation of an independent European Central Bank.[67] Although more research needs to be carried out on the role of AMUE, it is at least evident that a large section of transnational business had effectively organized itself to help to set the agenda with regard to monetary union. Moreover, the close connections between the ERT and AMUE do suggest that it is by and large the same elite of European transnational capital that has constituted at least one powerful interest pushing for both Europe 1992 and EMU.

At a more abstract level, the (socioeconomic) content of Maastricht can be interpreted as reflecting the transnational configuration of social and political forces within the European political economy at the end of the 1980s. The Round Table here represented important sections of the ruling elite within that configuration and, as such, was one important forum from which that elite could shape the debates that at the ideological level conditioned the political bargaining process. However, it was in the run-up to Maastricht that the social democratic project led by Delors also temporarily gained momentum and at least partly helped to set the agenda for Maastricht, even if that agenda in the end largely failed to materialize.[68] Maastricht was neither a triumph for Thatcherite hyperliberalism, nor the social democratic vision nor, for that matter, the neomercantilist strategy, but in fact contained elements of all three rival projects, even though it was biased in favour of the neoliberal project given the neoliberal orthodoxy underpinning the convergence criteria of EMU. Since Maastricht, however, the evolving European regime of socioeconomic governance has witnessed a further shift towards 'disciplinary neoliberalism' as the austerity race to meet the convergence criteria put even more people out of work and placed further strain on the welfare state. The EU further integrated itself into a global free trade regime under the new World Trade Organization (WTO) and 'competitiveness' – increasingly narrowly defined as the freedom for transnational capital to maximize (short-term) profit – became the primary 'benchmark' for European public policy. Below I will argue that in the construction of this new European order we can once more observe the political and ideological agency of the ERT.

The ERT's neoliberal offensive: shaping the discourse of European socioeconomic governance

After Maastricht the ERT's neoliberal shift has been further consolidated as is revealed by reports that have increasingly come to focus on deregulation, labour market flexibility and downsizing the public sector, along with even more unequivocal expressions of its commitment to global free trade.[69] With regard to ERT's strengthened free trade orientation, the crucial battle was probably that over the conclusion of the Uruguay Round of the General Agreement on Tariffs and Trade (GATT) talks in December 1993, which in retrospect probably signalled the final defeat of the 'Europrotectionists', both within the Round Table and the European capitalist class more widely.[70] After having reached internal unity on this point, the Round Table subsequently intensified its lobby campaign for a speedy conclusion of the trade negotiations and was probably one of the more important actors instrumental in changing the position of the French government.[71] According to the then director of the GATT, Peter Sutherland, 'the ERT was active and supportive of the Uruguay Round at the later stage when I was at the WTO'.[72] The post-Maastricht period also witnessed a deepening of the consensus in favour of monetary union, with the Round Table becoming more active in supporting this project.[73] The crises of the European Monetary System in 1992 and 1993 convinced, in particular, the Germans that the 'Deutschmarkzone' did not provide sufficient stability. Moreover, the neoliberal wing of the Round Table has also come to be more convinced of the virtues of EMU, principally because of the 'salutary' disciplinary effects the EMU criteria have so far had, and continue to have, on the socioeconomic policies of Europe's national governments.[74]

In short, the emphasis on the positive role of market forces has never been so strong as in current Round Table discourse. The ERT of today stresses that we live in a new world, in which 'nothing can be done today the same way as we did it yesterday; that is what we mean by "flexibility" and "freedom"'.[75] It is in the area of social and labour market policies that ERT's discourse has become most explicitly neoliberal. Well aware of the negative employment effects of the cost-cutting accumulation strategies that their companies have now adopted, the ERT capitalists in a 1993 report gloomily warned that 'a hard core of persistent unemployment

134 Bastiaan van Apeldoorn

will remain into the next century', but added that this core might yet be reduced if Europe is willing to 'flexibilize and upgrade the supply of labour'.[76] The former is designed primarily in terms of external flexibility, which means that the burden of adjustment will have to be carried by labour as the ERT itself is in fact frank enough to admit: '[a] very large amount of the effort to adjust European labour markets will rely on labour'.[77] In the end, the desired 'adaptation' of labour implies a fundamental restructuring of state–society relations. Again, the ERT is well aware of this and, speaking the language of hegemony, it appeals for the creation of a 'new social consensus':

> Enabling Europe to return to high employment growth requires more than replacing policy instruments, it calls for a change of our economic and social structures. But governments are only able to change structures when there is a *new social consensus*, i.e. the convergence on principles and, ultimately, agreement on the goals for that change among the social partners, governments, the opinion leaders and, ultimately, population ... We need a consensus on the European level that *only a healthy, efficient and competitive private sector is able to provide sufficient jobs, and that markets should be left to allocate labour efficiently.* [78]

Creating this new consensus means that the existing 'distorted [*sic*] social balance' has to be changed.[79] A key concept in the discourse within which this nascent hegemonic project of Europe's transnational capitalist class is articulated is that of 'competitiveness'. Competitiveness has come to function as such a key concept because of its potential to represent the 'general interest' as it appeals equally to neoliberals, neomercantilists and social democrats alike. But what competitiveness actually means, and how it has to be achieved, is an open question decided in concrete struggles. Below I argue that competitiveness is increasingly being defined in neoliberal terms and that the ERT has been one important forum promoting such a definition.

The new competitiveness discourse

Competitiveness has become the keyword not only in ERT's discourse, but in socioeconomic discourse at large. The argument put forward here is that the ERT has been one of the more important 'authors' of this competitiveness discourse within the European context. The first testimony (at the EU level) of the power of this discourse was the Delors' White Paper on 'Growth, Competitiveness and Employment', which has since become one of the main intellectual reference points in the socioeconomic policy debate within the EU.[80] Different pieces of evidence suggest that the ERT had a significant input into the development of this key Commission document.[81] At the press conference after the December 1993 Brussels summit at which Delors had presented his White Paper, the then Commission president recalled his consultation with industry and the support he had received for his proposals from the ERT.[82] The week before Delors had also participated in the press presentation of the ERT report *Beating the Crisis*, which was conceived as its contribution to the Commission's future economic strategy.[83] As a senior ERT official commented upon the relation between these two reports:

> It was very parallel, and we saw their drafts and they saw our drafts. And one of my friends, a very senior official in the Commission, he said to me, there is basically no difference between them ... very similar, growth, investment, competitiveness, and employment. What we have tried to do is to get these things fixed together in people's minds ... the message is the same, these things all go together, you won't fight unemployment if you don't fight for competitiveness, you won't get growth if you don't have investment.[84]

Indeed, careful reading of the two reports does reveal some striking similarities. Most importantly, they share the basic premise that higher growth and employment can only be achieved through promoting the competitiveness of European industry. Moreover, the strategy (with regard to these objectives) outlined by the White Paper also echoes that of *Beating the Crisis*. In the Commission document, the road to higher employment follows a strategy based on the three 'inseparable elements' – a 'macroeconomic framework which instead of constraining market forces ... supports them', structural adjustment of policies 'aimed at increasing the competitiveness of European industry and at removing the rigidities which are curbing its dynamism' and 'active policies and structural changes in the labour market and in the regulations'.[85] Just as the concept of industrial policy is recast in a more liberal frame, so is the Delorist vision of a 'social Europe' further watered down.

Notwithstanding this, Delors's Paper was still largely an attempt at a compromise between neoliberals and social democrats.[86] Since then, however, competitiveness has increasingly been defined in neoliberal terms within the Commission's policy discourse. As indicated, the ERT has constituted a key forum within which this neoliberal competitiveness discourse has been articulated. A senior ERT official explained the process as follows:

> [t]he members of the European Round Table perceive it as their role to make some input into policy making at the European level on those issues which are of crucial importance for the economic strength of Europe, what we are now calling the sort of general term of competitiveness. *And competitiveness is now a useful word but it is really like a paper bag into which you put things.* [87]

What the ERT has been trying to put in the bag – that is, the meaning it has sought to attach to the concept of competitiveness – is increasingly neoliberal in origin. The past is revealing here. Although competitiveness as a political catchword has only recently risen to its current heights, it was already much talked about in the 1980s. However, the meaning of competitiveness then was still primarily bound up with a neomercantilist ideology in which it meant being able to compete in the global marketplace by first shielding oneself from the forces of global competition in order then to enter the fray on the basis of increased strength achieved partly through *non-market* means. Now, however, competitiveness means survival of the fittest in the fully open environment of a global free market in which competitive performance is what the market measures it to be.

The ERT's promotion of this concept of competitiveness has certainly contributed to its wider acceptance within European governance. A first testimony to this was the setting up by the EU of a 'Competitiveness Advisory Group' (CAG) in the beginning of 1995, just over a year after the ERT had first proposed the creation of such a group.[88] The CAG membership consists of CEOs, as well as leading trade union representatives and other 'eminent persons' (usually former politicians), but is dominated by the former group.[89] At the time of its founding, three ERT members (Barnevik, Maljers and Simon) joined the 13-member council and at present Marco Tronchetti Provera (of Pirelli) maintains the links between the two groups. It should not surprise us therefore that the 'advice' this group has so far given (in six-monthly reports to the European Council) closely resembles that of the ERT, with both the Round Table and the CAG spreading the new competitiveness gospel.[90] As a senior official of the ERT remarked, 'one thing that is quite important in this whole scenario is multiplicity of messages and delivery systems around the whole theme'.[91]

As an operationalization of its competitiveness ideology, the ERT has, in tandem with the CAG, started to promote the concept of 'benchmarking' vis-à-vis the Commission and the member states. Benchmarking means 'measuring the performance' of individual firms, sectors, but also of nations against that of the 'best competitors' in the world.[92] After launching the idea, the Round Table organized several seminars with Commission and government officials to promote the concept.[93] In its report *Benchmarking for Policy-Makers*, the ERT is very explicit about how policy makers should 'measure' competitiveness: the country or (macro) region that is most competitive is the country that is most successful in attracting mobile capital. As the report put it, 'governments must recognise today that every economic and social system in the world is competing with all the others to attract the footloose businesses'.[94] That the expected outcome of this competition for transnationally mobile capital will be a deepening of neoliberal restructuring transpires from the kind of 'benchmarks' that are, for instance, proposed with regard to the policy goal of creating employment: the level of 'labour costs ... the flexibility of labour ... working and factory hours ... termination costs'.[95] The Maastricht criteria are also mentioned as a successful application of the benchmarking concept.[96] At the same time, the ideological potential of a concept like benchmarking, and indeed its capacity to appeal to a wider set of forces within society and to incorporate them into the emergent hegemonic bloc, is also not lost on the Round Table capitalists as the report stresses that benchmarking is 'not just an analytical device' but also 'carries a symbolic message':

At a time when the European model of society is experiencing some difficulties, and change may be perceived as painful (though not nearly so painful as the results of not changing), the role of symbols in mobilising human effort may become more important, and benchmarking can be part of this.[97]

Competitiveness and benchmarking have also accordingly become the key concepts within the public (socioeconomic) policy discourse of the EU. Analysing the policy documents of the Commission one also sees how these concepts are mobilized to promote a programme of neoliberal restructuring aiming to remove, in the words of the Director-General for Industry, the still remaining 'rigidities and distortions ... that prevent Europe from fully exploiting its potential'.[98] The ERT's promotion of the concept of benchmarking vis-à-vis the Commission has been particularly successful. In the same month that the ERT published its report the Industry Directorate-General came out with a document entitled *Benchmarking the Competitiveness of European Industry* in which it suggested that benchmarking should be used as a central policy guideline at all levels of EU governance.[99] In a follow-up communication the Commission explicitly acknowledged the input of the ERT as the first business organization to draw the Commission's and the Council's attention to the benchmarking concept.[100] In this communication – and at the request of the Council of Ministers[101] – the Commission launched a number of concrete initiatives to put the concept into practice, including the establishment of a 'High Level Group on Benchmarking', made up of 'experts' from industry, and the initiation of a number of so-called pilot projects in different member states to start identifying Europe's 'weaknesses and inefficiencies' at the enterprise, sectoral and public policy level (or what is referred to as 'framework conditions').[102]

Invoking the inevitability of globalization and 'hence' the need for adaptation, the Commission defines benchmarking as a tool for improving competitiveness and for promoting 'the convergence towards best practice'.[103] This involves the global 'comparison of societal behaviour [sic], commercial practice, market structure and public institutions'.[104] As the 'High Level Group on Benchmarking' – chaired by a board member of Investor, the investment company controlling the global Wallenberg empire – makes clear in its first report, the object of all these 'comparisons' is to promote rapid 'structural reforms' that will allow Europe to adapt to the exigencies of globalization: 'this involves further liberalization, privatization ... more flexible labour laws, lower government subsidies, etc.'.[105] Similarly, the Commission identifies labour market reform as a 'vital factor for the competitiveness of European industry', calling for 'a radical rethink of all relevant labour market systems – employment protection, working time, social protection, and health and safety – to adapt them to a world of work which will be organised differently'.[106]

Conclusion

To sum up, then, the social purpose of the new Europe is increasingly oriented to serve the interests of a globalizing transnational capitalist class. This article has argued that the European Round Table has developed into a key elite organization articulating and defining the interests of this class and propagating them vis-à-vis the European institutions and within public debate. As such, it has been claimed that the ERT has played a significant role in mediating the material and ideological power of this transnational class and thus in contributing to the neoliberal transformation of European order. Nevertheless, capital too, and in particular industrial capital, cannot live by the logic of what Karl Polanyi called the self-regulating market alone, but needs supporting government policies and social (non-market) institutions in order to accumulate wealth.[107] These conflicting requirements of capital may work themselves out in different ways, depending on the prevalent configuration of social forces. Given the preponderance of globalizing transnational capital within that configuration the conflict for now is settled in favour of 'the principle of economic liberalism' and all its socially uprooting effects.[108] Still, at least within continental Europe, the neoliberal project has yet fully to disembed the European market economy from its postwar social and political institutions. On the one hand, primacy lies with freedom of capital and markets, implying that the postwar 'European model' needs to be fundamentally restructured. On the other hand, it is recognized that this restructuring process cannot take place overnight and that it will have to be a gradual process in which a high degree of social consensus is maintained. These limits to a fully fledged (laissez-faire) neoliberalism are even acknowledged by the ERT, which, after all, is predominantly a club of transnational *industrial* capitalists[109] who tend to be more aware (than financial capitalists) of the social requirements of the reproduction of capital. Thus, notwithstanding its neoliberal competitiveness discourse, the ERT also still calls for a *European Ordnungspolitik* clearly more in tune with the German model of Rhineland capitalism than with the (UK) neoliberal model. Moreover, in spite of the opposition that the ERT has waged against EU social policies, it is also keen to preserve the ideology and practice of 'social partnership', thus rejecting a fully fledged neoliberal (Anglo-Saxon) model of industrial relations.[110]

Still, this articulation of the original neoliberal project with some elements of what were originally opposing projects (neomercantilism and transnational social democracy) thus far seems to be more of a hegemonic strategy of incorporation that seeks to further the neoliberal agenda than one that offers genuine prospects for a substantive 'embedding' of the new European market. In other words, the limited elements of 'embeddedness' that we may discern in the ERT's discourse seem to be primarily oriented towards the interests of globalizing transnational capital. The question remains, then, as to what extent the social purpose of the emergent European order may yet be constructed on a different ideological basis than that contained in the idea that the ultimate 'benchmark' for the 'performance' of a society is its ability to accumulate wealth in private hands. The answer depends at least in part upon the extent to which labour, as well as other groups that lose out in the neoliberal globalization process, will be able to form a stronger countervailing power at both the national and European levels. From a critical perspective, the examination of these possibilities, however remote they

Transnational class agency, European governance **139**

may presently seem, should be a necessary complement to the research agenda that has informed this discussion of the ideological power of Europe's emergent transnational capitalist class.

Notes

1 An exception is formed by O. Holman (1992), Transnational class strategy and the new Europe, *International Journal of Political Economy* 22(1): 3–22. For the best documented study of the role of the ERT in the Europe 1992 programme, see M.G. Cowles (1994), *The Politics of Big Business in the European Community: Setting the Agenda for a New Europe*, unpublished PhD Dissertation, The American University. See also M.G. Cowles (1995), Setting the agenda for a new Europe: The ERT and EC 1992, *Journal of Common Market Studies* 33(4), 501–26; N. Fielder (1997), *Western European Integration in the 1980s: The Origins of the Single Market* (Berlin: Peter Lang); and W. Sandholtz and J. Zysman (1989), 1992: Recasting the European Bargain, *World Politics* 42: 95–128. The research on the ERT presented in this article has been conducted for the author's PhD Dissertation (van Apeldoorn, *Transnational Capitalism and the Struggle over European Order*, unpublished PhD Dissertation, European University Institute, 1999). The lion's share of the research material consists of about two dozen interviews with (former) members, senior officials and so called 'associates' of the ERT. Unless indicated otherwise, all interviews cited have been conducted by the author. The interviews were conducted in the native language of the interviewee (either English, German, French, Dutch, or Italian); translations (of quotations) into English are my own.
2 A good introduction to the 'neo-Gramscian school' of International Relations is provided by S. Gill (Ed.) (1993), *Gramsci, Historical Materialism and International Relations* (Cambridge: Cambridge University Press). See also K. van der Pijl (1989), *Transnational Classes and International Relations* (London: Routledge) and R.W. Cox, with T. Sinclair (1996), *Approaches to World Order* (Cambridge: Cambridge University Press).
3 The intergovernmentalist perspective has been most developed by Andrew Moravcsik. See his *The Choice for Europe* (Ithaca, NY: Cornell University Press, 1998). A recent collection of essays by authors working from a supranationalist perspective, which draws in part on earlier neofunctionalist theories, can be found in W. Sandholtz and A. Sweet Stone (Eds) (1998), *European Integration and Supranational Governance* (Oxford: Oxford University Press).
4 Borrowing the words of John Ruggie (1982), International regimes, transactions and change: Embedded liberalism in the postwar economic order, *International Organization* 36(2): 382.
5 The rationalist assumptions are strongest and most explicit in the (liberal) intergovernmentalism of Moravcsik (see his *Choice for Europe*). Neofunctionalists and later supranationalists have always been drawn from time to time to the role of ideas and values in supporting the European integration process, but without asking the question what kind of ideas support what kind of European order.
6 See, for instance, Sandholtz and Zysman and their interpretation of the ERT, with regard to its role in the 1992 process, as a 'political interest group [constituted] by community action' and used, as such, by the EC to push through its programme (Sandholtz and Zysman, 1992: 117).
7 There are now about 45,000 TNCs in the world (up from 7000 in 1970), together controlling US$3.2 trillion in foreign direct investment stock (up from US$282 million in 1975). Indicating the present centrality of TNCs in the world economy, it is estimated that the 600 largest TNCs are producing more than a fifth of the world's real net output of industrial production, whereas about 40 per cent of employment in the industrialized world depends directly or indirectly on TNCs. See *World Investment*

140 Bastiaan van Apeldoorn

Report 1997: Transnational corporations, market structure and competition policy (United Nations 1997).

8 The two most important works of van der Pijl in this respect are his (1998), *Transnational Classes and International Relations* (London: Routledge) as well as his (1984), *The Making of an Atlantic Ruling Class* (London: NLB).

9 L. Sklair (1997) Social movements for global capitalism: The transnational capitalist class in action, *Review of International Political Economy* 4(3), 520.

10 Most fundamental are the functional difference between financial and industrial capital as well as differences in what we could call the geographical scale of operation of capital, where, even within the elite of large transnational corporations, we find important differences as some firms are more global than others (which may limit their transnational activities only to a single region of the global economy). Cf. van der Pijl, *Transnational Classes*.

11 For Gramsci, hegemony signified a mode of governance that rests upon a set of institutionalized practices and norms 'freely accepted' by subordinate groups but nevertheless expressing a structure of domination. See A. Gramsci (1971), *Selections from the Prison Notebooks* (London: Lawrence and Wishart): 169–70 and *passim*.

12 Here I draw upon van der Pijl (*Transnational Classes*, esp. ch. 4) as well as Stephen Gill (1990), *American Hegemony and the Trilateral Commission* (Cambridge: Cambridge University Press).

13 Cf. W. Streeck and P.C. Schmitter (1991), From national corporatism to transnational pluralism, *Politics and Society* 19(2): 133–64.

14 S. Gill (1998), European governance and new constitutionalism: Economic and Monetary Union and alternatives to disciplinary neoliberalism in Europe, *New Political Economy* 3(1): 5.

15 Wisse Dekker, quoted in Industrialists drive for a stronger Europe: Interview with Professor Dr Wisse Dekker, *Europe 2000* 2(2): 18.

16 Monod, quoted in ERT (1992), *European industry and the developing world: A dialogue between partners* (Brussels: European Round Table of Industrialists): 1.

17 Letter from Dr Helmut O. Maucher to the author, dated 12 June 1997.

18 On the ERT's formation, and the role of Davignon, see also Cowles, *The Politics of Big Business*: chs 3 and 4. As Cowles and others have also stressed, UNICE's relative weakness was one background factor against which we have to understand the formation of the ERT. Davignon, who for years had been trying to strengthen the ties between business and the EC executive, also did not find UNICE a suitable interlocutor for the EC as he regarded it more as a traditional lobby club than as a 'partner with which a dialogue could be developed' (interview with Etienne Davignon by author and Otto Holman, Brussels, 6 June 1993).

19 These are the words of co-founder Wisse Dekker, quoted in 'Industrialists drive for a stronger Europe': 17.

20 The ERT meets in a plenary session twice a year, but the existence of a steering committee (the organization's leadership), a Brussels-based secretariat, numerous working groups on different policy themes and the assistance of so-called 'associates' (also often senior managers from ERT companies) ensure a more continuous activity of the group.

21 In terms of organization the ERT is very small and non-bureaucratic, but a key role is played by a secretary-general and an assistant secretary-general.

22 Interview, Brussels, 24 May 1996. My emphasis.

23 *Financial Times*' Europe 500 at www.ft.com/ftsurveys/ft5_eur.htm

24 *Fortune*'s 1998 Global 500 at http://cgi.pathfinder.com/fortune/global500

25 One indicator of this internal coherence and the networking by which it is supported can be found in the high number of ERT members that are 'outside directors' of other ERT companies. See van Apeldoorn, *Transnational Capitalism*: ch. 4.

26 Streeck and Schmitter, From national corporatism to transnational pluralism. The number of 'interest groups' seeking to influence European policy making has grown

dramatically since Europe's *relance* in the mid-1980s and is now estimated by the Commission to total about 3000, including over 500 European and international federations. See J. Greenwood (1997), *Representing Interests in the European Union* (London: Macmillan): 3.

27 In the growing literature on organized interests in the EU, part of the debate has come to revolve around the question of whether these emerging supranational patterns of interest representation are either (neo)corporatist or pluralist. See, for example, S. Mazey and J. Richardson (Eds) (1993), *Lobbying in the European Community* (Oxford: Oxford University Press) and J. Greenwood, J. Grote and K. Ronit (Eds) (1992), *Organized Interests and the European Community* (London: SAGE). I maintain that the ERT fits neither 'model' well.

28 It should be pointed out that, in fact, this was a gradual development and that what follows is an interpretation of the ERT of today. Moreover, as we shall see later on, the early ERT could not yet function as an elite organization for Europe's transnational capitalist class because initially its membership was too narrowly concentrated in certain sectors of European industry.

29 Interview, Essen, 4 September 1996.

30 Interviews.

31 Interview with senior German ERT associate, Brussels, 30 May 1996.

32 Interview, Antwerp, 21 May 1996.

33 Telephone interview, 27 January 1998.

34 Or, as in the words of one long-serving ERT associate, who drew the comparison with the US Business Roundtable (which has four times as many members as the ERT), the ERT is 'less interested in specific themes ... within the life of the firms [and more] interested ... in themes of the medium-long term, that is to say, themes that concern the future of Europe', whereas its US counterpart is 'much more lobbyistic'. Interview, Ivrea, 2 December 1997.

35 Interview, London, 12 September 1996.

36 On the concept of agenda setting, see Cowles, *The Politics of Big Business*.

37 K. Richardson (1989), Europe's industrialists help shape the Single Market, *Europe*, EC Commission Office, Washington, DC, December. Direct contacts between ERT members and political leaders have, according to one ERT official, been especially developed under the chairmanship of Jérôme Monod (from 1992 to 1996), who, with his own political past and continuing strong links to French politics and politicians, further fostered this mode of communication. It was 'under Monod that the idea of going to see Juppé, Kohl, and so on [became normal practice]. That was very much Monod's habit, to pick up the phone [and say] OK, we go and see somebody, we go and see Balladur to get the Uruguay Round tied up'. Interview, Brussels, 24 May 1996.

38 This tradition was first established with Delors and continued with subsequent Commission President Jacques Santer. Interview with senior ERT official, 24 May 1996.

39 Former Commission President François-Xavier Ortoli was also a member for a short period in the early 1990s.

40 Interview, Ivrea, 2 December 1997.

41 See, respectively, A. Moravcsik (1991), Negotiating the Single European Act: National interests and conventional statecraft in the European Community, *International Organization* 42(1): 19–56; and Sandholtz and Zysman, 1992.

42 A similar approach has been recently advocated by L. Hooghe and G. Marks in (1999), 'The making of a polity: The struggle over European integration', in H. Kitschelt *et al.* (Eds), *Continuity and Change in Contemporary Capitalism* (Cambridge: Cambridge University Press): 70–97. Hooghe and Marks, however, do not propose a theoretical framework to understand which actors play what role in the struggle over European integration and what might account for the outcome of that struggle.

43 For a more elaborate analysis of these three projects and of the context in which they developed, see van Apeldoorn, *Transnational capitalism* ch. 3.

142 Bastiaan van Apeldoorn

44 See, for an account of this strategy, J. Pearce and J. Sutton (1986), *Protection and industrial policy in Europe* (London: Routledge & Kegan Paul).
45 See G. Ross (1995), *Jacques Delors and European Integration* (Cambridge: Polity).
46 This division of European capital is an adaptation from one proposed by Holman in Transnational class strategy and the new Europe.
47 For a more elaborate analysis of this early ERT strategy and how it was bound up with the structural composition of its membership, see van Apeldoorn, *Transnational Capitalism*: ch. 5.
48 ERT, *Foundations for the Future of European Industry*, memorandum to EC Commissioner Davignon, 10 June 1983.
49 An argument that is also made more elaborately by Cowles, *The Politics of Big Business*: ch. 4 (also Cowles, Setting the agenda). Moravcsik, *Choice for Europe*: ch. 5, denies the initiating role of the ERT in this respect, but fails to come up with convincing evidence contradicting that of Cowles.
50 ERT (1985), *Changing Scales* (Roundtable of European Industrialists): 3, 15.
51 See Cowles, *The Politics of Big Business*: ch. 4. See also A. Krause (1991), *Inside the New Europe* (London: Harper-Collins).
52 Telephone interview with Peter Sutherland, 27 January 1998. In order to help to keep momentum behind the implementation of Europe '92, the ERT set up a 'watchdog' committee, the Internal Market Support Committee, whose members (all prominent Round Table members) had many private consultations with both the EC and with national government leaders, top-level meetings that were supported by 'thousands of contacts on an *ad hoc* basis' between ERT associates and Community officials. Interview with Wisse Dekker by author and Otto Holman, Eindhoven, 6 September 1993.
53 Including CEOs from these sectors within the ERT. Interviews.
54 See B.T. Hanson (1998), What happened to Fortress Europe? External trade policy liberalisation in the European Union, *International Organization* 52(1): 55–85.
55 One prominent representative of ERT's neoliberal wing at that time, the then chairman of Unilever, Floris Maljers, in fact indicated that the 'struggle between liberals and protectionists' became a constant feature of the internal policy debates at the end of the 1980s and beginning of the 1990s. Interview by Otto Holman and author, Rotterdam, 3 September 1993.
56 For evidence on the 'globalization' of ERT's membership, see van Apeldoorn, *Transnational Capitalism*: ch. 6. The biggest sudden change in the composition of membership was due to a merger in 1988 with another, but largely ineffectual, transnational business forum, the *Groupe des Présidents*, whose membership included more truly global TNCs and which thus had a more liberal and free-trade orientation. Interviews.
57 ERT (1991), *Reshaping Europe* (Brussels: European Round Table of Industrialists).
58 Interviews.
59 See, for a detailed analysis of these and other factors, W. Sandholtz (1993), Choosing Union: Monetary politics and Maastricht, *International Organization* 47(1): 1–39.
60 Apart from communicating its neoliberal views through its reports and through other channels, at several critical moments the ERT also intervened directly to halt the construction of 'Social Europe'. For instance, as chairman of the ERT, Wisse Dekker sent a letter to Commission President Delors and all 12 EC ambassadors rejecting the proposed European Company Directive, arguing that industrial relations should remain at the national level. See M. Rhodes (1991), The social dimension of the Single European Market: National versus transnational regulation, *European Journal of Political Research* 19(2), p. 260.
61 Interview with senior ERT Official, Brussels, 27 April 1993.
62 Interview with Maljers (by Otto Holman and author), Rotterdam, 3 September 1993.
63 Ibid. A senior official of the ERT also recalls a lengthy meeting between an ERT delegation and the then prime minister Ruud Lubbers at the time of the Dutch presidency under which Maastricht was concluded. Interview, 24 May 1996.
64 http://amue.lf.net

65 *Agence Europe*, No. 4728, 22 February 1988.
66 Moravcsik, *Choice for Europe*, pp. 393, 434.
67 *Agence Europe*, No. 4811, 25 June 1988.
68 See, for a more elaborate discussion, Van Apeldoorn, *Transnational Capitalism*: ch. 7. See also Ross, *Jacques Delors*.
69 See, for instance, ERT (1993), *Beating the crisis: A Charter for Europe's industrial future* (Brussels: European Round Table of Industrialists).
70 This was at least the perception of former ERT Vice-Chairmen Floris Maljers (interview by Otto Holman and author, Rotterdam, 3 September 1993) and David Simon (interview, London, 12 September 1996).
71 At least, according to a senior ERT official, who related that the ERT, then chaired by Frenchman Jérôme Monod, met with French prime minister Balladur to discuss with him how the French government could say 'yes' to the conclusion of the Uruguay Round (which is what it wanted to do but did not know how to effect given domestic opposition) without angering public opinion, and particularly the farm lobby too much. Interview, Brussels, 24 May 1996.
72 Telephone interview with Peter Sutherland, 27 January 1998.
73 Thus, in a letter sent by the ERT to all the heads of state and government on the eve of the Madrid European Council of December 1995, the ERT reiterated its full support for monetary union and asked the government leaders to ensure 'monetary stability based on economic convergence and financial discipline'. Mimeo, letter dated 17 October 1995 and signed by Jérôme Monod, then Chairman of the ERT. A copy of the letter was also sent to Commission president Jacques Santer and the issue was discussed with him a few weeks later.
74 As a current prominent ERT member notes, 'Maastricht already has had its biggest effect. It would never have come to such a convergence if it had not been for the Maastricht criteria. Belgian politics [for instance] is unthinkable without Maastricht, then we would not have any brake on making big deficits.' Interview, Antwerp, 21 May 1996.
75 ERT, *Beating the Crisis*: 28.
76 ERT (1993), *European Labour Markets: An Update on Perspectives and Requirements for Job Generation in the Second Half of the 1990s* (Brussels: European Round Table of Industrialists), pp. 8 and ii.
77 Ibid., p. 16.
78 Ibid., p. 9. Emphasis in the original.
79 Ibid., p. ii.
80 European Commission (1994), *Growth, competitiveness, employment: The challenges and ways forward into the 21st Century* (Brussels: Office for Official Publications of the European Communities).
81 In the view of former ERT Vice-Chairman André Leysen the White Paper can be taken as a good example of ERT's influence. Interview, Antwerp, 21 May 1996.
82 *Agence Europe*, No. 6127, special edition, 12 December 1993.
83 *Agence Europe*, No. 6122, 6 December 1993.
84 Interview, Brussels, 24 May 1996.
85 European Commission, *Growth, Competitiveness, Employment*, p. 61.
86 This point is also made by Ross, *Jacques Delors*, pp. 224–5.
87 Interview, Brussels, 24 May 1996. My emphasis.
88 ERT, *Beating the Crisis*: 27.
89 For a list of present and former members as well as other information on the CAG, see http://europa.eu.int/comm/cdp/cag
90 See its first four reports, as collected in A. Jacquemin and L. R. Pench (Eds) (1997), *Europe competing in the global economy: Reports of the Competitiveness Advisory Group* (Cheltenham: Edward Elgar).
91 Interview, Brussels, 24 May 1996.

144 Bastiaan van Apeldoorn

92 ERT (1994), *European Competitiveness* (Brussels: European Roundtable of Industrialists), p. 4.
93 Interviews. See also *Agence Europe*, 23 November 1996.
94 ERT (1996), *Benchmarking for policy-makers: The way to competitiveness, growth and job creation* (Brussels: European Round Table of Industrialists), p. 15.
95 Ibid.: 13. 96.
96 Ibid.: 18.
97 Ibid.: 17.
98 Director-General for Industry, Stefano Micossi (1997), in the 'Preface' of European Commission, *The competitiveness of European industry* (Brussels: Office for Official Publications of the European Communities), p. 5.
99 European Commission, *Benchmarking the competitiveness of European industry*, Com (96) 436 Final, 9 October 1996, pp. 16 and ff.
100 European Commission, *Benchmarking: Implementation of an instrument available to economic and public authorities*, Com (97) 153/2, 16 April 1997: 3.
101 At the Industry Council of 14 November 1996. The Council recently called again upon the EC 'to ensure the ongoing development of benchmarking' at all levels. See European Commission, *Bulletin EU*, 4–1999, point 1.3.79.
102 Commission, *Implementation*.
103 Commission, *Benchmarking*: 16, and Commission, *Implementation*.
104 Commission, *Implementation*: 3.
105 High Level Group on Benchmarking (1999), First Report by the High Level Group on Benchmarking, *Benchmarking Papers*, No. 2, European Commission, Directorate-General III, p. 13.
106 European Commission, *Benchmarking*, p. 11. See also European Commission, *Benchmarking*: ch. 4.
107 K. Polanyi (1957), *The great transformation: The political and economic origins of our time* (Boston, MA: Beacon Press).
108 Ibid., p. 132.
109 Although in the case of some key ERT members the phrase 'finance capitalists' would be more correct given the links these industrialists have (via interlocking directorates) to financial institutions.
110 For a more elaborate analysis of these 'limits to neoliberalism' in ERT's current discourse, see van Apeldoorn, *Transnational Capitalism*: ch. 8.

Acknowledgements

For useful comments and suggestions, I am grateful to Colin Crouch, Stephen Gill, Otto Holman, Thomas Risse, Wolfgang Streeck, the editors of *New Political Economy* and two anonymous referees.

6

ASYMMETRICAL REGULATION AND MULTIDIMENSIONAL GOVERNANCE IN THE EUROPEAN UNION (2004)

Otto Holman

On the eve of the June 1998 Cardiff European Council summit, the former Chancellor of Germany, Helmut Kohl, and the French President, Jacques Chirac, sent a letter to the host of the Cardiff meeting, UK Prime Minister, Tony Blair.[1] In this joint letter, they expressed their concern about centralized decision making in Brussels and the European Commission's power. Both leaders had their own particular reasons to sign the letter. Chirac was rather annoyed by the interference of the European Commission in the allocation of World Cup tickets, while Kohl's position was in part the result of recent Commission decisions in the field of Competition Policy and in part aimed at neutralizing the Euro-sceptics in his right-wing coalition. It was this short-term expediency – in the case of Kohl very much related to the upcoming general elections in September that year – that caused one (anonymous) senior Commission official to speak of the 'new populism' in France and Germany (quoted in *Financial Times*, 16 June 1998).

Yet, the language used in the letter, its resemblance to previous statements (notably in the years before and after the signing of the Maastricht Treaty in 1992) and its firm incorporation into 'Euro-speak' ever since, suggest that something more was/is at stake than just short-term expediency. France and Germany explicitly rejected the idea of a European super-state and called for a debate on the future of the European Union (EU) and, more specifically, for a future decision-making structure that would be closer to the European citizens and respect political and cultural diversity in an enlarged union. At the very heart of the letter was the principle of subsidiarity, a concept that had re-entered the European debate at the end of the 1980s as part of the Delors strategy to Europeanize economic, monetary *and* social policies. A Dutch commentator at the time stated that this stress on subsidiarity was misleading and in fact distracted from the real question; the discussion should be centred on 'what's to be done' instead of 'who does what'. A transparent, political debate on the future of Europe involving European citizens,

146 Otto Holman

and their European and national representatives, was far more important than discussing the formal competences of the different (sub)national and European decision-making institutions. The latter would merely prolong the habit of European elites to take decisions behind closed doors while simultaneously pretending to operate *bürgernah* [close to the citizens – editors] (Sampiemon 1998).

Three years later, at the December 2001 European Council summit in Laeken, the 14 leaders of government and the French head of state agreed on starting a constitutional Convention in 2002, with the aim of creating a more democratic union, of bringing the EU closer to its citizens. It was concluded that many people were opposed to a 'federal super-state' and that the EU should not intervene 'in every detail' in matters best left to the elected representatives of member states or regions. In other words, the European Convention should draft a constitutional framework for a new model of European governance based on a narrow, bottom-up interpretation of the principle of subsidiarity. In June 2004, at the European Council summit in Brussels, agreement was reached about the text of the Constitutional Treaty. Right after the summit, the now 25 political leaders tried to convince their national constituencies that they had gained the maximum possible in the tough bargaining over the final, compromise-ridden text. Vital national interests were effectively defended and important policy areas – notably social policy – would be protected from supranational interference through the constitutionalization of competences at the lowest possible level of decision making. In an enlarged Union of 25 Member States, the idea of a federal super-state 'is a Eurosceptic fantasy, not a Europhile ambition', according to a British commentator (Peel 2004).[2]

In this article, I will identify this way of legitimizing recent institutional steps in European integration by national political elites as a more structural instance of 'new populism', as integral part of the unfolding mode of asymmetrical regulation and multidimensional governance in the EU. By regulation I mean, following Giandomenico Majone, the 'sustained and focused control exercised by a public agency, on the basis of a legislative mandate, over activities that are generally regarded as desirable to society' (Majone 1996: 9). If we take the Single Market as an example, we can assume that the free market activities since the mid-1980s are regulated in a would-be European society that 'generally' considers free market integration through European (re)regulation as an activity worthwhile in itself and 'hence in need of protection as well as control' (Majone 1996). Similarly, we can look at the European Central Bank as a public agency that exercises sustained and focused control over activities which have an impact on, for instance, price stability. The same can be said, finally, for activities in the field of social policy. Maintaining social cohesion, or guaranteeing a certain degree of social protection, can be generally regarded as desirable to society. The problem is, however, that (re)regulation at the European level in terms of single market and monetary integration causes deregulation at the national level in social terms. Asymmetrical regulation, then, not only refers to the discrepancy between European economic and monetary free market regulation, on the one hand, and the lack of social regulation (or harmonization) at the European level, on the other, but – more importantly – to the adverse impact of economic and monetary integration at the European level on social cohesion at the national level.

Multidimensional governance refers to the more comprehensive process of building a new European polity or, more specifically, a novel form of bourgeois domination in the transnational heartland of European production and finance. Governance refers to the organization of collective action through formal and informal institutionalization (institutions being 'the rules of the game that permit prescribe, or prohibit certain actions', see Prakash and Hart 1999: 2, and *multidimensional* governance in the EU refers to a process that is constituted in a social space transcending national borders and takes place simultaneously in subnational, national and supranational arenas, cf. Overbeek 2003: 4). Governance is thus about control and authority but – unlike 'government' in democratic polities – not necessarily about legitimacy and democratic accountability. Here the New Populism comes in: by introducing a vaguely defined concept like subsidiarity into the European Treaties and by using consultancy terms like best practice and benchmarking particularly in the field of social policy, the illusion of self-determination (and, hence, the illusion of democratic accountability at the national level under the heading of 'bringing the EU closer to its citizens') is maintained while creepingly empowering a European 'invisible hand'. It is this emerging and novel form of multidimensional governance in the European Union that we will turn to in the next section.

Multidimensional governance in the European Union

From an institutional perspective, governance in the EU is much more complex, and hybrid, than the anti-federalist rhetoric of national politicians suggests. Indeed, European integration theory has clearly moved beyond the well-known debate between supranational and intergovernmental institutionalists in the late 1980s and early 1990s (for an overview of this debate, see Rosamond 2000). This renewed interest in European integration theory was directly caused by the relaunch of European integration through the European Commission's White Paper on the completion of the internal market (1985) and the signing of the Single European Act (1986). After more than a decade of 'eurosclerosis', this unexpected revival of European integration heralded a short interval of 'europhoria', a period of unreflected optimism about the process of European integration – a mood in which, for some, even a federal Europe seemed possible in the near future. This period came to an end with the agreement on the Treaty of Maastricht in December 1991.[3] Since then, the theoretical debate on European integration has moved into the direction of a more eclectic approach. Not a single scholar still believes in an incremental, almost automatic process towards a federal Europe. And an increasing number of scholars seem to accept that nation-states are not the sole actors in EU decision making and that interstate bargaining is only part of a much more complex system of multilevel governance (MLG; a term first coined by Marks et al. 1996). The EU's hybrid nature is characterized by the existence of overlapping competencies among multiple levels of governance and by the interaction of political actors across those levels. MLG has become a common sense notion in mainstream integration literature.

148 Otto Holman

Although the MLG literature contributed to a better understanding of the institutional structures of the EU, some important corrections to this common-sense notion have to be made. As Bastiaan van Apeldoorn rightly pointed out, the bulk of mainstream integration literature is focused on *how* the structures of European governance are functioning, without raising the questions of *why* this multilevel system has emerged and *what kind* of European Union it seeks to promote (van Apeldoorn 2002: 5). One way of illustrating this point is to look at the specific nature of European integration thus far. It is as much about economic and monetary supranationalization (involving the creation of supranational structures of regulation and surveillance) as it is about strict intergovernmentalism, notably in the related social policy area. This comes close to what Paul Kapteyn calls 'the stateless market' (Kapteyn 1996). In short, European integration is about negative integration – i.e. the removal of all barriers to the free movement of goods, capital, services and (to a lesser extent) persons – and much less so about positive integration – i.e. the creation of new policy domains at the supranational level. 'Multilevel' then also means that some areas are moved to the supranational level while others are strictly reserved to national authorities claiming national sovereignty. One wonders why.

Part of the answer to this question is related to a second phenomenon. Part and parcel of multilevel decision making is the principle of *political* spillover. This refers to the fact that non-state actors (usually called 'lobby groups') move their lobbying activities to the European level in response to an increase in the policy-planning and law-making powers of notably the European Commission. It makes no sense to lobby at the national level when decision making is – or at least starts – in Brussels. In theory this seems a quite reasonable conclusion. But in practice we see an unequal distribution of 'capabilities to act' at the European level, an unequal access to the cupola of European decision making and – most importantly – an unequal outcome as far as agenda setting, policy planning and decision making are concerned. The post-war development of the welfare system – and, more specifically, the concomitant redistribution of income and decommodification of labour – was primarily the result of a class compromise between capital and labour, or more concretely, the outcome of concerted actions between organized labour and business in the context of Atlantic Fordism. If we look at the role of organized labour since the crisis of Fordism in the 1970s and 1980s, we see a dramatic decline in union density, negotiating power and capacity to act (see Ebbinghaus and Visser 1999). At the European level this is even more true, especially when compared to the extent in which European capital successfully organized itself in transnational planning bodies like the European Round Table of Industrialists (ERT; see van Apeldoorn 2002). In the absence of a strong institutional representation of labour at the European level, European capital is optimally using the 'multilevel playing field' that has been created within the European Union to fully implement its own neoliberal project and to arrange its own regional cohesion (Holman and van der Pijl 2003). If we compare the more recent role of trade unions to the one they played in the first two decades after World War II, we witness a comprehensive shift from demand-side to supply-side corporatism (both primarily at the national level), the latter reflecting the – albeit reluctant – participation of the cadres of national trade unions in the process of neoliberal restructuring (see Falkner 1997).

These two corrections – the asymmetrical nature of European regulation, premising supranational free market regulation over national social regulation, and the asymmetrical spillover of social actors to the European level – are a first step in answering the aforementioned questions of why MLG has emerged and what kind of EU it seeks to promote, i.e. in discovering the social purpose of MLG. In developing this argument further, I will first introduce the three interrelated components of what I prefer to call multi*dimensional* governance in Europe. My claim is that the EU is increasingly dominated by a New Trias Politica: the European Court of Justice (ECJ), the European Commission in close co-operation with organized business and the Council of Ministers. In the following, I will connect each of these three institutions to one particular component of multidimensional governance.

New constitutionalism and the European Court of Justice

First, European governance is characterized by what Stephen Gill calls new constitutionalism: the separation of 'economic policies from broad political accountability in order to make governments more responsive to the discipline of market forces, and correspondingly less responsive to popular-democratic forces and processes' (Gill 2001: 47). New constitutionalism within the European Union is very much related to the completion of the single market in the 1980s and early 1990s. One particularly strong example is the principle of mutual recognition that was originally formulated by the ECJ in the famous case Cassis de Dijon (1979) but introduced as a general principle to complete the internal market. According to this principle – which was intended to abolish technical barriers (such as national regulations related to health, safety and environmental standards, and to consumer protection) – products that are lawfully manufactured in one country must be admitted in other member states, irrespective of whether it complies with existing legislation in that member state or not. In more general terms, the political significance of this judgement of the ECJ boils down to the primacy of European over national law, of the Community's *acquis communautaire* over national legislators. In the words of Fritz Scharpf: 'By judicial fiat ... the freedom to sell and consume had achieved constitutional protection against the political judgement of democratically legitimised legislatures' (Scharpf 1999: 56). This first component of multidimensional governance is thus very much related to one of the pillars of the New Trias Politica: the role of the ECJ and the new constitutionalism enshrined in the European Treaties. The ECJ is first and foremost the European institution which guarantees a fair economic playing field or – in less neutral terms – ensures the free movement of market forces in a deregulated single market. It does not have substantial jurisdiction outside the first Pillar of the Maastricht Treaty, but it does play a central role in compelling compliance by member state governments with respect to the Community's *acquis communautaire* (which in turn is mainly concerned with the completion of the single market, and its institutional underpinnings).

Private–public partnerships: the European Commission and European business

A second feature of multidimensional governance in Europe is the phenomenon of private–public partnerships which has emerged – and to some extent been institutionalized – in the course of the 1990s. By this, we mean the informal and formal structures (or networks) where Chief Executive Officers (CEOs) of European capital, politicians and high representatives of the European cadres meet each other. It is particularly the agenda-setting and policy-planning capacity of these networks that is of importance here. And this is as much about decision making as it is about non-decision making: keeping specific policy areas or topics from the European agenda is as important as keeping the momentum of neoliberal restructuring and disembedding free market capitalism (under the banner of competitiveness).

The partnership between the European Commission and the aforementioned ERT is perhaps one of the most striking (and influential) examples in this respect. The European Commission is of particular importance in its policy-planning capacity and in its role as the *Guardian of the Treaties*. As far as the former task is concerned, the Commission operates in close co-operation with organized business. The ERT is a privileged agenda-setting and policy-planning group, privileged in its access to European institutions and member state governments and in its capacity to influence the European agenda. The relationship between the two can best be described as a 'symmetrical interdependent' one: the Commission and the ERT need each other in the realization of their respective goals. Already in the early years of its existence, a member of the Delors cabinet referred to the ERT in the following way: 'We see this group as a very useful bunch of people. These men are very powerful and very dynamic. They seed us with ideas. And, when necessary, they can ring up their own prime ministers and make their case' (quoted in Merritt 1986: 22). In other words, the Commission could (and can) use the members of the ERT in its attempt to strengthen its position vis-à-vis the member states, both in its policy-initiating and innovating capacity. On the other hand, the ERT needs the Commission because of its role as executive and co-legislature at the European level. The fact that the Commission has 'a quasi-monopoly of policy initiation and innovation inside the Community' (Church and Phinnemore 1994: 271) makes it the very political addressee of numerous interest groups. And again, among these interest groups the ERT is *primus inter pares*.

It is now generally acknowledged that the ERT played an important role in the relaunch of European integration in the 1980s, both with respect to the completion of the internal market and the development towards EMU (see Cowles 1994; Holman 1992; van Apeldoorn 2002). After Maastricht, the agenda-setting and policy-planning activities of the ERT shifted from a more comprehensive approach (including all the major issues of European integration) to an approach focused on the much more limited competitiveness discourse. Most of the reports of the ERT published after 1991 have European competitiveness as a central theme, with a strong emphasis on deregulation and labour market flexibilization. In the words of the former Secretary General of the ERT, Keith Richardson, 'the competitiveness of European business must be strengthened by making it possible to build an integrated free market economic system, with a maximum of flexibility and a minimum of regulation'; and more explicitly,

> jobs cannot be created by laws or by writing some new clause or chapter into the Treaty of Maastricht. What is urgently needed is the deregulation of labour markets and better education and training. New jobs will then follow from economic growth and the creation of wealth by business.
>
> *(Richardson 1997: 64–5)*

In 1995, then, the relationship between the European Commission and the ERT was institutionalized with the creation of the Competitiveness Advisory Group (CAG). As a co-initiative of the then German Commissioner for industry, Bangemann, and the ERT, the CAG would 'act as a watchdog, by subjecting policy proposals and new regulations to the test of international competitiveness' (ERT 1994: 3).

It is important to note that the emergent system of private–public partnership is by no means restricted to the EU level. The creation of the CAG coincided in time with the establishment of the Transatlantic Business Dialogue. This transatlantic network of representatives of the US government, the European Commission and American and European business leaders aims at deregulating transatlantic trade while covering such dispersed areas as genetically modified products and the next World Trade Organization free trade round (Cowles 2001). This example points at another difference with the MLG literature, which tends to concentrate on how the internal structures of European governance are functioning. A closer look at the way European governance is unfolding in reaction to (and as part of) global processes of neoliberal restructuring will bring us closer to an answer to the question of why this multilevel system has emerged and what kind of EU it seeks to promote (see below).

The new populism

Before we turn to this 'social purpose', a third component of multidimensional governance has to be introduced. Here the Council of Ministers, or better the representatives of national governments, comes in. As we indicated above, the new constitutionalism is very much about bypassing popular-democratic forces and processes, against the political judgement of democratically legitimized legislatures. This raises the question of how national governments try to find support among their respective national constituencies for the ongoing process of free market integration. The way national governments 'sell' neoliberal restructuring through multidimensional decision making to their national citizens can be best described in terms of the rise of a new populism.

The Council of Ministers is the ultimate decision maker and legislature (together with the European Parliament, since the introduction of the co-decision

152 Otto Holman

procedure) and controls – i.e. checks and restraints – the Commission. Its role as the guardian of the member states' interests has been effectively – and voluntarily – eroded since the ratification of the Single European Act in 1987, though primarily in the field of free market integration. Instead of being the political voice of culturally and historically distinct constituencies at the member state level, whose primary aim is to avoid integrational steps which run counter to the 'general interest' of the respective peoples, since the mid-1980s, the Council of Ministers (and the European Council) has increasingly become the European institution par excellence which defends and legitimizes the ongoing process of negative integration – and the concomitant processes of economic deregulation, privatization and labour market flexibilization – to the national constituencies while upholding the illusion of national sovereignty in other important areas. The rhetorical language of national governments in defence of national interests, values, identities and peculiarities is part of this illusion. In reality, however, a novel form of multidimensional governance is emerging, of which the new populism is an integral part, which supports the interests of an increasingly cohesive, transnational class of capital owners – embedded in transnational networks of political elites, bureaucracies and think tanks.

In a classical study of the phenomenon of populism, Ernesto Laclau came to a rather visionary conclusion:

> The emergence of populism is historically linked to a crisis of the dominant ideological discourse which is in turn part of a more general social crisis ... It is true that the long process of expansion of the forces of production which characterised Europe in the stage of monopoly capitalism increased the system's ability to absorb and neutralise its contradictions. But is also true that each time the capitalist system has experienced a serious crisis in Western Europe, various forms of populism have flourished. We need only think of the crisis after the First World War which produced the triumph of fascism, the world economic crisis which led to the ascent of Nazism, *and the world recession today that is accompanied by the multiplication of regionalisms that tend to be expressed in ideologies which make of populism a central moment.*
>
> *(Laclau 1977: 175–6, italics mine)*

Writing well before the relaunch of European integration in the second half of the 1980s, Laclau could not possibly foresee the impact of the global crisis of restructuring on European 'regionalism'. Neither could he realize in 1977 that the 'world recession of today' would turn into a deep, structural crisis, into a fundamental transformation of the global political economy, and into a dramatic transformation of national, social and cultural structures. The changing class relations underlying these transformations, and particularly the shift from the post-war Keynesian–Fordist class compromise to the neoliberal discipline of capital, could not be envisaged in the 1970s. In fact, resistance among organized labour and (part of) European capital substantially delayed neoliberal restructuring in the continental member states of the

European *Community*. It was only after the Treaty of Maastricht established a European *Union* that European integration became the vehicle of neoliberal restructuring. More specifically, the agreement on – and the subsequent move to – Economic and Monetary Union was a decisive step in finally breaking the resistance of labour and Fordist industry. It was only then that a direct appeal to 'the people' against established ideology took full shape. To understand why this direct appeal to the people is necessary in the EU of today, we need to introduce the notion of 'mobilization without integration'. But before that, we need to say a word about the general applicability of the notion of populism.

According to Pierre-André Taguieff, populism is not confined to specific movements, discourses or stages of capitalist development.

> Populism can only be conceptualised as a type of social and political *mobilization*, which means that the term can only designate a *dimension* of political action or discourse. It does not embody a particular type of political regime, nor does it define a particular ideological content. It is a political style applicable to various ideological frameworks.
>
> *(Taguieff 1995: 9)*

In this article, the New Populism in today's Europe is viewed as an integral component of what we referred to as multidimensional governance, and a dimension of the more comprehensive discourse of neoliberalism. It is a political style which attempts to reconcile supranational, economic and monetary integration with the illusion of national self-determination in dismantling (or in the words of today's leaders: modernizing) post-war welfare state structures. And it is a political style that presents emerging structures of new constitutionalism and public–private partnership as serving the general interest. The general interest is then defined in terms of improving competitiveness in a global setting.

Let us return for a moment to the analysis of Laclau. In discussing the theory of transitional stages as developed by Gino Germani, he distinguished four 'asynchronisms', i.e. co-existing elements which belong, respectively, to the two poles of the transitional stage (in the case of Germani's study traditional and industrial society). Here I will focus on two asynchronisms, the geographical and institutional ones (quoted in Laclau 1977: 147–50), and apply them to the present situation in the EU.[4] In my view, the heartland of European capitalism is witnessing a fundamental transition from a nationally embedded, Keynesian–Fordist class compromise to a new, transnational hegemonic configuration based on neoliberal restructuring, or, perhaps even more important, from an industrial to a post-industrial society. In this context, the two asynchronisms come fully to the fore.

First, the geographical one refers to the co-existence of central and peripheral states, rich and poor regions, and included and excluded social groups (participating in the 'new' and the 'old' economies, respectively). In the European Union of today, net-paying countries co-exist with the so-called cohesion countries (Spain, Portugal, Greece and Ireland) and this geographical asynchronism has become much more problematic after the 'big bang' enlargement towards Central and Eastern Europe. If we look at the sub-national, regional level, disparities between the richest and poorest regions are even bigger. Moreover, 25 years of structural policy in the EU has not reduced this gap in any substantial way. Finally, we may refer to the 'split-level' societies (or to use an old term from development theory: dual societies) that are emerging in Europe: an ever bigger gap between the winners and losers of free market integration, between the employed and unemployed, and between the 'new middle classes' and an underclass of migrant workers. In geographical terms, this gap is manifested by the physical segregation in urban conglomerates.

Institutional asynchronism refers to the co-existence of institutions corresponding to different phases. Here we may think of the co-existence of the institutions of national civil societies which played a prominent role during the phase of Keynesian–Fordist class compromise (political parties, trade unions, etc.), on the one hand, and the new structures and institutions of multidimensional governance in the EU, on the other. This brings us back to the notion of mobilization without integration. In the words of Laclau:

> By *mobilisation* is understood the process whereby formerly passive groups acquire *deliberative* behaviour (i.e. intervention in national life, which may oscillate between inorganic protest movements and legalised activity channelled through political parties). By *integration* is understood that type of mobilisation: (1) which is carried out through existing politico-institutional channels and is thus legalised by the regime in power; (2) in which the regime's framework of legitimacy is implicitly or explicitly accepted by the mobilised groups, such that the rules of the game of the existing legality are accepted.
>
> *(Laclau 1977: 148–9)*

An excellent example of mobilization and integration going hand in hand is the post-war Keynesian–Fordist symbiosis between organized capital and labour. The present situation in the EU shows an entirely different picture. As a result of the geographical and institutional asynchronisms, mobilization through integration is impossible in the present system of multidimensional governance in Europe. One of the consequences of this situation is the emergence of xenophobic, nationalist movements in a number of EU member states and the rise of an 'inorganic protest movement' commonly referred to as 'anti-globalists'. For the purpose of this article, however, it is important to note that the elites of the new Europe try to overcome the impossibility of 'mobilisation carried out through integration' by appealing directly to 'the people'. New populism must then be seen as a new type of social and political mobilization without integration. It is 'new' since it uses the structures of Europe's multidimensional governance and it is 'new' because it attempts to articulate different visions of the world – the one of an emerging power bloc at the transnational European level and the ones of the different 'peoples' of Europe – in such a way that their potential antagonism is neutralized. To quote Laclau once more, populist discourses 'constitute the complex of interpellations which express the "people"/power bloc contradiction as distinct from a class contradiction' (Laclau 1977: 167). And this is exactly what is at stake when we talk about mobilization without integration in the present system of multidimensional governance in the EU.

In the next section, we will try to show that the New Trias Politica of the European Union attempts to articulate a transnational class discourse aimed at recommodification – and, hence, further exploitation – of labour by mobilizing the 'peoples' of Europe – and, more particularly, the new middle classes – behind 'a new strategic goal for the next decade: to become the most competitive and dynamic knowledge-based economy in the world capable of sustainable economic growth with more jobs and greater social cohesion' (Lisbon European Council 2000: 2). It will be argued that this competitiveness discourse forms an illustration of what we here referred to as new populism inasmuch as it attempts to mask the class contradiction inherent to the process of neoliberal restructuring through neutralizing the potential antagonism between the 'peoples of Europe' and the transnational power bloc.

Constitutionalizing social policy: the new populism at work

After having outlined the notion of multidimensional governance, we have to emphasize the mutually reinforcing character of these three dimensions, which are 'superimposed dimensions of reality, where "facts" pertinent to one dimension only acquire their full meaning if they are considered against the background of the other dimensions' (Overbeek 1990: 87). In a similar way we can distinguish the three pillars of the New Trias Politica – the judiciary, the legislature and the executive – while at the same time realizing that these three powers strongly overlap in practice (like in most national polities). We can now turn to the multi-dimensionality of European restructuring and the consequences of asymmetrical regulation in terms of social deregulation nationally. In order to do so, I will first look into the direct impact of supranational economic and monetary regulation on the manoeuvring space of national governments, both in macro-economic and monetary and, as a consequence, in social terms.

In a speech held in 2001, the Dutch Commissioner for Internal Market Affairs, Frits Bolkestein, directly referred to the above quote from the presidency conclusions of the Lisbon European Council in March 2000. The EU's ambition to have the most competitive economy in the world in 2010 ('more competitive, that is, than the American economy') implied that

> we must leave the comfortable surroundings of the Rhineland and move closer to the tougher conditions and colder climate of the Anglo-Saxon form of capitalism, where the rewards are greater but the risks also ... We must avoid the resurgence of the Scylla and Charybdis of the past. These Scylla and

156 Otto Holman

Charybdis are economic nationalism and corporatism, respectively. Economic nationalism has taken the form of the so-called 'golden-shares', which are used to ward off foreign purchasers of domestic stock. Corporatism means the belief that management knows better what is good for shareholders than they themselves.

(Bolkestein 2001)

In order to meet the objective of competitiveness, Bolkestein argued, governments of member states would have only one category of measures left: micro-economic supply-side structural adjustment. This is because of EMU. It goes without saying that the governments of the eurozone can no longer resort to competitive devaluations. But they have also lost the possibility to influence their economies by monetary means. It is the ECB that sets the interest rate to ensure the stability of prices. In order to avoid misunderstanding, he added that 'the interest rate cannot serve two masters: the economic cycle and the stability of prices. It is the latter which must rule' (2001). Finally, and as a result of the Stability and Growth Pact, governments have – by and large – lost the instrument of fiscal policy. In the absence of a strong European government with strong redistributive powers, structural imbalances between member states can only be neutralized through adjusting product and labour markets. In short, the structural improvement of the micro-economic supply side is the only thing left to governments. The following quote indicates what Bolkestein had in mind:

Now micro-economic supply side structural adjustments are painful. It is no use denying this. That is why they are politically unpopular and thus difficult to carry out. Most people are conservative. Why should things change? Aren't they well off as it is? Why must they do things differently? Won't the future bring more uncertainty? Most trade unions are also conservative. They want to remain within the safe and cosy confines of what has come to be known as 'the Rhineland model' of capitalism, in which not shareholders but stake-holders are cherished and consultation takes place at numerous round tables.

In order to increase competitiveness, this 'corporatist atavism' has to be challenged. One does not have to have great imagination to see that Bolkestein referred – first and foremost – to the adjustment of labour market structures, i.e. to more flexible labour markets. If Europe wants to take the Lisbon ambitions seriously, there is no other option than to dismantle the 'cosy' welfare structures of the Keynesian–Fordist era. Most importantly, economic and monetary regulation at the European level leave national governments no other choice than to embark on this shift from demand-side to supply-side corporatism. These bold statements (from a commissioner who used to play the Eurosceptic card – under the slogan 'Europe is done' – while still leader of the Dutch Liberal Party) draw a direct link between EMU and the 'need' for labour market flexibility. As such they form a nice illustration of asymmetrical regulation: in the absence of supranational regulation in the field of social policy, the only other option left is national decline in a globalizing world (or, worse, economic nationalism). But the 'need' to impose micro-economic supply-side structural adjustments on reluctant social partners is one thing, the actual implementation of welfare state reforms is a totally different thing. Here, again, Europe offers a helping hand.

In order to fully grasp this last point, we have to emphasize that the relation between EMU and employment/unemployment goes much deeper than suggested by Bolkestein. It is no coincidence that the move towards EMU in the course of the 1990s went hand in hand with skyrocketing unemployment rates in the eurozone countries. A number of cause–effect relations can be discerned: the convergence race between the member states of the EU to meet the nominal, macro-economic criteria had a negative impact on employment creation; as a result of (the prospect of) monetary integration, a spectacular increase in (cross-border) take-overs and mergers took place, almost always coinciding with massive labour shedding; as a result of this concentration and centralization of capital in Europe, shareholder values have become more important, which in turn has led to labour shedding as a means to restore confidence among shareholders; since EMU did and does not include fiscal harmonization, fiscal (or regime) competition has become one of the leading practices in today's Europe, resulting in lower taxes on capital and, at least until the mid-1990s, higher taxes on labour.

But facilitating the flexible hire and fire of people at the member state level was not an easy task. In order to co-ordinate national efforts in this field, a European Employment Strategy came into effect in the second half of the 1990s. In retrospect, it can be concluded that the so-called open method of co-ordination of national employment and labour market policies was first enshrined in the 1997 Treaty of Amsterdam. As a direct consequence of the treaty's new employment chapter, the European Commission was asked to distil from a best-practice comparison specific but non-binding (read: open) recommendations on the basis of equally non-binding employment policy guidelines. To date, four broad guidelines structure the European Employment Strategy (which were initially formulated at the Extraordinary European Council Meeting on Employment in Luxembourg in November 1997):

- improving employability, inter alia by moving from passive to active labour market policies and promoting life-long learning. Active labour market policies include reforms of tax and social security policies (aiming at an increase of the gap between minimum wages and unemployment benefits), making it 'more attractive' for the unemployed to take up jobs;
- developing entrepreneurship by making it easier to start up and run businesses and making the taxation system more employment-friendly;
- encouraging adaptability of businesses and their employees by modernizing the organization of work, including flexible working arrangements, and by incorporating into national law more adaptable types of contract;
- strengthening the policies for equal opportunities: tackling gender gaps, reconciling work and family life and facilitating reintegration into the labour

158 Otto Holman

market. This objective seems first and foremost directed at increasing employment rates in Europe.

These employment guidelines are drawn up at Community level and then translated into National Employment Action Programmes. In 1999, a Peer Review Programme started. This 'dissemination of best practices of member states in labour market policies has the overall aim of enhancing transferability and mutual learning processes and promoting greater convergence towards the main EU goals' (http://p eerreview.almp.org/en/principles.htm, 29 November 2001). As indicated above, these 'main EU goals' were reformulated at the Lisbon European Council meeting of March 2000 as 'a new strategic goal for the next decade: to become the most competitive and dynamic knowledge-based economy in the world capable of sustainable economic growth with more jobs and greater social cohesion'.

At the very heart of the open method of co-ordination (of employment and labour market policies) is the concept of benchmarking. This concept originally refers to the use of best practice in management strategies, i.e. learning from the performance of 'best competitors' in a continuous attempt to increase competitiveness. Since the mid-1990s, it has been consistently promoted by the ERT in its deliberations with the European Commission. In a 1996 report called *Benchmarking for policy-makers*, the ERT defined benchmarking as

> a simple, flexible and above all dynamic process. It helps companies and governments to compare their own performance with the best in the world, and to motivate everybody concerned to do better ... No organisation today can afford to rest on its laurels in a world where last year's achievements are already gathering dust, remote and irrelevant ... Benchmarking succeeds because it works with human nature. It doesn't simply tell people to do better, it shows them how to do so by demonstrating what other people are doing ... Benchmarking is non-stop. It is a tool to bring about the continuous improvement and adaptation which are the only means to survival in a continually changing world.
>
> *(ERT 1996: 5)*

Benchmarking for policy-makers in the field of employment and labour market policies then primarily boils downs to scanning the world (i.e. introducing Anglo-Saxon practices of internal and external labour market flexibilization), to motivating workers to do better by reducing social protection, to enhance individual competition (as part of human nature) and to adaptation in a continuous survival of the fittest.

In such a continually changing world, social cohesion is reduced to mere statistics. It is about increasing employment rates and gross domestic product per capita levels, first and foremost by making Europe 'the most competitive and dynamic knowledge-based economy in the world'. If we accept, on the other hand, a definition of social cohesion as 'the political tolerability of the levels of economic and social disparity that exist and are expected in the European Union and of the measures that are in place to deal with them' (Mayes 1995: 1), we may come to entirely different conclusions. In the end, political tolerability is tested during elections. And national political elites are well aware of this fact of life.

That is why the European Employment Strategy attempts to reconcile supranational, economic and monetary integration with the illusion of national self-determination in 'modernizing' the so-called European social model. In the words of the Lisbon European Council, 'achieving the new strategic goal will rely primarily on the private sector, as well on public–private partnerships. It will depend on mobilizing the resources available on the markets, as well on efforts by member states.' In terms of governance, however,

> A fully decentralised approach will be applied in line with the principle of subsidiarity in which the Union, the Member States, the regional and local levels, as well as the social partners and civil society, will be actively involved, using variable forms of partnership. A method of benchmarking best practices on managing change will be devised by the European Commission network-ing with different providers and users, namely the social partners, companies and NGOs.
>
> *(Lisbon European Council 2000)*

It is this uneasy combination of public–private partnerships at the European level (agenda setting and policy planning) and national governance (implementation) that is at the heart of the new populism in Europe. In an 'integrated market governed by fragmented sovereignty', as Wolfgang Streeck argues, 'the wielders of that sovereignty compete with one another, in part for the respect of their citizens ... but most importantly for the allegiance of mobile production factors' (Streeck 1997: 3). The 'open method of co-ordination' of labour market policies is perhaps one of the best examples of this: in keeping up the illusion of the 'persistent plurality of national citizenship regimes' it introduces mechanisms of regime competition in the field of social policy. More specifically, peer pressure and recommendations from the European Commission are used to make domestic political and social relations more fluid and more adaptable to the exigencies of European capital. Or to put it differently, the open method of co-ordination is a process of

> construction, diffusion and institutionalization of procedures, policy para-digms, styles, 'ways of doing things' and shared beliefs, which are first defined and consolidated in the making of EU decisions and then incorporated in the logic of domestic discourse, identities, political structures and public policies.[5]
>
> *(Radaelli 2003: 30)*

In our terms, then, it is about mobilization without integration and it is about separating employment and labour market policies from broad political account-ability in order to make national governments more responsive to the discipline of market forces (the 'new constitutionalism'). The European Employment Strategy is

160 Otto Holman

certainly not a supranational policy, but neither is it strictly intergovernmental of nature. The open method of co-ordination underlying this strategy is a new political style which successfully attempts to reconcile supranational, economic and monetary integration with the illusion of national self-determination in dismantling (or, in official discourse, modernizing and flexibilizing) post-war welfare state structures.

Concluding remarks

In the past, enlargement has been the most formidable obstacle to social policy integration (as an alternative to asymmetrical regulation). The successive enlargement rounds did not only bring together different welfare states with different institutional practices in the field of social policy broadly defined, but did also dramatically increase the gap between rich and poor member states in terms of expenditures on social protection as a percentage of gross domestic product (see Scharpf 2002: 646). In fact, every new round of accession agreements reduced the possibility of an effective harmonization of social policies at the European level. The recent big bang enlargement towards Central and Eastern Europe will make the prospect of future harmonization even more unlikely. Indeed, one could argue that one of the consequences of the enlargement strategy of the EU (and particularly its stress on the economic Copenhagen criteria) – i.e. a relative cut in social expenditure in most of the applicant countries – has further increased the social gap between rich and poor countries (and regions) in an enlarged union (see Holman 2001).

In this sense, enlargement towards Central and Eastern Europe will further obstruct any attempt to overhaul the European system of asymmetrical regulation:

- it will consolidate the gap between supranational regulation in the field of single market and monetary integration, on the one hand, and national (de) regulation in social affairs, on the other, and hence consolidate the unlinking of economic and social policies; and
- it will consolidate (if not further) the link between (re)regulation in the field of single market and monetary integration at the European level, on the one hand, and deregulation of labour market structures, on the other, and hence consolidate (if not further) the linking of the *consequences* of different policies.

To some, enlargement may have been the vehicle to prevent social harmonization, but the completion of the single market and – perhaps more importantly – the move towards monetary union can be held responsible for the externally induced restructuring of welfare state regimes at the national level. The recent conflict between the re-elected Schröder government and the German trade unions over the proposed labour market reforms and the social conflict in France over the proposed pension reforms are two important illustrations of this.

In terms of our discussion of the emerging model of multidimensional governance in the EU, developments within the European Convention point at a further institutionalization of this model. The final text of the Constitutional Treaty is based on the conclusions of the different working groups of the Convention. Particularly the working groups on the Principle of Subsidiarity, on Economic Governance, and on Social Europe have played an essential role in constitutionalizing the twin principles of subsidiarity and benchmarking. The working group on Social Europe concluded that existing competences of the EU in the social field were adequate and 'that action at the European level should focus on issues related to the functioning of the single market and/or areas with a considerable cross-border impact'. It further supported the inclusion of the open method of co-ordination in the Treaty. But this provision 'should indicate clearly that the open method of co-ordination cannot be used to undermine existing Union or Member State competence' (Secretariat of the European Convention 2003). One of the main conclusions of the working group on Economic Governance was that the 'current structure whereby exclusive competence for monetary policy within the Eurozone lies with the Community, exercised by the ECB ... and competence for economic policy lies with the Member States, should be maintained' (Secretariat of the European Convention 2002a).

In both cases, the status quo of asymmetrical regulation is thus prioritized and, indeed, incorporated (read: constitutionalized) into the Constitutional Treaty, notably in the articles III-101 (employment) and III-104 (social policy), where it is stated that 'European laws or framework laws may establish ... measures designed to encourage co-operation between Member States' but that such laws shall not include any 'harmonisation of the laws and regulations of the Member States'. It is no exaggeration to conclude that the three defining elements of a political community, based on three kinds of integration, as pointed out by the federalist Amitai Etzioni (i.e. an effective control over the means of violence, a centre of decision making that is able to affect significantly the allocation of resources and rewards throughout the community, and the dominant focus of political identification for the large majority of politically aware citizens; see Etzioni 1965: 4), did not form part of the guiding principles of the (majority of the) national and European representatives to the Convention. In fact, the working group on the Principle of Subsidiarity proposed the reinforcement of the application of the principle of subsidiarity in its restricted, narrowly defined meaning (i.e. a laissez-faire, bottom-up concept of subsidiarity; Secretariat of the European Convention 2002b).

The compliance with this bottom-up division of competences is subject to judicial review by the European Court of Justice, and guaranteed by the Constitutional Treaty. By simultaneously constitutionalizing the limited Community competences in social affairs, this reinforcement of the application of the principle of subsidiarity boils down to the continuation of the mechanisms of asymmetrical regulation in the foreseeable future. To put it in other words, by using the populist argument against an 'oversocialized' Hobbesian conception of a would-be controlling (European) state, echoing the Thatcherite opposition to even a minimal move towards Social Europe, an 'undersocialized' Lockean conception of the national state has been the outcome of the constitutional deliberations in the European Convention (cf. Etzioni 1988: 8). This may be accepted by the different constituencies of the EU as long as the 'geographical asynchronism', as referred to in section 3, can be neutralized by measures that are in place to deal with existing – or expected – levels of economic and social disparity between and within member states. For the moment, developments point in another direction. If at some point in the history of European integration the national welfare state may have been the most important obstacle to social policy integration (or harmonization), it is the victory of transnational market forces and the mechanisms of asymmetrical regulation and multidimensional governance that makes it the most vulnerable institution in the European Union of today

Postscript

Two core concepts in my 2004 article, namely, 'asymmetrical regulation' and 'new populism', foreshadowed in a way what Dani Rodrik famously described as 'the inescapable trilemma of the world economy'. He posited the incompatibility of democracy, national sovereignty and economic and monetary integration, asserting that 'we can combine any two of the three, but never have all three simultaneously and in full' (Rodrik 2007). Applied to contemporary Europe: if we want more or deeper economic and monetary integration we must either cede some democratic accountability or some member state sovereignty.

The architects of the post-Cold War completion of the Single Market and creation of the monetary union led us to believe that they could square the circle. Liberalization, privatization and deregulation through reregulation at a higher level were deemed necessary to boost economic growth and create more jobs at home. The relaunch of European integration was presented as a second 'European rescue of the nation state' (Milward 1994), albeit under different, neoliberal circumstances. In the context of multi-level governance, economic and monetary regulation at the European level and social regulation at the national level became two sides of the same euro. This 'division of labour' between the New Trias Politica in Europe and national authorities was constitutionalized in the 2009 Treaty of Lisbon. This occurred basically according to the established practices as described in my article, including the co-ordinating task of the European institutions in streamlining national labour market policies.

The distribution of competences over different levels of decision making soon proved to be a case of top-down Europeanization in disguise. The appearance of sovereignty, and indeed the illusion of self-determination, in social affairs collided with the reality of deep economic integration in times of crisis. The sovereign debt crisis clearly showed the perverse effects of the 'stateless market' form of integration. It revealed that economic and monetary reregulation at the supranational level in the absence of political union effectively entailed social deregulation at the national level. Skyrocketing government debts were countered with the most extreme austerity measures since the crisis of the 1970s, notably in the so-called deficit countries. Traditional crisis management measures – government spending, protectionism, fixing of interest and exchange rates – were no longer possible or, at least, no longer deemed possible. In case of severe macro-economic imbalances, two instruments are left to the national sovereigns and both sets of measures may have negative social effects and/or result in a deterioration of social protection schemes. These are regulatory competition (for example, the downward adjustment of corporate tax rates) and so-called structural reforms. The latter basically involve bringing fiscal deficits down to zero and flexibilizing labour markets. The political platform on which Emmanuel Macron won the 2017 presidential elections in France included all three elements and is only one of many recent examples.

Deep economic and monetary integration thus eroded national sovereignty in macro-economic policy making directly and in social regulation indirectly. Contrary to what the democratic deficit literature (e.g. Føllesdal and Hix 2006) wants us to believe, democracy was not affected in this relaunching of European integration (Moravcsik 2002). Practices at the transnational or supranational level such as the political independence of the European Central Bank did not differ from (previously) existing national practices. However, the relaunch did cause a *social* deficit in a double sense: it effectively disempowered the post-war institutions of social integration and it dismantled post-war welfare state structures. In short, it facilitated 'social and political mobilisation without integration' (Holman, this volume, p. 154). My article focused on the (transnational) elite discourse of competitiveness and only mentioned in passing 'the emergence of xenophobic, nationalist movements'.

In 2003–2004, I did not foresee the triple crisis or, perhaps better, did not fully appreciate its potential effects on European integration. Institutional impasse, sovereign debt and the mismanagement of migratory flows have fuelled Euroscepticism to the extent that 'mobilization without integration' has become a real threat to the EU. In the meantime, the main political victim of this trend seems to be European social democracy. Shortly after publication, and juggling with the concept of populism in its 'old' and 'new' varieties, I once told an audience of Dutch social democrats that Wim (after Wim Kok, former prime minister (1994–2002) during the short interval of Third Way 'socialism' and leader of the Dutch Labour Party) had given birth to Pim (after Pim Fortuyn, the Dutch populist who was murdered in 2002). Rereading my 2004 article, I find elements of an explanation for the current demise of social democratic parties all over Europe. This also leads to a slight adjustment of Rodrik's trilemma: it is *social* democracy, not democracy, which does not match with deep economic integration and national sovereignty.

Notes

1 An earlier version of this paper was presented at the Conference on Global Regulation at the University of Sussex, 29–31 May 2003. I would like to thank Magnus Ryner, Jean-Christophe Graz and two anonymous reviewers for their valuable comments.
2 Not any more, one should add. A case in point is the recent turn of the (traditionally pro-European and federalist) Dutch labour party. The leader of the PvdA, and successor of Wim Kok, Wouter Bos, presented the new European strategy of his party in March 2004. His speech, titled *Beyond federalism: a new realism in Europe*, can be downloaded from his website www.wouterbos.nl (under 'speeches').

164 Otto Holman

3 In Maastricht all explicit references to what was left of the federalists' objectives were deleted from the draft treaty that was prepared under the Luxembourg and Dutch presidencies. The EU's 'federal goal', for instance, was changed in 'an ever-closer union among the peoples of Europe, in which decisions are taken as closely as possible to the citizen in accordance with the principle of subsidiarity' (Preamble of the Treaty on European Union).

4 The other two are labelled as sociological and motivational asynchronisms. Sociological asynchronism can be divided into 'objective' characteristics (employed or unemployed, occupation in different sectors of the economy) and 'subjective' ones: 'attitudes, social character, social personality' corresponding to 'advanced' and 'backward' stages, respectively. The latter one comes close to motivational asynchronism: 'because the same individual belongs to multiple different groups and institutions, asynchronism affects the individual himself. There co-exist in his psyche attitudes, ideas, motivations, beliefs corresponding to successive "stages" of the process' (Germani 1965, quoted in Laclau 1977: 148).

5 Editors' note: The original 1999 reference was to an unpublished draft text, which was eventually published in 2003.

References

van Apeldoorn, B. (2002). *Transnational capitalism and the struggle over European integration.* London: Routledge.

Bolkestein, F. (2001). European competitiveness. Speech for the Ambrosetti Annual Forum, 'Intelligence 2001 on the World, on Europe, on Italy'. Cernobbio, Italy, 8 September.

Church, C.H. and Phinnemore, D. (1994). *European Union and European Community. A handbook and commentary on the post-Maastricht treaties.* London: Harvester Wheatsheaf.

Cowles, M.G. (1994). *The politics of big business in the European Community. Setting the agenda for a new Europe,* PhD dissertation. Washington, DC: American University.

Cowles, M.G. (2001). The transatlantic business dialogue. Transforming the new transatlantic dialogue. In M.A. Pollack and G.C. Shaffer (Eds), *Transatlantic governance in the global economy* (pp. 213–233). Lanham, MD: Rowman and Littlefield.

Ebbinghaus, B. and Visser, J. (1999). When institutions matter. Union growth and decline in Western Europe, 1950–1995. *European Sociological Review* 15(2): 135–158.

ERT (1994). *European competitiveness. The way to growth and jobs.* Brussels: ERT.

ERT (1996). *Benchmarking for policy-makers. The way to competitiveness, growth and job creation.* Brussels: ERT.

Etzioni, A. (1965). *Political unification. A comparative study of leaders and forces.* New York: Holt, Rinehart & Winston.

Etzioni, A. (1988). *The moral dimension. Towards a new economics.* New York: Free Press.

Falkner, G. (1997). Corporatist governance and Europeanisation. No future in the multi-level game? *European Integration Online Papers* 1(11): 1–20.

Føllesdal, A. and Hix, S. (2006). Why there is a democratic deficit in the EU: A response to Majone and Moravcsik. *Journal of Common Market Studies* 44(3): 533–562.

Gill, S. (2001). Constitutionalising capital: EMU and disciplinary neo-liberalism. In A. Bieler and A.D. Morton (Eds), *Social forces in the making of the new Europe. The restructuring of European social relations in the global political economy* (pp. 47–69). Basingstoke: Palgrave.

Holman, O. (1992). Introduction. Transnational class strategy and the new Europe. *International Journal of Political Economy* 22(1): 3–22.

Holman, O. (2001). The enlargement of the European Union towards Central and Eastern Europe. The role of supranational and transnational actors. In A. Bieler and A.D. Morton (Eds), *Social forces in the making of the new Europe. The restructuring of European social relations in the global political economy* (pp. 161–184). Basingstoke: Palgrave.

Holman, O. and van der Pijl, K. (2003). Structure and process in transnational European business. In A.W. Cafruny and M. Ryner (Eds), *A ruined fortress. Neoliberal hegemony and transformation in Europe* (pp. 71–93). Oxford: Rowman & Littlefield.

Kapteyn, P. (1996). *The stateless market. The European dilemma of integration and civilisation.* London: Routledge.

Laclau, E. (1977). *Politics and ideology in Marxist theory. Capitalism, fascism, populism.* London: NLB.

Lisbon European Council (2000). *Presidency conclusions.* 23 and 24 March.

Majone, G. (1996). Regulation and its modes. In G. Majone (Ed.), *Regulating Europe* (pp. 9–27). London: Routledge.

Marks, G., Hooghe, L. and Blank, K. (1996). European integration from the 1980s: State-centric versus multi-level governance. *Journal of Common Market Studies* 34(3): 341–378.

Mayes, D. (1995). Introduction: Conflict and cohesion in the Single European Market. A reflection. In A. Amin and J. Tomaney (Eds), *Behind the myth of European Union. Prospects for cohesion* (pp. 1–9). London: Routledge.

Merritt, G. (1986). Knights of the Roundtable: Can they move Europe forward fast enough? *International Management26* July: 22–26.

Milward, A. (1994). *The European rescue of the nation-state*, 2nd ed. London: Routledge.

Moravcsik, A. (2002). In defence of the 'democratic deficit'. Reassessing legitimacy in the European Union. *Journal of Common Market Studies* 40(4): 603–624.

Overbeek, H. (1990). *Global capitalism and national decline. The Thatcher decade in perspective.* London: Unwin Hyman.

Overbeek, H. (2003). Transnational political economy and the politics of European (un) employment. In *The political economy of European employment* (pp. 1–10). London: Routledge.

Peel, Q. (2004). The personal spat that poisons Europe. *Financial Times*, 24 June.

Prakash, A. and Hart, J.A. (1999). Globalization and governance. An introduction. In *Globalization and governance* (pp. 1–24). London: Routledge.

Radaelli, C.M. (2003). The Europeanisation of public policy. In K. Featherstone and C. M. Radaelli (Eds), *The politics of Europeanisation* (pp. 27–56). Oxford: Oxford University Press.

Richardson, K. (1997). Het primaat van concurrentievermogen. Het Europese Bedrijfsleven en de Intergouvernementele Conferenie van 1996. In O. Holman (Ed.), *Europese Dilemma's aan het einde van de twintigste eeuw. Democratie, werkgelegenheid, veiligheid, immigratie* (pp. 58–67). Amsterdam: Het Spinhuis.

Rodrik, D. (2007). The inescapable trilemma of the world economy. http://rodrik.typepad.com/dani_rodriks_weblog/2007/06/the-inescapable.html (accessed 6 November 2017).

Rosamond, B. (2000). *Theories of European integration.* London: Macmillan.

Sampiemon, J.H. (1998). Manipulatie achter Europese façades. *NRC Handelsblad*, 19 June.

Scharpf, F.W. (1999). *Governing in Europe. Effective and democratic?*Oxford: Oxford University Press.

Scharpf, F.W. (2002). The European Social Model. Coping with the challenges of diversity. *Journal of Common Market Studies* 40(4): 645–670.

Secretariat of the European Convention (2002a). Final Report of Working Group VI on Economic Governance. Brussels: CONV 357/02, 21 October.

Secretariat of the European Convention (2002b). Conclusions of Working Group I on the Principle of Subsidiarity. Brussels: CONV 286/02, 23 September.

Secretariat of the European Convention (2003). Final Report of Working Group XI on Social Europe. Brussels: CONV 516/1/03, 4 February.

Streeck, W. (1997). Citizenship under regime competition. The case of the European Works Councils. *European Integration Online Papers* 1(5): 1–29.

Taguieff, P.-A. (1995). Political science confronts populism. From a conceptual mirage to a real problem. *Telos* 103: 9–43.

PART II
Critical commentaries

7

CLASS FRACTIONS AND HEGEMONIC CONCEPTS OF CONTROL

Andreas Bieler and Adam David Morton

From the seminal volume by Kees van der Pijl (1984) on *The making of an Atlantic ruling class* through Henk Overbeek's (1990) assessment of *Global capitalism and Britain's decline* to contributions by a younger generation on capital's role in European integration and the political economy of Sweden (e.g. van Apeldoorn 2002; Ryner 2003), the Amsterdam School (AS) has contributed significantly to our understanding of political economy. Rather than adopting a state-centric analysis of international politics, an uncritical liberal assessment of the assumed benefits of globalization, or an ahistorical emphasis on institutional structures, this group of scholars has revealed the underlying structural dynamics around capitalist social relations of production and how material interests have constituted neoliberal restructuring.

This short commentary outlines how academics from the AS have informed our analyses; critically engages with the notion that the AS constitutes a distinctive approach before warning against the very notion of 'school' formation; and concludes that, rather than employing the same set of inherited concepts, critical scholars today should embrace wider debates to offer a broader historical materialist perspective on the geopolitics of global capitalism.

Important influences

Embarking on our academic careers at the end of the 1990s, AS work provided a breath of fresh air in a situation where discussions of globalization were dominated by exchanges between state-centric neorealists and market-focused liberals. For Andreas, an article by Otto Holman (1992) proved crucial for his analysis of Austria's and Sweden's accession to the European Union (EU) in 1995 (Bieler 2000). While Andreas already recognized that social class fractions are the main collective actors to be investigated, how to identify them in concrete empirical research was

170 Andreas Bieler and Adam David Morton

another matter. Holman's interest in the links among rival comprehensive concepts of control, transnational class strategy, and European integration prompted him to produce four ideal typical fractions of capital based on their production sites and trading horizons: 1) import-competing producers of tradable goods for the domestic market; 2) import-competing producers of tradable goods for the European market; 3) export-competing producers of tradable goods for the world market; and 4) globally operating financial institutions (Holman 1992: 16). This allowed Andreas not simply to distinguish between national and transnational class fractions of capital and labour (reflecting the level at which production is organized) but to sub-divide the former into nationally oriented social forces, engendered by national production for the domestic market, and internationally oriented social forces, stemming from national production for export (Bieler 2000: 47). It was thereby possible to divide Austrian and Swedish capital and labour into meaningful class fractions for a heuristically powerful analysis of these two countries' accession to the EU.

For Adam, it was an article by Kees van der Pijl (1989) that first stimulated a focus on class, hegemony, and the states system within which to elaborate a historical materialist analysis of the historical sociology of state formation. Kees cited the following passage from Antonio Gramsci: 'It is in the concept of hegemony that those exigencies which are national in character are knotted together … A class that is international in character has … to "nationalise" itself in a certain sense' (Gramsci 1971: 241, Q14§68).

Thus, as van der Pijl (1989: 12; 1996: 307) commented, the struggle for hegemony involves 'translating' particular interests, from a particular form of state, into forms of expansion that have universal applicability across diverse states. Usually, it is within this nodal 'national' context that hegemony is initially constructed prior to outward expansion on a world scale and is associated with struggles over class hegemony. This approach has informed van der Pijl's expansive and wide-ranging contribution to Marxist historical sociology, especially in relation to the theory of passive revolution. For van der Pijl this condition refers to a process of 'molecular' class formation governed by the relations between different types of state (van der Pijl 1998: 82, 105). These coordinates inspired Adam's more detailed reconnaissance of the concept and condition of passive revolution as it emerges from Gramsci's *Prison notebooks* (Morton 2007). Furthermore, it was this theorization of passive revolution and its affinity with the structuring condition of uneven and combined development that enabled an expansive analysis of the historical sociology of modern state formation in Mexico (Morton 2013).

A distinctive Amsterdam School?

There is no doubt about the significance of the AS to debates in and beyond political economy from the 1980s onwards. We nonetheless remain deeply sceptical about the existence of a distinctive AS in international political economy. Embarking on our doctoral projects in the mid-1990s, we regarded the work by

Amsterdam colleagues as part of a broader, novel turn towards historical materialism inspired, especially, by the work of Robert Cox and others. Drawing on Marx, Kees van der Pijl (1984: 4) distinguished class fractions based respectively on productive capital, money capital and commodity capital, while Cox (1987: 359–60) emphasized the emergence of transnational capital, with Stephen Gill (1990) elaborating this in his work on the Trilateral Commission.

Nevertheless, one of the key novelties in such work was a shared focus on the agency of capital and labour that encouraged a focus on different class fractions. Thus, Cox argued already in 1981 that 'now, as a consequence of [transnational] production, it becomes increasingly pertinent to think in terms of a global class structure alongside or superimposed upon national class structures' (1981: 147). Admittedly, members of the AS speak about comprehensive concepts of control (e.g. van der Pijl 1984: 7–8) rather than struggles over class hegemony (Cox 1983: 168). Both emphases are, however, defined in a similar way and, in fact, are often used interchangeably (e.g. Holman 1996; Overbeek 1990: 26; Overbeek and van der Pijl 1993). Drawing also from Bob Jessop (1990: 201), this blended focus on comprehensive concepts of control and hegemonic projects is pivotal to our own understanding of contending fractions of capital and labour in relation to accumulation strategies and hegemonic projects within different capitalist type of states (see Bieler 2000: 47–51; Morton 2013: 111–13). Equally, Amsterdam scholars have drawn on the main division between national and transnational class fractions instead of van der Pijl's division (e.g. van Apeldoorn 2002). Finally, a key edited collection by Gill (1993), providing pivotal conceptual and empirical advances from the perspective of historical materialism – that proved highly significant for our personal academic development – brought together scholars from geographically diverse localities. In short, we have been unconvinced about the notion of a distinctive AS.

Similarly, at an epistemological level, we have doubts about the merits of 'school' formation as the basis for knowledge production and intellectual development. As Adam established as early as 2001, the formation of a 'school' of thought often implies the loss of critical theoretical development. For,

> the diversity of social relations becomes translated into a single category, preventing any serious discussion of assumptions, contradictions and differences which are thereby covered up. There is therefore the liability that the consolidation of a 'school' or '-ism' could disable and disempower what was empowering and interesting about the original insights in the first place.
>
> *(Morton 2001: 36).*

Most tellingly, to our knowledge, advocates of the AS have not responded to the serious criticism that they project too much class coherence to neoliberalization and especially the internal unity of transnational capital onto the global political economy. Likewise, to the same demand that analysis 'must give way to more active sorties against neoliberalism, and the analysis of concepts of control must beget original concepts of resistance' (Drainville 1994: 125), the response has been silence (e.g. Overbeek and van Apeldoorn 2012). In our view, post-disciplinary engagement across critical

172 Andreas Bieler and Adam David Morton

theories enables us to avoid any kind of ossification within a given conceptual framework and indicates the need to connect in *and beyond* the AS. It is this post-disciplinary engagement within and beyond historical materialist political economy which allows us to tackle issues of resistance, among others.

Engaging beyond the Amsterdam School

A first step in our wider engagements was a sympathetic critique of Open Marxism (Bieler and Morton 2003). While we rejected these scholars' state-centric analysis of developments at the international level, we have followed closely their conceptualization of how to understand the separation between the 'political' and the 'economic', or 'state' and 'market'. Unlike within feudalism, when lords expropriated surplus from peasants by direct political force, exploitation in capitalism is managed indirectly through economic means. With production organized around wage labour and the private ownership of the means of production, it seems less so that people are politically forced to work for someone else. Nevertheless, without access to means of production, in normal conditions workers are forced to sell their labour power to capital to ensure their survival. This is why Engels (1969: 343–4) regards them as, effectively, wage slaves.

More recently, this work and wider engagement with Robert Brenner's (1977) and Ellen Meiksins Wood's (1995) social property relations approach has allowed us to deepen our historical understanding of the emergence of capitalism in our joint monograph *Global capitalism, global war, global crisis* (Bieler and Morton 2018). As Hannes Lacher (2006) and Benno Teschke (2003) make clear, capitalism was born into a prior existing international states system. Elsewhere, Alex Anievas and Kerem Nişançıoğlu have unravelled the concrete dynamics of capitalist expansion using the concept of uneven and combined development to assess capitalism's encounter with non-capitalist spaces beyond a Eurocentric perspective (Anievas and Nişançıoğlu 2015). Our book emphasizes the internal relations of global capitalism, global war, and global crisis to analyse historical and contemporary themes on the expansion of capitalism through uneven and combined development (global capitalism), the role of the state and geopolitics (global war), and conditions of exploitation and resistance (global crisis) within the global political economy. Based on the philosophy of internal relations that is the hallmark of historical materialism, we understand the character of capital in such a way that the ties between the relations of production, state-civil society, and conditions of class struggle can be realized. Thus, the internal relations among global capitalism, global war, and global crisis are conceived to develop through struggle and resistance. This approach provides a novel intervention into theoretical debates on 'the international' in contributing to Marxism understood as a post-disciplinary 'family of approaches', as Ngai-Ling Sum and Bob Jessop usefully put it (2013: 10), rather than remaining within a single unified disciplinary straightjacket. This does not imply that the past and present work by colleagues from the AS is no longer relevant. Nevertheless, our experience shows that moving beyond the narrow confines of one's own circle leads to reinvigorated theoretical and empirical analyses.

References

Anievas, A. and Nişançıoğlu, K. (2015). *How the west came to rule: The geopolitical origins of capitalism.* London: Pluto.

van Apeldoorn, B. (2002). *Transnational capitalism and the struggle over European integration.* London: Routledge.

Bieler, A. (2000). *Globalisation and EU enlargement: Austrian and Swedish social forces in the struggle over membership.* London: Routledge.

Bieler, A. and Morton, A.D. (2003). Globalisation, the state and class struggle: A 'critical economy' engagement with Open Marxism. *British Journal of Politics and International Relations* 5: 467–499.

Bieler, A. and Morton, A.D. (2018). *Global capitalism, global war, global crisis.* Cambridge: Cambridge University Press.

Brenner, R. (1977). The origins of capitalist development: A critique of neo-Smithian Marxism. *New Left Review* 104: 25–92.

Cox, R.W. (1981). Social forces, states and world orders: Beyond international relations theory. *Millennium: Journal of International Studies* 10: 126–155.

Cox, R.W. (1983). Gramsci, hegemony and international relations: An essay on method. *Millennium: Journal of International Studies* 12: 162–175.

Cox, R.W. (1987). *Production, power and world order: Social forces in the making of history.* New York: Columbia University Press.

Drainville, A. (1994). International political economy in the age of open Marxism. *Review of International Political Economy* 1: 105–132.

Engels, F. (1969 [1847]). Principles of communism. In *Marx and Engels collected works*, vol. 6 (pp. 341–357). London: Lawrence and Wishart.

Gill, S. (1990). *American hegemony and the Trilateral Commission.* Cambridge: Cambridge University Press.

Gill, S. (Ed.) (1993). *Gramsci, historical materialism and international relations.* Cambridge: Cambridge University Press.

Gramsci, A. (1971). *Selections from the prison notebooks.* London: Lawrence and Wishart.

Holman, O. (1992). Introduction: Transnational class strategy and the new Europe. *International Journal of Political Economy* 22: 3–22.

Holman, O. (1996). *Integrating Southern Europe: EC expansion and the transnationalization of Spain.* London: Routledge.

Jessop, B. (1990). *State theory: Putting the capitalist state in its place.* Cambridge: Polity Press.

Lacher, H. (2006). *Beyond globalization: Capitalism, territoriality and the international relations of modernity.* London: Routledge.

Morton, A.D. (2001). The sociology of theorising and neo-Gramscian perspectives: The problems of 'school' formation in IPE. In A. Bieler and A.D. Morton (Eds), *Social forces in the making of the new Europe* (pp. 25–43). Basingstoke: Palgrave.

Morton, A.D. (2007). *Unravelling Gramsci: Hegemony and passive revolution in the global political economy.* London: Pluto Press.

Morton, A.D. (2013). *Revolution and state in modern Mexico: The political economy of uneven development*, updated edition. Lanham, MD: Rowman & Littlefield.

Overbeek, H. (1990). *Global capitalism and national decline: The Thatcher decade in perspective.* London: Unwin & Hyman.

Overbeek, H. and van Apeldoorn, B. (Eds) (2012). *Neoliberalism in crisis.* Basingstoke: Palgrave.

Overbeek, H. and van der Pijl, K. (1993). Restructuring capital and restructuring hegemony: Neoliberalism and the unmaking of the post-war order. In H. Overbeek (Ed.), *Restructuring hegemony in the global political economy* (pp. 1–27). London: Routledge.

van der Pijl, K. (1984). *The making of an Atlantic ruling class*. London: Verso.

van der Pijl, K. (1989). Ruling classes, hegemony and the state system: Theoretical and historical considerations. *International Journal of Political Economy* 19(3): 7–35.

van der Pijl, K. (1996). A theory of transnational revolution: Universal history according to Eugen Rosenstock-Huessy and its implications. *Review of International Political Economy* 3: 287–318.

van der Pijl, K. (1998). *Transnational classes and international relations*. London: Routledge.

Ryner, M. (2003). *Capitalist restructuring, globalization and the Third Way: Lessons from the Swedish model*. London: Routledge.

Sum, N.-L. and Jessop, B. (2013). *Towards a cultural political economy: Putting culture in its place in political economy*. Cheltenham: Edward Elgar.

Teschke, B. (2003). *The myth of 1648: Class, geopolitics and the making of modern international relations*. London: Verso.

Wood, E.M. (1995). *Democracy against capitalism: Renewing historical materialism*. Cambridge: Cambridge University Press.

8

LOSING CONTROL?

The Amsterdam School travels east

Dorothee Bohle

This commentary approaches the merits and some shortcomings of the Amsterdam School through the lens of Eastern Europe's neoliberal capitalist restructuring. Arguably, there is no other region in the world where the School's central concerns – transnational class formation, transnationalization of the state and the neoliberal concept of control – are as formative for its capitalism as in Eastern Europe. This is for two reasons. First, communism collapsed at a time when neoliberalism had consolidated internationally. Second, Eastern Europe's capitalist revolutions were revolutions without a national bourgeoisie. Together these factors had profound consequences for the emerging structures of East European capitalism. In those countries that joined the (outer rim of) the 'Lockean heartland' (van der Pijl 1998), the bourgeoisie became thoroughly transnationalized from the beginning and state institutions were more radically geared towards fostering transnational accumulation and subordinating labour than those in the West. As I will argue in this chapter, the Amsterdam School's toolkit is an enormous asset when analysing the emergence of capitalism in the region. However, there is a risk that its focus on transnational constellations of class power and elite agency overlooks important sites of conflicts and changes in capitalist power on the ground.

Transnational capital, international organizations and passive revolutions

Several authors have analysed the emergence of East-Central European capitalisms after the breakdown of communism through the analytic lens of the Amsterdam School. While their approaches somewhat differ, with authors drawing to different degrees on the first and second generation of the School, and on broader neo-Gramscian perspectives, most share several core arguments.[1] Most importantly, the East European transformations have been analysed as *passive revolutions*, i.e. as situations of radical change pushed by elites whose ideas do not stem from the domestic context but rather reflect international developments (Bohle 2006; Shields 2006, 2012). The argument here is that the breakdown of state socialism was of crucial importance for making the East European societies particularly receptive to Western ideas and projects. After the crisis of Fordism in the West, the end of import-substituting industrialization in the South, Eastern state socialism was the last attempt to organize and sustain a development project within the framework of the nation state that ultimately failed. Whereas the West underwent restructuring on a large scale and finally replaced the old Fordist model of development with a new, transnationally organized neoliberal one, Eastern Europe stagnated over the 1980s and experienced the total breakdown of its system. It is partly due to this uneven timing of crisis and restructuring that Western forces could extend their ideas, rules, norms and institutions and thus their interests to the East. Economic liberalism as an ideology became very attractive for these societies, because it constituted the most radical alternative to the existing socialist system. However, neoliberalism could neither be based on established societal groups nor around a specific national hegemonic project. The revolutions in Eastern Europe were, then, as often stated, bourgeois without a bourgeoisie. Instead of powerful economic groups, intellectuals and elites within the state became responsible for the neoliberal reforms (Eyal et al. 1998).

Second, these elites sought to buttress their neoliberal reform agenda with the support of international organizations. Initially, the International Monetary Fund and the World Bank were of crucial importance. From the second half of the 1990s, however, the European Union (EU) emerged as a crucial agent of neoliberal restructuring in the East. After the Single Market and the European Monetary Union, EU enlargement had become the next major project of the EU, shoring up its neoliberal outlook. The EU exported the core of its deregulatory programme, thereby opening the East for transnational capital. At the same time, it initially applied selective protectionism to shield Western companies and populations from the shock of enlargement. Increasingly, however, transnational capital used the Eastern production sites to put competitive pressures on wages, social policies and taxation in the West, while free movement of labour inflicted further strains on Western welfare states and working conditions (Holman 2004; Bohle 2006; Vliegenthart and Overbeek 2007).

Third, EU enlargement was also the main vector through which the East European capitalist class became transnationalized. The EU used membership conditionality and the instruments developed for the accession process to promote foreign capital inflows. In its accession partnerships and annual reports, the EU specifically suggested privatization via foreign ownership in several strategic sectors; and openness to foreign direct investment crystallized as one important condition for membership (Medve-Bálint 2014). The EU was also an early supporter of setting up national investment agencies, and trained their staff (Drahokoupil 2008). All this resulted in a massive inflow of foreign direct investment, turning Europe's eastern periphery into a heavily transnationally penetrated region.

Losing control? **177**

Neo-Gramscian scholarship has taken great pain to show how transnational capital has exerted structural and behavioural power in their host countries, influencing state strategies and social compromises. However, the focus on neoliberal restructuring through transnational capitalist forces, which the region surely epitomizes, has resulted in a somewhat simplistic picture of East European capitalism. At times, the scholarship reads as if transnational capital is all there is. Moreover, although social struggles loom large among the concerns of the Amsterdam School, current studies mostly pay no more than lip service to grassroots struggles.

Beyond hegemony: challenges to transnational neoliberalism

The Amsterdam School has often been criticized for being too focused on elite-driven hegemonic projects and practices, for conflating the structural and behavioural power of capital and for paying insufficient attention to divisions within the capitalist class, as well as to the social bases of resistance to neoliberal restructuring (e.g. Drainville 1994, Worth 2002). These criticisms are perhaps nowhere more warranted than for the analyses of Europe's eastern periphery, where unexpected developments have emerged recently, which are hard to fit in some respects with the Amsterdam School's specific analytical lens. The recent reconfiguration of capitalist power in Hungary illustrates this well. As is well known, the Hungarian parliamentary election in spring 2010 gave the right-wing nationalist FIDESZ party of Viktor Orbán an unprecedented two thirds majority in the Parliament. The government used this stellar victory to radically alter Hungarian political and economic institutions. One of the most intriguing initiatives has arguably been the government's 'fight against debt slavery', during which it imposed significant costs on the – mostly foreign owned – banks, and also renationalized some of them (Johnson and Barnes 2015). My point here is not that this has challenged the transnational character of Hungarian capitalism. But it amounts to a significant reconfiguration of class power, where groups associated with money capital and banks have lost important positions. In this respect, the concepts of a transnational capitalist class and an overarching concept of control seem to hide more than they explain. Certain groups of the transnational capitalist class are currently losing control and we need to know how this important shift could have happened and what its social base is. This requires a much more fine-grained analysis of the composition, alliances and conflicts within the Hungarian capitalist class.

A very similar point emerges when it comes to resistance and possible counter-hegemonic projects. Far too often, the turn to nationalism and far-right politics in the region are conceptualized as a simple reaction of the losers of neoliberal restructuring, that is, mostly workers made redundant and impoverished by radical reforms. However, this interpretation glosses over crucial questions of agency and the class base of nationalism and the far right. Thus, recent research on the Hungarian right has shown that far from being simply *reactive* to economic grievances, *proactive* agency matters; and, in this respect, middle classes are playing a key role in forging what they see as a counter-hegemonic project to that of the cosmopolitan and liberal elites. As

178 Dorothee Bohle

Greskovits (2017: 1) writes, the Hungarian right was rebuilt through a civil society movement, which was 'militant in terms of its hegemonic aspirations and collective practices; massive in terms of its membership and activism; middle-class based in terms of social stratification; and dominantly metropolitan and urban on the spatial dimension'. In this rebuilding, issues of dignity, status and identity have taken centre stage, with questions of material well being relegated to the background. Such issues raise intriguing questions about the relationships among agency, identity and class positions, which have not been adequately addressed in the framework of the Amsterdam School.

Overall, it seems to me that the Amsterdam School's expansion to the East bears witness to some of the weaknesses identified long ago by Drainville (1994: 114):

> But the bond between global circuits of social capital and global politics is more fragmented than the writings of open Marxism suggest, and the relationship between national social formations and the world economy less linear. The analysis of both requires a more careful historical exploration of the specificity of different sites of neo-liberalism … This is a picture that cannot be painted with the broad brush used by open Marxism. It is a meticulous work that needs to be alive to distinct historical structures.

To put it differently, in order not to fall victim to overgeneralizations, the Amsterdam School needs to descend from the lofty heights of the transnational to survey the local and everyday.

Note

1 This section draws on Holman (1998, 2001, 2004) and Vliegenthart (Vliegenthart and Overbeek 2007; Vliegenthart and Horn 2007), who analyse Eastern Europe from an Amsterdam School perspective; and Shields (2004, 2006, 2007, 2008, 2012) and Bohle (2002, 2006), who build on broader neo-Gramscian perspectives. These works focus on the Viségrad countries: Hungary, Poland, the Czech Republic and Slovakia.

References

Bohle, D. (2002). *Europas neue Peripherie: Polens Transformation und transnationale Integration.* Münster: Westfälisches Dampfboot.

Bohle, D. (2006). Neoliberal hegemony, transnational capital and the terms of the EU's eastward expansion. *Capital & Class* 30(1): 57–86.

Drahokoupil, J. (2008). *Globalization and the state in Central and Eastern Europe: The politics of foreign direct investment.* London: Routledge.

Drainville, A.C. (1994). International political economy in the age of open Marxism. *Review of International Political Economy* 1(1): 105–132.

Eyal, G., Szelényi, I. and Townsley, E.R. (1998). *Making capitalism without capitalists: Class formation and elite struggles in post-Communist Central Europe.* London: Verso.

Greskovits, B. (2017). Rebuilding the Hungarian right through civil organization and contention: The Civic Circles movement. RSCAS 2017/37. Florence: Robert Schuman

Center for Advanced Studies, European University Institute. http://cadmus.eui.eu/ha
ndle/1814/47245

Holman, O. (1998). Integrating Eastern Europe: EU expansion and the double transformation in Poland, the Czech Republic, and Hungary. *International Journal of Political Economy* 28(2): 12–43.

Holman, O. (2001). The enlargement of the European Union towards Central and Eastern Europe: The role of supranational and transnational actors. In A. Bieler and A.D. Morton (Eds), *Social forces in the making of the new Europe* (pp. 161–184). Basingstoke: Palgrave-Macmillan.

Holman, O. (2004). Integrating peripheral Europe: The different roads to 'Security and Stability' in Southern and Central Europe. *Journal of International Relations and Development* 7(2): 208–236.

Johnson, J. and Barnes, A. (2015). Financial nationalism and its international enablers: The Hungarian experience. *Review of International Political Economy* 22(3): 535–569.

Medve-Bálint, G. (2014). The role of the EU in shaping FDI flows to East Central Europe. *Journal of Common Market Studies* 52(1): 35–51.

van der Pijl, K. (1998). *Transnational classes and international relations*. London: Routledge.

Shields, S. (2004). Global restructuring and the Polish state: Transition, transformation, or transnationalization? *Review of International Political Economy* 11(1): 132–154.

Shields, S. (2006). Historicizing transition: The Polish political economy in a period of global structural change – Eastern Central Europe's passive revolution? *International Politics* 43(4): 474–499.

Shields, S. (2007). From socialist solidarity to neo-populist neoliberalisation? The paradoxes of Poland's post-communist transition. *Capital & Class* 31(3): 159–178.

Shields, S. (2008). How the East was won: Transnational social forces and the neoliberalisation of Poland's post-communist transition. *Global Society* 22(4): 445–468.

Shields, S. (2012). *The international political economy of transition*. London: Routledge.

Vliegenthart, A. and Horn, L. (2007). The role of the EU in the (trans)formation of corporate governance regulation in Central Eastern Europe: The case of the Czech Republic. *Competition & Change* 11(2): 137–154.

Vliegenthart, A. and Overbeek, H. (2007). Corporate governance regulation in East Central Europe. In H. Overbeek, B. van Apeldoorn, and A. Nölke (Eds), *The transnational politics of corporate governance regulation* (pp. 177–198). London: Routledge.

Worth, O. (2002). The Janus-like character of counter-hegemony: Progressive and nationalist responses to neoliberalism. *Global Society* 16(3): 297–315.

9

THE AMSTERDAM SCHOOL AS A POTENTIAL SOURCE OF INSPIRATION FOR CHINESE SCHOLARS

Bai Yunzhen

For Chinese scholars, the Amsterdam School (AS) has the potential to contribute greatly and comprehensively to International Relations (IR) and International Political Economy (IPE) by challenging the intellectual hegemony of realism and liberalism. It could, moreover, provide Chinese scholars with powerful analytical concepts and tools and the confidence to use them.

First, as we know, the AS approach is firmly grounded in the historical materialist tradition and attempts to 'develop a historically grounded conception of the *dialectical totality* of structure and agency' (Overbeek 2004: 114). It has also creatively applied this dialectical view of the changing capital relation and class forces to the transnational regional and global level. For Chinese scholars, then, the AS confirms the heuristic power of historical materialism and offers key theoretical insights into structure–agency relations.

Second, more specifically, Chinese scholars may use proven core concepts and analytical tools of the AS to analyse domestic and transnational capital accumulation and the emergence and evolution of transnational class relations. These concepts include fractions of capital, concepts of control, the cadre class, socialization, the Lockean heartland and Hobbesian contender states. One way for Chinese scholars to contribute to the further development of the AS would be to refine and reinterpret these concepts and apply them to their own historical and cultural context.

As van der Pijl commented, a 'contender state' 'must mobilise, from above, the society it controls in order to resist subordination to the combined forces, commercial and political, of the heartland' (2012: xxi). In fact, France, Germany, Japan and the USSR each interacted differently with the consolidation and expansion of the Lockean heartland, reflecting their respective contender experiences. This is an invitation to Chinese scholars to explore how China as another Hobbesian contender state has been differentially integrated into the transnational structures of hegemony in specific historical periods and how this has affected its own economic and political trajectory.

Third, there is the ontological inspiration. Class analysis is an important tool to undertake sophisticated analyses of how class forces make history but not in circumstances of their own choosing. The AS explores this in terms of, inter alia, how changing concepts of control may link the economic, political and social fields of social orders. While realist and, especially, liberal International Relations theorists recognize the relevance of non-state actors, their thinking remains largely state-centric. In other words, they emphasize the ontological primacy of the national state. In contrast, AS scholars reject this national state-centric approach in favour of research on the international expansion of capital accumulation, the historical formation of transnational classes and the internationalization of the state. They also give classes a key role in capitalist development and explore their role in accumulation at the national, international and transnational levels.

Fourth, more generally, Chinese scholars working in the discipline of IR or IPE tend to focus narrowly on the received tradition in these disciplines and are reluctant to put forward innovative ideas. The example of the trans-disciplinary scholarship of the AS, which critiqued realism and neo-realism and distanced itself from world systems theory in favour of a more explicit Marxist analysis of class structure and the internationalization of capital could encourage Chinese IR and IPE scholars to rethink their own research tradition and draw on other social science disciplines to help them escape the confines of these two disciplines.

Thus inspired, Chinese scholars could achieve three objectives. First, they could seek intellectual resources from Marx and other scholars in the Marxist tradition, fulfil the theoretical promise of historical materialism and reconstruct a more comprehensive grand theory of historical transformation. Second, on this basis, using the fundamental concepts of historical materialism and the distinctive concepts of the AS and neo-Gramscian scholarship more generally, they could explore the material linkage between the political and economic spheres and expand their research to the transnational class and struggles for hegemony. And, third, they could elaborate a grand theoretical agenda suitable for understanding China's global role.

The reception of the AS in China

While many Chinese scholars are familiar with Robert Cox's work, only a few have recognized the significance of the AS. Regrettably, AS studies remain untranslated into Chinese. Partly as a result, Chinese scholars often associate the AS with the work of Robert Cox and Stephen Gill but, thereby, neglect its distinctive concepts and arguments. Even when they do consider it, they disagree about the AS and its relation to neo-Gramscianism.

My Master's supervisor, Professor Wang Tiejun at East China Normal University introduced the AS into China through the works of Kees van der Pijl. He related this to the Coxian approach and then explored both his and Bastiaan van Apeldoorn's analyses of regional integration (Wang 2000, 2013). In his view, while

AS problems and methods offer valuable comments on traditional international relations theory, van der Pijl and colleagues overemphasize the class relationships in the Lockean heartland and Hobbesian contender states and neglect research on the many non-hegemonic countries and classes (Wang 2000).

My master's thesis summarized van der Pijl's ideas about transnational classes and used his historical sketch of four comprehensive concepts of control (liberal internationalism, state monopoly capitalism, corporate liberalism, and neo-liberalism) to analyse the capitalist class in the global political economy. In my view, van der Pijl mainly explores the formation of transnational social networks in terms of the dynamics of capital accumulation and the evolution of ideology. By comparison, Cox attends more to the internationalization of production and the state, emphasizing that material capabilities, ideas and institutions promote the formation of social forces. On this basis, he explores the historical formation and dynamics of world order.

In contrast, Zhang Jianxin, from Fudan University, argues explicitly that the AS makes a distinctive contribution to the neo-Gramscian school. In his opinion, whereas Cox starts with the social relations of production and regards the hegemonic historical bloc as their product, van der Pijl focuses on capital and grounds the transnational historical bloc in capital accumulation and circulation (Zhang 2011).

Influenced as they are by mainstream realist and liberal IPE, Chinese scholars seldom apply transnational historical materialism to analyse the global political economy. Thus the AS is rarely incorporated into International Political Economy (IPE) textbooks in the Chinese academy. Although the main IPE textbook in China (Wang Zhengyi's *General Theory of International Political Economy*) does address Marxism, it only includes dependency theory and world system theory. I was the first to introduce van der Pijl's work in a textbook on *Theories of International Relations* (2009), which highlights the empirical research, such as the European integration, globalization, and the American hegemony. Thus, one might conclude that the Chinese academic world is affected by the 'liberal heartland' and its 'soft power', despite being familiar with the historical materialist tradition. An exception is Li Bin, from Nanjing University, who uses Cox's world order approach to explore the role of social forces in world order and Chinese strategy (Li 2010).

China's global role and new research agendas

Based on a systematic and critical exploration of the AS and its key concepts, Chinese scholars should use its theoretical framework to analyse China's rise, East Asian regionalism and the influence of the US on the development of Asian political economy, particularly China's domestic and international political economy. This would promote theoretical innovation and enrich the research and knowledge generation in IPE in the Chinese academy.

More specifically, I see three ways in which AS insights may contribute to studying the political economy of China.

A first research agenda item is to combine traditional Chinese thought with the AS. While 'China would appear to be the primary contender today' (van der Pijl 2006: xii), its state-society complex is quite distinctive contender state. China is a contender state but also a modern Confucian-legalist state as well as a socialist state. Indeed, the ancient ideas of the Confucian-legalist state have significantly affected the evolution of the socialist state. This needs to be explored. Conversely, understanding the relationship between the heartland and the contender state from the Confucian perspective of the dialectic of reconciliation (also called Confucian dialectics) is also necessary and important. This dialectic of reconciliation emphasizes the conditional nature of social change in general and the importance of respectful reconciliation of antagonisms in a wider unity to prevent extreme confrontations. Thus, Chinese scholars should try to combine the dialectics of historical materialism with the dialectic of reconciliation to avoid a mechanical analysis of the heartland/contender state divide and reveal the dialectical nature of relations between China and the liberal heartland. Crucial here is recognition of the transnational expansion of capital beyond the West and its social/economical/political consequences.

A second agenda item is critical analysis of the legacies of Marx, Lenin, Gramsci and other historical materialist thinkers to promote further innovation in the AS. Chinese scholars are deeply read in Marx's key works as well as other classical Marxist texts. To this should be added key works in contemporary Marxism with Chinese characteristics, such as Mao Zedong's *On practice* and *On contradiction* and Xi Jinping's *The governance of China*.

Capital relations, forms of the state and politics and social institutions are highly variable across time and space, not only because of differing economic and political factors, but also because of different education and cultural traditions such as Confucianism. Exploring the historical dialectic of material production and inherited cultural traditions could well promote theoretical and epistemological innovation in the AS.

A third crucial issue is historically specific analysis of concrete issues in the current global conjuncture. Marx placed social class at the centre of his analysis of politics. China's regional and global role also depends not only on its 'cadre class' but also on mass action. China's developing regional and global roles interact with the consolidation and expansion of an internally differentiated Lockean heartland. Chinese and foreign scholars should investigate the challenges facing China's regional and global roles. Topics could include the impact of social forces in the process of East Asian integration, the transnational politics of the 'Belt and Road Initiative' (previously known as the Silk Road Economic Belt and the 21st-Century Maritime Silk Road), trans-Pacific relations, Asia–Europe relations and global governance and regulation.

On the one hand, Chinese scholars might combine AS theoretical insights with the Chinese strategic culture, which emphasizes the unity of opposites, self-discipline of moral thinking and governing based on Confucian dialectics. They could then discuss the dialectical relations among the four goals – economic, political, ethical, societal – of the 'Belt and Road Initiative' and the resulting interaction with Europe, which is the western pole of the Belt and Road programme. This would be explored against the backdrop of geopolitical and geo-economic dynamics including the evolving relationship between China and the US-led heartland.

On the other hand, perhaps non-Chinese (or non-China-based) scholars could employ AS concepts and approaches to analyse the role of social forces in East Asian regional cooperation. This would be a great echo of how the AS started with its project on the role of social forces in the making of European integration and contribute to comparative historical analysis of East Asian and European integration, their respective transnational dynamics and class character and the impacts of American hegemony on both integration processes.

To sum up, combining the Chinese traditional thought and model of political economic governance with a historical materialist approach would help to comprehensively understand China's global role, the struggles between the liberal heartland and the contender states, and rivalries among the contenders. This would further enhance the AS's move from abstract theorization and analysis to more concrete, historical analysis.

References

Bai, Y. (2009). *Introduction to International Relations Theoretical Schools* (Guójì guānxì lǐlùn xuéyuán jiéshảo). Hangzhou: Zhejiang People's Publishing House.

Li, B. (2010). Social forces, world order, and China's development (Shèhuì lìliàng, shìjiè zhìxù, zhōngguó fǎ zhǎn). *World Economics and Politics* 38(12), 119–36.

Overbeek, H. (2004). Transnational class formation and concepts of control: Towards a genealogy of the Amsterdam project in international political economy. *Journal of International Relations and Development* 7(2): 113–141.

van der Pijl, K. (1998). *Transnational class and international relations*. London: Routledge.

van der Pijl, K. (2006). *Global rivalries: From the Cold War to Iraq*. London: Pluto.

van der Pijl, K. (2012). *The making of an Atlantic ruling class*. London: Verso.

Wang, T. (2000). The theoretical innovation of neo-Gramscianism in IR (Xīn gé lán xī zhǔ yì duì guó jì guān xi lí lùn de chuàng xīn). *European Studies* 18(1): 14–19.

Wang, T. (2013). *Global production network and regional integration of Southeast Asia* (Quán qiú shēngchǎn wǎngluò hé dōngnányà dìqū yītǐ huà). Shanghai: Shanghai People's Publishing House.

Zhang, J. (2011). *The radical international political economy* (Jī jìn de guó jì zhèng zhì jīng jì xué). Shanghai: Shanghai People's Publishing House.

10

RECONSIDERING THE 'DANGEROUS LIAISONS' BETWEEN CHINA AND NEOLIBERALISM AND ITS IMPACT IN LATIN AMERICA AND CARIBBEAN COUNTRIES

Leonardo Ramos and Javier Vadell

This commentary reflects on rising China and its impact in Latin America and the Caribbean (LAC) region from an Amsterdam School (AS) perspective. The two key AS concepts used in our discussion of China below are 'contender states' (van der Pijl 1998, 2008) and 'comprehensive concepts of control' (CCCs). The latter have four important aspects. First, CCCs are 'expressions of bourgeois hegemony reflecting a historically specific hierarchy of classes and class fractions. [Second,] they express the ideological and, in a Gramscian sense, hegemonic structure of particular historical configurations of capital' (Overbeek and van der Pijl 1993: 5; cf. Bode, Chapter 1). Third, CCCs 'contain and give expression to the *content* of hegemony in specific historical periods' (Overbeek 2004: 128, italics in original). Fourth, a CCC 'provides a clue to understanding the nature of the relation between structure and agency', notably in terms of the dialectical relationship between the (structural) process of capital accumulation and the agency of concrete social forces (Overbeek and van der Pijl 1993: 5).

Thus considered, the AS contributes innovatively to a critical and dialectical understanding of structure-agency relations. It combines structural and conjunctural analysis with interest in how specific social forces struggle for hegemony and thereby seek to transform and consolidate specific forms of domination. In exploring this relationship, it both emphasizes the importance of conceptualizing capitalism as a global or *world-scale* phenomenon – like World Systems Theory – and highlights the 'historical specificity of *national* formations and of the state's role in the reproduction of capitalism' (Overbeek 2004: 121, italics in original). The distinction between the Lockean heartland and plural contender states reinforces this dialectical approach. This historicist and non-state-centric approach to hegemony, with its concern with the transnational nature of capitalist development, facilitates a more profound understanding of the nature, appeal and effects of neoliberalism and the possibilities of post-neoliberalism.

Neoliberalism is a complex phenomenon and its genesis in a hegemonic CCC has two interlinked aspects: first, it is a transnational process that involves local, national, macroregional and global forms of spatialization and, second, it is a class project. We developed a similar approach inspired in part by neo-Gramscian scholarship in an article on the Asian Consensus (AC) as network power (Vadell et al. 2014) – an approach that can be substantially strengthened by a dialogue with an AS perspective. This distinguished three theoretical – dialectically interrelated – levels of neoliberalism:

1. Global: this is represented by the transnational liberal historical bloc dominated by US-based transnational capital. This bloc is driven by and condensed in US state power, which emerged in the 1970s, and is accelerating neoliberal globalization and extending the reach of accumulation (Overbeek 2016: 311).

2. National: this concerns the specific models of development implemented by governments and associated social forces since the 1980s. Its dynamic reflects how political agents respond politically to the structural power of capital in their domestic realms. A useful notion to overcome methodological nationalism here – albeit with clear implications for other levels – is 'variegated capitalism' (Jessop 2011). This notion seeks to steer a middle path between World Systems Analysis and the methodologically nationalist focus of the 'varieties of capitalism' literature. It highlights the multiscalar nature of the global political economy and how different economic spaces are integrated into this changing system. This approach is also influenced by Jessop's strategic-relational perspective, which 'enhances the analytical grasp of social agency in empirical studies … by treating processes of ideational contestation led by groups of politically and ideologically conscious agents as a key analytical concern' (Mulvad 2015: 201). It indicates how local and national geographical scales result in part from ideational and material struggles over political-economic models (on China, see Mulvad 2015).

3. The agential level addresses how agents articulate and coordinate economic and political power networks by setting standards and promoting or transforming global regimes (Grewal 2008). These networks link the local/national and macroregional levels with global structures and superstructures. Following Grewal, this network power has been instantiated in North–North, North–South and South–South relationships in the most diverse aspects. Here we highlight the non-state-centric aspect of Grewal's networking framework – the state is seen in an extended, Gramscian sense, as a state/society complex (cf. Grewal 2008: 131–4). Seen in these terms, China's (re)emergence is intrinsically related to (transnational) state/society relations and has significant roots in and consequences for the crisis of the Washington Consensus and the emergence of a new network power, the AC. The latter supports China's rising power by embedding it in the Global South and other emerging countries and seeks to govern its spillover effects on the Global South.

The AC is a contemporary dynamic process of change in the international political economy that involves a mutation of the neoliberal hegemonic structure of the current hierarchical capitalist order. This mutation is anchored in China's projection of political power and its economic rise as a part of the core of the capitalist system. Above all, the AC is a dynamic commercial, financial, investment and foreign aid network power that interconnects China, Asia and the Global South as a whole (China-SCPRC 2014). It emerged after the 2001 economic crisis and was reoriented to a reformatted hegemonic neoliberal globalization disrupting the foundations of the Washington Consensus. Geopolitically, the rise of China also triggers a new contest over global natural resources and other strategic commodities. Furthermore, time-space compression and new technological advances have triggered new global standards of social and economic coordination.

In 2004 Joshua Ramo published *The Beijing Consensus*, with immediate repercussions. He identified three features that condition how a developing nation could find its own place in the global economy, based on China's development path: (1) constant innovation and experimentation; (2) an emphasis on the quality of life – especially equity and sustainability – in development issues; and (3) political 'self-determination' vis-à-vis World Bank and International Monetary Fund dictates. In fact, Ramo's definition describes a utopian model of development with strong normative elements rather than a new type of North–South relationship. Thus his model does not help us to understand the geopolitical and geo-economic implications of the unprecedented and growing economic interdependence between LAC and China, which is a complex process that involves far more than simply replicating the model of Chinese development (Vadell et al. 2014).

In this sense, the AC is a very useful concept to understand the new complementary and asymmetric relationship in the post-Washington Consensus era. It constitutes a new network power between China's state/society complex and some less developed regions, particularly countries in Africa and the LAC region, which can promote an alternative CCC with features of both hegemony and domination. Given China's expansion, the Global South must decide whether, and how, to exploit new possibilities of integration into the global economy by engaging in complementary trade with China and benefitting from Chinese investments and assistance. It therefore concerns the opportunities for and constraints on upward mobility (Li 2017) as potential peripheral or semi-peripheral actors in a new hierarchical structure. Henceforth, the great challenge to less developed state/society complexes is how to cope with the structural transformations that test their agential capabilities.

Thus, recent decades are calling into question the paradigmatic scale of neoliberalism as a CCC. China's political and economic ascendance is crucial here. The scope for 'globalization with Chinese characteristics' has been reinforced with the inauguration of Donald Trump as US President while China continues its path of gradual but constant economic expansion. This enhances Chinese influence in the global economic order and the gradual construction of a parallel system of global economic governance. The latter reflects the general hybrid trajectory of China's rise: adapting to the international liberal order yet maintaining state ownership in strategic economic sectors (de Graaff and van Apeldoorn 2017). This parallel system comprises: (1) the New Development Bank – formerly BRICS Development

Bank; (2) the Asian Infrastructure Investment Bank; (3) the Silk Road Fund linked to the Belt-and-Road-Initiative; and (4) the Free Trade Area of the Asia-Pacific, which are being developed without abandoning traditional economic institutions such as the International Monetary Fund and World Bank.

Since the 2008 economic crisis, China has come even closer to the developing countries through a strategy that is expressed in two ways. First, China's external policy prioritizes its relations with developing states. And, second, China views these as real or potential allies, particularly in the international political arena.

The LAC countries are an exemplary case. Most of the Western media (e.g. Carroll 2010; Larmer 2017) and some scholars (e.g. Jenkins et al. 2008; Svampa and Slipak 2015) have noted the risks of the LAC countries' new dependence in relation to China. Nevertheless, as Li (2016: 18) stated, 'the China–Latin America relationship is providing new economic opportunities and political manoeuvring spaces for the region'. Indeed, the LAC–China relation is far more complex than a dependency relationship and has opened new political opportunities to elites and social forces from the LAC countries.

In trade relations, for example, the bilateral trade between China and Latin America has accelerated since the early 2000s – from $12 billion in 2000 to $275 billion in 2013 (CEPAL 2015). China is now one of the most important destinations for LAC exports, as well as a crucial source of foreign direct investment into LAC countries. The period from 2008 to 2016 presents a trend to a commodity-extraction-based relationship between the LAC and China that, prima facie, is crystallizing as a new core-periphery network power, closely connected with the neoliberal CCC. That said, it is remarkable that China's Second Policy Paper concerning the LAC (Central People's Government of the People's Republic of China 2016) changes the focus of the partnership. It highlights the following areas for further cooperation: science, technology and innovation, information technology, energy and resources, infrastructure construction, agriculture and manufacturing. This not only indicates the particularities of the Chinese elite's political and economic orientation but also reveals the possibilities for LAC countries and their social forces to benefit from this changing relation.

To conclude, in undertaking such a dialogue with AS perspectives, our main concern is not whether the Chinese model per se is neoliberal. Instead, we advance two claims. First, the AC is part of the neoliberalization process that is unfolding on a global scale and, second, it is dialectically related to the limits, criticisms and resistance thereto. In these respects, the AS framework sheds new light on the limits and possibilities of the emerging relation between China as a contender state (van der Pijl 2017) and neoliberalism as an apparently consolidated CCC: how long could such a dangerous liaison be maintained without morbid symptoms for the global political economy as a whole – and China in particular? How could rising 'statist' Chinese elites (de Graaff and van Apeldoorn 2017) promote an integrated circuit of accumulation centred in the Asian region and how might this relate to US-centred global capitalism? What do these processes imply for the agential possibilities for the LAC state/society complexes? These and related questions not only critically highlight the content of hegemonic processes but also reinforce the continued pertinence of the AS for providing a critical international political economy perspective – one that offers significantly important insights into contemporary transformations in the global political economic order.

References

Carroll, R. (2010). China pours its wealth into Latin America. *Guardian*, 18 April.

Central People's Government of the People's Republic of China (2016). China's policy paper on Latin America and the Caribbean. Available at: www.china.org.cn/world/ 2016-11/24/content_39777989.htm

CEPAL (2015). Primer Foro de la Comunidad de Estados Latinoamericanos y Caribeños (CELAC) y China. Explorando espacios de cooperación en comercio e inversión. Available at: www.cepal.org/es/publicaciones/37577-primer-foro-la-comunidad-estados-la tinoamericanos-caribenos-celac-china

China-SCPRC (2014). White paper: China's foreign aid. Available at: http://english.gov. cn/archive/white_paper/2014/08/23/content_281474982986592.htm

de Graaff, N. and van Apeldoorn, B. (2017). US elite power and the rise of 'statist' Chinese elites in global markets. *International Politics* 54(3): 338–355.

Grewal, D.S. (2008). *Network power: The social dynamics of globalization.* New Haven, CT: Yale University Press.

Jenkins, R., Dussel Peters, E. and Mesquita Moreira, M. (2008). The impact of China on Latin America and the Caribbean. *World Development* 36(2): 235–253.

Jessop, B. (2011). Rethinking the diversity of capitalism: varieties of capitalism, variegated capitalism, and the world market. In G. Wood and C. Lane (Eds), *Capitalist diversity and diversity within capitalism* (pp. 209–237). London: Routledge.

Larmer, B. (2017). Is China the world's new colonial power? *New York Times Magazine*, 2 May.

Li, X. (2016). The expansion of China's global hegemonic strategy: Implications for Latin America. *Journal of China and International Relations* 4(special issue): 1–26.

Li, X. (2017). The rise of emerging powers and China and the enlargement of 'room for maneuver' and 'upward mobility'. *Rising Powers in Global Governance.*

Mulvad, A. (2015). Competing hegemonic projects within China's variegated capitalism: 'Liberal' Guangdong vs. 'statist' Chongqing. *New Political Economy* 20: 199–227.

Overbeek, H. (2004). Transnational class formation and concepts of control: Towards a genealogy of the Amsterdam Project in international political economy. *Journal of International Relations and Development* 7(2): 113–141.

Overbeek, H. (2016). Globalizing China: A critical political economy perspective on China's rise. In A. Cafruny, L.S. Talani and G.P. Martin (Eds), *The Palgrave handbook of critical international political economy* (pp. 309–329). London: Palgrave-Macmillan.

Overbeek, H. and van der Pijl, K. (1993). Restructuring capital and restructuring hegemony: Neo-liberalism and the unmaking of the post-war order. In H. Overbeek (Ed.), *Restructuring hegemony in the global political economy: The rise of transnational neo-liberalism in the 1980s* (pp. 1–27). London: Routledge.

van der Pijl, K. (1998). *Transnational classes and international relations.* London: Routledge.

van der Pijl, K. (2008). China's challenge to the West in the 21st century. Working paper no. 1, University of Sussex: Centre for Global Political Economy.

van der Pijl, K. (2017). The BRICS: An involuntary contender bloc under attack. *Estudos Internacionais* 5(1): 25–46.

Ramo, J.C. (2004). *The Beijing Consensus: Notes on the new physics of Chinese power.* London: Foreign Policy Centre.

Svampa, M. and Slipak, A.M. (2015). China en América Latina: Del consenso de los commodities al consenso de Beijing. *Revista Ensambles* 2(3): 34–63.

Vadell, J., Ramos, L. and Neves, P. (2014). The international implications of the Chinese model of development in the Global South: Asian Consensus as a network power. *Revista Brasileira de Política Internacional* 57(special issue): 91–107.

11

SAYING GOODBYE?

Tracing my itinerary from Amsterdam to Beijing

Naná de Graaff

My introduction to the work of the Amsterdam School (AS) occurred during my master's study. After the initiation period, I gradually began to define my own position, profiting from the inspiration that the approach offers while also beginning to move beyond it. What follows is rather a personal account – fragments of an incomplete journey based on three critical exchanges, as I recall them, and the strands of research that I embarked upon as a result.

Three critical exchanges

But ... what about elites?

A first critical exchange concerned class and elites. Transnational capitalist class (formation; see, for instance, the contributions by van der Pijl, Overbeek and van Apeldoorn in the first part of this volume), was a concept whose empirical substance seemed highly attractive due to the evident concentration of political and economic power it indicated. 'But ...' was one of my first questions – at the time still a master's student – 'what is the difference between class and elites?' The only response at the time was that this was too complex a question and I would find out later. And I did, in a thin book by Tom Bottomore (1993): a key difference is that the class concept is embedded in solid theory explaining its sources of power, whereas elite theory just assumes these sources, and focuses on explaining and analysing the workings of elite power. Although this shows the theoretical limitations of elite theory, class theory seemed to me so burdened by a dichotomous abstraction and determinism that it tended to lack heuristic power when analysing the much more complex and multilayered reality of social power structures posed by contemporary capitalism.

But ... how can we tell?

A directly related concern I had with the grand theories and even grander analyses of transnational capitalist class formation, transatlantic ruling classes, the Lockean heartland and contender states, hegemonic projects and comprehensive concepts of control was a dearth of systematic empirical underpinning (although there were exceptions, like van Apeldoorn 2002). Rich in anecdotal historical evidence, these narratives captured my imagination and tapped into my political engagement, but I missed a precise and rigorous empirical and methodological foundation. What and who exactly belongs to the transnational capitalist class? How can we determine the boundaries – or even analyse the workings – of a 'comprehensive concept of control'? In other words, how do we operationalize these concepts to help us systematically collect data to underpin our grand narratives and theories?

But ... what about the Rest?

A third critical exchange sprang from the fundamental power shift occurring in the global political economy: the centre of power gravitating away from the Lockean heartland towards the East. Most of AS research and theory had focused on the West. This made sense in the era when most of the AS's vital concepts and theories were being developed but the ripples of neoliberal globalization were reaching far beyond the Western centres of power, engendering the so-called Rise of the Rest, pivotal to which was China's opening up and gradual integration into the world economy with its measured introduction of state-directed market reforms. This generated another set of critical questions that set the direction of my analytical compass: to what extent and how might the AS's key concepts and theoretical propositions apply to the non-Western rising powers? How would transnational capitalist class formation and the neoliberal hegemonic project be (re)shaped in a multipolar world? What would neoliberalism or a comprehensive concept of control 'with Chinese characteristics' look like?

Three strands of research

First, despite the limitations of elite theory alluded to above, I opted to focus on analysing corporate elite networks and their political impact, with a longer-term ambition to insert elite studies more prominently into debates in International Relations and International Political Economy, where I found this dimension largely missing. Second, I developed a strategy for systematic data collection on elites and firms, which I called biographical and organizational mapping (de Graaff 2013: 31–6). Third, I adopted social network analysis to help me analyse these data in a straightforward manner. Its basic premise is that studying the relations among actors matters more than comparing their individual attributes and that this enables a visualization and systematic analysis of these social relations (Wasserman and Faust 1994; Scott 1991).

A long tradition of 'power structure research' (Domhoff 2007) was waiting for me to build upon. Going back to the seminal sociological work of C. Wright Mills's study of *The power elite* (1956) that occupied key positions at the apex of US society, this tradition had generated a plethora of studies on corporate and political elites, and the power structures and networks they sustain, primarily through interlocking directorates and elite policy-planning networks, alternated with government positions. While much of this literature focuses on the US (Domhoff 1967), a thriving body of research has also evolved on transnational corporate elite networks and policy-planning elites (Carroll 2010), as well as European and national elite networks (Fennema 1982; Carroll et al. 2010, and for more recent work see Heemskerk's contribution in this volume).

Just like the AS, however, this literature had so far exclusively focused on the West. The rising power and influence of the quartet then popularly referred to as the BRICs (Brazil, Russia, India, China) highlighted the imperative to direct our analytical gaze beyond the West and start studying these emerging powers, China above all, their rising corporate elites and how they interacted with established elite power structures.

My PhD research (de Graaff 2013) therefore focused on emerging non-Organisation for Economic Co-operation and Development economies and their growing role in the global oil and gas market, which was, from the beginning, a highly politicized market. Moreover, the mounting power and influence of state-owned oil corporations in a market previously dominated by Western private oil majors indicated a re-articulation of state power and expansion of state-owned capital, which seemed to contradict prevailing expectations that the forces of globalization were progressively deterritorializing and transnationalizing world politics (e.g. Scholte 2000), accompanied by an erosion of state power in favour of private authority (Cutler et al. 1999). I found the non-Western state-owned oil corporations to be increasingly embedded in hybrid networks and alliances with Western private oil corporations (de Graaff 2011), whereas their directors (oil elites) remained largely detached from Western elite networks and – unsurprisingly – intimately connected to their respective states (de Graaff 2012), yet in a distinctly different way from US corporate elites (see below).

More generally, my study highlighted that the expansion of state-owned capital did not necessarily imply a reversal of the transnationalization and financialization of global oil markets – pivotal to world politics – but rather a deepening and extension of it, partly incorporating the emerging powers and its 'statist' capital. However, rather than diminishing state power, the latter was playing a vital, integral role in the globalization of capital (de Graaff 2013: 202).

This indicated a need to further explore and theorize the state's role in capital accumulation within twenty-first-century globalizing capitalism. This was even more urgent following the eruption of the global financial crisis (2007–2008) and the crucial role of states in saving 'too big to fail' (financial) capital and seeking to preserve neoliberalism through ever more severe austerity measures. Together with Bastiaan van Apeldoorn and Henk Overbeek, I embarked upon this project, leading to our co-edited volume, *Rebound of the capitalist state: The re-articulation of the state–capital nexus in global crisis* (van Apeldoorn et al. 2012).

Despite my fascination with emerging new (elite) power configurations due to a rising 'Rest', one could not ignore the still incumbent power of the West: the US. This then constituted a project that started with my master's thesis on neoconservative networks and their influence on foreign policy making in the Bush Administration, which formed the basis for the long-term collaboration with Bastiaan van Apeldoorn on corporate elite networks and post-Cold War US grand strategy. The first iteration of our project employed the concept of hegemonic projects to explore the networks of neoconservative intellectuals – and their linkages to dominant sections of US capital and think tanks. We concluded that, given the rising contradictions of US-led neo-liberal globalization, the neoconservatives' failure to formulate a successful neoconservative hegemonic project to preserve US primacy provided the structural context for Obama's call for change (de Graaff and van Apeldoorn 2011).

Our subsequent work (van Apeldoorn and de Graaff 2014, 2015) dropped this conceptual framework and theorized how the social background of foreign policy makers – especially their affiliation with corporate elite networks and policy-planning networks – shapes their worldview, which in turn influences the foreign policy they make (van Apeldoorn and de Graaff 2015: 16–30). In our extensive empirical study on top foreign policy makers in the post-Cold War administrations (Clinton, Bush and Obama) we found that more than two thirds of these officials had had previous top corporate affiliations – half of them engaged in a revolving door pattern – and a majority were extensively connected to a core network of foreign policy establishment think tanks, which are in turn extensively funded by large corporations (van Apeldoorn and de Graaff 2015: 62–98). A key conclusion was that the continuities in US foreign policy that we observed, and interpreted as an open door imperialist strategy aimed at the global expansion of US capital – through varying means – could be partly explained by the predominance of transnationally oriented capital that was present in these corporate elite networks closely entangled with the foreign policy establishment.

With the unexpected rise to power of Trump on a roaring anti-establishment message and with a fiercely nationalist 'America First' rhetoric, these longstanding elite power structures as well as the liberal internationalist Open Door foreign policy seem to be seriously challenged. This calls for an investigation into the potentially new (corporate and political) elite power structures that may be emerging in the wake of Trump and other populist and anti-establishment leaders in the US and beyond – as well as into the policies they will formulate and implement (for a first attempt, de Graaff and van Apeldoorn, forthcoming). In fact, this development might well stimulate the kind of studies that the AS generates and inspires.

Meanwhile, the research strands described above have in recent years merged into an expanding research agenda on China's rise within the liberal order (e.g. de Graaff 2014; de Graaff and van Apeldoorn 2017, 2018); investigating how China's economy and core industries are internationalizing and how this plays out within Chinese corporate and political elite networks; assessing how far they are integrating into the transnational power structures that have been dominant in the liberal order; and what the particular features of a state–capital nexus 'with Chinese characteristics' entail. This research agenda complements van der Pijl's (2012) and Overbeek's (2016) recent work on China by providing detailed empirical analyses of Chinese elite power structures based on network analysis and field interviews. Though not yet inclined to make any grand theoretical claims, I would agree that the Chinese political economy is – and will remain – distinctive for the foreseeable future, and will not be co-opted into the Lockean heartland (van der Pijl 2012). My findings so far, however, seem to suggest that Chinese 'statist' capitalism does not have one face – which ultimately will reject liberalization – but has *two faces*. Partly conforming to – even embracing – further liberalization, partly resisting this, in an attempt to keep state (party) control. This contradiction, or duality, will characterize China's rise and development within the liberal order – both internally and externally – and generates a hybridity that awaits both further empirical investigation and theorization. I hope it is here, on our way to Beijing, that our critical exchanges will continue.

References

van Apeldoorn, B. (2002). *Transnational capitalism and the struggle over European integration.* London: Routledge.

van Apeldoorn, B. and de Graaff, N. (2014). Corporate elite networks and US post-Cold War grand strategy from Clinton to Obama. *European Journal of International Relations* 20(1): 29–55.

van Apeldoorn, B. and de Graaff, N. (2015). *American grand strategy and corporate elite networks: The open door since the end of the Cold War.* London: Routledge.

van Apeldoorn, B., Overbeek, H. and de Graaff, N. (Eds) (2012). The rebound of the capitalist state: The rearticulation of the state–capital nexus in the global crisis. *Globalizations* 9(4).

Bottomore, T. (1993). *Elites and society*, 2nd ed. Harmondsworth: Pelican.

Carroll, W.K. (2010). *The making of a transnational capitalist class: Corporate power in the twenty-first century.* London: Zed.

Carroll, W.K., Fennema, M. and Heemskerk, E.M. (2010). Constituting corporate Europe: A study of elite social organization. *Antipode* 42(4): 811–843.

Cutler, C.A., Haufler, V. and Porter, T. (Eds) (1999). *Private authority and international affairs.* Albany, NY: State University of New York Press.

Domhoff, G.W. (1967). *Who rules America? Power, politics and social change.* Englewood Cliffs, NJ: Prentice Hall.

Domhoff, G.W. (2007). C. Wright Mills, power structure research, and the failures of mainstream political science. *New Political Science* 29(1): 97–114.

Fennema, M. (1982). *Networks of banks and industry.* The Hague: Martinus Nijhof.

de Graaff, N. (2011). A global energy network? The expansion and integration of non-Triad national oil companies. *Global Networks* 11(2): 262–283.

de Graaff, N. (2012). Oil elite networks in a transforming global oil market. *International Journal of Comparative Sociology* 53(4): 275–297.

de Graaff, N. (2013). Towards a hybrid global energy order: State-owned oil companies, corporate elite networks and governance. PhD dissertation, Vrije Universiteit Amsterdam, www.ubvu.vu.nl/dissertations/temp/temp06.pdf?CFID=3701153&CFTOKEN= 8fd1266cf25ed433-C062C4DB-B669-B347-C667A060BC4FD99A

196 Naná de Graaff

de Graaff, N. (2014). Global networks and the two faces of Chinese national oil companies. *Perspectives on Global Development and Technology* 13(5–6): 539–563.

de Graaff, N. and van Apeldoorn, B. (2011). Varieties of US post-Cold War imperialism: Anatomy of a failed hegemonic project and the future of US geopolitics. *Critical Sociology* 37(4): 403–427.

de Graaff, N. and van Apeldoorn, B. (2017). US elite power and the rise of 'statist' Chinese elites in global markets. *International Politics* 54(3): 338–355.

de Graaff, N. and van Apeldoorn, B. (2018). US–China Relations and the liberal world order: Contending elites, colliding visions? *International Affairs* 94(1).

de Graaff, N. and van Apeldoorn, B. (forthcoming). A Trumpian foreign policy elite? A network analysis of the Trump Administration and its implications for America's global role. *Global Networks*, special issue on transnational policy elites.

Mills, C.W. (1956). *The power elite*. New York: Oxford University Press.

Overbeek, H. (2016). Globalizing China: A critical political economy perspective on China's rise. In A. Cafruny, G. Pozo-Martin and L.S. Talani (Eds), *Handbook of critical international political economy: Theories, issues and regions* (pp. 309–329). London: Palgrave Macmillan.

van der Pijl, K. (2012). Is the East still Red? The contender state and class struggles in China. *Globalizations* 9(4): 503–516.

Scholte, J.A. (2000). *Globalization: A critical introduction*. London: Macmillan.

Scott, J. (1991). *Social network analysis: A handbook*. London: SAGE.

Wasserman, S. and Faust, K. (1994). *Social network analysis: Methods and applications*. Cambridge: Cambridge University Press.

12

REFLECTIONS ON THE AMSTERDAM SCHOOL AND THE TRANSNATIONAL CAPITALIST CLASS

William K. Carroll

Since the 1980s, the Amsterdam School (AS) has pursued an empirically rich and conceptually sophisticated research programme addressed to transnational class formation in the twentieth and twenty-first centuries. The programme has been cumulative, registering significant advances over time, as globalizing capitalism itself has shape-shifted. By placing the struggle for hegemony at the centre of an international political economy sensitive to national specificities, the AS has articulated a strong alternative, within International Relations, to neorealism and constructivism. But beyond that, it has contributed broadly to historical materialism as a transdisciplinary perspective in social science.

As a budding sociologist, I first became aware of this school through Henk Overbeek's (1980) *Capital & Class* article, 'Finance capital and the crisis in Britain' (see Chapter 3). His clear conception of finance capital as 'the integration of the circuits of money capital, productive capital and commodity capital under the conditions of monopolization and internationalization by means of a series of links and relationships between individual capitals' (1980: 102) influenced my dissertation research. But, whereas Overbeek's dissertation focused on, among other things, the role of City-based finance in Britain's decline, mine was a case study of Canada's post-war decades, through the late 1970s – when US-based investment was flooding in, even as Canada's own capitalists consolidated their networks of finance capital and, in later years, rapidly expanded abroad (Carroll 1986). Cutting against the grain of left-nationalist thought at the time, which characterized Canada as an anomalous 'rich dependency' (Panitch 1981), I argued that, in an era of capitalist globalization under the auspices of US hegemony, Canada's capitalist class had not sold out. On the contrary, it had retained a robust accumulation base in integrated circuits of industry and finance. Featured in my research as a marker of this capital integration was the dense network of interlocking directorates that drew Canada's capitalists into a corporate community.

198 William K. Carroll

I was further drawn to the AS perspective in the mid-1980s, as I turned simultaneously to Gramsci and to International Political Economy to better situate my work on Canada's capitalist class. In this regard, Bob Jessop's emerging strategic-relational approach, announced most succinctly in his 1983 *Kapitalistate* article, offered an appealing reading of Gramsci as a theorist of culture, politics and economics, of strategy and structure. Jessop introduced the concepts *accumulation strategies* and *hegemonic projects* as diagnostic tools that could throw light on the correlation of forces within specific conjunctures but also across broad eras.

My 1987–8 sabbatical in the Political Science Department at the University of Amsterdam, hosted by Meindert Fennema, facilitated a deeper engagement with the AS. On the one hand, I extended my research interest in interlocking corporate directorates to the transnational field, about which Fennema had published the seminal work as his dissertation (Fennema 1982). On the other hand, I began to work with some basic AS insights on fractions of capital and concepts of control, which helped specify the relationship between accumulation strategies and hegemonic projects. As Henk Overbeek comments (2004: 115), the notion of a comprehensive concept of control enables us to understand how strategic divisions in bourgeois politics and the structural dynamics of capital accumulation are interrelated. In this way, the fractionation of the capitalist class is understood as a moment of the underlying process of class formation, rather than as an aberration or an insignificant epiphenomenon.

Indeed, it is in making a concept of control *comprehensive* – 'an effective vector of class formation within and beyond the bourgeoisie' (van der Pijl 1984: 12) – that the level of fractional interests is transcended and, thereby, a general, hegemonic interest assembled. This is always as a contingent accomplishment. In this formulation, the interplay of structure and strategy is explicit, as illustrated, for example, in US-led, post-war corporate liberalism and the integrated, state-supported circuit of finance capital provided strategic and structural coordinates for an historic bloc that came to unify the North Atlantic, promoting capitalist internationalization on a regulated basis (van der Pijl 1989: 8). In the Canadian case, the transition to neoliberalism had as its centrepiece the construction of a continental free trade zone offering Canadian business access to the world's largest and most politically secure market while enhancing capital's structural power against local workforces and governments (Carroll 1990). Pursued more as passive revolution than as a Thatcherite 'two-nations' nationalist project (Jessop et al. 1988), deregulated continentalism yielded a formula for integrating the circuit of North American capital in such a way that Canadian-based financial groups could become 'direct participants on an equal footing with the American-based counterparts in a lucrative and politically stable field of accumulation' (Carroll 1993: 235).

In the 1990s, I began to map the contours of transnational capitalist relations in detail, in collaboration with Meindert Fennema. Our 2002 article revealed a modest increase between 1976 and 1996 in transnational interlocking among the world's largest corporations, occurring entirely within Europe and across the North Atlantic. My 2010 book, *The making of a transnational capitalist class* (TCC), whose title acknowledges a debt to both E.P. Thompson and Kees van der Pijl, focused on developments from 1996 through 2006, and again found a modest increase in transnational interlocking. The elite network remained centred on the North Atlantic, although across that decade corporations from a greater range of countries (including the semi-periphery) began to participate. Noting the important role that policy-planning groups such as the World Economic Forum play in fostering 'a transnational historic bloc of capitalists and organic intellectuals that builds consensus and exercises business leadership in the global arena' (2010: 228), the study also pointed to fractional divisions that limit the TCC's capacity to act fully as a class for itself. In this regard, I drew on van der Pijl's (1998) analysis of internationalization. Specifically, I argued that TCC formation 'takes place not as the unfolding of a borderless world ruled by capital but in the context of an ongoing tug-of-war between Lockean liberalization and Hobbesian territorialization, with alter-globalization thrusts from below opposing both options' (2010: 233).

This characterization is distinct from that of William Robinson (2004, 2012), who has portrayed the TCC (and an accompanying transnational state) as having already arrived. In subsequent reflections, I have argued for a more nuanced analysis, attuned to the interplay of national, regional and transnational political-economic relations (Carroll 2012). Bastiaan van Apeldoorn and Naná de Graaff's meticulous study of the US state–capital nexus was helpful in clarifying these relations. Where Robinson sees a homogeneous TCC whose interests are advanced by a transnational state in which the US state apparatus is the most powerful component, van Apeldoorn and de Graaff discern, at the heart of that apparatus, a distinct fraction of 'US-based transnational capital' – at once both national and transnational – whose interests are reflected in US grand strategy. The specific, territorialized project of US Open Door imperialism is not to construct a global order for the TCC. Rather, it 'is about serving *the general and long-term interests of US transnational capital*, that is, opening and keeping open the door not just for today's US corporations but also for the future' (van Apeldoorn and de Graaff 2012: 597). In this more nuanced perspective, capital's continuing national moorings are related dialectically to transnational circuits of accumulation; that is, capital is not in any simple sense bifurcated into 'national versus transnational'. And, if US-based capital and the US Open Door have led the way in elaborating a Lockean Heartland and absorbing Hobbesian challengers, the uneven and contradictory character of accumulation and state power cautions us against extrapolating from past to future – particularly in a conjuncture of 'Trumpism' – when, according to *Der Spiegel*, 'the West as an entity, it would seem, is disintegrating' (2017).

This brings me to a final pair of insights that I have taken from my engagement with the AS. Kees van der Pijl and Yuliya Yurchenko have traced neoliberalism's mutation from a 'systemic' phase, which restored profitability via real accumulation (partly through attacks on organized labour and social welfare), to 'predatory neoliberalism'. In the latter case, financialization creates an ever expanding volume of fictitious capital as 'real accumulation becomes a secondary consideration altogether' (2015: 503). When the bubble inevitably bursts, state bailouts displace financial crisis into a crisis of public finance; hence, 'austerity, the asset-stripping of entire societies ... becomes the downside of refuelling speculative money-dealing capital' (2015: 512). Societal asset stripping, in turn, provokes protective responses from below. Thus, as it becomes

200 William K. Carroll

more predatory, and as its base thins from an alliance of capital and the asset-owning middle classes to an exclusivist oligarchy, neoliberalism also becomes more authoritarian (Bruff 2014), ratcheting up the free market/strong state dynamic already salient in Thatcherism (Gamble 1988; Carroll and Sapinski 2016).

Finally, amid sharpening contradictions whose symptoms range from new renditions of authoritarian populism to such counterhegemonic initiatives as climate justice, I have turned to Kees van der Pijl's analysis of the transnational cadre, a class of 'knowledge workers', fluid in political perspective and entrusted with tasks of conception and direction in production and with broad normative integration. As capital becomes more visibly predatory, exhausting 'both the community/society and the natural substratum on which it feeds' (van der Pijl 1998: 30), the cadre 'may become receptive to arguments and forces emerging from the grassroots resistance to capitalist development' (van der Pijl 2004: 202). If, as van der Pijl (1998: 165) holds, 'the cadres are the *class which historically performs the role of shaping the structures for a classless society in the context of class society*', prospects for democratic transformation hinge on detaching cadre from the hegemonic bloc and creating a bloc that aligns community and organizational leaders, social professionals, scientists and engineers, artists, journalists and scholars with subalterns on the receiving end of domination (see Carroll 2013a, 2013b).

References

van Apeldoorn, B. and de Graaff, N. (2012). The limits of open door imperialism and the US state–capital nexus. *Globalizations* 9(4): 593–608.

Bruff, I. (2014). The rise of authoritarian neoliberalism. *Rethinking Marxism* 26: 113–129.

Carroll, W.K. (1986). *Corporate power and Canadian capitalism.* Vancouver: University of British Columbia Press.

Carroll, W.K. (1990). Restructuring capital, reorganizing consent: Gramsci, political economy, and Canada. *Canadian Review of Sociology and Anthropology* 27: 390–416.

Carroll, W.K. (1993). Canada in the crisis: Transformations in capital structure and political strategy. In H. Overbeek (Ed.), *Restructuring hegemony in the global political economy. The rise of transnational neo-liberalism in the 1980s* (pp. 216–245). London: Routledge.

Carroll, W.K. (2010). *The making of a transnational capitalist class: Corporate power in the twenty-first century.* London: Zed.

Carroll, W.K. (2012). Global, transnational, regional, national: The need for nuance in theorizing global capitalism. *Critical Sociology* 38: 365–371.

Carroll, W.K. (2013a). Networks of cognitive praxis: Transnational class formation from below? *Globalizations* 10: 651–670.

Carroll, W.K. (2013b). Whither the transnational capitalist class? *Socialist Register* 50: 62–88.

Carroll, W.K. and Fennema, M. (2002). Is there a transnational business community? *International Sociology* 17: 393–419.

Carroll, W.K. and Sapinski, J.P. (2016). Neoliberalism and the transnational capitalist class. In K. Birch, J. MacLeavy and S. Springer (Eds), *The handbook of neoliberalism* (pp. 25–35). London: Routledge.

Fennema, M. (1982). *Networks of banks and industry.* The Hague: Martinus Nijhof.

Gamble, A. (1988). *The free economy and the strong state.* London: Macmillan.

Jessop, B. (1983). Accumulation strategies, state forms, and hegemonic projects. *Kapitalistate* 10–11: 89–111.

Jessop, B., Bonnett, K., Bromley, S. and Ling, T. (1988). *Thatcherism: A tale of two nations*. Cambridge: Polity.

Overbeek, H. (1980). Finance capital and the crisis in Britain. *Capital & Class* 11: 99–120.

Overbeek, H. (2004). Transnational class formation and concepts of control: Towards a genealogy of the Amsterdam Project in international political economy. *Journal of International Relations and Development* 7(2): 113–141.

Panitch, L. (1981). Dependency and class in Canadian political economy. *Studies in Political Economy* 6: 7–33.

van der Pijl, K. (1984). *The making of an Atlantic ruling class*. London: Verso.

van der Pijl, K. (1989). Globalisation of class and state. Paper presented at the annual conference of the British Political Studies Association, University of Warwick, April.

van der Pijl, K. (1998). *Transnational classes and international relations*. London: Routledge.

van der Pijl, K. (2004). Two faces of the transnational cadre under neo-liberalism. *Journal of International Relations and Development* 7(2): 177–207.

van der Pijl, K. and Yurchenko, Y. (2015). Neoliberal entrenchment of North Atlantic capital: From corporate self-regulation to state capture. *New Political Economy* 20(4): 495–517.

Robinson, W.I. (2004). *A theory of global capitalism*. Baltimore, MD: Johns Hopkins University Press.

Robinson, W.I. (2012). Global capitalism theory and the emergence of transnational elites. *Critical Sociology* 38(3): 349–363.

Der Spiegel Online (2017). Merkel concerned G-20 summit could end in fiasco. 30 June, www.spiegel.de/international/world/eu-us-trade-conflict-threatens-to-escalate-ahead-of-g-20-a-1155342.html#ref=nl-international, accessed 19 July 2017.

13

ALTERNATIVE PERSPECTIVES ON EUROPEAN INTEGRATION

Alan Cafruny and Magnus Ryner

Starting with *A ruined fortress?* (Cafruny and Ryner 2003), continuing with *Europe at bay* (Cafruny and Ryner 2007), and culminating in *The European Union and global capitalism* (Ryner and Cafruny 2017), we have developed an historical materialist approach, broadly conceived, to the European Union (EU). Through a close critical engagement with various mainstream theoretical perspectives, we have tried to show that historical materialism provides a deeper and more comprehensive understanding of the origins of the EU, the transition to the neoliberal or second project of European integration, and its contemporary crisis. Our understanding of the dialectical interplay of integration and disintegration in Europe has been greatly influenced by scholars working within the Amsterdam School, notably Kees van der Pijl, Henk Overbeek, Otto Holman, and Bastiaan van Apeldoorn as well as by the French regulation school and (neo-)Gramscians, including most notably Bob Jessop, Robert Cox, and Stephen Gill.

Notwithstanding the proliferation of competing analytical models, mainstream International Political Economy (IPE) scholarship has not fundamentally transcended its original realist/idealist dichotomy. Thus, 'integration', which is fundamentally associated with the market and its administration, is understood as a largely self-stabilizing and benevolent process that expresses the inherent rational potentials of human nature. Power, arbitrariness, and special interests, by contrast, are associated with the state and the state system. The central debate is between 'optimists', 'pessimists', and 'middle positions' about the extent to which the former can assert itself given the constraints of the latter. Such a 'states and markets' approach to IPE has not developed an integrated political economy.

By contrast, critical IPE starts from the premise of an organic connection (albeit formal separation) among the state, inter-state relations, and capital. Imperialism does not derive from the logic of 'power', narrowly conceived, but rather reflects the ceaseless drive towards capital accumulation beyond the boundaries of the national territorial state in which it was formed and developed. However, if scholars of critical IPE do not fundamentally disagree about the origins of the contemporary capitalist state, there are nevertheless important differences in emphasis relating to the extent to which states are subsumed within broader transnational networks. In Volume I of *Capital*, Marx clearly showed that the development of capitalism was organically connected to the world market, as its presupposition and as its posit (result). However, there was not surprisingly a certain 'state centricity' in first-generation theories of imperialism. For these were developed during the second industrial revolution, characterized by huge publicly sponsored investments in social overheads, the relative decline of British imperialism, and the challenge of rising imperialist powers – the latter two changes culminating in World War I. Rudolf Hilferding (1910), Vladimir Illich Lenin (1917), Rosa Luxemburg (1913), and Nikolai Bukharin (1917) all emphasized inter-imperialist or inter-ruling class rivalry. They sought to locate the expansionary imperatives arising from within national capitalism in the tendency of the rate of profit to fall or overaccumulation and assumed that these expansionary drives would eventually lead to war. The exception to this apparent consensus was the German social democrat, Karl Kautsky, who argued that the world market had reached a stage where 'denationalized' combinations of capitalists had rendered inter-imperialist rivalry obsolete and, with it, war (Kautsky 1914). This dispute has, in some respects, been reprised in contemporary critical IPE.

The renaissance of Marxist scholarship in the 1960s and 1970s led to a new generation of theories of imperialism that sought to situate inter-state rivalry within profound changes in post-war capitalism. These theories highlighted the transnational linkages among ruling classes that had developed in the context of Atlantic Fordism, welfare state capitalism, the 'internationalization of the New Deal' (Panitch and Gindin 2013), and the supervisory leadership, or 'hegemonic', functions performed by the United States. Analysis of these enabled critical IPE scholars to develop novel approaches to analysis of the EU.

Whereas mainstream EU studies posited a largely internal ('sui generis') dynamic of integration, based above all on a functionalist logic, Marxist scholarship was more attuned to the US and global origins of the EU. Accordingly, they sought to situate economic and political processes of European integration within the framework of US imperialism and IPE. The central question thus became whether European capitalism could develop a sufficient internal coherence to emerge as an alternative global power centre. Ernest Mandel (1969) concluded that European capitalism was gradually amalgamating under the umbrella of the Common Market and, as it did so, the result was growing rivalry with the United States. By contrast, Nicos Poulantzas (1975) was more sceptical of the prospects for an internally coherent rival European centre emerging. Focusing on the implications of US leadership in key sectors for the structuring of the global economy and especially the growing significance of money capital, Poulantzas proposed the term 'internal bourgeoisie' (1975: 72–6) to describe the continuing subordination – and fragmentation – of 'fractions' of European capital, national capitalist classes, European capital in general, and, hence, the EU itself.

The core concept that the Amsterdam School uses to explore transnational class formation – comprehensive concepts of control – is informed by these insights, but it takes the argument further: in his seminal work, Kees van der Pijl (1984) placed the strategies of agents that form accumulation regimes and underpin successive hegemonies at the centre of analysis. He contended that the construction of US hegemony involved more than simply inter-state or inter-ruling class power relations, but in fact a system of transnational class formation. Drawing on the concept of 'societalization' (*Vergesellschaftung*), which Marx (1857) treated as a necessary counterpoint to the entropic and atomizing tendencies of commodification, van der Pijl argued that national bourgeoisies reordered their relations towards one another. They gradually ceased to relate to one another as if their rivals belonged to an external nature to be dominated or conquered, if necessary by war. Rather, transnational capitalist relations were, as Poulantzas had it, 'interiorized' (in the English translation, 'internalized') (1975: 46, 62, 72–6, 273). Hegemony in different periods, he continued, can be defined in terms of various 'comprehensive concepts of control' that bind capitalist classes together around a given regulatory-cum-governance project with the help of Gramscian organic intellectuals and cadres. After World War II, US planners expanded and deepened a 'Lockean heartland' that facilitated the evolution of a transnational civil society and international organization (van der Pijl 1998). Haunted by the 'nightmare of depression' (Williams 1972), they thus adopted a more comprehensive and liberal approach to the problem of international capitalist order, resurrecting the concept of the 'open door'.

Indeed, the foundation, development, and periodic expansion of European integration are fundamentally moments of the expansion of the transnational capitalist political economy, which has been in uneven formation since the Glorious Revolution, centred first around Great Britain and later around the United States (van Apeldoorn et al. 2003: 38–9).

It is to this project – rather than an inherent internal dynamic – that the EU owes its origins. Van der Pijl thus explained why it was possible for US and European ruling classes strategically to coordinate Fordist regulation on an Atlantic scale and, later, the measures that instituted transnational neoliberalism (see also Overbeek 1993).

In his seminal analysis of Europe's neoliberal relaunching, Bastiaan van Apeldoorn (2002) showed that transnational European class formation, led by the European Roundtable of Industrialists, was decisive in the formation of a single European market. The Roundtable unified European transnational capital around a neoliberal project that was successfully transmitted to policy makers. The question raised by van Apeldoorn's analysis, writing at a time of considerable optimism concerning the European project, was whether European transnational capital would cut the Atlantic umbilical cord and develop as a relatively autonomous centre of capital accumulation. Were there latent potentials in the federalist, dirigiste, and social democratic elements that Europe's capitalist class co-opted with a view to generating sufficient consent in an 'embedded neoliberal' power bloc?

If the Amsterdam School has shown conclusively that there are 'transnational power blocs', can it be said that there are also transnational classes into which

Alternative perspectives on European integration **205**

'national bourgeoisies' have been subsumed? Is Kautsky's concept of ultra-imperialism relevant in the present conjuncture? Scholars broadly associated with the Amsterdam School have demonstrated a certain ambiguity with respect to this question and are certainly not of one voice. Indeed, leading scholars have argued that an embryonic 'Atlantic ruling class' has emerged (e.g. van der Pijl 1984) without, however, eliminating global rivalries (van der Pijl 2006), and others have anticipated the development of an autonomous European transnational class (e.g. van Apeldoorn 2002; van der Pijl et al. 2011). Other neo-Gramscian scholars, such as Bieler and Morton (2015), have argued that 'one has witnessed the emergence of a transnational capitalist class (TCC) meaning that it is no longer possible to simply speak in terms of a rivalry between "German" capital, "French" capital, or "American" capital, etc.' (Bieler and Morton 2015: 105; see also Sklair 2001). Similar arguments have been made, inter alia, by Stephen Gill (1990), William Robinson (2004), van Apeldoorn (2004), and Hardt and Negri (2000). In general, then, the Amsterdam School has tended to focus on inter-capitalist cohesion. This is especially notable with respect to the EU.

Our own analysis has been more sceptical. Indeed, our main disagreement with the main body of the Amsterdam School concerns the scope and extent of inter-capitalist unity. Our work on the EU has emphasized 'uneven and combined development' as a destabilizing force within Europe itself. Thus, in *Europe at bay* (Cafruny and Ryner 2007) and *The European Union and global capitalism* (Ryner and Cafruny 2017) we stick closer to Poulantzas's original formulation. We find a world of rival capitalist ruling classes, albeit linked by concepts of control forged on a structurally selective terrain. Though we agree that states are by no means independent from these, they are not mere instruments of ruling class strategies. The concept 'comprehensive concepts of control' conflates important distinctions between 'accumulation strategies' and 'hegemonic projects' (Jessop 1983). Given their role in mediating between capital accumulation and mass legitimacy, states and inter-state dynamics impose further constraints on the integrating tendencies of capitalism that, in our view, the Amsterdam School underestimates.

Europe's present malaise can be explained largely in terms of the growing disunity of ruling classes within, respectively, the transatlantic and European spaces. In the former, the spread of finance-led neoliberalism across the Atlantic has served to erode European welfare capitalism. It does not – and probably cannot – dismantle the US-led transnational power bloc but rather redefines it in a more predatory and unstable fashion. Within the EU, the German ruling class has acquired (geo-economic) primacy. This is seen in its virtual monopoly of decision-making power over the Eurozone and in the long reach of production chains into Central and Eastern Europe, effectively subsuming and subordinating this region within the German industrial core. Notwithstanding this power, Germany appears incapable of forging an autonomous, integral hegemonic bloc that can resolve the growing crisis of neoliberalism on European terms. This is manifested in what we have called the 'ordo-liberal iron cage' and portends deepening conflict and disintegration.

References

van Apeldoorn, B. (2002). *Transnational capitalism and the struggle over European integration*. London: Routledge.

van Apeldoorn, B. (2004). Theorizing the transnational: An historical materialist approach. *Journal of International Relations and Development* 7(2): 142–176.

van Apeldoorn, B., Overbeek, H., and Ryner, M. (2003). Theories of European integration: A critique. In A.W. Cafruny and M. Ryner (Eds), *A ruined fortress?* (pp. 17–46). Lanham, MD: Rowman & Littlefield.

Bieler, A. and Morton, A.D. (2015). Axis of evil or access to evil: Spaces of new imperialism and the Iraq war. *Historical Materialism* 23(2): 94–130.

Bukharin, N. (1917). *Imperialism and the world economy*. London: Lawrence & Wishart.

Cafruny, A.W. and Ryner, M. (Eds) (2003). *A ruined fortress? Neoliberal hegemony and transformation in Europe*. Lanham, MD: Rowman & Littlefield.

Cafruny, A.W. and Ryner, M. (2007). *Europe at bay: In the shadow of US hegemony*. Boulder, CO: Lynne Rienner.

Gill, S. (1990). The emerging hegemony of transnational capital: Trilateralism and the global order. In D. Rapkin (Ed.), *World leadership and hegemony* (pp. 119–146). Boulder, CO: Lynne Rienner.

Hardt, M. and Negri, A. (2000). *Empire*. Cambridge, MA: Harvard University Press.

Hilferding, R. (2006 [1910]). *Finance capital: A study in the latest phase of capitalist development*. London: Routledge.

Jessop, B. (1983). Accumulation strategies, state forms, and hegemonic projects. *Kapitalistate* 10/11: 89–111.

Kautsky, K. (1970 [1914]). Ultra-imperialism. *New Left Review* 59: 41–46.

Lenin, V.I. (1917). *Imperialism: The highest stage of capitalism*. London: Lawrence & Wishart.

Luxemburg, R. (2003 [1913]). *The accumulation of capital*. London: Routledge.

Mandel, E. (1969). *Europe vs. America? Contradictions of imperialism*. London: New Left Books.

Marx, K. (1973). Introduction. In *Grundrisse: Foundations of the critique of political economy* (pp. 81–111). Harmondsworth: Penguin <1857>.

Marx, K. (1976 [1867, 1887]). *Capital*, Volume I. London: Lawrence & Wishart.

Overbeek, H. (Ed.) (1993). *Restructuring hegemony in the global political economy*. London: Routledge.

Panitch, L. and Gindin, S. (2013). *The making of global capitalism: The political economy of the American empire*. London: Verso.

van der Pijl, K. (1984). *The making of an Atlantic ruling class*. London: Verso.

van der Pijl, K. (1998). *Transnational classes and international relations*. London: Routledge.

van der Pijl, K. (2006). *Global rivalries from the Cold War to Iraq*. London: Pluto.

van der Pijl, K., Holman, O., and Raviv, O. (2011). The resurgence of German capital in Europe. *Review of International Political Economy* 18(3): 420–448.

Poulantzas, N. (1975). *Classes in contemporary capitalism*. London: New Left Books.

Robinson, W.I. (2004). *A theory of global capitalism: Production, class, and state in a transnational world*. Baltimore, MD: Johns Hopkins University Press.

Ryner, M. and Cafruny, A. (2017). *The European Union and global capitalism: Origins, development, crisis*. London: Palgrave.

Sklair, L. (2001). *The transnational capitalist class*. Oxford: Blackwell.

Williams, W.A. (1972 [1959]). *The tragedy of American diplomacy*, 2nd edition. New York: Delta.

14

NATIONALIST POPULISM WITHIN THE LOCKEAN HEARTLAND

Hans-Jürgen Bieling

Introduction: Locke versus Hobbes

The Amsterdam project has several distinctive conceptual elements. In addition to its roots in historical materialism, these include a transnational perspective, neo-Gramscian readings of hegemony and organic intellectuals, and a strong focus on the role of capital fractions in developing comprehensive concepts of control (Overbeek 2000: 60–6). A subsequent theoretical advance is the contrast between two kinds of state-civil society complexes. Alluding to classical social contract theory, Kees van der Pijl (1998, 2006) identifies a Lockean heartland and Hobbesian contender states. He regards the former as marked by extensive civil society relations, whose development is influenced by commercial orientations, possessive individualist thinking, concepts of self-regulation, and a rich ensemble of associations. The reproduction of civil society is stabilized by a liberal type of state, which rests on the rule of law, institutionalized checks and balances, reliable contractual relations, and rather limited capacities of state intervention. Based on the relative autonomy of state and market vis-à-vis each other, the ruling classes have delegated the function of governing to a governing class. Furthermore, the continuing interaction of state and civil society is embedded in a highly productive capitalist economy, extensive markets, and trade relations. Internationally, this is associated with the promotion of global civil rights and the ideology of liberal cosmopolitanism, flanked by a broad network of military bases. Initially, the Lockean heartland was centred in the Anglo-American world, before it penetrated and incorporated other regions such as continental Europe, where, however, possessive individualism was (and remains) tempered by stronger social orientations institutionalized in distinctive welfare regimes and corporatist forms of interaction.

In contrast to the Lockean heartland, the state-civil society complex of Hobbesian contender states is markedly more authoritarian. This mainly results from the relative economic backwardness of these countries. Their ruling classes and governing classes – in close alliance or as state classes – aim to catch up economically by developing stronger forms of state interventionism. The control dimension is not confined to the economy. It also embraces the infrastructure of civil society, that is, political parties, associations, academia or media, and the arenas of public communication. The state-controlled, often authoritarian political culture also influences external relations. Economically, the state classes in Hobbesian contender states tend to follow neo-mercantilist thinking and apply protectionist instruments; more generally, they are critical of liberal cosmopolitan concepts and disposed instead to defend national sovereignty and traditional international law.

This conceptual differentiation proved very useful for understanding the causes and the course of major structural conflicts within the global political economy over past centuries. Important examples include conflicts between the Anglo-American world and its former rivals such as France, Germany, Japan, or the Soviet Union. The more recent conflict dynamics in the Ukraine, between the European Union (EU) and Turkey, or between the US and China also fit broadly into this line of interpretation.

But there are also some problematic aspects. Thus, in general terms, the differentiation between the Lockean heartland and Hobbesian contender states may distract observers from analysing the grounding of the limits and contradictions of neoliberal globalization and neoliberal cosmopolitanism in processes emerging in the Lockean heartland itself. More specifically, focusing on elite networks and transnational relations and the tendency to neglect domestic class conflicts may well hinder our ability to study and interpret the rise of nationalist populism not only within the US and UK but also within the transformed EU. But these are surely important aspects of the current crisis tendencies in neoliberalism and indicate the inherent and contingent limits of the neoliberal transnational capitalist class even in its core region. In turn, this requires a greater emphasis on the contradictions and hegemonic struggles within the national settings of capitalism.

Capitalist contradictions and the nature of social conflicts

Kees van der Pijl has already provided a good starting point for analysing these contradictions and conflicts in his discussion of the distinctive features of the social class conflicts in different periods of capitalist development (1998: 36–49). Thus, for the eighteenth and nineteenth centuries, he identified a first period of unfolding proletarianization, primarily driven by primitive accumulation and the formal subordination of labour to capital. The precursor to this was a process whereby more or less autonomous workers such as craftsmen or peasants, and household members – women and children – were uprooted from traditional social relations and subjected to a new capitalist regime of control. This control regime was intensified in the late nineteenth and twentieth centuries, when the focus on relative surplus value extraction corresponded with a real subsumption of labour under capitalist control. This implied that the locus of social struggles moved into the arenas of work and production. Given the powerful political organization of labour, this move allowed the negotiation of more comprehensive social and labour regulation(s). The third period, beginning in the 1980s, not only involves the globalization of finance and production but also a deeper capitalist penetration and (re)commodification of the sphere of reproduction. So the nature of struggles has changed again. Different kinds of social movements – from trade unions to the anti-globalization movement or the churches – are increasingly concerned about social insecurity and the comprehensive commercialization of everyday life.

The changing nature of social struggles is certainly part of the changing dynamics and patterns of capitalist accumulation. However, it would be a mistake to confine the analysis just to this structural dimension. For, the social relations of production and reproduction also include the production of knowledge and certain moral values inscribed into institutionalized norms, regulations, and practices (Cox 1989: 39). In this sense, it seems useful to pay greater attention to the dimensions of the 'moral economy' (Thompson 1971). In capitalism this covers not only socio-economic relations but also modernized norms and commitments, particularly the cultural processes of sense making and the production of inter-subjective meaning. Such a wider understanding of the new quality of capitalist accumulation and the new forms of resistance has stimulated some critical scholars to reread Karl Polanyi (notably 2001). In addition to the concept of embeddedness, which implicitly includes moral economy aspects, attention was directed towards interpreting capitalist development as a 'double movement'. According to Polanyi, on the one hand, the principle of economic liberalism effectively promoted the myth of a self-regulating market and the ideal of laissez-faire politics and, in consequence, a social disembedding of economic relations; and, on the other hand, the principle of social protection provided a reference point for a counter-movement, which reacted to the devastating social and ecological effects of economic liberalism by suggesting a re-embedding of the capitalist economy.

In the past decades, for some observers, the concept of the 'double movement' has proved instructive for analysing and interpreting the emergence of the anti- and alter-globalization movement. More recently, however, it has seemed even more appropriate for understanding the rise of nationalist populism in large parts of the Organisation for Economic Co-operation and Development world, not least in the EU and the US. In other words, nationalist populism can be analysed and interpreted as a reaction and counter-movement to the social and cultural implications of the disembedding of economic relations induced by globalization and financialization (Saval 2016). Given increasing social inequality and insecurity, many people struggle very hard to cope with the precariousness of work and social life. Further concerned about the financial crisis and the crisis of migration regimes, they experience or fear a loss of control, of individual perspectives, and of tradition (Detje et al. 2017). In most societies, such fears and experiences and the manifold forms of social contempt generate feelings of anger (Hochschild 2016), which often are politically articulated by nationalist populist movements. Furthermore, these

210 Hans-Jürgen Bieling

movements strongly invoke the imaginary of national control and sovereignty and aim to reorder social protection in terms of exclusive nationalist solidarities.

A new political cleavage in the world of developed capitalism

None of this justifies a strict historical analogy to the fascist movements in the 1920s and 1930s, given the above-mentioned shift from classical imperialism to transnational capitalism as well as the strategic orientation of nationalist populist movements (Berman 2016). This means, to date, most nationalist populists seem to broadly accept most of the elements of representative and direct democracy. Sometimes, they pretend to strengthen or to apply the latter only, however, to weaken the role of intermediary civil society organizations. Furthermore, once in power, their political leaders seem less tolerant of liberal, rule of law-based principles such as political independence of courts, media, and science or, likewise, of freedom of speech and other individual and minority rights. Consequently, their actions contribute to an authoritarian transformation of political culture. This applies even more, if one considers the main programmatic priorities of nationalist populist movements. For, irrespective of national peculiarities, most such movements advance ethno-nationalist reasoning, criticism of multiculturalism, anti-Islamism, opposition to the EU (notably the European Monetary Union), migration, and a nationalist articulation of social issues.

In a way, the rise of nationalist populism reflects a new discursive cleavage between neoliberal cosmopolitanism and nationalist populism. While corresponding with most features of the Lockean heartland, neoliberal cosmopolitanism even goes beyond classic liberal cosmopolitan orientations, as it highlights economic principles such as the priority of investor rights, market competition, or economic non-discrimination and allows for the cross-border guarantee of individual civil rights and liberties by international or supranational organizations such as the United Nations or EU. In several regards, neoliberal cosmopolitanism should be conceived of as a transnational movement, which at least partially undermines the traditional self-understanding of the nation-state and puts the ideology of national sovereignty into question. It provokes, therefore, not only nationalist resistance from the side of Hobbesian contender states, often governed by authoritarian governments, but also increasingly within the Lockean heartland itself. This is illustrated by many movements, which emerged in response to defending national sovereignty and some forms of selective social protection in terms of trade policy, industrial policy, or social security provision. A social component is also there but it is harder to identify in the UK (United Kingdom Independence Party and the Brexit campaign) and the US (Tea Party and Donald Trump) than in continental Europe, where large parts of the working and middle classes feel increasingly represented by nationalist populist parties such as the Front National in France, the (True) Fins in Finland, the Sweden Democrats, the Freedom Party in the Netherlands, and the PIS in Poland or Fidesz in Hungary (Rydgren 2013).

The centrality of the new discursive cleavage between neoliberal cosmopolitanism and nationalist populism poses serious analytical and political challenges. Analytically, the rise of nationalist populism in the Lockean heartland suggests that the AS focuses too much on the role of transnational capitalist classes, their neoliberal think tanks, and strategic planning bodies and neglects the political articulation of the contradictions of neoliberal restructuring within domestic civil societies. As indicated, the Amsterdam Project includes some starting points for studying societal contradictions and struggles. Thus, besides conceptual reflections on the structural transformation of class struggle (van der Pijl 1998: 36-49), Otto Holman has identified a 'new populism' as a particular 'political style' intended to soften social discontent within the EU by, for example, promoting subsidiarity, intergovernmental coordination and the illusion of national self-determination (Holman 2004). This suggests that European politicians anticipated the recent wave of nationalist populist reactions. However, this is only half the story. For the AS still focuses mainly on the top-down political management of capitalist contradictions and tends to neglect bottom-up processes that involve the political articulation of social struggles within domestic, sometimes also transnational, arenas. Besides such analytical issues, the structuring role that the cleavage between neoliberal cosmopolitanism and nationalist populism performs for most public discourses is also politically highly problematic. For both orientations are specifically socially exclusive: whereas neoliberal cosmopolitanism marginalizes economically weaker groups, nationalist populism opposes immigrants, minorities, and civil rights movements. Furthermore, the new discursive cleavage generates a constellation in political movements and organizations that call for solidarity find it hard to be heard in the public or realize their demands. We need, then, political projects or initiatives that help to reopen the public sphere and undermine the prominence of these complementary forms of exclusion.

References

Berman, S. (2016). Populism is not fascism. *Foreign Affairs* 95(6): 39–44.

Cox, R.W. (1989). Production, the state, and change in world order. In E.-O. Czempiel and J.N. Rosenau (Eds), *Global changes and theoretical challenges*. (pp. 37–50). Toronto: Lexington Books.

Detje, R., Dörre, K., Kronauer, M., and Schumann, M. (2017). Zeitenwende oder. Zeit für eine Wende der Linken. *Blätter für deutsche und internationale Politik* 62(4): 97–103.

Hochschild, A.R. (2016). *Strangers in their own land. Anger and mourning on the American right*. New York: New Press.

Overbeek, H. (2000). Towards a neo-Gramscian theory of European integration. The example of the tax harmonization question. In H-J. Bieling and J. Steinhilber (Eds), *Dimensions of a critical theory of European integration* (pp. 59–81). Marburg: Forschungsgruppe Europäische Gemeinschaften, Philipps-Universität.

van der Pijl, K. (1998). *Transnational classes and international relations*. London: Routledge.

van der Pijl, K. (2006). *Global rivalries. From the Cold War to Iraq*. London: Pluto.

Polanyi, K. (2001 [1944]). *The great transformation*. Boston, MA: Beacon.

Rydgren, J. (Ed.) (2013). *Class politics and the radical right*. London: Routledge.

Saval, N. (2016). Polanyi in our times. *Nation*, 19–26 December.

Thompson, E.P. (1971). The moral economy of the English crowd in the eighteenth century. *Past and Present* 50: 76–136.

15

OUT OF AMSTERDAM!

Beyond the boundaries of (transnational) capitalist class formation

Laura Horn and Angela Wigger

The 'Amsterdam School', or 'Amsterdam Project' (AP), has made crucial contributions to understanding transnational capital and class agency in the transformation of contemporary capitalism. The invitation to consider its strengths, weaknesses, and relevance provides a welcome opportunity to rethink our intellectual and political linkages with the AP as past doctoral students of leading Amsterdam scholars, continuing friends and collaborators, and active scholars/teachers of a historical materialist perspective on Europe and European integration. This said, despite the formative influence and continued integration of the AP in our research, neither of us considers herself an AP scholar.

Our sympathetic critique develops in four steps. First, we interrogate the strengths and weaknesses of the notion of *comprehensive concepts of control* (CCCs) in empirical analysis, a core concept that we have both engaged with in detail but not applied in our work. Second, we question whether the AP has indeed crystallized into a school and relate this to the wider sociology of the academic field. Third, we problematize the ontological primacy that the AP gives to capital fractions. And, fourth, we locate the AP in the field of critical political economy (CPE) and its commitment to understanding and, ultimately, transforming contemporary capitalism.

Comprehensive concepts of control: going beyond theory

CCCs comprise 'frameworks of thought and practice by which a particular world view of the ruling class spills over into a broader sense of "limits of the possible" for society at large' (van der Pijl 1998: 51). As Overbeek observes, CCCs provide the crucial strategic link between structural changes in capital accumulation and capitalist class agency. The concept thereby enables the AP to navigate between the traps of structuralism and voluntarism (2004: 115, 119). The AP focus on fractionation, differentiating between, inter alia, the axes of productive and money capital and national and transnational capital, enables it to distinguish the contradictory interests and social antagonisms arising from different stages in the circuit of capital and show how these affect concrete instances of class formation. Moreover, as van Apeldoorn noted, 'concepts of control must be translated into state policy to become effective' (2004b: 155). Thus, he continues, CCCs comprise 'a particular configuration of social classes (and fractions thereof) that expresses itself at the ideational level and that gives "content to a historical state"'. The historically contingent articulation of CCCs mandates a clear methodological and empirical strategy (van der Pijl 1984). Analysing CCCs requires a formidable amount of research, engaging and triangulating various social scientific methods. Summarizing the resulting methodological challenges, Jessop and Sum (2017: 7) argue for a

> careful evaluation of their class relevance and class appeal in specific conjunctures and horizons of action [through] spatio-temporally nuanced analysis of relatively stable structures, changing conjunctures, the balance of forces, and successive offensive and defensive steps in the struggles between capital fractions and between the bourgeoisie and subaltern classes.

While the AP has made ground-breaking theoretical and conceptual contributions, there is an unstable balance between dense theoretical discussion and engagement with empirical material, and the general 'messiness' of social reality. The AP sometimes resolves this tension in favour of theoretical jargon. The concept of CCCs illustrates this; it remains empirically problematic. For, as Jessop and Sum (2017: 7) observe, the hegemony of a given CCC can only be established *ex post* and this requires a detailed account of why some CCCs become hegemonic and others fail. Thus, while theoretically the CCC concept offers a way to avoid determinism, this can only be delivered empirically through further methodological fine-tuning. Even key AP scholars use the concept as a theoretical linchpin without fully exploring its empirical potential in detailed analyses of class agency and class struggle.

Consequently, given the current fetishization of methods, AP's limited concern to integrate theoretical discussion and empirical analysis exposes it to the risk of being marginalized as a 'class conspiracy theory' – as a mainstream International Political Economy (IPE) colleague once generously warned us at an international conference. AP scholars know this, of course. Recent publications on neoliberalism in crisis, European Union integration, US foreign policy and transnational capitalism in general show real movement in this regard (Overbeek and van Apeldoorn 2012; van Apeldoorn 2013; van Apeldoorn and de Graaff 2016). However, in the spirit of friendly critique, we would highlight the need for *more* sustained empirical analyses. It is in concrete engagement with the social reality of contemporary capitalism, not in repeated self-referencing, that critical analysis fulfils its emancipatory commitment.

From the Amsterdam Project to the Amsterdam School myth

The genealogy of the AP has been well covered – perhaps surprisingly well for a group of researchers that is so limited in number that it can be comfortably seated around a table of one of Amsterdam's famous *bruin cafés* (traditional pubs). As its social genesis is already the stuff of legends, we focus on its status as a school and its positioning within CPE. In the 2004 *JIRD* special issue, van Apeldoorn insisted that the 'Amsterdam IPE project' is far from 'constituting a separate school – and certainly not aspiring to become one' (2004a: 110). Van der Pijl also emphasized that the AP 'cannot be considered anything even nearly deserving that label' (2004: 178). This assessment rests on a distinction between a project and a school; otherwise the two terms might also be conflated. Whereas a project consists of a series of individual contributions based on a shared theoretical framework or set of ideas, a school involves a far broader intellectual movement of followers and disciples that build on and/or develop further a distinct yet coherent approach. According to van Apeldoorn, the AP as a project reflects a 'specific endeavour to ground [analysis] ... in a particular class-theoretical framework' (2004a: 110). Within the wider terrain of CPE, this constitutes 'one particular contribution of what was originally a single group of researchers from the University of Amsterdam to what has since become a much broader perspective'.

Indeed, we see a strategic dilemma emerging for the overall coherence of the AP project and its status as a school. If it is codified and employed, for instance, in PhD projects without proper immanent critique and subsequent development, it risks becoming a stifling self-referential caricature of itself with faithful disciples rather than critical followers. Conversely, if it takes its epistemological commitments seriously, it must recognize the historically specific, transient, and problematic nature of its core concepts and seek to strengthen (and sublate) them by critical engagement with and articulation to other theoretical perspectives and currents. As van Apeldoorn et al. (2010) stress, CPE should be committed to evolving, open-ended, progressive research. Interestingly, while their contribution is an intervention in the 'transatlantic divide' debate within IPE, seeking to move beyond the British School, they do not mention the AP in this context. That we might have to rethink the practice of doing AP is suggested by the fact that only a few current (male) young scholars are working with an AP perspective. Its gendered nature is also revealed in this volume. Apart from six male pioneers, only a third of the commentators are female.

Broadening the Amsterdam Project ontology and overcoming left-wing conservatism

We agree with Montgomerie's cautioning that, 'however important our intellectual traditions are, they cannot stand in the way of progress and innovation within the critical school' (2017: 41). While she refers mainly to the need to include feminist methods to reveal the gendered nature of capitalism, her point also holds for the need for a subaltern perspective. The AP suffers from its almost exclusive focus on the internal fractionation of capital to the neglect of a similar fractionation of labour. The theoretical and analytical coverage of historically specific social *relations* of production surfaces merely as a macro-perspective, while social relations that may not be rooted in class, such as gender, race, age, or sexuality, remain obscure. While the latter categories might be less pertinent for the AP's ontological focus on fractions of capital, this does not excuse its continuing tendency to reduce social struggles to top-down arrangements securing domination within the state apparatus (see also Bailey et al. 2017).

This leads to the theoretical and analytical marginalization of clusters of class action that voice dissent, protest, disruption, and resistance, including capitalist as well as 'subaltern' classes excluded from the state institutional realm. It also leads to neglect of the combination of infrastructures of dissent and actual resistance that takes shape as concrete praxis-oriented activities. The ontological primacy that the AP gives to capital fractions may explain its overall neglect of, or pessimism about, emerging forms of resistance, which are perceived as limited or merely reactive. As an emancipatory project, the AP is theoretically committed to transformative agency; but, so far, it has not contributed to the politicization of social struggles and their resilience. Of course, many other researchers produce abstract forms of knowledge and broad theoretical discourses without leaving the comfort zones of critique of capitalism, but this does not absolve AP scholars from concern with their social function. To avoid 'left melancholy' (Brown 1999), we advocate broadening the AP ontology to class struggles from below. Coincidentally, its local mirror image, the *Amsterdam School*, an early twentieth-century intellectual group and political movement for socialist architecture, was devoted to decent working-class housing. Its beautiful buildings offer a poignant reminder of the need to anchor intellectual endeavours in concrete, emancipatory commitments.

Towards an emancipatory Amsterdam Project

AP scholars have presented incisive critiques of the orthodoxy in International Relations, IPE, and European integration theories. Contributions from AP scholars are seminal teaching materials for historical materialist perspectives (van der Pijl 2009; Overbeek 2012). While students find the fractionation perspective interesting and surprisingly accessible, they rarely adopt the distinctive AP perspective in their own work. In the marketplace of academic ideas, other historical materialist perspectives offer students an easier route to understanding contemporary capitalism. However, critical knowledge production that breaks with the ideological confines of neoliberal capitalism is crucial to political resistance to the power inequalities ingrained in institutions and their everyday routines. Universities, research institutes, and schools are a crucial battleground, especially as the social sciences are less than welcoming to Marxist perspectives. While AP scholars' efforts in this respect should be applauded, this has not been translated into a coherent strategy within or beyond the AP's 'core'. This is a pity as we consider the contributions of AP scholars of utmost importance to teaching Marxist perspectives in IPE in the continued engagement to challenge the dominance of Weberian, liberal narratives. We conclude with a plea for an AP that takes its critical commitments beyond theoretical paradigm maintenance, and for more empirical analyses to foster its overall positioning within a neoliberalized academic terrain. Accordingly, we invite the AP's core scholars to engage more with the vibrant, innovative CPE research community that exists outside Amsterdam today.

References

van Apeldoorn, B. (2004a). Guest editorial. Transnational historical materialism. The Amsterdam IPE project. *Journal of International Relations and Development* 7(2): 110–112.

van Apeldoorn, B. (2004b). Theorizing the transnational. A historical materialist approach. *Journal of International Relations and Development* 7(2): 142–176.

van Apeldoorn, B. (2013). The European capitalist class and the crisis of its hegemonic project. *Socialist Register* 50: 189–206.

van Apeldoorn, B. and de Graaff, N. (2016). *American grand strategy and corporate elite networks. The open door since the end of the cold war.* London: Routledge.

van Apeldoorn, B., Bruff, I. and Ryner, M. (2010). The richness and diversity of critical IPE perspectives. Moving beyond the debate on the 'British School'. In N. Philips and C. Weaver (Eds.) *IPE. Debating the past, present and future* (pp. 215–222). London: Routledge.

Bailey, D.J., Clua-Losada, M., Huke, N., and Ribera-Almandoz, O. (2017). *Beyond defeat and austerity. Disrupting the critical political economy of neoliberal Europe.* London: Routledge.

Brown, W. (1999). Resisting left melancholy. *Boundary 2* 26(3): 19–27.

Jessop, B. and Sum, N.L. (2017). Putting the 'Amsterdam School' in its rightful place. A reply to Juan Ignacio Staricco's critique of cultural political economy. *New Political Economy* 22 (3): 342–353.

Montgomerie, J. (Ed.) (2017). *Critical methods in political and cultural economy.* London: Routledge.

Overbeek, H. (2004). Transnational class formation and concepts of control. Towards a genealogy of the Amsterdam Project in IPE. *Journal of International Relations and Development* 7(2): 113–141.

Overbeek, H. (2012). Transnational historical materialism. Theories of transnational class formation and world order. In R. Palan (Ed.), *Global political economy. Contemporary theories*, 2nd ed. (pp. 162–176). London: Routledge.

Overbeek, H. and van Apeldoorn, B. (Eds) (2012). *Neoliberalism in crisis.* Basingstoke: Palgrave-Macmillan.

van der Pijl, K. (1984). *The making of an Atlantic ruling class.* London: Verso.

van der Pijl, K. (1998). *Transnational classes and international relations.* London: Routledge.

van der Pijl, K. (2004). Two faces of the transnational cadre under neo-liberalism. *Journal of International Relations and Development* 7(2): 177–207.

van der Pijl, K. (2009). A survey of global political economy. Centre for Global Political Economy, University of Sussex. Available at https://libcom.org/library/survey-global-political-economy (accessed 19 December 2017).

16

THE AMSTERDAM SCHOOL

Gender as a blind spot

Marianne H. Marchand

The Amsterdam School (AS) has brought significant and original insights to the study of international or global political economy regarding post-war political and economic transformations, especially those related to globalization. My chapter evaluates these contributions productively from a gender perspective. It argues that AS analyses of transnational class formation have largely failed to incorporate gender and other mechanisms of inequality such as race, ethnicity, and sexual orientation. To demonstrate this, I will focus on two foundational concepts that are central to AS interpretations of globalization: transnational class formation and the Lockean heartland of the capitalist order. My critique relies on several important tenets of feminist International Political Economy (IPE)/International Relations (IR), especially the concept of intersectionality, the interconnectivity between reproductive, productive, and virtual (RPV) economies, and insights from transnational or post-colonial feminism. I conclude with suggestions on how these deficits can be overcome within an AS framework and thereby improve the scope and explanatory power of the approach.

Feminist theory and the concept of intersectionality

A major theoretical contribution of feminist thought is the concept of intersectionality. Kimberlé Crenshaw (1991) introduced it to challenge the dominance of white, middle-class feminism. She argued that its identity politics failed to address intra-community differences:

> Although racism and sexism readily intersect in the lives of real people, they seldom do in feminist and antiracist practices. And so, when the practices expound identity as 'woman' or 'person of color' as an either/or proposition, they relegate the identity of women of color to a location that resists telling.
>
> *(Crenshaw 1991: 1242)*

218   Marianne H. Marchand

Crenshaw recognized three types of intersectionality that generate African-American women's invisibility: structural, political, and representational. Structurally, these women's experiences result from multiple, intersecting systems of domination. Politically, 'women of color are situated within at least two subordinated groups that frequently pursue conflicting political agendas' (1991: 1252). The social construction of women of colour is the third aspect. These insights inspired intersectionalist studies, including a subfield known as the 'politics of intersectionality' that focuses on the intricacies of how intersectionality works to disempower marginalized groups through an 'oppression Olympics' in which groups compete for 'the title of being the most oppressed in order to gain political support of dominant groups' (Wilson 2013: 2).

Thus, instead of creating allegiances and solidarities among marginalized groups, identity politics leads to contestations that may complicate their already marginalized or oppressed situation. To counter such situations, intersectionality has not only become an analytical tool, but a political strategy, too (Wilson 2013). This dual significance has made intersectional thought a dominant paradigm for feminist and gender studies.

Feminist IPE/IR and globalization

During the 1990s, feminist scholars and activists increasingly challenged fictitious boundaries between the national and international as they responded to globalization and encountered feminist activists from around the world. United Nations agencies were pivotal here in providing the physical and intellectual spaces, such as the Fourth International Women's Conference in Beijing, to facilitate such encounters and interactions.

Feminist IPE/IR soon became a serious voice in critical globalization studies. For instance, Saskia Sassen identified the gendered dimensions of resistance to the rearticulation of the global circuits of capital, including a 'feminization of survival' (Sassen 2002: 89–91). Marianne Marchand and Anne Sisson Runyan advocated the concept of global restructuring instead of globalization to facilitate a multi-sited, multi-speed, multi-layered, and multi-scalar gender analysis that addresses both productive and reproductive spheres. They claim that this allows us to analyse how the market, state, civil society, and militarism are embedded in and (re)constructed through these processes (2011: 7). Likewise, V. Spike Peterson (2003) proposed a comprehensive analysis of globalization that explores the mutual constitution and interaction of the RPV (or digital) economies. Through this framing, she emphasizes how the complexities of globalization are embedded in structural hierarchies and embodied in terms of, inter alia, race, ethnicity, class, and gender (Peterson 2003: 8).

Post-colonial and transnational feminism

While Crenshaw challenged the idea of a distinctive sisterhood among women living within one country, post-colonial feminism challenges the representation in dominant Western feminist work of 'Third World women' as subordinate,

The Amsterdam School and gender **219**

submissive, and not really emancipated (Mohanty 2003: 17–42). Likewise, transnational feminists argue that such representations disable cross-border organizing and solidarities and challenge the agenda-setting role of their counterparts in the Global North because it marginalizes their voices. Although transnational feminism has been criticized for prioritizing a cultural logic of representation over a political economy perspective (Mendoza 2002), it adds much to the insights of intersectionality and Peterson's notion of RPV framing through its focus on the negative effects of transnational capitalism, its challenges to the primacy of the nation-state, and its concerns about representations of 'Third World women'. Together, these provide the starting point for my dialogue with the AS.

The Amsterdam School: transnational class formation and the Lockean heartland

The AS is recognized for its critical and nuanced analyses of transnational class formation and, more recently, neoliberal globalization. However, class and class analysis remain a central point of departure. As Kees van der Pijl notes:

> Class denotes the aspect of agency producing and reproducing the structures of a society based on exploitation; put otherwise, by embodying the structural inequalities of the social order, classes constitute the living reality of these structures. Yet class is still a relatively abstract concept. It manifests itself usually in mediated forms, through all kinds of 'imagined communities'.
>
> *(1998: 31)*

In his analysis of the rise of transnational classes and their role in globalization, van der Pijl identifies several facilitating conditions. First, he argues that class formation in capitalism is related to the commodification of social relations and the disciplinary nature of capital as manifested in the three areas of 'original accumulation', 'the capitalist production process', and 'the process of social reproduction' (van der Pijl 1998: 36; more generally, 9–30).

Although the AS does consider the reproductive sphere and household level, it still lacks a well-developed gender analysis. The main reason for this is that it ignores intersectionality and subordinates gendered, racial, and other structural hierarchies to an overarching class hierarchy. For instance, citing Ken Post, van der Pijl notes that 'male dominance became structured into class societies' (1998: 35). This suggests that gender relations result from dominant class formations and have little or no autonomous grounding. From a gender perspective, this reductionist approach does not consider the importance of intersectionality among different structural hierarchies – which would reveal a range of complex connectivities and power dimensions.

Following Peterson's analysis, the reproductive sphere should not be relegated to extra-economic social relations but considered another economic dimension:

reproductive and informal labor in the reproductive economy is a condition of – and not coincidental to – the so-called productive economy. To adequately understand either economy, we must analyze their interaction. Indeed, some argue that economic analyses should start from the reproductive economy.

(Peterson 2003: 111–12)

In particular, the reproductive economy is important for global restructuring through its unpaid reproductive labour at the household level and through the informalization of economic activities (Peterson 2003). As feminist economists have shown, the structural adjustment programmes imposed on Latin American countries in the 1980s and 1990s would not have 'succeeded' had its negative side-effects not been absorbed by the reproductive economy. Poor women in these countries stepped up their reproductive labour at the household level and performed additional informal economic activities to make ends meet and avoid a complete breakdown of the social reproductive sphere (Benería 2003: 49–51).

The flexibilization of production, the main source of such informalization, is itself feminized as women tend to be the preferred type of labour for low-skilled, temporary, part-time, and low-wage jobs. Moreover, as Peterson writes, feminization does not just refer to women but all those activities or spaces that have a connotation of being subordinate or are associated with feminine characteristics (Peterson 2003: 61–4). In particular, the process of deindustrialization in the Global North, or Lockean heartland in AS terminology, has entailed a feminization of labour: with the Global North's lower-end service sector employing women and migrant workers often in precarious jobs, while the outsourcing of production to the Global South has resulted in more female workers being employed in manufacturing, especially in export-processing zones. In general, these subordinate or feminized flexible workers face deplorable working conditions, but are also pitted against each other, as recent elections in the United States have revealed. During his campaign, Trump attacked Mexican immigrants for being drug dealers, criminals and rapists, and stealing jobs from US workers; at the same time, he criticized North American Free Trade Agreement as an unfair trading agreement that enabled US jobs to be exported to Mexico and Canada. This illustrates what Wilson has labelled 'oppression Olympics'.

In its analysis of the Lockean heartland, the AS ignores the gendered and racialized nature of the flexibilization of production and accompanying informalization. It acknowledges tensions among productive and financial fractions of capital and associated transnational classes in the Lockean heartland but, in so doing, it invisibilizes other tensions resulting from intersecting mechanisms of inequality. For example, while (undocumented) migrant workers have become indispensable in many economic sectors, their presence has also generated a political and social backlash, as revealed in recent US elections. In addition, the AS invokes the dichotomous foundations used by modernization theory in its distinction between the 'modern' Lockean heartland and 'backward' Hobbesian contender states:

The Amsterdam School and gender **221**

The relative backwardness and social heterogeneity of the social substratum, the coincidence of several historical stages of social development within a single sovereign jurisdiction, sometimes further confounded by national/ethnic and religious divisions, all require the permanent presence and priority of the state as the driving force of economic development.

(van der Pijl 1998: 81–2)

Given this 'relative backwardness' of Hobbesian states, van der Pijl denies the possibility of homegrown social movements or an autonomous civil society in the Global South:

[s]ocial forces are shaped pre-emptively, often violently, from above, rather than formed organically on the ground of social development and production; accordingly, they remain dependent on the state for their existence – their 'class' organizations, parties, employer and even trade unions, are in effect state institutions.

(van der Pijl 1998: 82)

Moreover, it is suggested, any kind of contestation is confined within the state and cannot become transnational. Clearly these assumptions would be disputed by transnational post-colonial feminism, which forcefully critiques dichotomous constructions such as traditional-modern as well as homogenizing representations of 'Third World' actors as lacking emancipatory power or transnational organizational capacity. Latin American feminist transnationalism is exactly what Mendoza analyses (2002). Furthermore, Mohanty (2003) discusses feminist transnationalism in general terms, thereby directly challenging AS assumptions about the absence of autonomous, transnational organizing in Hobbesian states.

Final thoughts

This chapter set out to challenge the AS foundational concepts of transnational class formation and Lockean heartland from a gender perspective, by relying on the concept of intersectionality, Peterson's RPV framing, and the insights of transnational and post-colonial feminism. This challenge reveals three problems with the AS. First, it prioritizes class over other structural hierarchies and does not recognize that these have autonomous foundations. This explains why it cannot fully consider the intersectionalities among different structural hierarchies resulting in multiple, complex inequalities and power relations. Second, whereas the AS locates reproductive activities within the arena of social relations, feminist economists have convincingly shown their organic connectivity to the productive economy, considering them a separate dimension of the overall economy. Third, the AS still relies on dichotomous constructions such as traditional-modern when analysing politico-economic processes in the Global South and also denies the possibility for social movements to organize autonomously and transnationally. Yet writings by transnational and post-colonial feminists have demonstrated that such assumptions are erroneous and reflect (neo) colonial representations of the Global South's realities.

Where to go from here? It seems that the AS and a gender perspective as outlined in this chapter remain at odds. Yet, for the AS to develop a more comprehensive analysis it must recognize the multiple sources and forms of inequality, such as gender, race, ethnicity, etc. People's everyday lived realities result from the interconnectivities among different structural hierarchies. For instance, an undocumented female migrant working in hotel housekeeping faces multiple inequalities – that of gender, ethnicity, class, and nationality. To analyse her situation only through a class lens would miss the complex and overlapping inequalities of her oppression. In fact, her undocumented status or her ethnicity may marginalize her more than her class status. This is why we should all take intersectionality seriously in analysing power and inequality.

References

Benería, L. (2003). *Gender, development, and globalization: Economics as if all people mattered.* London: Routledge.

Crenshaw, K. (1991). Mapping the margins: Intersectionality, identity politics, and violence against women of color. *Stanford Law Review* 43(6): 1241–1299.

Marchand, M.H. and Runyan, A.S. (Eds) (2011). *Gender and global restructuring: Sightings, sites and resistances*, 2nd ed. London: Routledge.

Mendoza, B. (2002). Transnational feminisms in question. *Feminist Theory* 3(3): 295–314.

Mohanty, C.T. (2003). *Feminism without borders: Decolonizing theory, practicing solidarity.* Durham, NC: Duke University Press.

Peterson, V.S. (2003). *A critical rewriting of global political economy: Integrating reproductive, productive and virtual economies.* London: Routledge.

van der Pijl, K. (1998). *Transnational classes and international relations.* London: Routledge.

Sassen, S. (2002). Counter-geographies of globalization: Feminization of survival, in K. Saunders (Ed.), *Feminist post-development thought: Rethinking modernity, postcolonialism and representation* (pp. 89–104). London: Zed.

Wilson, A.R. (2013). Introduction, in *Situating intersectionality: Politics, policy and power* (pp. 1–10). Basingstoke: Palgrave-Macmillan.

17

THE AMSTERDAM SCHOOL, CRITICAL REALISM AND THE STUDY OF 'DEEP STRUCTURES'

Hubert Buch-Hansen and Juan Ignacio Staricco

Scholars associated with the Amsterdam School (AS) have produced a series of high-calibre studies of diverse politico-economic phenomena, including the formation of an Atlantic ruling class (van der Pijl 1984), British political and economic decline (Overbeek 1990), the transnationalization of Spain (Holman 1996) and the relaunch of European integration (van Apeldoorn 2002).[1] These and other important contributions established a sophisticated version of transnational historical materialism as an important alternative to mainstream approaches in International Political Economy. One of its distinctive features in this regard is its conceptualization of social structures. Our contribution focuses on how structure is studied in AS research and notes that such research has to a large extent not systematically explicated how to study structures empirically. We suggest that an alignment with critical realism could help to clarify AS's approach to social explanation.

AS scholars' account of structure transcends both *individualism* – whether the methodological individualism of (neo)realism and (neo)liberalism or the 'naïve idealism' of some types of constructivism – and determinist *structuralism* – as exemplified by world systems theory (cf. van Apeldoorn 2002: 13–4; Overbeek 2004: 116). Because the AS has examined class formation in capitalist social formations, social relations of production are the structure that has attracted the most attention. Within this realm, relevant cleavages – determining the distribution of material capabilities and its concomitant social positions – can be identified at two levels of abstraction. First is the main structural division in a mode of production that is determined by the opposition between those who control and supervise the process of production and those who execute the productive tasks (van Apeldoorn 2002: 3). Second, in concretizing their analysis of the capitalist class – though not of those in subordinate positions in this structure, the role of which is undertheorized (cf. Staricco 2017: 6) – the AS has adopted a fractionalist perspective, demarcating capitalist groups according to their function in the overall circuit of capitalist reproduction (Overbeek 2004: 128). The material conditions shared by individuals occupying similar structural positions form the basis for the possible emergence of common identities and interests. Here, the notion of 'comprehensive concepts of control' is fundamental because, while acknowledging the inherently political and ideological nature of class formation and struggles for hegemony, it also highlights the 'limits of the possible' inscribed in structures (cf. van der Pijl 1998: 6).

The transnationalization of class formation has become possible only as the relations of production have progressively transnationalized. Hence, in their empirical analyses, the AS scholars found it necessary to account for the main structural transformation that enables this process: the emergence of a globally integrated form of capitalism. How, then, should this and other deep structural transformations be studied empirically, according to AS scholars? Unfortunately, the landmark AS works do not directly answer this question. In fact, they generally do not explain in any depth why specific sources were chosen – a partial exception is van Apeldoorn (2002) – or why particular methods were used to analyse them. If AS scholars do not preach, how do they practice? After warning that 'the focus on statistics of international transactions ... tends to miss the qualitative dimension of globalization', van Apeldoorn (2002: 55–6) affirms that foreign direct investment could be considered as the most important indicator of the global integration of production. This is best evidenced in the constantly rising figures of foreign direct investment stocks that, driven by transnational corporations, has come to replace trade flows as the main force of global integration. Van der Pijl (1998: 54–8; see also 1984: 277–87) proposes to rely on 'profit distribution' as the key indicator for assessing the evolution of hierarchical and power relations among capital fractions. As 'the capacity of fractions of capital to appropriate a share of the total mass of profits shapes the sense of identity of a particular segment of collective capital with the momentary functioning of the system' (van der Pijl 1998: 58), it can be assumed that the most profitable fraction(s) will be better placed to unify the capitalist class – and lead the struggle for hegemony around its particular world view. These are just two examples of indicators used by AS scholars to study structures.

Given that they have produced rich empirical studies, we are not arguing that a lack of rigorous empirical research is the Achilles' heel of the 'Amsterdam project'. Yet, because its leading exponents have done little to expose their approach to empirical analysis, it tends to be less systematic than the empirical works of other leading scholars of transnational historical materialism. Two useful models for future AS-inspired empirical research on structures are, first, William K. Carroll's use of network-analytical methods in his insightful study of the formation of a transnational capitalist class (2010); and, second, William I. Robinson's use of diverse indicators to document its existence (2004). For Robinson, in addition to foreign direct investment, these indicators include growing foreign portfolio equity investments, 'cross-national M&As, strategic alliances, and interlocking transnational directorates, as well as worldwide subcontracting and outsourcing [and] the extension of free-enterprise zones' (Robinson 2004: 54).

More generally we suggest that, to provide a more systematic explanation and explicit justification of its analysis of structures, scholarship drawing on AS theory could benefit from an engagement with the philosophy of science known as critical realism (cf. Bhaskar 1979). It is important to note, though, that while most AS works do not refer to critical realism, some AS scholars have resorted to its social ontology for inspiration when conceptualizing the agency–structure relationship underlying the notion of class (see van Apeldoorn 2002: 21–2, 2004; see also Holman 1996: 7, 218). Beyond that, the AS has not been explicitly aligned with critical realism.[2] Yet, as critical realism and Marxism are compatible in many respects, much AS research appears broadly consistent with critical realism, laying the ground for a potentially fruitful complementarity.

At a minimum, such an engagement could make it clearer to scholars who encounter the AS for the first time how its theory might be used in empirical research. Advancing a relational conceptualization of structures, critical realists regard social reality as stratified: in addition to a surface level of manifest events and phenomena, reality contains a deep layer of underlying structures. In the words of Bhaskar, the principal founder of critical realism, it is to such 'structures of social relations that realism directs our attention … as the explanatory key to understanding social events and trends' (1989: 4). It is demanding to study these deep social structures but leading exponents of critical realism, not least Sayer (1992), have provided useful guidance on how structural analyses can be conducted. For critical realists, social explanation typically entails a retroductive move from observations of actual events and processes (economic crises, strikes, the adoption of new laws, democratization, etc.) to the generative mechanisms (including deep social structures) that combine to produce these surface phenomena. Retroduction involves reflecting upon what real structures and mechanisms must exist, *in all likelihood*, for the object of study to exist and display the actual properties that it does. Without using the term retroduction, Marx resorted to this mode of reasoning at times (e.g. 1965 [1867]). It involves using the method of abstraction – a method that some AS research utilizes (cf. van der Pijl 1984: passim, 1998: 57). Yet although critical realism is certainly inspired by Marx and his legacy in several respects, it is – unlike Marxism – a fully developed philosophy of science position.[3]

To illustrate how a critical realist research design could work backwards from some specific object of interest to the mechanisms and structures causing/sustaining that object, let us imagine that a researcher is interested in explaining the properties of a specific regulation that bears on capital accumulation or class domination. The first step could be to understand the content of the regulation, for instance by conducting interviews with policy makers, lobby groups, social movements, etc. and undertaking a discourse analysis. The next step could be to ask retroductive questions about the structural preconditions for the regulation to be the way it is, so as to generate some propositions as to why the regulation has this particular content. In this process, theory is crucial. From an AS perspective, this kind of regulation would be expected to reflect (albeit imperfectly) underlying power relations between capital fractions. The AS suggests that specific class fractions tend to have specific ideological inclinations organically related to the economic functions that they perform in the capital accumulation process (e.g. van der Pijl 1998: 49–53). Thus, if the regulation of interest is, say, strongly liberal in its content, this could lead to the proposition that it reflects the prevalence of money capital over industrial capital. To empirically assess this proposition, the researcher could analyse profit distribution data and other indicators mentioned above as well as using network analysis methods (elsewhere such methods have been argued to potentially resonate well with critical realism, cf. Buch-Hansen 2014). Much more could be said about how structural analysis can be conducted from a critical realist perspective, but the above will have to suffice as an indication of how a more comprehensive alignment with critical realism could be used by scholars applying AS theory to explicate (and, if needed, justify) their approach to social explanation.

In this contribution we have referred to the AS as if it were a currently existing 'school'. It should, however, be acknowledged that today few scholars identify with the AS label and that as such the AS may no longer exist. Although most members of the school have so to speak left the building, a group of researchers (ourselves included) continue to draw inspiration from contributions made by the original AS members. In this way, the 'Amsterdam project' lives on. Yet, if it is not to ossify in the long run, AS theory needs to attract new generations of students and researchers. One important precondition for this to be the case is – we suspect – that efforts are made to explicate how one can apply AS theory systematically in the study of deep structures. Here there is, as argued in this contribution, a potential for engaging with critical realism.

We conclude by underscoring that critical realism does not provide researchers with a 'cookbook recipe' on how to identify structures. On the contrary, critical realists oppose overly schematic models of social explanation, insisting that 'it is the nature of objects that determines their cognitive possibilities for us' (Bhaskar 1979: 31). This basic insight is lost on much contemporary social science, not least in the neo-positivist tradition: in many cases, research suffers from what could be called the disease of 'method mania', i.e. the delusion that the hallmark of good social science is the application of ever more sophisticated (quantitative) methods to ever larger datasets. In our view, the way forward for scholarship drawing on AS theory is not to enter the world of big data and sophisticated statistical methods: phenomena like transnational social relations, concepts of control, capital fractions, and hegemonic struggles are simply not objects that inherently lend themselves to this type of social research. The AS landmark works drew on qualitative sources as much as – or more than – on quantitative data. Furthermore, each of them has enriched our understanding of transnational social relations more than any number of fancy regression analyses could ever have done.

Notes

1 We are grateful to Bastiaan van Apeldoorn and Morten Ougaard for their insightful comments. Any remaining errors are our own.

2 Here we should mention that, in recent works, where he no longer identifies with the AS label, van Apeldoorn now draws more than before on insights from critical realism and explicates how deep structures are studied (e.g. van Apeldoorn and de Graaff 2015).
3 On the relationship between Marxism and critical realism, see, inter alia, the contributions to Brown et al. (2002). Bhaskar even suggests that 'Marx's work at its best illustrates critical realism; and critical realism is the absent methodological fulcrum of Marx's work' (1991: 143).

References

van Apeldoorn, B. (2002). *Transnational capitalism and the struggle over European integration.* London: Routledge.

van Apeldoorn, B. (2004). Theorizing the transnational. A historical materialist approach. *Journal of International Relations and Development* 7(2): 142–176.

van Apeldoorn, B. and de Graaff, N. (2015). *American grand strategy and corporate elite networks: The open door since the end of the Cold War.* London: Routledge.

Bhaskar, R. (1979). *The possibility of naturalism. A philosophical critique of the contemporary human sciences,* 1st ed. Brighton: Harvester Press.

Bhaskar, R. (1989). *Reclaiming reality. A critical introduction to contemporary philosophy.* Brighton: Harvester.

Bhaskar, R. (1991). *Philosophy and the idea of freedom.* Oxford: Basil Blackwell.

Brown, A., Fleetwood, S., and Roberts, J.M. (Eds) (2002). *Critical realism and Marxism.* London: Routledge.

Buch-Hansen, H. (2014). Social network analysis and critical realism. *Journal for the Theory of Social Behaviour* 44(3): 306–325.

Carroll, R. (2010). China pours its wealth into Latin America. *Guardian,* 18 April.

Holman, O. (1996). *Integrating Southern Europe. EC expansion and the transnationalization of Spain.* London: Routledge.

Marx, K. (1965 [1867]). *Capital,* Vol. 1. Moscow: Progress.

Overbeek, H. (1990). *Global capitalism and national decline.* London: Unwin & Hyman.

Overbeek, H. (2004). Transnational class formation and concepts of control. Towards a genealogy of the Amsterdam Project in international political economy. *Journal of International Relations and Development* 7(2): 113–141.

van der Pijl, K. (1984). *The making of an Atlantic ruling class.* London: Verso.

van der Pijl, K. (1998). *Transnational classes and international relations.* London: Routledge.

Robinson, W. I. (2004). *A theory of global capitalism. Production, class, and state in a transnational world.* Baltimore, MD: Johns Hopkins University Press.

Sayer, A. (1992). *Method in social science. A realist approach,* 2nd ed. London: Routledge.

StariccoJ.I. (2017). Class dynamics and ideological construction in the struggle over fairness. A neo-Gramscian examination of the Fairtrade initiative. *Journal of Peasant Studies,* available at https://doi.org/10.1080/03066150.2017.1337003

18

CONFRONTING GLOBAL GOVERNANCE AFTER THE HISTORICAL TURN IN INTERNATIONAL RELATIONS

Samuel Knafo

The late 1970s and 1980s 'open' forms of Marxism emerged that sought to capitalize on Marx's rich historicism and emphasis on class struggle. In International Relations (IR), the proponents of the historical turn sought to demarcate their position from the deterministic and reductionist approaches that had become associated with Marxism (Drainville 1994). The Amsterdam School (AS) was in the forefront here, building on Marx's insights in ways that few others did. Whereas neo-Gramscians arguably opted for a more Weberian framing to overcome determinism,[1] the AS still studied the changing modalities of class struggle (van Apeldoorn 2004). Its distinctive European viewpoint was evident both in its unique synthesis of various strands of continental Marxism and its interest in the distinctive trajectory of the European Union as a lens to view what would become a defining trend of neoliberalism: the rise of global governance.

Reflecting on the school's unique contributions, I examine three questions about class struggle under neoliberalism. Methodologically, how did AS negotiate the historical turn? Substantively, how have they studied transnational classes – a theme rightly considered a key contribution of the AS? Finally, I highlight an often neglected but vital contribution: the study of the emerging cadre class.

First, the AS has developed a flexible historical materialist framework for engaging with history. Its historicist orientation is exemplified in its core notion of 'concept of control'. This highlights intra-capitalist struggles to grasp how different class fractions may coalesce into different capitalist regimes of governance. This has yielded in-depth historical analyses (e.g. van der Pijl 1984, 2006; Overbeek 1990). It has fuelled a rich reflexion on the dynamics of socialization (*Vergesellschaftung*) under capitalism, well represented in Kees van der Pijl's *Transnational classes and international relations* (1998).

While these reflexions about class struggles are instructive, I wonder whether the approach went far enough in dealing with the historical turn. For it arguably failed

Confronting global governance **229**

to produce a clear methodological template to address the problem of reflexivity that initially prompted the wider historical turn in IR: the challenge of finding out what we ourselves take for granted and thereby reify. AS scholars hoped that, by turning to history to track the social construction of world orders, they could reveal their contingency. This historical constructivist turn helped to explain where social institutions or governance regimes (e.g. Atlanticism, neoliberalism) come from. But lacking a specific methodology for reflecting on what a given epistemic community takes for granted, the AS has risked reducing the historical turn to a simple call for exploring how things 'really' played out historically.

This limitation is exemplified in the AS's problematic treatment of agency. Agency is important for historical materialism, of course, and central to the historical turn. But recognizing that agency matters is different from specifying how this recognition would change how we historicize (Knafo 2010). Too often, historical materialists accommodate agency within what remains a structuralist perspective. It often simply amounts to making more space for social change without significantly changing the analysis. The AS, for example, rejects one-sided interpretations that privilege either agency or structure (Overbeek 2004) partly because it fears that overemphasizing agency may come at the expense of downplaying structural limitations (van Apeldoorn et al. 2008: 13). But doing so means that AS scholars can easily carry on with a structural analysis provided that they somehow acknowledge that agents can make a difference. AS scholars can thus extensively detail what actors do, but this can easily be interpreted as manifestations of structural trends and imperatives. It remains unclear then how this form of 'historicization' changes the broader and more established narratives that this turn to history was meant to challenge.

Take the concept of fraction of capital – a notion explicitly intended to capture class agency (Overbeek 1980). Drawing on Marx, AS scholars have reappropriated fractional analysis to identify proto-concepts of control corresponding ideal-typically to the interests of profit-producing or money capital and then explored how these are combined in comprehensive concepts of control as the basis for the historically specific class alliances that underpin specific capitalist regimes. In doing so, they insist that the relatively abstract concept of class fraction should not overdetermine the historical analysis. But concepts do set expectations that often trap scholars. Here it encourages AS scholars to assess capitalist regimes in terms of whether they favour the interests of specific, predefined fractions of capital. As Simon Clarke (1978) suggested in a critique of approaches that had been inspired by Poulantzas (1973), starting from predetermined, reified historical categories (such as fractions of capital) can hinder the analysis of social struggles despite one's commitment to remain true to history. A deductive template based on the logic of capital can easily lead scholars to abstract from concrete commercial, industrial or financial practices and specific institutional contexts *when seeking to characterize* capitalists in terms of fractions. AS scholars want to have it both ways when insisting that the concept of fraction of capital be established on the grounds of historical analysis while still retaining this concept to frame the analysis. This is an impossible wager.

230 Samuel Knafo

While AS scholars have not explicitly reflected on their uses of history, this does not mean that they must fall (or have fallen) into a structural trap. But it does make it hard to determine whether history serves *either* to add some details to a pregiven theoretical narrative *or* to substantially modify that narrative. Breaking this reifying gaze, I would argue, requires a more reflexive use of agency as a framing device. This means not just accounting for social change but, more importantly, establishing how the actions or innovations of key agents are surprising for their context. This systematic focus on the counterintuitive nature of history is necessary to break with linear accounts of history. It must establish why historical turning points cannot be derived from theoretical categories (see Knafo and Teschke 2017) to make a credible claim that it is tracking the making of history. Otherwise it remains too easy to fall back on a structural and reifying perspective.

This leads me to my second point about transnational classes (van der Pijl 1979) and the role of transnational processes of socialization in redefining class interests. The AS makes another important contribution in analysing how class formation occurs through articulating the internal (or national) and the external (international) aspects of socialization (Overbeek 1990). These analyses have produced rich social insights on globalization and the changing modalities of class struggle. However, by turning its gaze to transnational processes, the AS underestimates how this complicates the methodological task/challenge of contextualization. Again, it is one thing to state that the global economy is shaped through transnational processes, another to determine what can be known about them. This requires putting strategies and practices into context, but this is difficult to do when dealing with the scale of transnational processes. Social institutions are usually more localized or, at least, limited to a national scale. Seeking characterizations that apply across various national spaces thus often leads to generic social references, for example to capitalist (or financial) interests or to the promotion of markets, that are often deduced from general principles rather than properly historicized (see, for example, van Apeldoorn 2000 or Holman 2004).

This is not to say that AS scholars do not refer to specific developments or institutions. On the contrary, they have produced historically rich studies about these transnational processes (e.g. van Apeldoorn and Horn 2007). But the efforts to characterize the transnational class or other transnational actors tend to become generic because they are pursued largely in highly abstract terms. This is reflected in discussions of global governance that address neoliberal rhetoric regarding the construction of market rules or market-like logics, rather than starting from a historicized account of the social interests involved. As a result, class struggle appears all too familiar as researchers rely on the same generic baselines to explain the interests at stake. The limitation of this transnational viewpoint, I suggest, is reflected in the fact that the AS has been most successful precisely when it starts from the national and local in undertaking contextualization (for example, van der Pijl 2006).

It seems hard to avoid falling on one or the other side of the national-transnational divide. One cannot locate practices and processes in a transnational and national context at the same time. Either there is a transnational class, implying that national variations are minor, or national differences are significant enough to refute the idea of such a class. We must settle this issue because our choice determines what we use as a reference point for the analysis. AS scholars have tried to avoid this problem stating that the decision to look at the transnational and/or national depends on the case we study. By contrast, I do not think that the issue can be settled in these terms and the AS has little to say about how to negotiate this difficult determination. More important, I think, is a methodological consideration. Local or national perspectives provide richer perspectives on class struggle because they offer more institutional references for the work of contextualization.

My third point concerns a contribution too often neglected in International Political Economy scholarship: the emergence of a new class of cadres. Reflecting its long-standing interest in the making of the European Community/Union and its bureaucratic underpinning, the AS has long read neoliberalism as a product of a powerful tension between planning and market forms of socialization. This approach provides a powerful corrective to the tendency in International Political Economy literature to read public management as simply doing the deed for and on behalf – if not necessarily at the behest – of capitalists. But as van der Pijl shows, cadres confront complex tensions in using bureaucratic and managerial practices to construct social orders in the face of market dislocations (van der Pijl 2004). Whereas new public management is often read as an extension of corporate practice, and thus interpreted as a proxy for 'more markets', van der Pijl's fascinating account of the tensions that animate governance offers a more promising view on the crucial role of the new cadres in global governance.

This said, I would still call for a more historicist reading of this development. For the rich insights about the changing landscape of governance veer at times towards a theoretical and deductive treatment rather than a properly historical one. For example, van der Pijl's characterization of these cadres often revolves around their general function in reproducing capitalism, an account established at a theoretical level rather than based on concrete characterizations of their practices. As a result, he relies on abstract considerations about bureaucracies and governance that miss the specific nature of the new administrative practices that are now redefining governance. The rapid spread of new public management deserves a more concrete historical engagement concerned with the novelty and provenance of these practices, their complex transformations as they spread through various realms of governance and the complex politics they unleash as they are adopted outside of the United States where they arguably first emerged (see Knafo et al. forthcoming).

Note

1 Robert Cox, for example, used Gramsci to recast questions of international order in social terms (1983); but his main framework owed much to a Weberian methodology that explored the intersection of three key but often neglected dimensions of international relations: institutions, ideas and production (1981).

References

van Apeldoorn, B. (2000). Transnational class agency and European governance: The case of the European Round Table of Industrialists. *New Political Economy* 5(2): 157–181.

van Apeldoorn, B. (2004). Transnational historical materialism: The Amsterdam international political economy project. *Journal of International Relations and Development* 7(2): 110–112.

van Apeldoorn, B. and Horn, L. (2007). The marketisation of European corporate control: A critical political economy perspective. *New Political Economy* 12(2): 211–235.

van Apeldoorn, B., Drahokoupil, J. and Horn, L. (Eds) (2008). *Contradictions and limits of neoliberal European governance: From Lisbon to Lisbon*. Basingstoke: Palgrave Macmillan.

Clarke, S. (1978). Capital, fractions of capital and the state: 'Neo-Marxist' analysis of the South African state. *Capital & Class* 2(2): 32–77.

Cox, R.W. (1981). Social forces, states, and world orders: Beyond international relations theory. *Millennium: Journal of International Relations* 10(2): 126–155.

Cox, R.W. (1983). Gramsci, hegemony, and international relations: An essay in method. *Millennium: Journal of International Relations* 12(2): 162–175.

Drainville, A.C. (1994). International political economy in the age of open Marxism. *Review of International Political Economy* 1(1): 105–132.

Holman, O. (2004). Asymmetrical regulation and multidimensional governance in the European Union. *Review of International Political Economy* 11(4): 714–735.

Knafo, S. (2010). Critical approaches and the legacy of the agent/structure debate in international relations. *Cambridge Review of International Affairs* 23(3): 493–516.

Knafo, S. and Teschke, B. (2017). *The rules of reproduction of capitalism: A historicist critique*. Working paper 12, Center for Global Political Economy, University of Sussex.

Knafo, S., Dutta, S., Lane, R. and Wyn-Jones, S. (forthcoming). The managerial lineages of neoliberalism. *New Political Economy*.

Overbeek, H. (1980). Finance capital and the crisis in Britain. *Capital & Class* 11: 99–120.

Overbeek, H. (1990). *Global capitalism and national decline: The Thatcher decade in perspective*. London: Unwin & Hyman.

Overbeek, H. (2004). Transnational class formation and concepts of control. *Journal of International Relations and Development* 7(2): 113–141.

van der Pijl, K. (1979). Class formation at the international level. *Capital & Class* 9: 1–21.

van der Pijl, K. (1984). *The making of an Atlantic ruling class*. London: NLB.

van der Pijl, K. (1998). *Transnational classes and international relations*. London: Routledge.

van der Pijl, K. (2004). Two faces of the transnational cadre under neo-liberalism. *Journal of International Relations and Development* 7(2): 177–207.

van der Pijl, K. (2006). *Global rivalries: From the Cold War to Iraq*. London: Pluto.

19

NETWORK ANALYSIS AND THE AMSTERDAM SCHOOL

An unfulfilled promise?

Eelke M. Heemskerk

The role of network analysis in the Amsterdam School oeuvre

The Amsterdam School (AS) has made important and highly original contributions to our understanding of global power relations. Two of its attributed strengths are that it relies on detailed narrative accounts of rival capitalist strategies and policies, and that it analyses interpersonal networks, corporate ties, and material interdependencies. Nevertheless, given the AS concern for relating structure and agency, network analysis would be an excellent method to systematically and rigorously explore, corroborate, and test the AS conceptual framework. Why, then, is network analysis so rarely applied in AS writings? And what can we do to remedy this?

AS scholarly work has always had a keen interest in how corporate elite networks underpin class formation. In *The making of an Atlantic ruling class*, van der Pijl already noted the role of bankers and finance capitalists in the network of interlocking directorates between German banking and industry (1984: 266–7). But his account remained a narrative, lacking a systematic analysis of the corporate elite network structure. This reflects somewhat of an aversion amongst AS scholars towards apparently positivistic research methods such as network analysis. Henk Overbeek's doctoral dissertation did examine networks of interlocking directorates in Britain utilizing network analysis metrics such as density and degree (Overbeek 1988). However, he did not use available software and his analysis remained rather rudimentary. Bastiaan van Apeldoorn's seminal study on the European Round Table of Industrialists (2002) revealed many important properties of the European corporate elite but, like Overbeek, lacked systematic analysis of corporate networks. Two recent articles co-authored by van der Pijl described board interlocks, but again without making use of available software or network metrics (van der Pijl et al. 2011; van der Pijl and Yurchenko 2015).

234 Eelke M. Heemskerk

In contrast, Meindert Fennema's seminal dissertation did rigorously conceptualize the network of the transnational corporate elite (Fennema 1982; see also Chapter 4, this volume). When it appeared, however, this work was perhaps considered relevant to, but not an integral part of, the AS. Fennema and van der Pijl did initially co-author on neoliberalism and international bank capital (respectively, Fennema and van der Pijl 1987a; 1987b), with both publications combining van der Pijl's theoretical framework with Fennema's empirical results. However, the combination of a broad theoretical perspective and systematic use of large datasets ended. Fennema moved to other areas of research and van der Pijl continued in a historical and theoretical direction. More recently, Naná de Graaff has included thorough and systematic descriptive network analysis in her own work on global oil elites (2017) and, with Bastiaan van Apeldoorn, on US foreign policy (van Apeldoorn and de Graaff 2016 and 2017).

Network analysis is thus largely absent from the AS work, which is remarkable given the excellent fit with the AS conceptual framework, and surprising when we remember that the University of Amsterdam in the 1970s and 1980s was a hotspot of corporate network analysis (Fennema and Heemskerk 2018).

Why the Amsterdam School should embrace rigorous network analysis

Network analysis remained by and large an unfulfilled promise for the AS. This is unfortunate and should be remedied for at least three reasons. First, empirical network analysis can help to bolster and develop the AS body of knowledge. Because of the laborious nature of data collection, most early studies focused on board interlocks between the top 100 or 500 firms. However, the increasing availability of data and new data mining and analysis techniques have expanded research horizons. We can now study extremely large datasets covering millions of firms and measure corporate elite formation at an astonishingly high resolution, allowing for detailed questions, for instance on which industrial sectors are leading in moulding the transnational capitalist class. Recent work uncovered unprecedented levels of corporate ownership concentration in the USA, where the largest three institutional investors (BlackRock, State Street, and Vanguard) are now together the largest shareholder in 438 of the Forbes 500 (Fichtner et al. 2017: 313). However, such data require theoretical elaboration to contribute to meaningful social theory. For example, what does it mean when a few financial institutions emerge as dominant corporate owners? The AS theoretical perspective can integrate these empirical findings in a broader, carefully constructed historical theorization of the dynamics of global capitalism. Likewise, puzzling and unexpected empirical patterns may trigger a rethinking and updating of key AS concepts. This reciprocal dialogue between empirics and theory can situate changing corporate structures within broader historical patterns and align grand theory and empirical reality.

Second, the relatively limited interest in systematic empirical analysis left space for key original insights and concepts to be 'discovered' in other fields, without referencing the AS. For instance, the seminal notion of concepts of control is nowadays broadly attributed to Neil Fligstein, who coined a similar (but not identical) notion over a decade later (1993). Similarly, Mark Granovetter's seminal paper on embeddedness (1985) soon became a cornerstone of socio-economics. But his critique of undersocialized (i.e. structuralist) and oversocialized (i.e. actor-oriented) approaches recalls AS efforts to combine a Marxist analysis of the circuits of capital with a neo-Gramscian analysis of hegemonic strategies and fractional agency. Had the AS embraced a more accessible, recognizable method such as network analysis, its impact would probably have resonated far more widely.

Third, conversely, while there is now extensive systematic exploration of ever growing datasets of global corporate and elite intertwinement, many studies lack the firm theoretical underpinning necessary to conceptualize power in today's global political economy. Indeed, Mark Mizruchi recently identified two major pitfalls in empirical studies of corporate networks: 'the focus on description rather than explanation and the tendency for techniques and data analysis to run ahead of our ideas' (2016: 7). A (re) reading of some of the pioneering AS contributions might help to alleviate these risks.

Theory trumps empirical analysis?

One obstacle in this respect is the AS's particular understanding of social relations and the limits of quantitative methods in studying them. For many mainstream scholars, social relations are observable interactions that can be mapped and systematically analysed in rather precise network terms. However, the AS is generally sceptical of relying on empirical data. It echoes what Aaron Levenstein once said about bikinis and statistics: 'what they reveal is suggestive, but what they conceal is vital' (1951). Thus, AS scholars often note that social relations under capitalism may *not* be observable. As van Apeldoorn explains: 'Social relations of transnational production may link workers in New York with workers in New Delhi without any direct interactions ever going on between the members of these two groups'. Hence, 'social relations are hidden because within a stratified ontology they lie beneath the surface of events and actions at the level of "deep structures"'. He concludes that 'it is more the *quality* – that is, the nature of social relations – that counts than the *quantity* of interactions' (2004: 161, 162, italics original). Such a judgement easily leads to rejection of observable network relations as a key ingredient in systematic analysis of capitalist classes. This occurs when network analysis is used to '*justify* the attribution of class relevance to comprehensive concepts of control and their social bases' (Jessop and Sum 2017: 8, my italics).

Indeed, one might infer that, for the AS, an elegant theoretical understanding of global power and class relations rendered plausible by anecdotal examples of particular networks is more important than rigorous empirical analysis that may refute (parts of) their theory. Theory trumps data whenever one avoids grounding one's theory in prior systematic empirical analysis.

For example, van der Pijl et al. (2011) analyse board interlocks between 150 transnational corporations to argue that, from the early 1990s, German capital has moved to the centre of the North Atlantic network. They take this as evidence that Germany is increasingly speaking for Europe. Yet their analysis only focuses on those board interlocks where two firms share at least two directors. While this was common practice in the 1970s (see Stokman et al. 1985), two decades later such ties have become very infrequent. Germany, however, historically had exceptionally large corporate boards, which explains why by 2005 any remaining multiple ties disproportionately involve German firms. Studies on the European and global network taking into account the larger network structure do not confirm the rise of German capital (Carroll et al. 2010; Carroll 2013; Heemskerk 2011, 2013). A more elaborate, open-ended research design might have inspired van der Pijl et al. to revise their narrative. This would be consistent with the original critical spirit of the materialist interpretation of history and its aim to grasp the mechanisms of social power relations and domination through rigorous *empirical* analysis.

It is never too late for a second chance

It is not difficult to illustrate how the conceptual frame of the AS might be fruitfully enriched with emerging social network analysis techniques. One example would be the recent work of Babic et al. (2017). Building on core categories of the AS, they use network analysis to show that the role of state ownership in global capitalism cannot be grasped by mainstream conceptions of 'markets versus states'. Instead, this requires an analysis of how such ownership is embedded in broader relations of capitalist power, domination, and rival strategies in the global political economy. Another example is related to the work of van Apeldoorn and de Graaff (2016, 2017) on US foreign policy. They integrate highly original empirical analysis of politicians' career patterns and the revolving doors between business, politics, policy planning, and the military. This line of academic inquiry could benefit significantly from recent advances in the study of career patterns, most notably applying sequence analysis techniques originally developed for the study of DNA to understand how elites 'mature' (e.g. Coen and Vannoni 2016; Ellersgaard et al. 2016). This would directly contribute to understanding how organizational networks underlie or sustain particular policy orientations and concepts of control. A final example is the rise of Big Corporate Network Data. For instance, Heemskerk and Takes (2016) investigated the community structure of the global corporate elite among the largest 1 million firms worldwide. They find both a distinct and internally relatively cohesive Asian community and a core that still rests on the trans-Atlantic heartland of liberal capitalism. This speaks to the enduring relevance of the AS work on the transforming structures of global capitalism.

These are just three examples; many others could be given. For now, it suffices to say that much will be gained if the unfulfilled promise of combining (large-scale) network analysis with AS theoretical insights finally materializes. Network analysis would benefit from the theoretical rigour of AS work and its relevance to understanding global capitalism in the twenty-first century. And scholars working in the Amsterdam tradition could refine their analyses by drawing on empirically rich, theoretically relevant network studies. Were these synergies to be realized, a collection like this one, published in a couple of decades, would provide original research that combines thorough theoretical insight with both historical narratives and systematic, large-scale network analysis.

References

van Apeldoorn, B. (2002). *Transnational capitalism and the struggle over European integration*. London: Routledge.

van Apeldoorn, B. (2004). Theorizing the transnational. An historical materialist approach. *Journal of International Relations and Development* 7(2): 142–176.

van Apeldoorn, B. and de Graaff, N. (2016). *American grand strategy and corporate elite networks. The open door and its variations since the end of the Cold War*. London: Routledge.

van Apeldoorn, B. and de Graaff, N. (2017). Obama's economic recovery strategy open markets and elite power. Business as usual? *International Politics* 54(3): 356–372.

Babic, M., Fichtner, J., and Heemskerk, E.M. (2017). States versus corporations. Rethinking the power of business in international politics. *International Spectator*, https://doi.org/10.1080/03932729.2017.1389151

Carroll, W.K. (2013). *The making of a transnational capitalist class. Corporate power in the twenty-first century*. London: Zed.

Carroll, W.K., Fennema, M., and Heemskerk, E.M. (2010). Constituting corporate Europe. A study of elite social organization. *Antipode* 42(4): 811–843.

Coen, D. and Vannoni, M. (2016). Sliding doors in Brussels. A career path analysis of EU affairs managers. *European Journal of Political Research* 55(4): 811–826.

Ellersgaard, C.H., Larsen, A.G., Henriksen, L.F., and Lunding, J.A. (2016). Pathways to the power elite-career trajectories in the core of the Danish networks of power. *Sequence Analysis and Related Methods (LaCOSA II)*: 847.

Fennema, M. (1982). The international corporate elite. In *International networks of banks and industry* (pp. 83–102). The Hague: Martinus Nijhoff.

Fennema, M. and Heemskerk, E.M. (2018). When theory meets methods. The naissance of the field of corporate interlock research. *Global Networks* 18(1): 81–104.

Fennema, M. and van der Pijl, K. (1987a). *El triunfo del neoliberalismo* (collab. J. Ortega). Santo Domingo: Ediciones de Taller.

Fennema, M. and van der Pijl, K. (1987b). International bank capital and the new liberalism. In M.S. Mizruchi and M. Schwartz (Eds), *Intercorporate relations. The structural analysis of business* (pp. 298–319). Cambridge: Cambridge University Press.

Fichtner, J., Heemskerk, E.M., and Garcia-Bernardo, J. (2017). Hidden power of the Big Three? Passive index funds, re-concentration of corporate ownership, and new financial risk. *Business and Politics* 19(2): 298–326.

Fligstein, N. (1993). *The transformation of corporate control*. Cambridge, MA: Harvard University Press.

de Graaff, N.A. (2017). Oil elites and transnational alliances. In T. Lehman (Ed.), *The geopolitics of global energy. The new cost of plenty* (pp. 65–84). Boulder, CO: Lynne Rienner.

Granovetter, M. (1985). Economic action and social structure. The problem of embeddedness. *American Journal of Sociology* 91(3): 481–510.

Heemskerk, E.M. (2011). The social field of the European corporate elite. A network analysis of interlocking directorates among Europe's largest corporate boards. *Global Networks* 11(4): 440–460.

Heemskerk, E.M. (2013). The rise of the European corporate elite. Evidence from the network of interlocking directorates in 2005 and 2010. *Economy & Society* 42(1): 74–101.

Heemskerk, E.M. and Takes, F.W. (2016). The corporate elite community structure of global capitalism. *New Political Economy* 21(1): 90–118.

Jessop, B. and Sum, N.L. (2017). Putting the 'Amsterdam School' in its rightful place. A reply to Juan Ignacio Staricco's critique of cultural political economy. *New Political Economy* 22(3): 342–353.

Levenstein, A. (1951). Article in Leonard Lyons' syndicated US newspaper column, 'The Lyons' Den', November.

Mizruchi, M.S. (2016). The resurgence of élite research. Promise and prospects. A comment on the symposium. *Sociologica* 10(2). www.sociologica.mulino.it/doi/10.2383/85293

Overbeek, H. (1988). *Global capitalism and Britain's decline*. Doctoral dissertation, Universiteit van Amsterdam.

van der Pijl, K. (1984). *The making of an Atlantic ruling class*. London: Verso.

van der Pijl, K. and Yurchenko, Y. (2015). Neoliberal entrenchment of North Atlantic capital: From corporate self-regulation to state capture. *New Political Economy* 20(4): 495–517.

van der Pijl, K., Holman, O., and Raviv, O. (2011). The resurgence of German capital in Europe. *Review of International Political Economy* 18(3): 420–448.

Stokman, F.N., Ziegler, R., and Scott, J. (1985). *Networks of corporate power*. Oxford: Blackwell.

PART III

The Amsterdam School and the political economy of contemporary capitalism

20

A TRANSNATIONAL CLASS ANALYSIS OF THE CURRENT CRISIS

Kees van der Pijl

The crisis that became manifest in 2007–2008, from which, so far, no exit has been found, is a systemic crisis of the capitalist mode of production. It has opened an epoch of political decay fraught with grave dangers because of the simultaneous disruption of the biosphere by overpopulation, pollution, and climate change, and the risks of the proliferating 'War on Terror' sliding into a major inter-state war. The crisis is being perpetuated by the class fraction that caused it, i.e. *money-dealing capital* (speculative finance), which remains the directive force within the transnational capitalist system.

In contrast to a pluralistic understanding of rival class fractions competing for political influence in specific policy fields to advance their particular interests (criticized by Clarke 1978, referencing Poulantzas 1971 among other authors), the Amsterdam School proceeds from the assumption that one fraction guides the entire class structure for an extended period *through the propagation of its particular perspective as a concept of control*. During that period, the main classes and indeed society as a whole, voluntarily or for lack of an alternative, assimilate the underlying principles on which the dominance of a directive fraction rests, its preferred *modus operandi* and outlook, its 'logic', and regards them as normal.

What Marx wrote about classes in a political revolution, viz., that a particular class 'emancipates the whole of society *but only provided the whole of society is in the same situation as this class*' (1975: 184, emphasis added) – may also be claimed for fractions of the capitalist class. As capital is forced, time and again, to free itself from constraints that have accumulated to the point where its operation as a particular social configuration (a closed economy centred on production, or a 'financialized' one with production outsourced across the globe, etc.) becomes seriously compromised, an ascendant fraction may capitalize on a frustration felt well beyond its own ranks. However, since in a crisis, the fraction that has led the previous constellation into the quagmire usually continues to occupy the commanding heights (both in terms of material power and in an ideological sense), the necessary restructuring requires a 'disruptive contingency', an outside force or condition to break the mould and really dislodge it by rendering its directive principles unworkable or otherwise inappropriate. War and revolution, or the threat of either, have been such contingencies; since at least the 1970s the various forms of disruption of the Earth's biosphere should be added to the list (Houweling 1999; Newell 2012).

Class formation in the geopolitical economy

The disruptive contingencies impact on a specific 'geopolitical economy' (Desai 2013), centrally configured around a liberal, Lockean heartland of capital and successive contender formations. The epoch of a capitalist West occupying the commanding heights of the global political economy was inaugurated by the Anglo-Dutch alliance that helped the liberal Whigs to power in the British Isles and New England, the 'Glorious Revolution' of 1688 (Israel 2003). This event also accelerated the formation of a proletariat created as peasants were driven off common lands by the enclosure (privatization) movement (Thompson 1968: 237–43). The Dutch intervention was motivated by fear of the power of the strongest European power at the time, absolutist France, which under Louis XIV may be labelled the prototype of a contender to Anglophone supremacy. In contrast to the Lockean state/society complex of the heartland, French development was typically initiated *and sustained* as a state-guided process, condensing the ruling bloc into a state class. Its power derives from its control of the actual state, whereas the capitalist ruling class, because its power is social before it is political, not the other way around, usually leaves state management to an auxiliary governing class (see Figure 20.1 and the discussion below).

In the ensuing century, the Anglo-French contest was fought out on a global scale, notably in the Seven Years' War (1756–63). This momentous struggle forced major changes on both sides in the conflict – weakening Britain to the point where it had to relinquish the North American colonies (which then restored the Lockean principles) and throwing France into the convulsions of revolution (Kaufmann 1999; Godechot 1971). This then worked as a 'disruptive contingency', obviously closely connected to the heartland-contender structure. Henceforth, we may observe a degree of repetition of this pattern. The West evolves as a slowly expanding heartland of capital under successive concepts of control originating with changing fraction perspectives; facing it are contender states, all eventually defeated by the (laissez-faire, corporate, neo-) liberal West (for definitions, see Mirowski 2013: 38–41 and below). Paradoxically, their challenge to the Lockean heartland has worked to *stabilize* the prevailing configuration of forces in the West: the most recent example being that, as long as the Soviet contender bloc held out, it worked to rein in the destabilizing primacy of money-dealing capital and the predatory neoliberalism it has spawned.

The broken line between the contemporary West and the Brazil/Russia/India/China (BRICS)/Shanghai bloc is meant to indicate that its role as a contender is

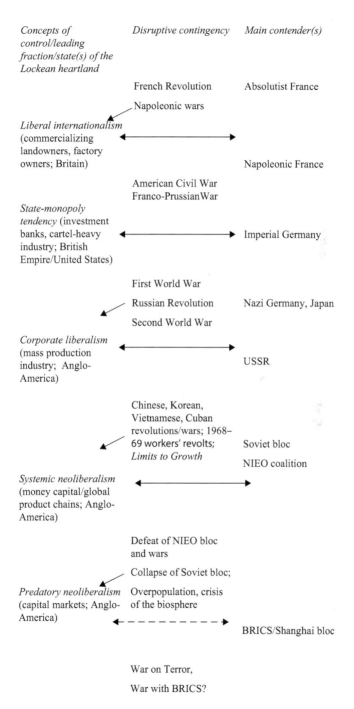

FIGURE 20.1 Successive class constellations in the West, 'disruptive contingencies', and contender formations

Note: NIEO = new international economic order

244 Kees van der Pijl

half-hearted because the state classes in the bloc do not oppose the capitalist West from an ideological vantage point. This adds to the instability already generated by post-1991 neoliberalism.

Fraction perspectives and politics

As Ries Bode argues in his foundational piece (Chapter 1), fractions of the capitalist class strive to develop their particular ideas on the political economy into concepts of control and make them *comprehensive*. This is made possible because under certain conditions such as the trend in profit distribution rewarding particular activities within the overall process of capital accumulation, the ideological dispositions of a given fraction acquire a rationality transcending its particular interests and are propagated as the objectively rational way forward. Via media, the political process and lobbying, the semblance of an identity between its particular interest and the general interest is created, 'the impression that it [is] the interests of this group that need to be courted in order for wider national economic success to be granted' (Atkinson et al. 2017: 190). This rationality is obviously most compelling for the ascendant fraction and its organic intellectuals (politicians, journalists, academics, etc.). However, in an epochal crisis to which a response must be found and which, as indicated, will usually involve external events and forces, its appeal spreads. Material and symbolic concessions to other fractions, strata, and social groups will be made to broaden the initial bloc of forces, to the point where a critical mass is mobilized and the remaining forces are too weak to develop a sufficiently relevant alternative.

Now, compared to the situation in the 1920s and 1930s that informed Bode's argument, or to Marx's original theses in *Capital*, fractions of capital are no longer neatly separated from each other institutionally, nor are they primarily national. In 1977 André Granou highlighted that the fraction of finance capital, comprising different forms of capital, was beginning to transcend the functionally distinct fractions; Henk Overbeek makes the same point in his *Capital & Class* piece reproduced in Chapter 3. Transnational 'finance capitalists' preside over integrated, densely interlocked networks of banks and industry, which remain centred in the North Atlantic heartland (Carroll 2010). These networks are marked by *constitutive internal contradictions* that the finance capitalists must arbitrate and seek to reconcile (Soref and Zeitlin 1987: 60–1). Yet they inevitably do so from a particular fractional perspective. To relate a concept of control to such a perspective it is not necessary that fractions operate as institutionally separate entities. If in the 1990s it was still found that non-financial companies used derivatives mainly for hedging against foreign currency risk, by the time of the 2008 crash they turned out to have been as deeply involved in the shadowy financial practices of actual shadow banks, and they still are (Allayannis and Ofek 1997: 1, 25; Rasmus 2016a: 218; Mirowski 2013: 318–19).

The class compromises that follow from a directive fraction or fraction orientation combine material and symbolic aspects in various ways, ultimately *condensed* at the level of states (Poulantzas 2008). In the process, class formation and fraction (re)alignment become expressly political in Gramsci's sense of 'bringing into play emotions and aspirations in whose incandescent atmosphere even calculations involving the individual human life itself obey different laws from those of individual profit, etc.' (Gramsci 1971: 140). Nonetheless, material rewards are necessary to lend stability to the set of compromises underpinning a concept of control. Without stable employment and productivity-linked wages, the intense animosity towards the Soviet bloc and/or communism that characterized the 1950s would not have continued. Indeed, that antagonism waned once inflation began to eat into wages and benefits. For when a concept of control loses its comprehensiveness and unravels, it will soon be recognized as the *particular* project of *special* interests and lose its common-sense quality. This helps to understand the rise of anti-capitalist militancy in the late 1960s, early 1970s, in combination with détente. The continued existence of the Soviet bloc nevertheless steadied the capitalist order, just as it would keep in place a particular, systemic variety of neoliberalism until it finally collapsed in 1991. For the West, state socialism was what Guy Debord calls 'an adversary that has objectively supported it by the illusory unification of all opposition to the existing order' (1994: thesis 111, translation adapted). This was no different for other contenders.

From corporate liberalism to neoliberalism

Wolfgang Streeck (2014) has analysed the current crisis as the exhaustion of the successive attempts to 'buy time' and thereby postpone the full impact of the crisis of corporate liberalism that began in the late 1960s. Until the financial crash of 2007–2008, ruling and governing classes in the West succeeded in salvaging a measure of class compromise at home by throwing money into the breaches – using inflation, state debt, and private debt. However, as I will argue, the class compromises through which this was achieved have become increasingly symbolic, with fewer and fewer material rewards for other fractions besides the speculators, let alone the majority of the population. Hence the fundamental political instability of the current configuration, aggravating its 'systemic fragility' (Rasmus 2016a).

Corporate liberalism is the liberalism governing relations between bodies internally organized along their own principles, so 'sovereign' in their own domains. It was based on the class compromise forced on capital by organized labour, with the presence of a strengthened Soviet bloc adding its weight to the new balance of forces. Decolonization further undermined the West's pre-eminence in the global political economy. Capital had to operate within a narrow bandwidth, counteracting the appeal of the planned economy whilst simultaneously accommodating democratic demands that required *emulating* the Soviet model in terms of social security, employment, and other alluring aspects of state socialism. The anti-communist campaign of the first Cold War, besides disciplining the workforce, served this purpose.

In the terms introduced above, the fraction of capital positioned centrally in this set of intersecting influences, lending substance to the original New Deal and post-war Marshall Plan projections of a corporate liberal social contract, was *productive capital*. The class compromise at the heart of the corporate liberal concept of control was that between capital and organized labour in production, sharing productivity gains through collective bargaining. In this sense, we can speak of an epoch of democratic capitalism, at least for the North Atlantic political economy – not for Vietnam, or Indonesia, and other areas for which no parallel division into sphere of interest had been agreed. This period corroborates the thesis that, in capitalism, democracy depends not on the bourgeoisie but on organized labour (Rueschemeyer et al. 1992).

The strike wave across all developed capitalist economies in 1968 and 1969, signalled to the capitalist class that social protection and countercyclical crisis management had lasted too long and that the manoeuvring space for further concessions had closed. Capitalists now began to prepare to void the post-war social contract, abandoning their erstwhile passivity and restoring their capacity to actively shape social relations (Streeck 2014: 25–6). In hindsight, this prepared the ground for replacing corporate liberalism by neoliberalism but, initially, the West passed through a first episode of 'buying time'. The collapse of the Bretton Woods system in 1971–73 greatly increased liquidity in the world economy – a process continuing today and ultimately spawning a financial elite powerful enough to take over from productive capital altogether (Rasmus 2016a: 182–3).

The inflationary 1970s initially allowed the class compromises of the corporate liberalism to be prolonged. In the United States the productive perspective echoed in the 1975 proposal for a national planning body (Panitch and Gindin 2012: 143). Britain's entry into the European Community in 1973 was likewise motivated by the Tory government's expectation that it would stimulate Britain's *industrial* modernization (Overbeek 1990: 157). Yet signs were that the consolidation of capitalist property relations would require a downscaling of democracy. A seminal report to the Trilateral Commission, formed in the early 1970s to explore a coordinated way out of the crisis, proposed to reduce 'the demand load on states' as a result of the post-war class compromises, dubbed an excess of democracy (Crozier et al. 1975; cf. Gill 1990). On the edges of the liberal heartland a series of overtly counterrevolutionary interventions restored order the hard way: coups in Greece and Turkey, military dictatorships in Chile, Uruguay, and Argentina, the strategy of tension in Italy and other instances of terrorism by the North Atlantic Treaty Organization (NATO) secret army, 'Gladio', and transatlantic neo-Nazi networks linked to it (Ganser 2005; Teacher 1993).

The Mont Pèlerin Society (MPS), the anti-Keynesian pressure group of Friedrich Hayek, Milton Friedman, and Karl Popper, was directly involved in the neoliberal experiments by the new Latin American dictatorships, whose shock treatment of society allowed a radical make-over (Klein 2007; Walpen 2004; an overview of MPS branches is in Mirowski 2013: 44–6). In the United States, the MPS broadened its monetarist perspective into a comprehensive stance by linking up with the Heritage Foundation, a US think tank and pressure group seeking to roll back the 'excess of democracy'. It too was founded in the early 1970s by direct mail experts with backing from far-right multimillionaires; it was credited with writing the script for the Reagan Administration. Its president, Ed Feulner, Jr., in 1978 became treasurer of MPS; Feulner was vocal in attacking the connection between inflation and Third

World industrialization and Soviet bloc modernization strategies under the new international economic order and détente (Feulner 1976: 66; Mayer 2016: 77–91). In the same period a reconstituted Committee on the Present Danger clamoured for ending détente and resuming the arms race, heralding the constitutive union between money capital and coercion that was to crystallize later (Scheer 1982).

These different initiatives culminated in 1979 when NATO took the decision to introduce new attack missiles in Western Europe and Paul Volcker, appointed by President Carter as head of the Federal Reserve, used a series of interest rate hikes to undermine the anti-Western positions financed by inflationary credit (Panitch and Gindin 2012: 142, table 6.2). Thus, a protracted process of rolling back socialist or quasi-socialist states and social forces was set in motion. Alexander Haig, Ronald Reagan's first secretary of state, questioned the legitimacy of a 'Third World' in-between East and West and denounced 'national liberation' as 'terrorism'; his successor, George Shultz, in January 1984 even claimed that the partition of Europe after the war had 'never been recognised by the United States' (cited, respectively, in van der Pijl 2006: 231, 203). Thus, they signalled that the international compromises on which the post-war world order had also been based no longer applied.

From systemic to predatory neoliberalism and crisis

The 'Volcker Shock' threw the world into a debt crisis – in some cases, a terminal crisis – forcing all states to reorient to exports to service the hard-currency debt with which they found themselves saddled (cf. Greider 1989: 75, 101 and passim). The United States again occupied centre-stage, this time as what Yanis Varoufakis calls the 'Global Minotaur', devouring the world's financial and material surpluses. The attack on organized labour, prominent on the MPS agenda right from its first meeting in 1947, was now put into practice (Cockett 1995). Already by the mid-1980s, the United States had reduced wage growth to less than 2 percent per annum, when the great battles with the unions in Britain and elsewhere were just beginning (Varoufakis 2013: 104–5). Parallel to raising the rate of exploitation, the replacement of social protection by 'workfare' policies was meant to keep the growing surplus population tied to the discipline of the labour market (Soederberg 2014: 58). Paradoxically, new groups entering the work force, such as women or the young, often accepted part-time and flexible jobs from a desire to balance work with other concerns (Streeck 2014: 31). 'May 68' also added pleasure-seeking hedonism and individualism to intensive consumption, soon to be made cheaper by overseas production.

With the sovereignty of organized labour suspended, a narrower, substitute compromise with asset-owning middle classes emerged in the course of a parallel assault on the sovereignty of the large corporation. As Gérard Duménil and Dominique Lévy highlight, it took the form of:

> a strict alliance with top management … achieved by paying out astounding remunerations, as 'wages' and 'stock options'. Asset owners were given the

248 Kees van der Pijl

chance to profit from capital incomes and asset price rises, either directly or through mutual and other investment funds.

(2004: 30)

Thus, the outlines of a new concept of control radically different from the post-war social contract were becoming evident. As Volcker would put it himself in 1985, the new hegemonic formula was perhaps 'not implemented as smoothly as it could have been ... [but] there is ... more emphasis on market orientation ... more concern and effort to reduce the proportion of government in GNP, more emphasis on private initiative'. Neither was this shift confined to the United States; it extended, in Volcker's words, 'to France and the developing world' (cited in Gill 1990: 114).

However, if the repression of finance was to be relaxed, *all aspects of that regime had to be loosened*. So not just investment funds to start up new production, but also free-floating, money-dealing capital, targeted by the Glass-Steagall Act of 1933, the centre-piece of the New Deal in the United States. Its particular perspective survived Keynesianism as 'micro-economics'; materially, money-dealing capital effectively hibernated, notably in the 'Eurodollar' market in the City of London (Burn 2006). Hence, the *rentiers*, whose income derives from this form of financial activity and whom Keynes had recommended for euthanasia in the *General Theory*, were making a comeback, along with the ending of financial repression (Keynes 1970: 376; Morris 1982). Already in 1974, new legislation allowed US retirement benefits to be securitized. This cleared the way for the 1980 Banking Act, which removed the control of money creation by the Federal Reserve. Banks were henceforth permitted to tap into financial markets, borrow from pension funds and mutual funds, and turn their debt into securities. Out of this arose the phenomenon of the 'shadow bank', exempt from deposit rules, but offering a broad range of financial services (Chesnais 2011: 37–8).

By the time Thatcher and Reagan won their elections, financial incomes were rising sharply. In the United States, 'The big acceleration ... began around 1979 or 1980. During the period of the Volcker monetary policy of high real interest rates and the Reagan policy of large budget deficits, the *rentier* share leaped' (Epstein and Power 2002). With it came 'the search for short-term havens in highly liquid assets, instead of seeking opportunities for long-term productive investment' (Naylor 1987: 13). Pioneered in the United States, shadow banks, whether 'basic', 'hybrid', or other (see the list in Rasmus 2016a: 224), collected funds from investors, broke them up into $100,000 lots to qualify for federal deposit insurance, and then sold them on to whoever offered the highest interest rate. As financial radio show host James Jorgensen commented at the time, 'In many respects, we've come full circle to the bargain-hunting 1920s ... except for one big difference: The risk-takers today are playing with money that's federally insured' (Jorgensen 1986: 20). Tax revolts against the universal welfare state meanwhile led to relaxing the fiscal burden on upper income groups and business; governments in due course reduced taxation and then borrowed from those it no longer taxed (Chesnais 2011: 113; Rasmus 2016a: 303). Yet it took until the USSR collapsed and the main

Transnational class analysis of the current crisis **249**

contender that had kept the *systemic* variety of neoliberalism in place was removed, before financial asset investment rose to become the main directive force in the capitalist West.

The epochal shift within neoliberalism after 1991

The implosion of the Soviet bloc was not just a world historic event for the societies affected and for Third World states and social forces enjoying its protection. It also transformed capitalism by replacing systemic neoliberalism by a crisis-prone, predatory variety obeying the logic of money-dealing capital. Coming on top of the opening of China and the doubling of the global labour supply from 1.5 to more than 3 billion people, the lowering of the red flag on the Kremlin triggered an epochal rise in foreign direct investment once the threat of nationalization was removed (Dzarasov 2014: 26–7; Delgado Wise and Martin 2015: 70).

As the socially protective state withered away around the globe, undermined by debt and ideological corruption, populations came to face transnational capital directly, no longer in a relation mediated by states (Vieille 1988: 247). Workers in the West were placed under draconian work obligations enacted under Clinton and other exponents of the 'radical centre' in the 1990s. Production was restructured along 'global commodity chains' serving the West (Merk 2011). Cheap goods from production outsourced to Latin America, East Asia, and Eastern Europe to some extent compensated for falling wages; the remaining shortfall was covered by debt (Soederberg 2014: 58–61, 88; Rasmus 2016a: 236–7). Large corporations operating circuits of productive capital in the process came to adopt the perspective of 'commercial enterprises or consultancies, which select the most competitive components from the programmes of the international manufacturers' (Junne 1979: 74). However, the narrowing of the global consumer market led to an overaccumulation of capital fuelling financial asset investment handled by banks and shadow banks. As Ruslan Dzarasov documents, 'in the 2000s net dividends reached sums twice those for investment in fixed assets' (Dzarasov 2014: 31).

In the course of the 1990s the vantage point of ascendant money-dealing capital, or in contemporary lingo, 'trade in financial services' (characterized by Jack Rasmus as a 'chasing yield psychology', Rasmus 2016a: 233) became the lodestar for the reconfiguration of capital by crowding out other considerations of maintaining capitalist class rule. It resonated in the popular mindset as an immersion in 'risk society' (Beck 1986). Such risks included major environmental disasters such as the 2010 Deepwater Horizon oil spill as a consequence of BP's singular focus on yield (Dzarasov 2014: 33–4). Operating at arms' length from material production, the commercial perspective of money-dealing capital is preoccupied by buying cheap and selling dear, with an eye to 'rent extraction through financial arbitrage and innovation'(Jessop 2013: 264). Peter Gowan captures the shift when he writes that 'trading activity here does not mean long-term investment … in this or that security, but buying and selling financial and real assets *to exploit—not least by generating—price differences and price shifts*' ('speculative arbitrage') (Gowan 2009: 9,

250 Kees van der Pijl

emphasis added). 'Proprietary trading' (speculating not just on commission but also with a bank's own or leveraged money and deposit base), Gowan relates, was pioneered by John Meriwether at Salomon Brothers; in 1994, he set up his own hedge fund, Long Term Capital Management, with two 'Nobel' laureates in economics.

However, as the speculative financial sphere ballooned, the insurance risks increased as well (Nesvetailova 2010: 9–13). So, when Long Term Capital Management crashed in 1998, it had to be bailed out with the help of Alan Greenspan's Federal Reserve – taking moral hazard to new heights. The bailout 'allowed the financial turmoil to transmute into yet another stock market/housing bubble' (Rude 2008: 211). Financial crises that had hitherto been contained, like the savings and junk bond crises in the United States, now turned global, with the Asian meltdown and multiple sovereign debt crises in Mexico, Russia, Argentina, and elsewhere. The combined assets of shadow banks, 'strip-mining' entire economies, to use Jack Rasmus's phrase, by 2005 exceeded regular bank assets. Certainly. the amounts are estimates and the boundary line between the two categories is not strict, since commercial banks also extend credit to shadow banks. Yet if we take the shadow banks as representing the fraction of money-dealing capital, and the central bank-regulated bank sector as money capital representing capital in general, the fact that, in 2007, according to the Fed's own *Flow of Funds* figures, the latter controlled approximately \$10 trillion in assets in the United States, against \$13 trillion for basic shadow banks (hedge funds, investment banks, pension funds, etc., amounting to one fifth of global shadow bank assets at the time), gives a sense of the paramountcy of the money-dealing fraction on the eve of the financial crash (Rasmus 2016a: 217–22).

The other fractions aligned on this particular perspective by various routes, such as the adoption of a commercial perspective by transnational corporations, referred to above. With the working class weakened and organizing along class lines suspect as a road to serfdom (the title of Hayek's neoliberal manifesto of 1943), middle-class social movements for a time continued the progressive thrust of the previous decade. The campaign against new NATO nuclear missiles in Europe in the early 1980s would be a case in point. It was followed by a benevolent, albeit passive response to Gorbachev's turn to open-ended democratization of the Soviet bloc and an end to the Cold War, before dissipating into various gender identity movements no longer connected to a desire for overall social change. From a postmodern perspective, there is no meaning in the historical process; there is only an endlessly revolving present, mirroring the new volatility of finance and the time horizon of money-dealing capital (Harvey 1989).

In the global, *geo*-political economy, shocks of the magnitude of the Asian Crisis and subsequent meltdowns would not remain confined to the sphere of fiscal or monetary policy. In June 1991, US presidential hopeful Bill Clinton submitted to what the *New York Times* later called a 'job interview' with Wall Street bankers, the politically most prestigious segment of the shadow bank sector (this segment has been described as 'Wall Street Democrats'; Ferguson and Rogers 1986). They included Clinton's eventual Treasury Secretary, Robert Rubin of Goldman, Sachs, and set the agenda for the new administration's fiscal and monetary policies. However, Wall Street at that point also became closely involved with the US aerospace industry, which was embarking on a series of mega-mergers (Lockheed and Martin, Boeing-Rockwell-McDonnell Douglas, Raytheon and Hughes) in response to the Soviet demise. Along with oil companies eying the energy riches of the former Soviet republics in the Caucasus and Central Asia, this welded together a bloc of forces that, by Clinton's second term, was geared to an offensive posture in Europe. At the State Department, Richard Holbrooke, an investment banker himself, was entrusted with the Yugoslavia portfolio, which eventually led to NATO interventions in Bosnia and in Serbia over Kosovo and parallel NATO expansion, violating agreements with Gorbachev in 1991 (van der Pijl 2006: 261–79; Sarotte 2014). The continuing receptiveness among the Western middle class to 'humanistic' interpretations of foreign policy meanwhile had moved from resistance to nuclear rearmament to support for 'humanitarian intervention', for which the Carnegie Endowment had produced the justification in a 1992 report co-authored by Holbrooke (Johnstone 2016: 43–4).

By now the contours of the concept of control that would guide the West to the crisis of 2008 and hold the globe to ransom afterwards were clearly evident. Risk taking, originating with money-dealing capital, came to include political-strategic forward pressure into the defunct Soviet bloc, not least to prevent an autonomous German-led move into the vacuum. NATO strategy, reflecting the social reality of 'rampant globalization' and a 'new kind of capitalism' – 'a reality that reinforces the *Zeitgeist* of the risk society' (Williams 2009: 5, 11, 25), fuelled economic and political brinkmanship reinforcing each other (Nederveen Pieterse 2007).

Perpetuating the crisis under the auspices of money-dealing capital

When the mortgage-backed securities business began to falter during 2007 and US house prices actually started to fall in January 2008, the speculative bubble burst. A series of bankruptcies or near bankruptcies led the UK and US governments to respond by bailing out the affected institutions. Table 20.1 lists its main moments.

Already in the primaries, Obama won the support of billionaire money dealer George Soros and hedge fund tycoon Paul Tudor Jones, who feared the crisis might spin out of control. Following their lead, the top Wall Street investment banks (alongside Google, Microsoft, and Time Warner and a handful of Ivy League universities) gave large sums to Obama's campaign against the hapless John McCain. Goldman Sachs, which played a key role through former head Hank Paulson at the Treasury already, was the second largest donor to the Obama candidacy; JP Morgan Chase was fifth and Citigroup seventh, with Swiss UBS and Morgan Stanley also in the top 20 (Navidi 2017: 173–4; OpenSecrets.org 2017).

TABLE 20.1 Key moments in the UK/US financial crisis, state intervention, and corruption, 2007–2008

Date	Event	State intervention	Specifics; instances of collusion
Feb 2007	HSBC $10.5bn loss on mortgage subsidiary		Largest investor in US sub-prime
April 2007	New Century Financial files for bankruptcy		Specialized in sub-prime
June 2007	Bear Stearns closes two hedge funds		First to securitize sub-prime mortgages
Sept 2007		Fed rate from 5% to 4.75%	
Sept 2007	Northern Rock close to bankruptcy		5th largest UK mortgage lender
Feb 2008		£50bn aid package, nationalized	
March 2008	Bear Stearns taken over by JPMorgan Chase		JPMorgan CEO on New York Fed Board, takeover managed by BlackRock
April 2008		Purchase backed by $30bn of Fed loans Fed rate down to 2%	
July 2008	Wachovia $8.9bn loss Fannie Mae/Freddie Mac solvency warning		Holding 5 out of $12 trillion mortgage market
Sept 2008		FDIC forces sale to avoid failure FM/FM nationalized	Nationalized under pressure from Chinese investors in FM/FM
Sept 2008	Collapse of IndyMac, taken over by OneWest; Lehman Bros bankrupt; Merrill Lynch taken over by Bank of America;	IndyMac Federal Bank for bad assets Fed decides to sacrifice Lehman	7th largest mortgage lender
	AIG near bankruptcy;	$85bn rescue package in exchange for 80% Fed share	New York Fed president major AIG investor; rescue funds paid out to Goldman Sachs, Merrill Lynch/Bank of America, SocGen, Deutsche, Barclays
	HBOS taken over by Lloyds TSB; Wachovia taken over by Wells Fargo	FDIC OK with Wells Fargo	HBOS largest UK mortgage lender Citigroup claims damages after Wachovia takeover denied; Tim Geithner, head of New York Fed, supports Citi

Transnational class analysis of the current crisis **253**

Date	Event	State intervention	Specifics; instances of collusion
	Washington Mutual taken over by JPMorgan Chase		
	Bradford & Bingley part-taken over by Santander	Part-nationalized	Largest UK buy-to-let mortgage lender
		US Treasury package of $700bn to buy up toxic debts	Secretary Paulson former head of Goldman Sachs; Fed emergency lending outsourced to JPMorgan, Morgan S, Wells Fargo
Oct 2008	Stock market collapse	Rescue packages Ford, GM, Chrysler	Barack Obama elected with support from Goldman Sachs, JPMorgan, Citigroup
Dec 2008			Geithner nominated treasury secretary

Source: Nesvetailova 2010: 27–37; Mirowski 2013: 185–6, 192, 231; Gamble 2009: 21–34; *Wikipedia*

Note: FDIC = Federal Deposit Insurance Corporation

However, the relationship between the new president and the financial world soon deteriorated. When Obama, enjoying the support of a Democratic congress for the first two years, closed a tax loophole specifically benefiting private equity and hedge fund operators, Stephen Schwarzman of the Blackstone private equity firm (he compared the measure to Hitler's invasion of Poland) crossed over to the ultra-conservative camp of the fossil fuel billionaires, Charles and David Koch (Mayer 2016: 253–4). The Dodd-Frank Wall Street Reform and Consumer Protection Act, with its transparency rules and provisions for regulating the commodity futures derivatives trade (eventually enacted in mid-2010) and the even more threatening Volcker rule, only further alienated the investment bankers. Volcker, the one-time architect of systemic neoliberalism, wanted to limit proprietary trading to 3 percent of core assets. The rule was projected to come into force in 2015 (Clapp and Helleiner 2012: 191–2; Rivlin and Hudson 2017). In 2009 Volcker and his one-time boss, David Rockefeller, also joined the Institute for New Economic Thinking, set up by Soros and managed by a former manager of one of the latter's hedge funds (Navidi 2017: 17, 212; Mirowski 2013: 2–6, 240).

Other components of what might have been a bloc of forces seeking a return to a less rapacious political economy included the New America foundation, originally established in 1999. It was sponsored by the Ford Foundation, Google and its former CEO, Eric Schmidt, and the Gates Foundation of Microsoft founder Bill Gates, all prominent supporters of Obama's 2008 campaign as well (New America 2017). Similarly long-term-oriented forces were behind the Center for American Progress, also initially funded by Soros and by aerospace giant Northrop Grumman (van Apeldoorn and de Graaff 2016: 200–1). The Princeton Project for National

Security, sponsored by the Ford Foundation, Carnegie Endowment, the German Marshall Fund, and David Rubinstein of the Carlyle Group, envisaged a return to the central notion of a Lockean heartland, the core concept running through Anglo-American international thinking from the beginning (Parmar 2012: 249; van der Pijl 2014). Anne-Marie Slaughter became Hillary Clinton's director of policy planning and eventually went on to head New America from 2013 (on her corporate connections, cf. Gill 2012: 514). Other foreign policy think tanks were the Center for a New American Security (funded and led by prominent aerospace and defence companies) and the Phoenix Initiative linked to it, again with Slaughter in a key role (van Apeldoorn and de Graaff 2016: 201, 206–7). However, the disastrous regime change in Libya bankrupted the idea, championed from these quarters, of using IT and social media ('smart power') to stop China in Africa (Campbell 2013; Johnstone 2016).

In the absence of a 'disruptive contingency' derailing the forces behind predatory neoliberalism, the sustained bailout worked to actually reinforce them. Volcker's influence was confined to the initial period, and Wall Street money dealers soon gained the upper hand again. Obama's chief of staff, Rahm Emmanuel, had spent the Bush years as managing director of Wasserstein Perella; Treasury Secretary Tim Geithner as head of the New York Fed had been the spokesman for the finance community all along, notably for Citigroup. Institutions with personal connections to him saw their fortunes vary with the prospects of his nomination (Navidi 2017: 45; van Apeldoorn and de Graaff 2016: 215, cf. 194). Once in office, Geithner instructed one of his Wall Street acquaintances, Larry Fink of BlackRock, a 'passive index fund' (another form of shadow bank), to analyse and sell $30 billion worth of risky mortgage securities. He then asked Fink to do the same for AIG's mortgage securities (Rügemer 2016: 75; Navidi 2017: 30–1). These commissions helped BlackRock grow spectacularly. On the eve of the financial crisis, the most centrally located controlling firms in the world economy (with Barclays at no. 1) already included two passive index funds, State Street (no. 5) and Vanguard (no. 8) (Vitali et al. 2011: 33), but BlackRock soon overtook them. By mid-2016, it had $4.5 trillion in assets under management (Vanguard, $3.6 trillion and State Street, $2.6 trillion) and had risen to the no. 1 controlling firm in the United States (Fichtner et al. 2016: 8–9, 16). By comparison, PIMCO, the world's largest bond fund, has $2 trillion under management; the largest hedge fund, Bridgewater, $150 billion (Navidi 2017: 66–7, 70).

The BlackRock saga is just one spectacular example of how the money-dealing fraction (shadow banks, regulated banks dealing with them, and their billionaire and multimillionaire clients) came out stronger by being saved and/or enlisted in rehabilitating the sector that had precipitated the descent into the crisis. 'The success of the rescue operations', François Chesnais writes, 'has allowed them to preserve their domination' (Chesnais 2011: 66). In fact, *after* the banks had been saved, the provision of free liquidity through quantitative easing and near zero interest rates continued. Peddled under the manifestly false pretence that easy money would get the banks to resume lending to the real economy (an argument at best valid under the systemic variety of neoliberalism left well behind), the estimated \$25 trillion extra liquidity thrown in across the globe after the crisis only fuelled the ongoing bonanza for the super-rich. Since 2010 they have seen 'more than \$5 trillion ... distributed in stock dividend payouts and stock buybacks alone in the US ... in the past two years at a rate of more than \$1 trillion a year' (Rasmus 2016b). Austerity is the price paid by society to keep the enrichment process at the top going. From the perspective of predatory neoliberalism, this is entirely rational, since the operation is aimed at

> bailing out investors and restoring capital incomes for the entire class of financial investors. By funnelling money and liquidity through the private banks, into the hands of investors and speculators, the objective was to boost stock, bond, derivatives and other speculative investment markets ... It was about restoring the [financial elite's] wealth and assets not just rescuing their banks.
>
> *(Rasmus 2016a: 264)*

In 2010 the shadow banking system was again 20 percent larger than the regulated banking sector (Chesnais 2011: 72–3). Three years later shadow banks globally controlled \$75.2 trillion, up from \$26 trillion in 2002. One third of the total is domiciled in the United States (\$25 trillion), against the largest 38 US regular banks commanding \$10.5 trillion at most (Rasmus 2016a: 221–2, table 12.1). The Western heartland remains at the centre because here the shadow bank sector, money-dealing capital, relies on a 'network of equity ties linking the world's largest financial players, i.e. financial intermediaries and sovereign investors "of last resort"' (Pistor 2009: 553).

As a result, there has occurred what Thomas Piketty calls, 'an oligarchic type of divergence, that is, a process in which the rich countries would come to be *owned by their own billionaires*' (Piketty 2014: 463, emphasis added; cf. Freeland 2012). This process received a huge boost in January 2010, when the US Supreme Court in the *Citizens United* case ruled that corporations are entitled to free speech as much as individual citizens. This removed the spending limits on politicians and political issues for US billionaires and multimillionaires, as long as they took the trouble of passing their money through dedicated 'super PACs' ('Political Action Committees', Mayer 2016: 227–9). On this new legal basis, the Koch brothers, who in the previous years had built up a far-right billionaire network, threw their weight behind Mitt Romney in the presidential election of 2012 (after the candidate reversed his viewpoint on global warming). Since Dodd-Frank and the envisaged Volcker rule already led Wall Street to abandon the Obama ticket (Romney's first five donors were Goldman Sachs, Bank of America, Morgan Stanley, J.P. Morgan Chase, and Wells Fargo; OpenSecrets.org 2017), this stacked the odds against the incumbent. Yet Obama won, because he recruited Bill Gates and others for his own super PAC, whilst the superrich on the far right supported different candidates. Thus, the casino mogul and Israel hardliner, Sheldon Adelson, backed Newt Gingrich, and mutual fund multimillionaire Foster Friess, Christian conservative Rick Santorum (Mayer 2016: 317–18, 320).

The net result, however, is that the US political system has become the playground of individual billionaires and the investment banks and funds serving them. Cut off from any domestic productive base as much as from the broader middle class, the predatory neoliberalism espoused by money-dealing capital tends to concentrate political struggle at the top, subject to the ideological whims of individual money magnates. They can even mobilize apparent grassroots discontent, as the Tea Party phenomenon demonstrates (Mayer 2016: 165ff.). Both at the top and the bottom, 'growing disparities in wealth have reawakened class tensions; and political pragmatism has been losing ground to ideological extremism' (Kupchan and Trubowitz 2007: 9).

In the Eurozone, the money-dealing fraction is also outpacing the regulated bank sector again (cf. Lautenschläger 2017: 9, graph). Here too, the most conspicuous shadow bank in handling the crisis was Goldman Sachs. Its executives and board members popped up wherever critical measures were in order: apart from 'technocratic' prime ministers in Greece and Italy appointed under European Union (EU) pressure (Lukas Papademos and Mario Monti, respectively), Antonio Borges, responsible for Europe at the International Monetary Fund, Karel van Miert, Otmar Issing, and Petros Christodoulou in various roles, and of course, Mario Draghi at the European Central Bank (Independent 2011; Rivlin and Hudson 2017). Outgoing EU Commission president Barroso did not have to think long where to move to either and succeeded Peter Sutherland as president of Goldman Sachs International in 2016. As special representative of the UN secretary-general for international migration, Sutherland exhorted the EU to open its borders; Draghi's predecessor at the European Central Bank, Jean-Claude Trichet, in 2011 sketched the ideal society awaiting new arrivals: 'the elimination of automatic wage indexation clauses … firm-level [wage] agreements … the liberalisation of closed professions … the privatisation of services currently provided by the public sector', and so on and so forth (cited in Dumini and Ruffin 2011).

The election of the maverick billionaire, Donald Trump, to the US presidency in November 2016 fits the trend. Stacked with other billionaires and intent on continuing the bonanza for the super-rich, possibly to the point of a US sovereign default, Goldman Sachs is again prominently represented, notably with Stephen Mnuchin as Treasury Secretary and Gary Cohn as chief economic advisor. 'Prior administrations often had one or two people from Goldman serving in top positions. George W. Bush at one point had three. At its peak, the Trump administration effectively had six' (Rivlin and Hudson 2017). In June 2017, the same authors relate, Mnuchin's department issued a statement of principles concerning financial regulation that was focused on promoting 'liquid and vibrant markets' and included a call 'to ease capital requirements and substantially amend the Volcker Rule'.

Authoritarian oligarchic rivalry

As money-dealing capital can no longer offer any compromises to the population at large, it replaces material rewards and side payments with a political aesthetics, arousing fear over terrorism, fostering xenophobia, and demonizing selected foreign leaders – turning oligarchic rule into straightforward authoritarianism (Deppe 2013). The 'politics of fear' goes hand in hand with the contamination of the public sphere by distortion and misrepresentation of fact by the governing classes and media. Gramsci characterizes this as the intermediate phase of 'corruption/fraud', in between consent and coercion, when hegemony is out of reach but overt force still risky (Gramsci 1971: 80 n.; Liguori and Voza 2009: 167). It generates a favourable environment for the rise of right-wing populist and neo-Nazi parties and war propaganda. Politics itself has become suspect in the neoliberal mindset as the idea gains ground that the 'markets' arbitrate claims to wealth and power through general rules, whereas 'politics' distorts this rationality by introducing power and connections (Streeck 2014: 62).

In response to the Trump victory in the 2016 presidential election, Wall Street Democrats and the media they dominate launched a campaign to blame Russia for the unexpected failure of Hillary Clinton's presidential bid. The accommodation with Moscow promised by Trump hence remained out of reach. The hardening of the Democratic stance has also transpired in the formation of the Alliance for Securing Democracy in which the Trilateral/New America tendency has merged with the NeoCon forces of the Project for the New American Century. The Alliance for Securing Democracy is a transatlantic initiative under the umbrella of the German Marshall Fund and is led by a former foreign policy advisor to Hillary Clinton, Laura Rosenberger, and a NeoCon stalwart, Jamie Fly (Greenwald 2017; ASD 2017). In hindsight one might consider the 2016 contest as a choice between a high-risk confrontation with Russia or new wars in the Middle East and, possibly, East Asia.

Trump's America First policy and the prompt withdrawal from the Transatlantic Trade and Investment Partnership (TTIP) and Trans-Pacific Partnership (TPP) projects, meanwhile, should not be read as isolationism. These treaties are not merely about 'free trade', but project a comprehensive sovereignty of capital *enforceable against states*. The Canada–Europe Comprehensive Economic Trade Agreement and the EU–Japan Economic Partnership Agreement, committing the EU and Canada and the EU and Japan, respectively, to secure such enforcement also for US companies, but without TTIP or TPP foreign capital, will not enjoy the same privilege in the United States. Likewise, in the International Criminal Court the United States has itself obtained immunity and the withdrawal from the largely symbolic Paris Climate Agreement can also be viewed from that angle. In the domain of global surveillance, as revealed by Edward Snowden, the United States and its heartland allies (the 'Five Eyes') already occupy such a sovereign position (Greenwald 2014).

The extent to which the primacy of money-dealing capital will continue no longer depends on the West alone. It is also turning into a struggle between capital fractions in China. Contender states always prioritized production, but under corporate liberalism and the systemic variety of neoliberalism until 1991, the Western heartland retained a strong productive base, too. In the current configuration of forces, finance reigns supreme in the West, with information technology and defence (often privatized) as auxiliary forces. They have left the quest for meaningful social compromise behind and waging the 'War on Terror' unlike past contests for industrial primacy does not require a material capacity to galvanize society. 'The threat posed by international terrorism is sporadic and elusive,' Charles Kupchan and Peter Trubowitz write. 'The most effective countermeasures include law enforcement, intelligence gathering, and covert operations – activities that entail bureaucratic coordination, but not national mobilization' (Kupchan and Trubowitz 2007: 29).

Beijing responded to the 2008 crisis with a massive infrastructure investment programme to the tune of 45 percent of gross domestic product (Rasmus 2016a: 145). In 2013, when the export-led boom and related commodities boom that benefited key suppliers to China (including the other members of the BRICS quintet and other 'emerging economies') subsided, president Xi Jinping announced two pillars of an alternative, production-centred international order: the *One Belt, One Road*, 'New Silk Road' project (OBOR) and the Asian Infrastructure Investment Bank. 'By the construction of new infrastructure corridors spanning across the Eurasian landmass in the form of highways, railways, industrial parks, and oil and gas pipelines, OBOR is connecting for the first time in the modern era landlocked regions of hinterland China and Russia and Central Asia republics with the sea ports,' writes William Engdahl. For the novelty of the OBOR project is the combination of land corridors with sea lanes, thus checkmating the century-old strategy of disrupting Eurasia's economic ascent by stoking conflict between Western Europe and Russia, backed up by Anglo-American naval supremacy (Engdahl 2016).

However, a series of reforms after 2010 opened the Chinese financial system to shadow banks. Chinese shadow banks in 2013 held around $6.5 trillion in assets, accounting for 30 percent of accumulated Chinese debt, against $26 trillion for regular banks (Rasmus 2016a: 223). Much will depend on the struggle between this project and the financial elite associated with it, the latter in alliance with its US counterpart. 'The United States,' write Sit Tsui and his associates,

> would counter the OBOR effort by strengthening its alliance with capital interest blocs within China – both inside and outside the ruling clique – to reassert its influence over China's future development policy. Indeed, in this respect the United States has already had much success: the Chinese financial bureaucracy accedes to the unwavering primacy of the United States as the world's central bank, making it unlikely to question, much less undermine, U. S. leadership in the global order.
>
> *(Sit et al. 2017: 37)*

At the Chinese Communist Party Congress in November 2017 it would seem the two fractions of the state class have struck a deal, although time alone will tell what will come of the further liberalization of the Chinese financial sector and its opening to foreign investment.

Today, choice, risk, and the subordination of any collective concern to the pursuit of individual or narrow group interest pervade every aspect of social life. That is why there is no basis to expect 'solutions' to the crisis to be found within capitalism, only beyond it, by ditching the logic of private appropriation entirely. This should not be construed as an adventurous leap into the dark but conceived in steps allowing the orderly transition towards an equitable, socially and ecologically responsible society. Given the authoritarian and bellicose drift of the contemporary capitalist order the obstacles to achieving such a transition are obviously momentous.

References

Allayannis, G. and Ofek, E. (1997). *Exchange rate exposure, hedging, and the use of foreign currency derivatives*. New York: Stern School of Business.

van Apeldoorn, B. and de Graaff, N. (2016). *American grand strategy and corporate elite networks. The open door since the end of the Cold War*. London: Routledge.

ASD (2017). *Alliance for Securing Democracy*, http://securingdemocracy.gmfus.org/ (accessed 15 November 2017).

Atkinson, R.; Parker, S., and Burrows, R. (2017). Elite formation, power and space in contemporary London. *Theory, Culture and Society* 34(5–6): 179–200.

Beck, U. (1986). *Risikogesellschaft. Auf dem Weg in eine andere Moderne*. Frankfurt: Suhrkamp.

Burn, G. (2006). *The re-emergence of global finance*. Basingstoke: Palgrave-Macmillan.

Campbell, H. (2013). *Global NATO and the catastrophic failure in Libya. Lessons for Africa in the forging of African unity*. New York: Monthly Review Press.

Carroll, W.K. (2010). *The making of a transnational capitalist class. Corporate power in the 21st century*, with C. Carson, M. Fennema, E. Heemskerk, and J.P. Sapinski. London: Zed.

Chesnais, F. (2011). *Les dettes illégitimes. Quand les banques font main basse sur les politiques publiques*. Paris: Raisons d'agir.

Clapp, J. and Helleiner, E. (2012). Troubled futures? The global food crisis and the politics of agricultural derivatives regulation. *Review of International Political Economy* 19(2): 181–207. DOI: 10.1080/09692290.2010.514528

Clarke, S. (1978). Capital, fractions of capital and the state. 'Neo-Marxist' analysis of the South African state. *Capital & Class* 5: 32–77.

Cockett, R. (1995). *Thinking the unthinkable. Think-tanks and the economic counter-revolution, 1931–1983*. London: Fontana.

Crozier, M., Huntington, S.P., and Watanuki, J. (1975). *The crisis of democracy. Report on the governability of democracies to the Trilateral Commission*. New York: New York University Press.

Debord, G. (1994 [1967]). *The society of the spectacle*. New York: Zone Books.

Delgado Wise, R. and Martin, D.T. (2015). The political economy of global labour arbitrage. In K. van der Pijl (Ed.), *Handbook of the international political economy of production* (pp. 59–75). Cheltenham: Edward Elgar.

Deppe, F. (2013). *Autoritärer Kapitalismus. Demokratie auf dem Prüfstand*. Hamburg: VSA.

Desai, R. (2013). *Geopolitical economy. After US hegemony, globalization and empire*. London: Pluto.

Duménil, G. and Lévy, D. (2004). Neo-liberal dynamics. Towards a new phase? In K. van der Pijl, L. Assassi and D. Wigan (Eds), *Global regulation. Managing crises after the imperial turn* (pp. 28–42). Basingstoke: Palgrave-Macmillan.

Dumini, A. and Ruffin, F. (2011). Enquête dans le temple de l'Euro. *Le Monde Diplomatique*, November. CD-ROM ed. 1954–2011.

Dzarasov, R. (2014). *The conundrum of Russian capitalism. The post-Soviet economy in the world system*. London: Pluto.

Engdahl, F.W. (2016). The Eurasian century is now unstoppable. *Russia Insider*, 4 October, http://russia-insider.com/en/politics/eurasian-century-now-unstoppable/ri16800 (accessed 16 November 2017).

Epstein, G. and Power, D. (2002). The return of finance and finance's returns. Recent trends in rentier incomes in OECD countries, 1960–2000. *Research Brief, Political Economy Research Institute* 2, November.

Ferguson, T. and Rogers, J. (1986). *Right turn. The decline of the Democratic party and the future of American politics*. New York: Hill and Wang.

Feulner, E.J., Jr. (1976). *Congress and the new international economic order*. Washington, DC: Heritage Foundation.

Fichtner, J., Heemskerk, E.M., and Garcia-Bernardo, J. (2016). *Hidden power of the Big Three? Passive index funds, re-concentration of corporate ownership, and new financial risk*. Working paper. University of Amsterdam, CORPNET (28 October).

Freeland, C. (2012). *Plutocrats. The rise of the new global super rich and the fall of everyone else*. London: Allen Lane Penguin.

Gamble, A. (2009). *The spectre at the feast. Capitalist crisis and the politics of recession*. Basingstoke: Palgrave Macmillan.

Ganser, D. (2005). *NATO's secret armies. Operation Gladio and terrorism in Western Europe*. London: Frank Cass.

Gill, S. (1990). *American hegemony and the Trilateral Commission*. Cambridge: Cambridge University Press.

Gill, S. (2012). Towards a radical concept of praxis. Imperial 'common sense' versus the post-modern Prince. *Millennium. Journal of International Studies* 40: 505–524.

Godechot, J. (1971). *France and the Atlantic revolution of the eighteenth century, 1770–1799*, trans. H.H. Rowen. London: Collier Macmillan.

Gowan, P. (2009). Crisis in the heartland. Consequences of the new Wall Street system. *New Left Review* 55: 5–29.

Gramsci, A. (1971 [1929–1935]). *Selections from the Prison Notebooks*, trans. and ed. Q. Hoare and G.N. Smith. London: Lawrence & Wishart.

Granou, A. (1977). *La bourgeoisie financière au pouvoir et les luttes de classes en France*. Paris: Maspero.

Greenwald, G. (2014). *No place to hide. Edward Snowden, the NSA and the surveillance state*. London: Hamish Hamilton.

Greenwald, G. (2017). With new D.C. policy group, Dems continue to rehabilitate and unify with Bush-era neocons. *Intercept*, 17 July, https://theintercept.com/2017/07/17/with-new-d-c-policy-group-dems-continue-to-rehabilitate-and-unify-with-bush-era-neocons/ (last accessed 17 November 2017).

Greider, W. (1989). *Secrets of the temple. How the Federal Reserve runs the country*. New York: Simon and Schuster Touchstone.

Harvey, D. (1989). *The condition of postmodernity. An enquiry into the origins of cultural change*. Oxford: Blackwell.

Houweling, H.W. (1999). The limits to growth na ruim 25 jaar. Een realistische terugblik op een doem-scenario. *Transaktie* 28(1): 71–105.

Independent (2011). What price the new democracy? Goldman Sachs conquers Europe. *Independent*, 18 November.

Israel, J.I. (2003 [1991]). The Dutch role in the Glorious Revolution. In J.I. Israel (Ed.), *The Anglo-Dutch moment. Essays on the Glorious Revolution and its world impact* (pp. 105–162). Cambridge: Cambridge University Press.

Jessop, B. (2013). Credit money, fiat money and currency pyramids. Reflections on financial crisis and sovereign debt. In G. Harcourt and J. Pixley (Eds), *Financial crises and the nature of capitalist money* (pp. 248–272). Basingstoke: Palgrave-Macmillan.

Johnstone, D. (2016). *Queen of chaos. The misadventures of Hillary Clinton.* Petrolia, CA: CounterPunch Books.

Jorgensen, J. (1986). *Money shock. Ten ways the financial marketplace is transforming our lives.* New York: American Management Association.

Junne, G. (1979). Internationalisierung und Arbeitslosigkeit. Interne Kosten des 'Model Deutschland'. *Leviathan. Zeitschrift für Sozialwissenschaft* 7(1): 57–78.

Kaufmann, E. (1999). American exceptionalism reconsidered. Anglo-Saxon ethnogenesis in the 'universal' nation, 1776–1850. *Journal of American Studies* 33(3): 437–457.

Keynes, J.M. (1970 [1936]). *The general theory of employment, interest and money.* Basingstoke: Macmillan.

Klein, N. (2007). *The shock doctrine. The rise of disaster capitalism.* Harmondsworth: Penguin.

Kupchan, C.A. and Trubowitz, P.L. (2007). Dead center. The demise of liberal internationalism in the United States. *International Security* 32(2): 7–44.

Lautenschläger, S. (2017). *Pro-cyclicality and interconnectedness in the financial sector. The European perspective* (Joint BoE-HKMA-IMF Conference, November 8–9, Washington DC). Frankfurt: ECB.

Liguori, G. and Voza, P. (2009). *Dizionario Gramsciano 1926–1937.* Rome: Carocci.

Marx, K. (1975 [1843]). Critique of Hegel's Philosophy of law. In *Marx-Engels Collected Works*, vol. 3 (pp. 3–129). London: Lawrence & Wishart.

Mayer, J. (2016). *Dark money. The hidden history of the billionaires behind the rise of the radical right.* New York: Doubleday.

Merk, J. (2011). Production beyond the horizon of consumption. Spatial fixes and anti-sweatshop struggles in the global athletic footwear industry. *Global Society* 25: 73–95.

Mirowski, P. (2013). *Never let a serious crisis go to waste. How neoliberalism survived the financial meltdown.* London: Verso.

Morris, J. (1982). The revenge of the rentier or the interest rate crisis in the United States. *Monthly Review* 33(8): 28–34.

Navidi, S. (2017). *$uperhubs. How the financial elite and their networks rule our world.* Boston, MA: Brealey.

Nederveen Pieterse, J.P. (2007). Political and economic brinkmanship. *Review of International Political Economy* 14(3): 467–486.

Nesvetailova, A. (2010). *Financial alchemy in crisis. The great liquidity illusion*, with R.P. Palan. London: Pluto.

Newell, P. (2012). *Globalization and the environment. Capitalism, ecology and power.* Cambridge: Polity.

New America (2017). *New America Foundation*, www.newamerica.org (accessed 15 November 2017).

Naylor, R.T. (1987). *Hot money and the politics of debt.* London: Unwin Hyman.

OpenSecrets.org (2017). *Top contributors. Presidential races 2008, 2012* (separate entries), www.opensecrets.org/ (accessed 4 November 2017).

Overbeek, H. (1990). *Global capitalism and national decline. The Thatcher decade in perspective.* London: Unwin Hyman.

Panitch, L. and Gindin, S. (2012). *The making of global capitalism. The political economy of American empire.* London: Verso.

Parmar, I. (2012). *Foundations of the American Century. The Ford, Carnegie and Rockefeller Foundations in the rise of American power.* New York: Columbia University Press.

van der Pijl, K. (2006). *Global rivalries from the Cold War to Iraq.* London: Pluto.

van der Pijl, K. (2014). *The discipline of Western supremacy*, vol. 3 of *Modes of foreign relations and political economy.* London: Pluto.

Piketty, T. (2014). *Capital in the twenty-first century*, trans. A. Goldhammer. Cambridge, MA: Harvard University Press.

Pistor, K. (2009). Global network finance: Institutional innovation in the global financial market place. *Journal of Comparative Economics* 37(4): 552–567.

Poulantzas, N. (1971). *Pouvoir politique et classes sociales*, 2 vols. Paris: Maspero.

Poulantzas, N. (2008 [1976]). The political crisis and the crisis of the state, trans. J.W. Freiburg. In J. Martin (Ed.), *The Poulantzas reader. Marxism, law and the state* (pp. 294–322). London: Verso.

Rasmus, J. (2016a). *Systemic fragility in the global economy*. Atlanta, GA: Clarity Press.

Rasmus, J. (2016b). Why Trump won – and what's next. *CounterPunch*, 10 November, www.counterpunch.org/2016/11/10/why-trump-won-and-whats-next/ (accessed 22 September 2017).

Rivlin, G. and Hudson, M. (2017). Government by Goldman. *Intercept*, 17 September, https://theintercept.com/2017/09/17/goldman-sachs-gary-cohn-donald-trump-administration/ (accessed 25 September 2017).

Rude, C. (2008). The role of financial discipline in imperial strategy. In L. Panitch and M. Konings (Eds), *American empire and the political economy of global finance* (pp. 198–222). Basingstoke: Palgrave-Macmillan.

Rueschemeyer, D., Stephens, E.H., and Stephens, J.D. (1992). *Capitalist development and democracy*. Chicago, IL: University of Chicago Press.

Rügemer, W. (2016). BlackRock-Kapitalismus. Das neue transatlantische Finanzkartell. *Blätter für deutsche und internationale Politik* 61(10): 75–84.

Sarotte, M.E. (2014). A broken promise? What the West really told Moscow about NATO expansion. *Foreign Affairs* 93(5): 90–97.

Scheer, R. (1982). *With enough shovels. Reagan, Bush, and nuclear war*. New York: Random House.

Sit, T., Wong, E., Lau, K.C., and Wen, T.J. (2017). One Belt, One Road. China's strategy for a new global financial order. *Monthly Review* 68(8): 36–45.

Soederberg, S. (2014). *Debtfare states and the poverty industry. Money, discipline and the surplus population*. London: Routledge.

Soref, M. and Zeitlin, M. (1987). Finance capital and the internal structure of the capitalist class in the United States. In M.S. Mizruchi and M. Schwartz (Eds), *Intercorporate relations. The structural analysis of business* (pp. 56–84). Cambridge: Cambridge University Press.

Streeck, W. (2014). *Buying time: The delayed crisis of democratic capitalism*. London: Verso.

Teacher, D. (1993). The Pinay Circle Complex 1969–1989. *Lobster. Journal of Parapolitics* 26: 9–16.

Thompson, E.P. (1968). *The making of the English working class*. Harmondsworth: Penguin.

Varoufakis, Y. (2013). *The global minotaur. America, Europe and the future of the global economy*, rev. ed. London: Zed.

Vieille, P. (1988). The world's chaos and the new paradigms of the social movement. In Lelio Basso Foundation (Ed.), *Theory and practice of liberation at the end of the twentieth century* (pp. 219–256). Brussels: Bruylant.

Vitali, S., Glattfelder, J.B., and Battiston, S. (2011). The network of global corporate control. *PLOS ONE* 6(10): 1–6. Including supporting information: The network of corporate control. http://journals.plos.org/plosone/article?id=10.1371/journal.pone.0025995 (accessed 4 November 2017).

Walpen, B. (2004). *Die offenen Feinde und ihre Gesellschaft. Eine hegemonietheoretische Studie zur Mont Pèlerin Society*. Hamburg: VSA.

Williams, M.J. (2009). *NATO, security and risk management: From Kosovo to Kandahar*. London: Routledge.

21

PUTTING THE AMSTERDAM SCHOOL IN ITS PLACE

Bob Jessop

Introduction

The Amsterdam School (AS) can be explored as a social construct, a theoretical approach, and a political project. It had already formed before it was first construed as one of seven major schools in the *regulation approach* in my contribution to the First International Conference on Regulation Theory, held in June 1988 in Barcelona (Jessop 1988, 1990). Each regulation approach has its own prehistory, key foundational moments and contributors, and subsequent branching trajectories. Only the Parisian approach has consistently conceived itself as a school, namely, *l'école de la régulation* (the regulation school). In contrast, the key figures in the Amsterdam theoretical approach and its associated political project did not initially conceive themselves as a school, other than jokingly;[1] and founding members initially rejected my proposed characterization of them as the AS. Two alternatives suggested by its members were the Dutch 'branch' of transnational historical materialism (THM) (Overbeek 2000) and the Amsterdam Project in International Political Economy (IPE) (van Apeldoorn 2004; Overbeek 2004). For the sake of convenience and self-consistency, and in line with practice in this book, this chapter will continue to use the term Amsterdam School.

There are other ways to put the school in its place vis-à-vis other heterodox theoretical paradigms and political projects. This would lead to different construals. A second example concerns the enduring interest of the AS in *European integration*. In 1974, a small group of students and teachers in International Relations (IR) at the University of Amsterdam embarked on a teaching research project on 'Social Forces in Western European Integration' in the 1940s–1950s, its economic and political antecedents from the 1920s onwards, and its subsequent development into the 1970s (Overbeek 1990: xvii; van der Pijl 1998: 1). Indeed, relating the AS both to European integration and critical IPE are its founding figures' preferred ways of

264 Bob Jessop

putting the AS in its place. In contrast, my framing in relation to the regulation approach is an outsider's perspective.[2] Regarding European integration, Kees van der Pijl's first book (1978) addressed US influence in the European economy and European integration. Another stimulus was Gerd Junne's research in Berlin and Konstanz before he moved to Amsterdam in 1979: this had employed sectoral analysis and studied internationalization, including the internationalization of the state in a European context (for example, Schlupp et al. 1973; see also his foreword to this volume). AS research was extended to the roles of individual countries in European integration, successive stages in the accession process, and, more recently, to the economic, financial, and political crises of European integration and their reflection in legitimation crises and different forms of popular discontent. Furthermore, beside its analyses of regulation in terms of the articulation of local, sectoral, national, European, and international concepts of control, it has studied the changing forms of multi-level government and governance in Europe and, more recently, corporate governance at the national and transnational levels. Despite the empirical extension and conceptual deepening of its work on European integration – or, perhaps better phrased, because of their proven real heuristic and explanatory power, the initial key concepts have remained stable, persistent features of the AS and continue to demarcate it from other approaches.

Third, the AS can be related to the field of heterodox *global political economy* that emerged in the 1980s. Here it has been described as one variant of THM. Ryner et al. once noted the existence of

> distinct but commensurate research programs and orientations at the University of Amsterdam, the European University Institute in Florence, and York University in Toronto. Although there are significant differences among the contributors, they share a common commitment to a critical-theoretical analysis of transnational relations
>
> *(1998: 4)*

York University provided Robert W. Cox's academic home during 1977–92 as he made his most influential contributions to a critical, neo-Gramscian IPE. Van Apeldoorn studied in Amsterdam and the European University Institute, Ryner was a researcher in all three places. Overbeek also noted that AS work on the state had been sharpened and deepened in dialogue with Cox, Stephen Gill, and other scholars from York (Overbeek 2004: 125–6; cf. 2003: 24). Moreover, in his introduction to this volume, he recalls fruitful dialogues and academic exchanges between Amsterdam and Toronto in global political economy more generally.

Fourth, in other but related respects, the AS can also be placed in the study of the rise and consolidation of *neoliberalism and its varieties*. Amsterdam research on neoliberalism as a concept of control as a response to the crisis of Fordist corporate liberalism that reflected the rise of money capital began in the 1980s. Cases included Britain, West Germany, Belgium and the Netherlands, Austria, Sweden, the USA, Canada, as well as the European Union (EU). This approach differs radically from, and explicitly critiques, mainstream debates between neorealists and neofunctionalists. It calls for attention to the material and social bases of support for this concept of control and how it could be articulated to other concepts in more comprehensive concepts of control (CCCs). Other key questions concerned the varieties of neoliberalism, its transnational character (van Apeldoorn 2000, ch. 2, and 2002), its periodization (e.g. the shift from systemic to predatory neoliberalism; see van der Pijl, this volume), and the eruption of the crisis in and/or of neoliberalism at different scales of accumulation and resulting efforts at crisis management and their mediation through state power (Overbeek and van Apeldoorn 2012). As the preceding quotation indicates, the four major thematic foci of the AS are interrelated and co-evolving.

These four ways of putting the AS in its place guide the first half of this chapter. Interestingly, all four are mentioned as key themes and sites of debate in Overbeek's magisterial review of its development (2004). Overall, his review can be read as a first and comprehensive attempt to put it in its place in IPE. The second half deals with three issues: first, the school's metatheoretical assumptions and approach to theory development and empirical analysis; second, a more systematic account of its general features; and, third, based on the critical commentaries of the AS in Part II, its alleged weaknesses and how they might be resolved. The chapter ends with some brief recommendations.

The Amsterdam School and other regulation schools

In my initial account of different schools in regulation theory, the Amsterdam approach merited identification and inclusion because, like other schools, it was contributing to a broad, continuing, and progressive research programme in critical political economy that was opposed to mainstream scholarship in economics, IR, and political economy. It qualified as regulationist on three main grounds: first, methodologically, it worked with a scientific-realist ontology and epistemology inspired by Marx; second, its approach to theory building and presentation relied on a method of 'articulation'[3] combined with empirical analysis; and third, substantively, it sought to explain the improbable reproduction of the capital relation and the alternation of periods of relative integration, crisis periods, and the rise of new stable configurations (van der Pijl 1984, 1989, 1998, 2001; Overbeek 1990; Overbeek and van der Pijl 1993; and the discussion below). However, reflecting different theoretical backgrounds, state traditions, varieties of capitalism, and empirical concerns, there are five major areas of difference between the Amsterdam and Parisian schools:

1. It focused on *societalization* rather than political economy – let alone the economy in its narrow sense; from the start, it engaged not only in the critique of the economic and political aspects of the capitalist mode of production but also in a critique of the anatomy of bourgeois society and its increasing subordination to the logic of capital at diverse but interconnected scales up to the global.

266 Bob Jessop

2. It considered state formation and inter-state politics in more sophisticated ways and far greater detail. This reflected its roots in political science, IR, and IPE rather than, as with the Parisian School, economics, planning, and engineering. The AS is similar in this regard to German regulationists, such as Joachim Hirsch (see Hirsch 2000 for a comparison of materialist state theory and French regulation theory; cf. Jessop 1990 and Jessop and Sum 2005).
3. It highlighted class strategies, class formation, and the emergence of power blocs and historical blocs that consolidate these strategies rather than focusing on macro- and meso-economic relations and the 'chance discoveries' (*trouvailles*) (Lipietz 1993) of appropriate modes of social regulation in pre-defined institutional fields.
4. It explored these issues by anticipating, citing, and then drawing substantially on Gramsci's concept of hegemony and explored how different fractions struggled to define the 'general [societal] interest' of capital by formulating CCCs as an organic moment of specific capitalist configurations in the sense that they help to organize and direct (or lead) bourgeois hegemony in ways that can consolidate current or potential forms of accumulation and societalization (van der Pijl 1984: 7, 20–1; 1998: passim; Overbeek 2000: 186; on organic ideologies, see Gramsci 1971: 376–7).
5. It considered the role of money capital (especially in its concrete form of high finance)[4] and of an emerging transnational productive fraction alongside other fractions of capital (including landed capital) (Bode 1979; van der Pijl 1984: 7–20; Overbeek 1990: 23–5). In contrast, early work in the Parisian School focused mostly on the distinction between industrial and financial capital within national economies (France, the USA).

The AS focused on how different economic spaces have been integrated at different times into the world market as the ultimate horizon of capital accumulation. This can be seen in Bode's analysis of Dutch capital in the inter-war period (Bode 1979, and Chapter 1, this volume) and the post-war fate of Europe's coal and steel sector (Bode 1975, as summarized in Overbeek 2004: 117–18). The rest is history, starting with van der Pijl's analysis of US plans for Europe (1978), reprised in Chapter 2. This encouraged studies of the international or transnational as well as national moments of class strategies and struggles over CCCs plus their associated state forms. This gives the AS a distinctive position in regulation theory. However, as early and later Amsterdam scholars did not engage much with the Parisian, Grenoblois, or German schools or aim to contribute to the regulation approach, this may not, with hindsight, be the best way to locate it within the social sciences.

European integration

Overbeek's authoritative survey recalls that the AS emerged from collaborative research at the University of Amsterdam on European integration in opposition to the prevailing mainstream approaches of federalism and neofunctionalism (2004: 116–20).

Putting the Amsterdam School in its place **267**

The project on social forces in the making of Western European integration first focused on the interwar period, as processes of class formation were shaped from the 1920s onwards by its integration into the circuits of an emerging Atlantic Fordism.[5] Building on Bode (1975), van der Pijl (1978) explored how, under pressure from the Americans and by consent of European politicians, who backed a pragmatic variant of European federalist idealism, heavy industry in Western Europe was placed under joint European control through the European Coal and Steel Community. This overcame the industrial disputes between, especially, France and Germany; and facilitated the recovery of the European economy (cf. Chapter 2).

The dynamics and crisis tendencies of European integration have been a continuing theme in AS research, extending roles of individual countries in European integration; the accession of Southern European states and Central and Eastern European states (e.g. Holman 1993, 1996, and 2001) and to the Europeanization of CCCs (van Apeldoorn 2002). A key question is how these developments reflect and refract changing class projects, how these are contested within and outside EU institutions, how they involve imperial rivalries and international competition, and, in part, how they trigger and react to resistance and resentment from subaltern forces. Examples of such work are the chapters by Overbeek, van Apeldoorn, and Holman; and the two co-authored critical commentaries by Andreas Bieler and Adam Morton and by Alan Cafruny and Magnus Ryner. Amsterdam scholars have also analysed the crisis in the EU – and the 2000 Lisbon agenda – consequent upon the global financial crisis and Eurozone crisis and the associated attempt to relaunch the European project in the form of the Europe 2020 project, on which see, respectively, van Apeldoorn et al. 2010, and Overbeek and van Apeldoorn 2012. A series of edited collections and journal special issues have pursed these themes, drawing not only on researchers from different generations of the AS but also those close to it in the broader field of THM. A further set of questions included:

> To what extent are neoliberal hegemony, internationalization of the state, and Europeanization 'different sides of the same coin'? To what extent are the processes riddled with tensions, contradictions, and antagonisms? And could the 'internationalization of the state' and Europeanization even contain the seeds of a tendency that may undermine the predominant tendency toward a transnational neoliberal hegemony in Europe and the world order?
>
> *(Ryner et al. 1998: 3–4)*

These comparative and historical analyses have covered different policy fields, the wider politics of European integration, the nature of the European polity, and its changing modes of government and governance. The key concepts in all these analyses are rooted in Ries Bode's work, van der Pijl's first two books, and Gramsci's work on Americanism and Fordism, historical blocs, hegemony, and passive revolution, but they also integrate other relevant concepts to enhance and deepen the analysis. But it is the elaboration of the original concepts that distinguishes AS analyses from other approaches to European integration.

268 Bob Jessop

A related project was the 2004–2009 programme of the Amsterdam Research Centre on Corporate Governance Regulation (van Apeldoorn et al. 2003). Based on earlier AS work, van Apeldoorn and Overbeek conceived this with Andreas Nölke, who was at the Vrije Universiteit van Amsterdam in 2001–2007 and wrote his *Habilitationsschrift* there (Nölke 2004). The programme yielded four doctoral projects: Angela Wigger (2008; see also Buch-Hansen and Wigger 2011), Laura Horn (2009, 2011), Arjan Vliegenthart (2009), and James Perry (2009);[6] and an edited volume on the IPE of corporate governance regulation (Overbeek et al. 2007).

When the project ended in 2009, core members of the team dispersed to different universities in different European countries and began cooperating with other colleagues on other projects – repeating a pattern that Overbeek described in his introduction to this volume. But 'there was enough in our interests to maintain some sort of permanent affiliation: this was done through the creation of a virtual research network, the Amsterdam Research Center for International Political Economy (www.arcipe.eu), which our newest recruit, Naná de Graaff, also joined' (Overbeek and van Apeldoorn 2012: xi). The network discovered shared interests in the crisis in the neoliberal global order precipitated by the deepening disorder in the world's financial markets. This reflects a Phoenix-like return to the concerns of pioneering texts (e.g. Overbeek 1990: 7–9 and passim; van Apeldoorn 2002).

The Amsterdam project in international political economy and transnational historical materialism

The AS has a different genealogy, a different set of sources, and, in part, different foci from other THM variants. Its main arguments were inspired by other theoretical paradigms in the 1970s, some years before Cox first attracted serious attention in the mid-1980s for his critical approach to IPE (Cox 1977, 1981, 1983, 1987).[7] While Bode's foundational article (1979) did not mention Gramsci, two other early studies reprinted in this volume did integrate his ideas in rudimentary form (van der Pijl 1979; Overbeek 1980), while the books building on these articles gave Gramsci a more explicit role (van der Pijl 1984: 20–1 on Americanism and Fordism; Overbeek 1990: 28–9 on hegemony). His analyses were even more central to van der Pijl's analysis of *Transnational classes and international relations* (1998). Other key influences were Marx's work on circuits of capital and the world market; revisionist Cold War historiography, which explored US imperialism in the postwar world (e.g. Kolko and Kolko 1972); a project led by Frank Deppe at Marburg University on the European Economic Community (e.g. Deppe 1975; see also Bieling et al. 1993); and Junne's new curriculum in Amsterdam, which included dependency theory and world system theory and was based on his past research in Berlin and Konstanz (Overbeek 2004: 204; Jessop and Sum 2005: 26–7). There was also lively interest in Marxist debates on the world market in Germany, and in France, especially on the internationalization of capital, its fractions, and generations (Palloix 1971, 1973, 1974).[8] Another influence was Nicos Poulantzas, who identified the rise of an internationalized interior (or domestic) bourgeoisie in the (then) current phase of

Putting the Amsterdam School in its place **269**

imperialism and a matching trend to the internationalization of the state (1975, 1978).[9] AS scholars also engaged with British and US work on colonialism and imperialism.

Although Cox employed key concepts from Gramsci's prison writings (hence his designation as the founder of the Italian School[10] in IPE), he viewed Marxist political economy less favourably.[11] This marks a key difference from the AS approach. In addition, the latter studied the specificity of transnational class formation and transnational hegemony rather than, as in the Italian School, just rescaling selected Gramscian concepts from the national to international level.[12] This approach was adumbrated by Kees van der Pijl in his first book (1978; see Chapter 2) and elaborated in his 1984 book on Atlantic Fordist class formation (cf. Overbeek 1990: 84–100). These contrasting trajectories are reflected in five thematic clusters that distinguish the AS's place within THM:

1. Reflecting the Marxian emphasis on the world market, it posits that capital has always been international or, rather, non-national. Marx's comments on the tendential unity of the world market and the continuing plurality of territorial states also inform AS work on the changing relationships among global, transnational, and national scales of accumulation and societalization reflecting different modes of insertion into the international division of labour and/or inter-state hierarchies. A concern with how internal and external factors interact to shape capitalist regimes is reflected in the dialectical articulation of two notions of hegemony: a system of class rule and a power relationship among states (Overbeek in Chase-Dunn et al. 1994: 368). These aspects reflect the 'classical core' of the AS: the political articulation of class interests by capital fractions and fractions of the bourgeoisie, rival CCCs, hegemony, and historical bloc.

2. There is the analysis of segments, currents, fractions of capital and concepts of control, and class formation at different scales of mobilization at the political and ideological as well as economic level (van der Pijl 1984; Overbeek 1990). This remains an important theoretical move, as van der Pijl explains: 'the fraction concept can help to connect economics and politics in a way which cannot be achieved by either a monolithic concept of capital with a big "C" … or the politicism of mainstream IR, in which states are the privileged or even exclusive actors' (1998: 3). This distinctive focus is reflected in the AS's spiral movement between concept formation and historical research (see below). A key aim is to identify rival CCCs based on different syntheses of more immediate (or economic-corporate) concepts that reflect specific hierarchies of classes and class fractions (Overbeek and van der Pijl 1993: 3).

3. The relation between the world market and territorial states is explored, following van der Pijl, focusing on 'state-society complexes' (cf. Cox 1981), in terms of the differential articulation of capital/capitals to the state system. He distinguishes a relatively unified Lockean heartland organized in the shadow of the hegemony of the CCC and military-diplomatic power of a leading state; and a plurality of Hobbesian contender states that promote the interests of

home-based capitals vis-à-vis other contender states and the heartland. These positions are associated with different state forms. While liberal states, a pluralistic power bloc, a separation between ruling class and governing class, and self-regulating civil society based on civil law characterize the 'Lockean heartland' of advanced capitalism, 'Hobbesian' states are led by a dominant economic-political class – or state class – that seeks to penetrate and mobilize the economy and wider society through central planning and coercion in pursuit of catch-up development (van der Pijl 1989, 1998, 2007a). State–civil society relations are an important theme (e.g. Holman on their rearticulation following the collapse of the Francoist regime, 1993). Subsequent work has extended to Europe's semi-periphery and periphery, work on contender states (see de Graaff, Chapter 11), the rise of China (van der Pijl 2006: 297–335; 2007a; Overbeek 2012; de Graaff and van Apeldoorn 2018), and different grand strategies to promote, adapt to, or resist US imperial domination (respectively, van Apeldoorn and de Graaff 2015; and de Graaff and van Apeldoorn 2017).

4. The AS also has a relatively distinctive take on the internationalization of the state and its role in underpinning transnational hegemony (de Graaff 2014; Carroll et al. 2010). This is a prominent theme in critical IPE but was already implicit in the AS concern with transnational class formation and the role of national territorial states, inter-state cooperation, and transnational governance regimes in promoting the conditions for accumulation on a world scale. Newer AS themes in this regard are multi-level and multi-spatial metagovernance, new forms of global governance, including new regulations for corporate governance, and, of course, the return of the capital–state nexus (Holman 2004; van Apeldoorn et al. 2010; Overbeek 2012; and van Apeldoorn et al. 2013).

5. Inspired by van der Pijl, there is also strong interest in the cadre class and the different roles that its members could play, whether as leading figures in developing concepts of control and CCCs, coordinating or governing different institutions and networks, attempting to secure social cohesion by managing the evolving contradiction between the private and the social, and acting as relays of class strategies across different domains and sites of struggle (see, for example, van der Pijl 1993: 33–43, 1998: passim; and 2007a, 2007b). These roles remind one of Gramsci's concept of organic intellectuals and their expanded role in the enlarged state (*lo stato allargato*) that developed in the inter-war period and subsequently; and his remarks about the need for an appropriate balance – or fixed proportions – among different layers of functionaries in parties, bureaucracies, and other organizations (Gramsci 1971: 60–1, 191–2, 210–11, 228, 418).

Neoliberalism

The critique of transnational neo-liberalism in the 1990s can ... be seen as the culmination of the genesis of the AP [Amsterdam Project], the analysis in which all

> of the diverse theoretical influences came together in a coherent and distinctive research programme.
>
> *(Overbeek 2004: 129)*

The AS explains the rise of neoliberalism in terms of the economic, social, and political restructuring that began in the 1980s in response to the 1970s crisis in world capitalism. The latter affected the social relations of production, the composition of the historical bloc and its concepts of control, the role of the state, international regimes, and other aspects of the post-war order (Overbeek and van der Pijl 1993: 14). As such, it could be described, in Gramscian terms, as a series of organic crises. Later work sees the varieties of neoliberalism experience similar organic crises followed by attempts at restoration and renewal (Overbeek and van Apeldoorn 2012: 3ff.). Throughout its 'life course', from genesis to maturity and crisis, neoliberalism is analysed as a *transnational* political class project designed to restore capitalist class power, developing in different ways in the Lockean heartland and its outposts (e.g. Australia), in the semi-periphery (e.g. Chile), and periphery (e.g. on Latin America and the Caribbean, Fennema and van der Pijl 1987). In the periphery, it was imposed through disciplinary neoliberalism (on which, see Gill 1995; and van der Pijl 1998: 47). Although it has a different face in each country, it should not be studied as the sum of basically unrelated individual national developments. Rather, reflecting the AS rejection of the ontological primacy of a pre-given world systems logic and the methodological privileging of national economies and states, it studied neoliberalization in terms of the variegated development of a novel CCC or, as Fennema and van der Pijl express it in Spanish, a 'cosmovisión' (1987: 39ff.).

This variegation arises because 'transnational money capital and globally-operative productive capital manifests itself at national level as a set of intricate mediations between the logic of capital and the historical reality of national political and social relations' (Overbeek 1993: xi; cf. Overbeek and van der Pijl 1993: 15; Overbeek and van Apeldoorn 2012). The emergence of a new CCC does not eliminate competition, rivalries among capitals as 'hostile brothers' (Marx 1998: 252), fractional conflicts, or contradictions. These all remain and are reflected in a pool of competing concepts of control and even rival CCCs that provide sources of flexibility and margins of manoeuvre when crises in (rather than of) neoliberalism emerge. As it evolved through trial-and-error experimentation and became consolidated as the 'new normal', it gained a systemic and systematic character, albeit one that developed unevenly across different spheres and countries. It represented the interests of money capital as the form assumed by the most abstract and mobile form of capital and transnational profit-producing capital with its interests in exploiting ever wider markets and overcoming state-imposed barriers and other fetters that inhibit this expansion. New constitutionalism (Gill 1998; van der Pijl 1998: 47) played a role in consolidating neoliberalism and providing it with institutional and legal underpinnings that might insulate it against challenges from resistance and counter-hegemonic movements (Overbeek and van Apeldoorn 2012). Another result is the emergence of global governance and recurrent, but

272 Bob Jessop

typically failing, attempts to govern the course of world market integration and its wider repercussions (Overbeek 2010).

On a European plane, this theme is prominent in the discussion of European integration, especially developments such as the European Monetary Union and, more recently, the response to the Eurozone crisis (e.g. Overbeek and van Apeldoorn 2012). It is also seen in analyses of neoliberal imperialism (van Apeldoorn 2010). However, another aspect is the tendency towards a parasitic neoliberalism because the interests of transnational circulating capital are being pursued at the expense of productive capital, subordinate classes, and the environment (see Fennema and van der Pijl 1987: 11, 29–40; and van der Pijl 2015 and Chapter 20, this volume). This reflects a rentier perspective that is no longer concerned to balance the interests of money capital and profit-producing capital and, in whatever way, secure the interests of total social capital. This triggered a legitimacy crisis for neoliberal projects when the 2007–2008 financial crisis erupted but, given the weakness of rival CCCs and of socialist alternatives, there was time and space for concerted efforts by the state to limit financial reform, relaunch neoliberal 'reforms', and impose austerity in the Lockean heartland.

Philosophical and theoretical considerations

When the AS was emerging, as indicated above, its Marxist foundations were emphasized more than they are today. Moreover, alongside Marx's substantive texts, references were made to the metatheoretical and methodological discussions in the 1857 Introduction (1986b) and elsewhere. While these issues are less foregrounded nowadays, AS work still explores the political economy of capitalism and the anatomy of bourgeois society. Its theoretical approach could be described as logical-historical – although Amsterdam scholars have not used this description.[13] This approach involves theoretically guided comparison to move stepwise from abstract-simple categories to concrete-complex analyses of specific cases to establish how the social world comprises a 'rich totality of many determinations and relations' (Marx 1986b: 37). In other words, concepts get progressively and coherently refined as they are applied across a range of historical cases with a view to producing a consistent account of specific cases in which commonalities and differences have their proper weight. This is seen in Bode's founding Dutch article (1979) and the first two English books (van der Pijl 1984; Overbeek 1990).

Writing in the *Grundrisse*, Marx observed that, 'when we speak of capital here, it is still only a name' (1986a: 193). Its determinations as capital remained to be elaborated step by step. In the *Grundrisse*, he listed the following determinations:

> (1) General concept of capital. (2) Particularity of capital: circulating capital, fixed capital. (Capital as means of subsistence, as raw material, as instrument of labour.) (3) Capital as money. II. (1) *Quantity of capital. Accumulation.* (2) *Capital measured in terms of itself. Profit. Interest. Value of capital,* i.e. capital in distinction from itself as interest and profit. (3) *The circulation of capitals:* (a) Exchange of

Putting the Amsterdam School in its place **273**

capital with capital. Exchange of capital with revenue. Capital and *prices*; (ß) *Competition of capitals*; (7) *Concentration of capitals*.

(1986a: 194; cf. 1986b: 45).[14]

Some of these abstract themes are evident in Bode (1979), notably 'capital in general' (the general concept of capital) versus 'particular capitals', different positions in the transformation process and social metabolism of use values, profit, interest, forms of competition between particular capitals, circulation, concentration, and centralization. He also distinguishes the skill levels of the labour force and the geographical orientation of sectors and firms (see Chapter 1).

As the spiral of scientific enquiry continues, analytical categories are continually redefined. For, 'concepts are never introduced once-and-for-all at a single level of abstraction' (Aglietta 1979: 15).[15] Thus, introducing *Capital*, vol. III, Marx reported that it:

> must locate and describe the concrete forms which grow out of the *movements of capital as a whole* ... The various forms of capital, as evolved in this book, thus approach step by step the form which they assume on the surface of society, in the action of different capitals upon one another, in competition, and in the ordinary consciousness of the agents of production themselves.
>
> *(Marx 1998: 27)*[16]

This stepwise process is reflected in successive refinements. For example, Overbeek distinguishes the pure capitalist mode of production from the social formation of historical capitalism (1990: 14–16); and the functional distinction between money capital/productive capital from the institutional division between banking and industrial enterprises (1990: 24). Likewise, following Bode, Overbeek and van der Pijl distinguish abstract *capital fractions* from more concrete *class fractions* (van der Pijl 1984: 3–8; Overbeek 1990: 26–71; van der Pijl 1998); and, discussing economic and political strategies, both scholars contrast ideal-typical proto-concepts, competing CCCs, and the hegemonic CCC that characterizes specific historical capitalist constellations at different scales of accumulation and class rule (van der Pijl 1984: 1–28; Overbeek 1990: 26–8). Van der Pijl takes this approach to concept development even further in unfolding the concrete complexities of the world market and territorial states in terms of economic, politico-military, and diplomatic foreign relations, starting from the contradiction of the commodity form, in line with Marx's approach in *Capital* (2007a: 623ff.).

These concepts are then further refined through yet more detailed '*historical* as well as a *transnational* analysis' concerned with specific multi-layered spatio-temporal conjunctures that can extend to larger than national complexes of states and societies and entire historical eras (van der Pijl 1998: 3, italics in original; on periodization, see below). In this provisional, fallible two-way spiral process, 'the objective is the development of concepts and not the "verification" of a finished theory' (Aglietta 1979: 66). Empirical evidence still has a key role in building and evaluating theory.

274 Bob Jessop

This involves another spiral in which theoretical and evidential statements are compared and modify each other, resulting in a continual, dialectical transformation of concepts through their repeated confrontation with more empirical evidence. Eventually, theory is no longer helpful. 'The last mile in social analysis, in other words, may have to be covered without actual theory' (van der Pijl 2007b: 17). These dialectical phases are crucial for scientific development and 'make theory something other than the exposition of conclusions already implicitly contained in an axiomatic system' (Aglietta 1979: 15–16; cf. Marx on 'the assimilation and transformation of perceptions and images into concepts', 1986b: 38). In short, theory is an open process, not a final product. So concepts and theoretical arguments should not be applied too hastily and/or unthinkingly in cookie-cutter fashion.

This implies that research can proceed at different levels of abstraction and complexity. Occam's razor applies here. That is, research design and explanations should be as simple as possible but as complex as necessary. These two conditions are equally important. Together, they rule out that any adequate explanation is as good as any other at any given level of abstraction or complexity. For, as the analysis becomes more detailed, it should be possible to respecify an explanation along the same lines. This excludes some explanations that appear valid at earlier steps in an analysis. So, one should not criticize the AS (or other paradigms) for failing to explain phenomena that are more concrete or more complex than those that provide its initial research questions – provided that the proposed explanation can be elaborated without contradicting it, as opposed to supplementing and rounding it out. Conversely, an explanation will be considered inadequate if extending it to a lower level of abstraction contradicts the initial explanation.

Distinctive features of the Amsterdam School

How many scholars make a school is debatable – especially as the latter rarely embodies a unified and fully coherent theoretical system. For, as it expands, the thinking of its individual adherents also changes, new adherents introduce further variety, other adherents disperse, and favoured definitions, conceptions, theories, and historical explanations begin to diverge (cf. Overbeek's Introduction). This is especially likely where, as with the AS, there is no 'school textbook' that sets out the core concepts, assumptions, and arguments of the approach. A possible exception is van der Pijl's *Transnational classes and international relations* (1998), which is the most cited of all AS publications in general[17] and in the preceding critical commentaries.[18] There it contrasts with the Parisian regulation school, which has its textbooks, surveys, association, yearbooks, conferences, and authoritative interpreters as well as a rich and diverse range of publications that orient themselves, even when they disagree, to the canonical texts. Conversely, diversity aligns the AS with THM more generally, which is also a loose research programme. In these terms, who is a member is best left to a process of intellectual (self-)identification with the AS metatheoretical framework (Overbeek 2004: 134n.).

Combining key themes from Part I, comments in foundational texts, the major surveys by Overbeek and van Apeldoorn, more recent studies, critical summaries by informed outsiders (such as the present author and Ngai-Ling Sum), the commentaries in Part II, and my attempt to put the AS in its place in relation to four heterodox fields of work in critical political economy, I now discuss the distinctive features of the AS (see Table 21.1). It should be emphasized that this is an outsider's perspective, written for this concluding chapter, and almost certainly imparts more reflexivity and coherence than there was at any point during its uneven development. Its purpose is stock taking rather than historical reconstruction and will serve to orient recommendations for taking the AS further. Features covered in other chapters or above are presented briefly to allow more extended comments on other features.

Principal concern

The principal concern in the 1970s and 1980s can be described, from an outsider's perspective informed by hindsight, as the improbable integration of the circuits of capital in space-time given the multiple separations in the technical and social division of labour, the resulting different, potentially antagonistic interests of different fractions of capital, the unevenness of capital accumulation, and the differential insertion of national markets into the world market. Some of these themes are already evident in Bode (1979) and they have been systematically developed in later work, with or without the original Marxian foundations in the critique of the capitalist mode of production and the anatomy of bourgeois society.

Entry point and key concepts

To explain this improbable integration, which is reflected in periods of relative disintegration, crisis, and transitions, the AS builds on Marx's analysis of the circuits of capital to identify different clusters of immediate capitalist interests and, at a high level of abstraction, posits two ideal-typical proto-concepts of control. These are the liberal concept and productive proto-concepts, which correspond to the general interests of money and profit-producing capital, respectively (see van der Pijl 1979; Overbeek 1980; van Apeldoorn 2000 – all republished in this volume). In Gramscian terms, they could be understood as the critically reflexive 'spontaneous philosophies'[19] of these two class fractions performing these functions in the circuits of capital. These proto-concepts inform, in turn, the analysis of class strategies, whether of *fractions of capital* with specific direct political interests in specific kinds of state intervention or *fractions of the bourgeoisie*, which compete to define the general interests of capital from a distinct fractional perspective and give them a national-popular dimension to attract mass support (cf. Bode 1979). CCCs can become hegemonic where they combine mutually compatible blueprints for handling relations among various fractions of capital and for conducting labour relations (van

276 Bob Jessop

der Pijl 1984: 31ff.; 1998: 4–8; cf. Overbeek 1990: 26; 2004: 118; Overbeek and van der Pijl 1993: 4). Which CCC becomes hegemonic depends on 'the current tendency of capital accumulation and social development ... and also, in the final analysis, by the purely political qualities of those élites in mobilising the passions and aspirations of the population at large' (Overbeek and van der Pijl 1993: 4). This enables them to 'crowd out' rival CCCs until the hegemonic CCC in turn unravels (ibid: 4; see also Overbeek and van Apeldoorn 2012).

To win hegemony, CCCs must meet two conditions. First, they should have 'objective comprehensiveness (i.e., coverage of labour process, circulation relations, profit distribution, and state and international power relations)' (Overbeek and van der Pijl 1993: 4). And, second, they should secure an appropriate balance between the '"systemic" requirements of capital accumulation and its concrete, momentary needs' (ibid.). In other words, it should overcome the contradictions of previous regimes and offer a new social consensus. In this context, van der Pijl distinguishes hegemonic CCCs from 'revolutionary myths' that lacked internal logic and a social base (1989: 30). Such analyses illustrate Gramsci's distinction between 'historically organic ideologies, those, that is, which are necessary to a given structure, and ideologies that are arbitrary, rationalistic and "willed"' (1971: 376–7).

Transnational class formation and class strategies

The AS also stresses the state's central role in implementing CCCs at home and relaying transnational concepts – or resisting their penetration (for example, Holman 1996; van der Pijl 1989, 1998). The analysis of these emerging CCCs highlights the dialectic of structure and agency (or, again, class position and class agency). As van Apeldoorn observed:

> to constitute themselves as a class, capitalists somehow have to 'discover' their common interests and construct a shared outlook and identity that transcends the narrow view of their position as individual and competing capitalists. The moment of class agency – or the process of class formation is thus always a political process in which capitalists transcend the logic of market competition and reach a temporary unity of strategic orientation and purpose, enabling them to articulate (vis-à-vis other social classes or groups, as well as vis-à-vis the state) a 'general capitalist interest' ... [M]embers of a class have to imagine themselves as part of a wider (possibly transnational) community in order to constitute themselves as a class actor.
>
> *(2004: 155)*

In this regard, Amsterdam scholars note that socio-economic imaginaries have a crucial constitutive role in class formation. CCCs are organized around a constellation of interests that either did not exist before or previously had less weight in society. They do not have pre-given interests; nor do they circulate monolithically around the world, but they are always adapted to local circumstances (Fennema and van der Pijl

Putting the Amsterdam School in its place 277

TABLE 21.1 Distinctive features of the Amsterdam School in global political economy

Principal concern	Improbable (inter-scalar) integration of the circuits of capital
Entry point	Integral *class-theoretical* analysis of rival concepts of control tied to the positions and interests of differently conceived and constructed fractions in multi-scalar circuits of capital
Analytical horizon	Transnational class formation in a world market structured through a dominant CCC that reflects the interests of one capital fraction and wins support from other fractions and subaltern social forces
Key concepts	Circuits of capital, fractions of capital, productive and money proto-concepts of control, synthetic CCCs, variations in the capital–labour relation, articulation of geo-economics and geopolitics, Lockean heartland versus Hobbesian periphery, imperialism, militarism
Methods	Narrative strategic and policy analysis oriented to class formation, historical analysis of key events or crises that confirm or reorient hegemony of capital fraction, network analysis to support identification of class fractions
Primary agents	Rival fractions of capital, their allies, and intellectual supports oriented to imagined communities of interest
Class struggle	Alternation of periods of bourgeois offensive (oriented to hegemony) and of bourgeois defence (resort to force)
Periodization	Inter-woven temporalities, including *la longue durée*, long waves, short-term cycles, specific conjunctures Historical succession of hegemonic CCCs and associated struggles plus their effects in/on inter-scalar relations

1987: 40–1). They must proceed beyond narrow economic-corporate interests and find expression in policies, politics, and proposals for political reorganization if they are to be condensed into the formation of fractions of capital and fractions of the bourgeoisie (Bode 1979; cf. Overbeek 1990: 24).

To decipher the objective significance of CCCs for valorization and class domination requires careful evaluation of the class relevance and class appeal in specific conjunctures and regarding spatio-temporal horizons of action (cf. van der Pijl 1984: 7–34 and passim; Overbeek 1990; van Apeldoorn 2002). Thus, as van der Pijl notes, 'fractions can only be observed *in action* – the notion as such is "indeterminate and must be complemented by strategies that impart some substantive coherence to what would otherwise remain formal unities" (Jessop 1983: 89)' (1998: 50). Thus, the objective significance may often emerge only *ex post* especially given the complexities of crisis conjunctures and the performative role of CCCs in helping to resolve them and steer future strategies.

Indeed, crises can be an important steering mechanism. They reveal where corrective action or structural reorganization is required because the right balance had not been struck or is no longer adequate. Even so, crises are not moments of epiphany that provide instant diagnoses and scientific solutions. Class agency and struggle remain essential to win hegemony for a concept of control that has broad appeal and is also adequate.

278 Bob Jessop

Societalization (*Vergesellschaftung*), sometimes translated as socialization, is another primary concept. It refers to the impact of capital accumulation on the overall social formation, through processes such as commodification, the formal or real subsumption of ever wider social spheres under the logics of valorization and competition, changing forms of individuality and sociality, and the changing articulation between class relations and other kinds of social division and differentiation. The AS consistently treats the economic and political spheres as dialectically interrelated moments of the reproduction of the capitalist mode of production and capitalist societalization. This indicates that the AS has an essentially anti-economistic understanding of the dynamic of capitalism and is one of its key features. This is also seen in another primary concept, which emerges from the creative extension of Marx's comments on the world market and plurality of territorial states rather than his critique of political economy. This is the distinction between Lockean heartland and Hobbesian contender states. As this is discussed above, I do not dwell on it here.

Methods

Guided – but not constrained – by its core concepts, the AS gives detailed historical analyses of capital accumulation, class formation, societalization, and inter-state relations. It uses mixed methods, drawing on relevant historical and contemporary sources, including interviews (e.g. van Apeldoorn 2000, Chapter 5, this volume); and provides thickly descriptive strategic and narrative policy analyses focused on its core theoretical and political concerns. It also employs relevant data, such as profit rates, party funding and affiliations, lobbying activities, membership of think tanks and private associations, and so on; and it uses network analysis to map connections within and across different fractions of capital. These methods are then combined in various ways to explore and relate different aspects of the dialectic of structure and agency or, expressed differently, of path dependency and path shaping.

Primary agents

Many kinds of agents or social forces are involved in the making of capital accumulation and societalization and the contestation over rival concepts of control. These must be real agents, not abstractions or fields of conflict. As van der Pijl comments:

> the West, capital and, certainly, the hegemonic structure into which they are welded together are not as such actors. They denote fields of action which in combination reveal a certain orientation and sense of direction; but the actually directive social forces, the ruling classes, first of all, are constantly engaged in shaping this orientation and direction.
>
> *(2007a: 626)*

In this context, AS historical studies show how CCCs are created and promoted by organic intellectuals, party politicians, union leaders, central bankers, diplomats, experts, international fora such as the World Economic Forum that 'operate within the heartland, but also on its perimeter, as interfaces with the aspiring bourgeoisie from the contender states (van der Pijl 2006: 18), corporate lobbies, leading industrialists, bureaucrats, political pundits, international magazines, private lobbies such as the Bilderberg Group and Trilateral Commission,[20] and diverse other social agents across quite different social fields, geographical scales, and sites of struggle. Key agents in the 'inner circles' of leading fractions of the bourgeoisie are often active across formal institutional and organizational boundaries rather than confined to one institution or organization. As Bode (1979) noted, the success of CCCs depends critically on the presence of the hegemonic fraction's representatives in multiple political parties. As Gramsci once noted, the state 'is the entire complex of practical and theoretical activities with which the ruling class not only justifies and maintains its dominance but manages to win the active consent of those over whom it rules' (1971: 244). This involves far more than interlocking directorates. It extends to parallel power networks that connect major economic and political power centres. Moreover, besides building institutionalized class compromises, a vital aspect of winning consent concerns the rendering invisible, wherever possible, of class rule. For CCCs' capacity to win hegemony in 'the political business cycle' also depends on finding ways to disguise for a time a specific, asymmetrical conception of the general capitalist interest as a general social or national interest (cf. Overbeek 1990: 16–20, 25–29, 45; van der Pijl 1984: passim; 1998: 4–5; 2012: xvi–xvii; Overbeek and van der Pijl 1993: 4).

Periodization

A key aspect of the dialectic of structure and agency concerns the conditions in which social forces can make a difference. This puts periodization firmly on the AS agenda. However, there is no master periodization that holds for all cases. Rather, as Otto Holman remarks:

> Theoretical and empirical analysis must precede periodization. Moreover, periodization is a way of ordering the past from the viewpoint of the present, reflecting our present knowledge of the past, helping to understand our present situation without offering us more than a tendential insight into future developments.
>
> *(1993: 137)*

This is reflected in the AS approach to historical analysis. Bode related changes in domestic and foreign policy orientations in key segments of the Dutch ruling class to different stages in the inter-war period (1918–39). Overbeek's thesis explores class formation and political struggles in terms of the conjunctural, multi-layered interweaving of different histories with their own rhythms and durations: (1) long

280 Bob Jessop

waves of capitalist development, class formation, associated 'generations of the bourgeoisie', and world leadership in the inter-state system; (2) a medium-term perspective on stages of development, concerned in his case with the post-war period; and (3) short-term crisis dynamics (1990: 3–4, 11–23, 31–4). He combines the abstract analysis of circuits of capital, long waves and cycles, ideal-typical proto-concepts as interpretive and calculative framework of leading politicians and CCC. Van der Pijl explores this further in terms of the long-run sequencing pattern of the formation of the Lockean heartland and Hobbesian contender states (2007a: 620ff.). This is also reflected in a succession of more national and international CCCs. Only in historically specific periods do capital and capitalist relations become more nationalized economically and politically. The two main examples in the Lockean heartland are the inter-war period of state (monopoly) capitalism and the period of post-war corporate liberalism (e.g. van der Pijl 1984: 76–106, 214–41; Overbeek 1990: 4, 33, 63–70; Overbeek and van der Pijl 1993; van der Pijl 1998, 2007a; Chapter 20).

The long-run perspective of the AS generates rich analyses of the interweaving of processes with different temporal rhythms as its aficionados explore the contested succession of rival CCCs in different phases of capitalist development and/or in different economic and political spaces. An example is a model of phases in the life course of neoliberalism proposed by Overbeek and van Apeldoorn: (1) a crisis of the previous hegemonic project; (2) struggles leading to a new CCC; (3) its normalization with the aid of new constitutionalist changes that stabilize it and insulate it from challenge; (4) maturity accompanied by accumulating contradictions and crisis tendencies; and (5) a crisis in/of the neoliberal project (2012: 7–8).

Finally, Gramsci's pioneering analyses of hegemony are reflected in AS research on the changing modalities of bourgeois class struggle over CCCs in the Lockean heartland, with alternating offensive and defensive moments. Offensive phases are more oriented to securing hegemony through coalition building that transcend special interests, using flexible methods; defensive phases more oriented to force (e.g. van der Pijl 1984: 3–4 and passim; 1998: 50). These phases are related in turn to types of resistance, respectively reformism and anarcho-syndicalism (van der Pijl 1998: 50, citing Lenin 1963 [1910]).

With and beyond the Amsterdam School

A research programme can develop in three ways: (1) incremental empirical extension, which may include the adoption of new methods of inquiry as well as employing existing concepts to generate hypotheses for new themes or topics; (2) progressive conceptual deepening, including the development of concepts at more concrete-complex levels of analysis; and (3) ruptural theoretical – or even meta-theoretical – redefinition that challenges one or more of the foundational assumptions, core concepts, or explanatory principles (Jessop and Sum 2005: 219–20). From its inception in the late 1970s, the AS has certainly developed by extending its empirical horizons and adopting new methods of inquiry. There has also been

Putting the Amsterdam School in its place **281**

progressive conceptual deepening, as shown by the distinction between Lockean heartland and Hobbesian contender states. Ruptural theoretical redefinition is less evident. I now use this typology to review the commentaries in Part II and assess how they fit into this schema. Even the more critical pieces explicitly acknowledge some valuable contributions to radical IR and global political economy or, as with Naná de Graaff or Marianne Marchand, take them for granted to focus on specific theoretical or empirical deficits. My summary therefore highlights challenging criticisms rather than endorsements.

Several commentaries note that the AS, regardless of whether they see it as a school, has been a progressive research paradigm. Among the areas of empirical extension that were noted are: more differentiated analyses of fractions and subfractions of capital; the study of Southern Europe and East and Central Europe; more detailed engagement with the relations between global, triadic, continental, and national scales of accumulation; neoliberal restructuring; the rise of right-wing populism and nationalism; and an acknowledgement of the role of war in capital accumulation. In terms of methods, Naná de Graaff noted that the empirical underpinnings of the approach are weak, prompting her to turn to social network analysis and other techniques. Eelke Heemskerk proposed even greater use of network analysis, lest theory trump empirical analysis. He nonetheless mentioned the potential reciprocal gains that might come from combining rich network studies using the latest techniques and AS theoretical rigour to produce sound hypotheses for future research. And Samuel Knafo asks whether it is possible to study the transnational capitalist class (TCC) without examining specific local sites where actual social agents operate and reproduce capitalist rule.

Regarding conceptual deepening, a few contributors note that this has occurred; but others suggest important areas where it is lacking to the detriment of AS research. These include: more recognition of uneven and combined development; going beyond a dichotomous account of class relations; examining how national bourgeoisies are subsumed – or not – into transnational power blocs; the potential or actual incoherence of CCCs and their relation to divisions or shifts within the TCC; the contradictions and limits of neoliberal globalization within the Lockean heartland and its impact on the TCC; the sources of nationalism and populism as reactions to neoliberal cosmopolitanism; and the need to incorporate the theoretical and political implications of an 'intersectional' approach into the analysis of TCC formation and the Lockean heartland.

More challenging still are suggestions that conceptual deepening is required that would entail what I categorize as ruptural (meta)theoretical redefinitions. Theoretically, these suggestions include: the need for theoretical concern with subaltern groups and counter-hegemony rather than elite-driven hegemonic projects; a turn from the fractionation of capital to the internal fractions of labour; and concern with the local and everyday rather than the global and rarefied world of transnational elites. Metatheoretically, Laura Horn and Angela Wigger highlight the need to find the right balance between dense theoretical jargon and the messiness of the actual social world. Other contributors suggest the potential of a philosophy of IR

282   Bob Jessop

(Bieler and Morton); or that of critical realism, with its depth ontology and method of retroduction, which can theoretically posit and empirically explore deep structures and also identify how agency contributes to their reproduction and transformation (Buch-Hansen and Staricco).[21] Finally, Knafo argues that the Amsterdam scholars must engage more systematically and reflexively with the historical turn. They should avoid taking the existence of capital fractions for granted and focus on the scope for historical contingency in the forces and causes of capitalist development.

As an informed and sympathetic outsider who has drawn on AS work in his own theoretical, historical, and comparative analyses, I endorse the positive evaluations of the AS's theoretical and empirical development and suggestions for further empirical extension. The proposals for progressive conceptual deepening are also welcome – although some pioneering and/or recent studies already seem to have addressed some of these issues. More challenging, of course, are the proposals for (meta)theoretical developments that might produce ruptures in the AS theoretical paradigm. Progressive ruptures are welcome. There is certainly a risk of ossification if a school distances itself from parallel currents in THM (Bieler and Morton) or in 'Open Marxism' and a historicized critical political economy (Knafo), or, again, when it does not engage in critical dialogue with other vibrant currents in critical political economy (Horn and Wigger).

I am not convinced, however, that a philosophy of IR can help to advance the Amsterdam project – *if* that implies a totalizing perspective that highlights the logically necessary over the historically contingent aspects of capital accumulation and societalization in a world where strategies and crisis construals can be hotly contested. Given their most recent book (2018) as well as past research, however, I doubt whether this is what Andreas Bieler and Adam Morton are proposing. Moreover, as Overbeek observed, the AS rests on 'a historically grounded conception of the *dialectical totality* of structure and agency' (2004: 114, italics in original; cf. 119, 123). This is close to the open Marxism that Bieler and Morton endorse. Regarding critical realism, I have long considered Marx as a critical realist *avant la lettre* and, as my analysis of the metatheoretical underpinnings of the AS suggested, it has implicit critical realist aspects. It makes sense, then, to make this more explicit. Indeed, this would be advanced by rereading much Amsterdam research – from Ries Bode onwards – in the light of the new field of historical-materialist policy analysis (e.g. Brand 2013; Leubolt 2014). For this also seems to have been anticipated by the AS as indicated, indeed, in the comments on van Apeldoorn's analysis of European integration offered by John Kannankulam and Fabian Georgi (2012: 21–3).

Three areas for further conceptual deepening

If I may abuse my role as co-editor in this concluding chapter and provide my own critical commentary, I would identify three areas where the AS could benefit from progressive conceptual deepening inspired by compatible theoretical and

Putting the Amsterdam School in its place **283**

methodological currents. These areas are: the nature of the contradictions of capital accumulation and societalization and their implications for the adequacy and limits of CCCs in regularizing and normalizing class domination; the semiotic as well as material mediation of struggles over rival CCCs; and the nature of variegated capitalism in the world market.

First, conflicts, contradictions, and crisis tendencies figure regularly in AS analyses and even in the titles of articles and edited collections. These are understood in the Marxian sense of dynamic contradictions in movement at the heart of the capital relation and, as such, as mainsprings of capitalist development. Among AS scholars, Kees van der Pijl is most explicit about this. He recalls that Volume I of *Capital* begins with the commodity form, which comprises a contradictory unity of use value and exchange value (van der Pijl 2009: 4, 206–12; cf. 2007b). Marx then proceeds, of course, to unfold many further contradictory social relations in the capitalist mode of production from the contradictions in the commodity form and, albeit less systematically, in capitalist social formations. Thus, Marx's analysis 'builds towards an ever-more concrete understanding (moving *from the abstract to the concrete*) by bringing in ever further complications and real additions' (van der Pijl 2009: 207). Contradictions also provide a theoretical link between structural and agential analysis. On my reading of Marx's work, structural contradictions express themselves as sites of strategic dilemmas; and different proto-concepts of control and synthetic CCCs provide different answers on how to handle these dilemmas (Jessop 2013). Likewise, van der Pijl notes that a contradictory 'structure is dynamic, because from its perception as contradictory, follows human action to overcome it; this action, in turn, brings out the limits of the possible inherent in the prevailing social relations' (2010: 24). His analyses explore the historicized contradictions not only in the changing relation among forces and relations of production but also in the field of foreign relations due to the 'separate political existence and common humanity' (2007b: 144).

Given the emphasis on the historical specificity of modes of production, social formations, inter-state relations, rival CCCs, and so on, one should not expect a general, let alone a transhistorical, theory of structural contradictions and strategic dilemmas. Nonetheless, as Henk Overbeek notes, quoting Lucien Sève: 'when the attempt to grasp the essence of things leads us invariably to contradiction, it is because contradiction is the essence of things' (Sève 1975: 676, Overbeek's translation; Overbeek 2005). Thus, it is worth exploring contradictions and dilemmas more systematically for specific capitalist constellations, including how they are handled for a time by displacing or deferring them, and how they cumulate to precipitate crises that reveal the structural and historical limits to the hegemony and adequacy of specific CCCs in and beyond their respective hegemonic spheres. Such an approach is already well advanced in AS work on the varieties of neoliberalism and could be broadened in future work.

Second, Amsterdam scholars recognize rival elaborations of the two proto-concepts of control in different periods and that, given rival syntheses, not all CCCs can or do succeed. But how is success to be explained? There is a risk that the explanation works

284 Bob Jessop

backwards from identifying the successful CCC to explain its conditions of success without explaining why alternative projects fail.[22] The final explanation is grounded in the organic character of the CCC – its capacity to reconcile the structurally 'necessary' with more contingent conjunctural factors at relevant scales of economic and political organization. This will also depend on the qualities of political, intellectual, and moral leadership of rival fractions (cf. Overbeek and van der Pijl 1993: 4). This is consistent with Gramsci's analysis of hegemony. Thus, a typical AS explanation provides a dense historical account of the succession of hegemonic CCCs and their later decomposition, relies on a detailed narrative account of rival strategies and policies (including their repurposing), and draws on analysis of interpersonal networks, corporate ties, and material interdependencies to justify the attribution of class relevance to CCCs and their social bases. All of this reflects the AS focus on class relations, interests, and strategies.

Where I suggest such analyses can be deepened is through a critical semiotic as well as materialist analysis of how and why some CCCs, strategies, and policies prove more successful. Such analyses are now being developed (e.g. Overbeek and van Apeldoorn 2012, Introduction) and should be taken further. This would be in line with Gramsci's own analyses of hegemony rooted in his education in historical and spatial linguistics and development of what Peter Ives calls 'vernacular materialism' (Ives 2004). It would also require closer engagement with the continuing dialogue between rival (comprehensive) concepts of control and the world of everyday experiences and common sense that is central to winning hegemony. An additional benefit here would be bringing subalterns back in, as recommended in some of the critical commentaries.

Third, given its criticisms of world systems theory à la Wallerstein and dependency theory as well as of methodological nationalism, and given its stress on the tendential unity of the world market and the continuing plurality of territorial states, there is real potential for the AS to use its core concepts to go beyond the interrelations among varieties of neoliberalism (or, following Brenner et al. 2010, 'variegated neoliberalization') to consider the multi-scalar, multi-spatial relations among varieties of capitalism. I analyse this in terms of variegated capitalism (Jessop 2012) but, rereading some pioneering AS research for this conclusion, I now see that this concept was already implicit in van der Pijl (1979, Chapter 2, this volume). He wrote that:

> sections of the bourgeoisie, related to fractions of social capital, are distributed unevenly within different national states (in the sense of trade and transport being predominant in the Netherlands, banking in Switzerland, finance capital in Germany, etc.). Hence, not only will the pattern of internationalization from each country differ depending on the overall stage, but domestic class relations too, will affect, and be affected by, internationalization in quite dissimilar ways ... [T]he role of the state and the structure of the state apparatus differ with each type of internationalization.
>
> *(van der Pijl, Chapter 2, pp. 88)*

Putting the Amsterdam School in its place **285**

This comment not only concerns varieties of capitalism as conventionally understood but also how they are interrelated and co-evolve in mutually constitutive fashion in an emerging world market that is shaped by a dialectic of intertwined internal and external factors.

This is further explicated in Overbeek's survey of the AS. He wrote:

> The conceptualization of capitalism as a global phenomenon does not imply, as it does for WST [World System Theory], that the processes of class formation 'on the ground' are simply determined by the 'external' dynamics of the world-economy. We also need an understanding of the historical specificity of *national* formations and of the state's role in the reproduction of capitalism.
>
> *(2004: 121)*

Thus, if we want to analyse the emerging dynamic of the world market, we must consider the 'international division of labour', the 'insertion' of national economies in the world market, and, in complementary fashion, the situation of national class structures in the global class structure. Conversely, acknowledging the AS critique of world systems theory, the international division of labour must be conceived as the 'vehicle' through which production relations spread and class formation is 'nationalized', that is, the process whereby global class formation is articulated with the processes of nation building and state formation (Overbeek 2004: 121).

Conclusions

> GPE as understood here, however, self-consciously cuts across the disciplinary organisation of the social sciences. It opens up new possibilities for investigation and insight although it also is bound to provoke distrust among academic authorities and mainstream academics. The reason for this, I have come to believe, is because contesting the disciplinary organisation of the sciences (social as well as natural science) *amounts to resisting a more fundamental discipline, the discipline imposed by capital on society.*
>
> *(van der Pijl 2009: vii)*

This claim reveals the third aspect of the AS mentioned at the start of this chapter: its character as a *political project* rooted in the 1970s that has consistently engaged in the critique of exploitation and domination, including, notably, in different periods and phases of imperialism in the context of the developing world market. The political contestation of the rule of capital was at the heart of the earliest AS work (see Overbeek 2004) and is re-emphasized in several of the critical commentaries. It reflects the dialectical intertwining of theory and practice evident in what van Apeldoorn (2004) has described as the commitment of the AS to a philosophy of praxis – an echo of Gramsci's integral analysis of political economy, the state in its inclusive sense and the modalities of the exercise of state power, and of the intellectual and moral dimensions as well as the political moment of class struggle, broadly conceived. Indeed, if one wanted to put the AS in its place in the field of

286 Bob Jessop

critical social science, it could well be in terms of its growing critical engagement with the concepts, concerns, and legacy of Gramsci's philosophy of praxis, its capacities to apply his insights in new theoretical and political contexts, and its creative development of new, but commensurable, concepts and analyses for the contemporary era. This overarching approach would also provide the links that connect its contributions in the four areas identified above: the regulation approach, European integration studies, THM, and the analysis of neoliberalism.

The full breadth and depth of its studies is not fully appreciated due to selective reading based on a few key texts – often related to the period when readers were receiving their own post-graduate training and the contexts in which they read them. But it is important to put the overall development of the AS in its place in relation to other currents in critical IR, critical IPE, and, I would add, critical political ecology. This will provide numerous stimuli to extend its work empirically, to deepen it conceptually by engaging with theoretically compatible approaches and learning from those that are less compatible, and, perhaps, to enable metatheoretical and theoretical ruptures. Reading recent work by Amsterdam scholars and their close colleagues and the critical commentaries in this volume, key areas where progress can be made in dialogue with other approaches include: further exploration of the internationalization of the state, the historical specificity of finance-dominated accumulation, the contradictions and crisis tendencies of neoliberalism, a critical dialogue between historical materialism and critical semiotic economy, the dangerous turn to coercion and other forms of domination in the international order in the face of a crisis of US hegemony and the post-Washington Consensus, the rise of Brazil/Russia/India/China and the scope for China to redefine transnational class relations, and, finally, an account of the growing threats not only to capital accumulation but to humankind itself in capital's immanent drive to self-expansion at the expense of sustainable nature–society relations. These are challenges that no school, however large and well integrated, could – or should seek to – confront alone. For members, adherents, and interested followers of the AS in particular, they are challenges best met in and through critical and reflexive collective endeavours.

Notes

1 Overbeek noted that Bode, Fennema, van der Pijl, and others have 'sometimes jokingly been called the "Amsterdam School"' (Overbeek 1993: x). This seems to have been self-irony (cf. Overbeek's Introduction to this volume).
2 This path dependency, an outsider position, and a long-term interest in different regulation schools shaped my past comments on the AS; this chapter is far broader in scope.
3 Articulation is not a simple logical process of unfolding more concrete concepts from an abstract starting point along a single (albeit ramified) plane of analysis. It combines concepts developed along one plane of analysis (abstract → concrete) with concepts from different analytical planes (simple → complex) to get closer to an existing world as experienced by social actors. This approach is seen in (neo-)Gramscian accounts of political *class* domination in terms of hegemony as the exercise of 'political, intellectual,

and moral leadership' oriented to the 'national–popular' as well as 'economic–corporate' interests (Jessop 1982: 213–20).

4 Money capital is the most abstract and general form of capital but takes different concrete forms. One of these is high finance (Overbeek and van der Pijl 1993: 4).

5 Gramsci explored this in *Quaderno 22*, on Americanism and Fordism (1971: 277–318).

6 Henk Overbeek, personal communication; he also notes that none of the authors mentioned opted to employ a coherent and explicit AS framework. Angela Wigger and Laura Horn do refer on their personal websites to being inspired by, amongst others, the historical-materialist tradition (www.ru.nl/personen/wigger-a/;http://forskning.ruc.dk/site/en/persons/laura-horn(8d17a6a5-aee0–42d3–92cf-d152b46cae48).html).

7 Bode drew on German Marxism and Ernest Mandel; Overbeek's PhD (1988) cites British and German Marxists plus Gramsci's *Prison notebooks*; van der Pijl mentions Gramsci in his 1979 piece (Chapter 3) and draws further on the Italian's work in his analysis of the Atlantic ruling class (1984). Cox (1977) is little cited; his influence in neo-Gramscian IPE starts with his 1981 and 1983 articles and 1987 book. On 9 January 2018, Google Scholar, with all its limitations, recorded citations of 165, 4643, 2041, and 2937, respectively, for Cox's three texts.

8 An excellent overview of Palloix's work, which indicates the convergent interests with the AS, and includes out-of-print publications, is at www.christianpalloix.com/. Although based in Grenoble, Palloix did not belong to the Grenoblois regulation school; indeed, his work pre-dated its rise. German regulationism, which shares the Amsterdam and *Grenoblois* concerns with changes in the world market, is another case of parallel development.

9 On German and French theories of internationalization and the world market, see respectively: Deubner et al. 1979 and Busch 1981.

10 Germain and Kenny (1998) claim that this label is misleading, as the Italian School is not a school and contains no Italians.

11 This was partly a reaction to the dominance in the 1970s–1980s of structural Marxism.

12 Later research shows this was a better reading of Gramsci's view of scale (Jessop 2006).

13 Although van der Pijl (2009: 210) comes close, referring to logical-analytical and historical moments of Marx's thought.

14 Marx provided similar but not identical lists in other preparatory texts for *Capital*.

15 Aglietta is, of course, the pioneer theorist of the Parisian approach, not an Amsterdam scholar; but the methodological principles are the same and also derive from Marx's work.

16 Van der Pijl (1998: 57) cites a shorter extract from a different translation of volume III.

17 Google scholar gives 989 citations for *Transnational Classes and International Relations* and 714 for *The Making of an Atlantic Ruling Class*. Van Apeldoorn's book on *Transnational capitalism and the struggle over European integration* had 619 citations (as of 20 January 2018). This measure surely has problems but, *faute de mieux*, it is a useful indicator of influence in broad fields of study.

18 *Transnational classes* was highlighted 9 times, *Transnational capitalism* 6 times, *Making* 4 times, and Overbeek's *Global capitalism* 4 times. No commentator mentions Bode. This validates the editors' wish to translate his foundational article.

19 For Gramsci, spontaneous philosophy comprises ways of thinking, feeling, and acting implicit in language, routine practices, and conceptions of the world from a particular viewpoint, reflecting the particular grouping to which one belongs. A 'conception of the world is a response to certain specific problems posed by reality, which are quite specific and "original" in their immediate relevance' (1971: 324). However, spontaneous philosophies must be subject to critical awareness and reflection to guide coherent action and, eventually, to become the basis for winning hegemony (1971: 323–5, 419–25). Likewise, Overbeek and van der Pijl remark that 'functions give rise to common orientations, interest definitions, and collective experiences' (1993: 4). Proto-concepts are ideal types that help to interpret spontaneous economic-corporate positions and understand the development of CCCs.

288 Bob Jessop

20 Cf. Fennema and van der Pijl (1987: 41).
21 Van der Pijl explores capital–state relations as internally rather externally related and also refers to the deep structure of 'the exploitative transformation (socialization) of nature' by historical humanity that shapes 'economic, political and foreign (international) relations' (2007a: 621; cf. 1998).
22 This problem is especially evident in Laclau and Mouffe (1985) on hegemony.

References

Aglietta, M. (1979). *A theory of capitalist regulation: The USA experience*. London: New Left Books.

van Apeldoorn, B. (2000). Transnational class agency and European governance: The case of the European Round Table of Industrialists. *New Political Economy* 5(2): 157–181; Chapter 5, this volume.

van Apeldoorn, B. (2002). *Transnational capitalism and the struggle over European integration*. London: Routledge.

van Apeldoorn, B. (2004). Theorizing the transnational: A historical materialist approach. *Journal of International Relations and Development* 7(2): 142–176.

van Apeldoorn, B. (2010). Beyond neoliberal imperialism? The crisis of American empire. In H. Overbeek, B. van Apeldoorn, and N. de Graaff (Eds), *The state–capital nexus in the global crisis: Rebound of the capitalist state* (pp. 207–228). London: Routledge.

van Apeldoorn, B. and de Graaff, N. (2015). *American grand strategy and corporate elite networks: The open door since the end of the cold war*. London: Routledge.

van Apeldoorn, B., Drahokoupil, J., and Horn, L. (Eds) (2010). *Contradictions and limits of neoliberal European governance: From Lisbon to Lisbon*. Basingstoke: Palgrave Macmillan.

van Apeldoorn, B., de Graaff, N., and Overbeek, H. (Eds) (2013). *The state–capital nexus in the global crisis: Rebound of the capitalist state*. London: Routledge.

van Apeldoorn, B., Nölke, A., and Overbeek, H. (2003). *The transnational political economy of corporate governance regulation: A research outline*. Amsterdam: Vrije Universiteit.

Bieler, A. and Morton, A.D. (2018). *Global capitalism, global war, global crisis*. Cambridge: Cambridge University Press.

Bieling, H.J., Deppe, F., and Röttger, B. (1993). *Weltmarkt, Hegemonie und europäische Integration: Kritische Beiträge zur Theorie der internationalen Beziehungen*. Marburg an der Lahn: Forschungsgruppe Europäische Integration.

Bode, R. (1975). *De lotgevallen van een sector* [The fate of a sector]. Amsterdam: University of Amsterdam, unpublished manuscript.

Bode, R. (1979). De Nederlandse bourgeoisie tussen de twee wereldoorlogen. *Cahiers voor de politieke en sociale wetenschappen* 2(4): 9–50; Chapter 1; this volume.

Brand, U. (2013). State, context and correspondence: Contours of a historical-materialist policy analysis. *Österreichische Zeitschrift für Politikwissenschaft* 42(4): 425–442.

Brenner, N., Peck, J., and Theodore, N. (2010). Variegated neoliberalization: Geographies, modalities, pathways. *Global Networks* 10(2): 1–41.

Buch-Hansen, H. and Wigger, A. (2011). *The politics of European competition regulation: A critical political economy perspective*. London: Routledge.

Busch, K. (1981). Internationale Arbeitsteilung und Internationalisierung des Kapitals: Bemerkungen zur neueren französischen Weltmarktdiskussion. *Leviathan* 9(1): 12–43.

Carroll, W.K., Fennema, M., and Heemskerk, E.M. (2010). Constituting corporate Europe: A study of elite social organization. *Antipode* 42(4): 811–843.

Chase-Dunn, C., Taylor, P., Giovanni Arrighi, G., Cox, R., Overbeek, H., Gills, B., Gunder Frank, A., Modelski, G., and Wilkinson, D. (1994). Hegemony and social change. *Mershon International Studies Review* 38(2): 361–376.

Cox, R.W. (1977). Labour and hegemony. *International Organization* 31(2): 386–424.

Cox, R.W. (1981). Social forces, states and world orders: Beyond international relations theory. *Millennium* 10(2): 126–155.

Cox, R.W. (1983). Gramsci, hegemony and international relations: An essay in method. *Millennium* 12(3): 162–175.

Cox, R.W. (1987). *Production, power, and world order: Social forces in the making of history.* New York: Columbia University Press.

Deppe, F. (Ed.) (1975). *Europäische Wirtschaftsgemeinschaft (EWG): Zur politischen Ökonomie der westeuropäischen Integration.* Reinbek bei Hamburg: Rowohlt.

Deubner, C., Rehfeldt, U., Schlupp, F., and Ziebura, G. (Eds) (1979). *Die Internationalisierung des Kapitals: Neue Theorien in der internationalen Diskussion.* Frankfurt: Campus.

Fennema, M. and van der Pijl, K. (1987). *El triunfo del neoliberalismo*, collab. J. Ortega. Santo Domingo: Ediciones Taller.

Germain, R. and Kenny, M. (1998). Engaging Gramsci: International relations theory and the new Gramscians. *Review of International Studies* 24(1): 3–21.

Gill, S. (1995). Globalisation, market civilisation and disciplinary neoliberalism. *Millennium* 24(3): 399–423.

Gill, S. (1998). New constitutionalism, democratisation and global political economy. *Pacifica Review: Peace, Security and Global Change* 10(1): 23–38.

de Graaff, N. (2014). The hybridization of the state-capital nexus in the global energy order. *Globalizations*, 9(4): 531–545.

de Graaff, N. and van Apeldoorn, B. (2017). US elite power and the rise of 'statist' Chinese elites in global markets. *International Politics* 54(3): 338–355.

de Graaff, N. and van Apeldoorn, B. (2018). US–China relations and the liberal world order: Contending elites, colliding visions? *International Affairs* 94(1): 113–131.

Gramsci, A. (1971). *Selections from the prison notebooks.* London: Lawrence & Wishart.

Hirsch, J. (2000). The concept of materialist state theory and regulation theory. In J.D. Schmidt and J. Hersh (Eds), *Globalization and social change* (pp. 101–114). London: Routledge.

Holman, O. (1993). Transnationalism in Spain: The paradoxes of socialist rule in the 1980s. In H. Overbeek (Ed.), *Restructuring hegemony in the global political economy: The rise of transnational neo-liberalism in the 1980s* (pp. 134–161). London: Routledge.

Holman, O. (1996). *Integrating Southern Europe: EC expansion and the transnationalization of Spain.* London: Routledge.

Holman, O. (2001). The enlargement of the European Union: Towards Central and Eastern Europe: The role of supranational and transnational actors. In A. Bieler and A.D. Morton (Eds), *Social forces in the making of the new Europe* (pp. 161–184). Basingstoke: Palgrave-Macmillan.

Holman, O. (2004). Asymmetrical regulation and multidimensional governance in the European Union. *Review of International Political Economy* 11(4): 714–735; Chapter 6, this volume.

Horn, L. (2009). *The transformation of corporate governance regulation in the EU.* Doctoral dissertation, Vrije Universiteit Amsterdam.

Horn, L. (2011). *Regulating Corporate Governance in the EU: Towards a Marketization of Corporate Control.* Houndmills: Palgrave Macmillan.

Ives, P. (2004). *Language and hegemony in Gramsci.* London: Pluto.

Jessop, B. (1982). *The capitalist state: Marxist theories and methods.* Oxford: Martin Robertson.

Jessop, B. (1983). Accumulation strategies, state forms, and hegemonic projects. *Kapitalistate* 10: 89–111.

Jessop, B. (1988). Regulation theories in retrospect and prospect. Paper presented at the First International Conference on Regulation Theory, Barcelona, June.

Jessop, B. (1990). The regulation approach in retrospect and prospect. *Economy & Society* 19 (2): 153–216.

Jessop, B. (2006). Gramsci as a spatial theorist. *Critical Review of International Social and Political Philosophy* 8(4): 421–437.

Jessop, B. (2012). The world market, variegated capitalism, and the crisis of European integration. In P. Nousios, H. Overbeek, and A. Tsolakis (Eds), *Globalisation and European integration: Critical approaches to regional order and international relations* (pp. 91–111). London: Routledge.

Jessop, B. (2013). Revisiting the regulation approach: critical reflections on the contradictions, dilemmas, fixes, and crisis dynamics of growth regimes. *Capital & Class* 37(1): 5–24.

Jessop, B. and Sum, N. (2005). *Beyond the regulation approach: Putting the economy in its place in political economy.* Cheltenham: Edward Elgar.

Kannankulam, J. and Georgi, F. (2012). Die Europäische Integration als materielle Verdichtung von Kräfteverhältnissen: Hegemonieprojeke im Kampf um das 'Staatsprojekt Europa'. *Arbeitspapier* 39.

Kolko, G. and Kolko, J. (1972). *Limits of power: The world and United States foreign policy 1945–1954.* New York: Harper & Row.

Laclau, E. and Mouffe, C. (1985). *Hegemony and socialist strategy.* London: NLB.

Lenin, V.I. (1963 [1910]). Differences in the European labour movement. In *Collected Works*, vol. 16 (pp. 347–352). Moscow: Progress Publishers.

Leubolt, B. (2014). History, institutions, and selectivities in historical-materialist policy analysis: A sympathetic critique of Brand's State, context and correspondence. *Österreichische Zeitschrift für Politikwissenschaft* 43(3): 309–318.

Lipietz, A. (1993). From Althusserianism to 'regulation theory'. In E.A. Kaplan and M. Sprinker (Eds), *The Althusserian Legacy* (pp. 99–138). London: Verso.

Marx, K. (1986a). *Economic manuscripts of 1857–58* (first version of *Capital*). London: Lawrence & Wishart.

Marx, K. (1986b). Introduction. In *Economic manuscripts of 1857–58* (first version of *Capital*) (pp. 17–48). London: Lawrence & Wishart.

Marx, K. (1998). *Capital, Volume 3. The process of capitalist production as a whole.* London: Lawrence & Wishart.

Nölke, A. (2004). *Transnationale Politiknetzwerke: Eine Analyse grenzüberschreitender politischer Entscheidungsprozesse jenseits des regierungszentrischen Modells.* Habilitationsschrift, Fakultät für Sozialwissenschaften und Philosophie der Universität Leipzig.

Overbeek, H. (1980). Finance capital and the crisis in Britain. *Capital & Class* 11: 99–120; Chapter 3, this volume.

Overbeek, H. (1988). *Global capitalism and Britain's decline.* Doctoral dissertation, Universiteit van Amsterdam.

Overbeek, H. (1990). *Global capitalism and national decline: The Thatcher decade in perspective.* London: Unwin Hyman.

Overbeek, H. (1993). Preface. In *Restructuring hegemony in the global political economy: The rise of transnational neo-liberalism in the 1980s* (pp. ix–xi). London: Routledge.

Overbeek, H. (2000). Transnational historical materialism: theories of transnational class formation and world order. In R.P. Palan (Ed.), *Global political economy: Contemporary theories* (pp. 168–183). London: Routledge.

Overbeek, H. (2003). Globalization, neoliberalism and the employment question. In *The political economy of European employment: European integration and the transnationalization of the (un)employment question* (pp. 13–28). London: Routledge.

Overbeek, H. (2004). Transnational class formation and concepts of control: Towards a genealogy of the Amsterdam Project in international political economy. *Journal of International Relations and Development* 7(2): 113–141.

Overbeek, H. (2005). Class, hegemony and global governance: A historical materialist perspective. In A.D. Ba and M.J. Hoffmann (Eds), *Contending perspectives on global governance: Coherence, contestation, and world order* (pp. 39–56). London: Routledge.

Overbeek, H. (2010). Global governance: From radical transformation to neo-liberal management. *International Studies Review* 12(4): 697–702.

Overbeek, H. (2012). Sovereign wealth funds in the global political economy: The case of China. In H. Overbeek, B. van Apeldoorn, and N. de Graaff (Eds), *The transnational politics of corporate governance regulation* (pp. 138–160). London: Routledge.

Overbeek, H. and van Apeldoorn, B. (2012). Introduction: The life course of the neoliberal project and the global crisis. In *Neoliberalism in crisis* (pp. 1–20). Basingstoke: Palgrave-Macmillan.

Overbeek, H. and van der Pijl, K. (1993). Restructuring capital and restructuring hegemony: Neo-liberalism and the unmaking of the post-war order. In H. Overbeek (Ed.), *Restructuring hegemony in the global political economy: The rise of transnational neo-liberalism in the 1980s* (pp. 1–27). London: Routledge.

Overbeek, H., van Apeldoorn, B., and Nölke, A. (Eds) (2007). *The transnational politics of corporate governance regulation*. London: Routledge.

Palloix, C. (1971). *L'économie mondiale capitaliste*. Paris: Maspero.

Palloix, C. (1973). *Les firmes multinationales et le procès d'internationalisation*. Paris: Maspero.

Palloix, C. (1974). *Le processus d'internationalisation dans la sidérurgie et les industries mécaniques et électriques*, vol. 1. Grenoble: Institut de recherche économique sur la production et le développement.

Perry, J. (2009). *Global private authority and corporate governance*. Doctoral dissertation, Vrije Universiteit Amsterdam.

van der Pijl, K. (1978). *Een Amerikaans plan voor Europa: Achtergronden van het ontstaan van de EEG*. Amsterdam: Socialistische Uitgeverij.

van der Pijl, K. (1979). Class formation at the international level. *Capital & Class* 9: 1–21; Chapter 2, this volume.

van der Pijl, K. (1984). *The making of an Atlantic ruling class*. London: NLB.

van der Pijl, K. (1989). Ruling classes, hegemony, and the state system: Theoretical and historical considerations. *International Journal of Political Economy* 19(3): 7–35.

van der Pijl, K. (1993). The sovereignty of capital impaired: Social forces and codes of conduct for multinational corporations. In H. Overbeek (Ed.), *Restructuring hegemony in the global political economy: The rise of transnational neo-liberalism in the 1980s* (pp. 28–57). London: Routledge.

van der Pijl, K. (1998). *Transnational classes and international relations*. London: Routledge.

van der Pijl, K. (2001). International relations and capitalist discipline. In R. Albritton, M. Itoh, R. Westra, and A. Zuege (Eds), *Phases of capitalist development: Booms, crises and globalizations, cycles* (pp. 1–16). Basingstoke: Palgrave.

van der Pijl, K. (2006). *Global rivalries from the Cold War to Iraq*. London: Pluto.

van der Pijl, K. (2007a). Capital and the state system: A class act. *Cambridge Review of International Affairs* 20(4): 619–637.

van der Pijl, K. (2007b). *Nomads, empires, states: Modes of foreign relations and political economy*, vol. I. London: Pluto.

292 Bob Jessop

van der Pijl, K. (2009). A survey of global political economy. Centre for Global Political Economy, University of Sussex, available at https://libcom.org/library/survey-global-p olitical-economy (accessed 19 December 2017).

van der Pijl, K. (2010). Historicising the international: Modes of foreign relations and political economy. *Historical Materialism* 18(2): 3–34.

van der Pijl, K. (2012). Introduction. In *The making of a transatlantic ruling class*, 2nd ed. London: Verso.

van der Pijl, K. (2015) Varieties of capitalism or dominant fractions? Two forms of money capital in the current crisis. In R. Westra, D. Badeen and R. Albritton (Eds), *The future of capitalism after the financial crisis: The varieties of capitalism debate in the age of austerity* (pp. 39–55). London: Routledge.

Poulantzas, N. (1975). *Classes in contemporary capitalism*. London: NLB.

Poulantzas, N. (1978). *State, power, socialism*. London: Verso.

Ryner, M., Overbeek, H., and Holman, O. (1998). Guest editors' introduction. *International Journal of Political Economy* 28(1): 3–11.

Schlupp, F., Nour, S., and Junne, G. (1973). Zur Theorie und Ideologie internationaler Interdependenz. Internationale Beziehungen als System. In K.J. Gantzel (Ed.), *Politische Vierteljahresschrift Sonderheft* (pp. 245–307). Opladen: Westdeutscher Verlag.

Vliegenthart, A. (2009). *Transnational forces and corporate governance regulation in Central Europe.* Doctoral dissertation, Vrije Universiteit Amsterdam.

Wigger, A. (2008). *The European Commission, a supranational political entrepreneur in global competition governance? The pro-active role of the Commission's DG Competition in the global convergence in competition governance.* Doctoral dissertation, Vrije Universiteit Amsterdam.

INDEX

Note: Page numbers printed in **bold** refer to a major discussion of a given topic. Specific page numbers (e.g. 5–8) indicate that the discussion continues over the relevant pages; non-specific page numbers indicate several separate references on two (f.) or more (ff.) pages (5f. or 8ff.). The index is thematic so that entries sometimes refer to a relevant theme rather than an exact use of a given word concept or phrase. Authors are indexed only when they are directly quoted or discussed at length not when they are simply cited in support of one or another argument

Agency, *see* ideological agency, political agency, structure–agency
Aglietta, Michel 5, 272f, 287n
Agricultural capital 22, 27, 33f, 40ff, 73
Agriculture, 40, 65, 73, 188; Dutch 27, 33f, 37ff, 45f, 49f
Althusser, Louis 4f, 59f
Americanism and Fordism (Gramsci's text) 3, **63–66**, 267f, 287n
Andreff, Wladimir 5
Argentina 246, 250
American capital 3, 10, 59, 62, 66–67, 74ff, 84, 89–92, 194, 198
Amsterdam School, in architecture 4, 12n, 214
Amsterdam School, in international political economy xix–xx, **1–8**, 170–2, 197ff, 214–5, 263–5, 268–70; and Chinese IPE 180–5; elite focus 177, 192ff, 215; and eurocentrism 192; and European integration 266–8; everyday life 178; and gender 217ff; and historical turn 228ff; and identity politics 178, 222–3; and method 213ff, 224ff, 230, 233ff, 272–4, 278, 281f; and neoliberalism 270–2;

Open Marxism 171–3, 282; and regulation approach 265–6; structure–agency dialectics 185f, 229ff; Transnational Historical Materialism 3–4, 282
van Apeldoorn, Bastiaan 5, 9, 12–3n, 148, 192ff, 199, 204, 213f, 223ff, 227n, 233, 235f, 264, 275, 276, 282
Asia 70, 181–3, 187f, 236, 249f, 251, 257f
Asian Consensus **186–7**
Asian crisis 250
Atlantic unity **58–63**. *See also* circuit of capital, Atlantic; comprehensive concept of control
Atlanticism 60ff, 75, 228
Austerity 35, **75–6**, 133, 193, 199, 255, 278

Banking capital 23–4, 33–4, 44, 52ff, 70, **80–6**, 89, 97n, 102, 105, 177, 233, 243–4, 250, 256, 273. *See also* financial capital
Baran, Paul A. 5, 30
Belgium 41, 44, 95, 103, 108f
Belt-Road Initiative (China), *see* One Belt, One Road
Bhaskar, Roy 225f, 227n

294 Index

Bieling, Andreas 10
Bode, Ries xix, 4, 8, 287n
Bolkestein, Frits 155–7
Bourgeoisie, **28–9**, 284; American **59–63**;
  Atlantic **58–61**, 62ff, 73, 192, 198, 205;
  Catholic 41, 45; Dutch, 21–2, 28–32,
  35f, 50ff; Eastern Europe 175f; European
  59–60; German 23; internal (or interior)
  59, 203, 268, 281, 284; international 58;
  national 203ff, 281; solidarity 23. *See also*
  currents, political; fractions, of
  bourgeoisie
von Braunmühl, Claudia 5
BRIC(S) 193, 242f, 258, 286
Britain, *see* United Kingdom
British capital 80ff, 86ff, 95
Bukharin, Nikolai I. 2, 82, 203
Büsch, Klaus 5, 29, 287
Bush, George W. 194, 256

Cadre class 150, 180, 183, 200, 204, 228,
  231, 270
Calvinism, *see* Protestantism
Canada 197f, 220, 257, 264
Capital, in general 24, 87, 203, 206, 250,
  273. *See also* agricultural capital; American
  capital; British capital; commercial capital;
  finance capital, industrial capital; money
  capital, money-dealing capital;
  profit-producing capital, transnational
  capital
Capital–labour relation 62, 63, 65, 80, 208,
  277. *See also* labour; labour movement;
  trade unions
Caribbean 185–9, 271
Carter, Jimmy 75
Catholicism and Dutch politics **34–7**, 40,
  51–4
Central banks 46, 86–8, 132, 146, 163,
  247ff, 256, 258, 279
Centralization of capital 28, 81–4, 92, 157
China xx, 10, **180–4**, **185–9**, 192–5, 208,
  242, 249, 254, 258, 270
Christian Democracy 68, 70, 73
Christian Historical Union 31, 34–6,
  40, 50ff
City of London 81, 84, 95f
Circuit of capital 28–9; Atlantic **62ff**, 67;
  integration of 60–7 passim 74, 82ff, 96,
  188, 197f, 275
Civil society xx, 154, 159, 172, 178, 207–11
  passim, 204, 218, 221, 270
Class agency **121**, 171, 175, 178, 212–3,
  219, 229, 235, 276–7

Class analysis 58ff, **76n**, 219f, 222, 241,
  269f, 276–8. *See also* circuit of capital;
  fraction
Class antagonisms 30–1, 121, 155
Class compromise 52f, 62f, 65, 68, 73, 76,
  79f, 85 ff, **152–4**, **241–6**, 247, 279
Class formation 121, 170, 192, 194, 204,
  219ff, 224, **242–4**, 269f
Class struggle 51, 58, 65; and competition
  32; and state intervention 32. *See also*
  competition; state, modes of intervention,
  struggle
Clinton, Hillary 254, 257
Clinton, William J. (Bill) 194, 249ff
Colijn, Hendrikus 35, 37, 43–4, 47, 53
Cold War 31, **60–1**, 69, 71, 73ff, 91, 162,
  193, 244, 250
Colonial capital 22, 25, 34, 41ff, 52, 69f, 80,
  84, 86, 90, 94
Commercial capital 27f, 32–3, 52, 68; scope
  for hostility to working class 52
Communism 68–9, 75f, 175, 245, 258
Competition 25–30, 32–7, 54, 80, 86, 127ff,
  158, 210, 267, 273, 278; currency 24;
  regulatory 163
Competition policy 145
Competitiveness 52, 75, 87f, 90ff, 119–20,
  123, 127, **133f**, 153–60 passim, 176. *See
  also* discourse
Comprehensive concept of control xix, 1–2,
  4f, **8**, **31–2**, **50–1**, 55, 170, 177, **185–6**,
  187, 192, 198, 204f, 207, **212–3**, 224,
  235, 244–5, 265–7, 269–73, **276–84**;
  neoliberal xx, 11, 175, 187. *See also
  Herrschaftsynthese*
Concept of control 11, 171, 180f, 198, 228,
  235, 241, 244f, 265, 277f; European 264;
  international 264; national 264; neoliberal
  11, 175, 188, 248, 251, 264. *See also*
  proto-concept of control
Concentration of capital 28, 81, 84, 92, 95,
  157, 251, 273
Connally, Tom 72
Constructivism 2f, 197, 223, 228f
Contender states, *see* Hobbesian
  contender states
Contradictions, 9, 59, **208–11**, 273, **283**; in
  corporate networks 244; in hegemonic
  bloc 24, 44, 51, 155, 208; in
  neoliberalism 155, 194, 208, 211, 267,
  281, 286; political 39, 76, 78; societal 31
Corporate governance 270
Corporate liberalism 182, 198, 243, 245ff,
  257, 264, 280

Corporatism 52ff, 55, 62, 68, 75, 122, 125, 148, 156, 207. *See also* neo-corporatism

Cox, Robert W. xix–xx, 3, 5–6, 12n, 171, 181, 203, 210, 232n, 264, 268–9, 287n

Crenshaw, Kimberlé 217f

Crisis 69, 162, 275ff, 283; 1920–3 (Europe) 33, 35f, 152, 244; 1930s 22, 24ff, 32, 43, 51, 63f, 85f, 244; 1960s–'70s (UK) 81–3, 92, 95f; 1970s–'80s (Europe) 135, 148, 152, 162, 176, 271; 1990s–2000s (Asia) 187, 250; agricultural 49; climate 10, 163; in corporate liberalism 245, 264; debt 162, 247; European integration 267; Eurozone 272; financial 11, 199, 209, 251ff, 272; fiscal 199; global 172; global financial crisis 9, 188, 193, 244, 267; hegemonic 257, 280, 286; ideological 152, 163; legitimacy 272; migration 209; neoliberal 205, 208, 213, 241ff, 265f, 268, 271, 280; in Soviet bloc 249, 251; systemic 241; of Washington Consensus 186

Counter-hegemony 177, 200, 271, 281

Crisis-management 38, 43, **63–5**, 82, 92, 95, 212, 244–6, 251–4, 258–9, 265, 271; European Union 135ff, 267, 272; financial crisis 244–6, 251–4; Netherlands 32–5, 44, 51

Critical realism 181, **222–6**, 282

Critical theory (Frankfurt School) 3

Currency 24, 48, 247

Current, political 21, 31, 33ff, 41ff, 49, 51, 53f, 269

Cycles, economic 23–4, 35, 41, 43, 81, 156, 277, 280; political business cycle 279

Davignon, Etienne 124, 127, 129, 132, 140n

Deflationary policy 34, **43–54**, 70, 80, 84, 93

Delors, Jacques 126, 128, 131–2, 134–5, 145

Deubner, Christian 5

Dependent development 24

Deregulation 11, 128, 133, 146, 150ff, 155, 160

Devaluation 34, 44–50 passim, 88f, 93f, 154

Disciplinary neoliberalism 122, 133, 271

Discourse 119f, 127f, 152, 192, 211, 225, 277, 284; competitiveness **134–7**, 150–1, 163; neoliberal 10, **133–4**, 153, 211; populist **154–5**, 210

Division of labour 25, 29, 41f, 65, 269, 275, 285

Double movement 199–200, 209

Elites 191–2, 235–6

Emmanuel, Rahm 254

Engels, Friedrich 2, 172

England, *see* United Kingdom

Employment policy 40, 47, 87–89, 93ff, **134–6, 157–61**, 158–60

Enlargement of EU, 176; Eastern 9, 154, 175–8; Southern xv, 9, 160

Erhard, Ludwig 70, 73, 77n

European Economic Community 29, 60–1, 66, **71–4**, 80, 89, 92–5

European integration xix, 8f, 11; and role of USA 10

European Monetary Union **131–3**, 143n, 153, 156f, 160–2, 176, 205, 210, 256, 267, 272

European Round Table of Industrialists 5, 9, **119–38, 148–51, 158**, 204, 233

Eurozone, *see* European Monetary Union

Fascism 30, 60, 62, 66f, 67, 152, 243, 253, 270

Feminism 3, 214, **217–8;** methods 214

Fennema, Meindert 4, 5, 9, 12–13n, 29, 198, 234, 276

Finance capital 4, 11, 38, 44, 60ff, 64, **81–4**, 88, **94–7**, 102–4, **105–6**, 114, 129, 144n, 197–9, 220, 233f, 241 245ff, 266, 284. *See also* banking capital

Finance-led accumulation 11, 205, 250–8, 257f, 286

Fordism 63–73 passim, 75, 79–80, 85ff, 148, 152–4, 176, 203f, 243, 264, 267–9. *See also* Americanism and Fordism

Foreign direct investment 26, 50, 67, 74, 258

Foreign policy 30, **40–4, 59–61**, 66, 80, 87–90, 94, 251, 254, 257, 279,

Fraction 1, 4–5, 8, 22, **28–31**, 60, 63–5, 68, 70, 76, 80–3, 87, 121, 129, 169–70, 185–6, 198–9, 224ff, 229, **269**, 275, 277; Atlantic 29; autonomous 25; of bourgeoisie 5, 8, 22, **31–2**, 54f, 66, 269, 275ff; capital vs class fractions 273; China 257f; commodity fraction 171; European 29, 203; Europeanist 129f; finance fraction 4, 62, 81, 220, 241, 244; globalist 129, 131; hegemonic (or directive) 241, 244, 266, 279; landed fraction 266; liberal 61–2; money fraction 171, 275; money-dealing fraction 241, 250, 256; national fraction 170, 203, 213, 284; productive fraction 25, 81, 171, 213, 220, 266, 275; ruling class fractions 8; transnational fraction 170, 199, 213;

296 Index

US-based transnational fraction 199. *See also* agricultural capital; banking capital, circuit of capital; commercial capital, finance capital; industrial capital; money capital; money-dealing capital; monopoly capital; productive capital; profit-producing capital; transnational capital

Fractional compromise 54, 131

Fractional struggle (Dutch bourgeoisie **32–54**)

Fractions of labour 215, 281

France 21, 61, 67f, 74, 93, 101, 103, 145, 160, 180, 209, 242f, 267

Frank, André Gunder 5

Franklin, Marianne 1

Free trade **32–41**, 43f, 47–8, 54, 66–71 passim, 73, 74–5, 79, 90f, 133–6, 142n, 198. *See also* protectionism

Galtung, Johann P. 5

de Gaulle, Charles 68, 73, 90–4 passim, 97n

Geithner, Tim 252–54

Gender 157, 213–4, **216–21**, 250

German capital 60ff, 67, 71ff, 82f, 102, 233ff, 284

German ruling class 205

Germany 67, 145, 180, 208, 267; Dutch–German relations 22–5, 29, 37–44

Gill, Stephen 3, 5, 12n, 171, 181, 202, 264, 271

Global South 186–7, 220–1

Gold Standard 40, 46, **48–50**, **84–6**

Google xx, 251, 253

Governance 119, 147, 161, 184, 187, 228ff, 264, 270; corporate 114, 264, 270; European **120–39**, 146–49, 152ff, 159. *See also* multidimensional governance, multilevel governance, regulation, asymmetrical, and regulation

Governing class 207, 242, 245, 257, 270. *See also* ruling class

Gowan, Peter 249–50

de Graaff, Naná 13n, 199, 213, 234, 236, 268, 281

Gramsci, Antonio 3, 4, 63–6, 170, 183, 244, 257, 266f, 276, 279f, 284ff, 287n

Granou, André 244

Great Britain, *see* United Kingdom

Greenspan, Alan 250

Heath, Edward (Ted) 93–5

Heemskerk, Eelke 114, 281

Hegemonic bloc 136, 183, 199, 204, 253f

Hegemonic project 1, 176, 192ff, 198, 205, 273ff, 280

Hegemony 4, 5, 21, 32, 44, 52,54, 69, 75, **121**, 134, 138, **140n**, 153–4, **170–1**, 177, 180f, 185, 197f, 204, 211, 213, 224ff,248, 257, 266ff, **269**, 273ff, 278ff, 283ff, 286–7n; neoliberal 186–7, 267; transnational 153; United States xx, 184, 197, 203, 286. *See also* comprehensive concept of control; counter-hegemony; struggle, hegemonic

Herrschaftssynthese xix

Hilferding, Rudolf 2, 4, 81f, 203

Hirsch, Joachim 30, 55n, 266

Hirschfield, Hans Max 32–40, 44, 47–50 passim

Historical bloc 186, 266–9, 271

Historical materialism 59, 119, 169–72, 180–4, 197, 201ff, 215, 228–9, 286. *See also* transnational historical materialism

Historical materialist policy analysis 282

Historical turn 10, 170, 178, **228–31**

Hobbesian contender states xx, 5, 8, 10, 180, 182, 199, **206–8**, 210, 220–1, 270, 277–81 passim

Historicism 58

Holman, Otto 1, 4, 5, 9, 142n, 169f, 202, 211, 270, 279

Horn, Laura 13n, 210, 230, 281f, 287n

Hungary 177–8, 210

Identity politics xx, 178, 217f

Ideology 21, 31, 35, 52, 59–60, 119–21, **127–32**, **136–9**, 152–53, 176, 210, 224–6, 244, 269. *See also* competitiveness; discourse; hegemony; neoliberalism; neomercantilism

Ideological agency 119, **133**

Imperialism 2, 4, 44, 58, 61, 64, 203f, 211, 277; American 66, 202, 268, 270; British 203; classical 60, 91, 210; German 243; neoliberal 272; open door 194, 199; rentier 67

Imperial preference 44, 86, 89

Imperial rivalries 59, 72, 74, 203, 267, 270

Industrial capital 25, 46, 50–4, **61–2**, 73, 82, 84, 93–4, 126, 138, 226; scope for compromise with working class 52. *See also* class compromise, productive capital, profit-producing capital

Integration, European 5, 8ff, **71–74**, 90f, **119–22**, **127–9**, **146–55**, **162–3**, 170, **202–5**, 212, 215, 263f, **266–8**, 272, 282, 286; Imperialist 58f

Intellectuals 63, 198–9, 204, 207, 212, 244, 270, 279

Intergovernmentalism 120, 127f, 147f, 212

Interlocking directorates 5, 9, **82–4**, 88, 92, **95–7**, **100–17**, 193, **197–9**, 224, 233–6, 244, 279. *See also* network analysis
International Monetary Fund 188–8
International relations, feminist 217f
Internationalization 5, 25, 28, 60, **66–73**, 82f, 284; of bourgeoisie 66fff; of capital 59f, 82, 95, 182, 198f, 268; of credit and finance 24, 61; of New Deal 202; of production 28, 60, 79; of state 59, 66, 76, 182f, 264, 267, 269–70, 286
Intersectionality 215, **217–22**, 281

Japan 83, 87, 123, 128ff, 180, 208, 243, 257
Jessop, Bob 3, 12n, 171f, 176, 198, 202, 205, 213, 235
Junne, Gerd 264, 268

Kautsky, Karl 203, 205
Kennedy, John F. 63, 67, 72ff, 77n, 91
Keynes, John Maynard 50, 65, 101, 248
Koch Brothers (Charles, David) 253, 255
Kohl, Helmut 141n, 145

Labour government (UK) 86–8
Labour market 11
Labour movement 47, **50–4**, 69, 92. *See also* labour, organized; trade unions
Labour, organized 51, 68ff, 94f, 208, 245ff
Labour power (including skill) 29, 62, 79; reproductive 220
Labour process 59, 80
Laclau, Ernesto 152–5, 288n
Latin America 67, 185–9, 220, 246, 249, 271
Law, David 3
Law of value 29. *See also* valorization
Lenin, Vladimir Illich 2, 4, 60, 76n, 81f, 183, 203
Li, Bin 183
Liberal internationalism 182
Liberal parties 33, 40, 42, 50, 53, 68, 156
Liberalism 39, 61f, 67, 70f, 74f, 139, 176, 209, 222. *See also* corporate liberalism; neoliberalism
Lipietz, Alain 5, 266
Lockean heartland xx, 5, 8, 10, 175, 180ff, 185, 192, 195, 199, 204, **207–11**, **219–20**, 242f, 254, 269–72 passim, 277f, **280–1**
Luxemburg, Rosa 2, 4, 203

Maastricht Treaty **129–33**, 133
Macron, Emmanuel 163
Management functions, executive vs supervisory 100–4

Mandel, Ernest 3, 5, 28, 203, 287
Marchand, Marianne 1, 10, 218, 281
Marshall Plan 68–71
Mass production, *see* Fordism
Marx, Karl 2, 4, 12n, 59, 101, 183, 203f, 225
Marxism 21, 58, 170, 181–3, 203, 215, 225, 235, 272; classical 2ff, 30, 183; and critical realism 227n; Soviet 2, 21, 58; Western 2, 7. *See also* Historical materialism, Open Marxism
Methodological nationalism 58, 181, 186, 212, 230–1, 271, 284
Mexico 220, 250
Miliband, Ralph 4
Mohanty, Chandra Talpade 219, 222
Monetary policy 39, 47, 49f, 88, 248ff
Money capital 8, 45f, 50, 60–3, **81–2**, 171, 177, 198, 203, 226, 229, 247, 264, 266, **271–5**, 277, **287n**
Money-dealing capital 11, 199, **241–3**, **248–57**. *See also* banking capital, finance capital, money capital
Monopoly capital 21, 29ff, 64f, 82, 84f, 91, 96, 152, 197
Montgomerie, Johnna 214–5
Morton, Adam David 12n, 205, 282
Multidimensional governance 146–55
Multilevel governance **147–9**, 151, 270
Murray, Robin 5

Nationalism 61, 154, 157, 163, 177, 194, 198, 210, 281. *See also* populism
Nationalization of industry 88
NATO 73f, 246f, 250f. *See also* Cold War
Nazism, *see* fascism
Neo-corporatism 122
Neo-Gramscianism xix, 11, 119, 139n, 175, 177, 182f, 186, 202, 205, 207, 228, 235, 264, 269, 286n
Neoliberal cosmopolitanism 10, 208ff, 281
Neoliberalism xx, 5, 9f, 119, 122, **128–32**, 134ff, 148f, 151ff, 171, 182, 185ff, 192ff, 202, 228ff, 242, 245ff, 264, **267–72**, 280, 284; finance-led 205; transnational 177f, 204; *See also* comprehensive concept of control, neoliberal disciplinary neoliberalism; predatory vs systemic neoliberalism
Neomercantilism **129–32**, 134, 136, 138, 208
Netherlands, the 60, 70, 77n, 102f, 114, 264, 284; higher education system 5–7
Network analysis 5, 9,11, **193–5**, 226, **233–7**, 277–8, 281

298 Index

Network power 186
Networks 82ff, **94–7**, 104–4; international
104–16; national 108–9, 114, 116;
transnational 152, 202
Neusüß, Christel 5
New constitutionalism 80, 122, **149ff,
155–60**
New Deal 63ff, 69, 80, 203, 245, 248
New public management 7, 231
Nixon, Richard 71, 74f, 93
Nölke, Andreas 268

Obama, Barack 194, 251, 253ff, 268
One Belt, One Road (Belt-Road Initiative)
183, 188, 258
Ontology 2ff, 10, 181, 212, **214–5**, 235,
265, 271, 282
Open Marxism 172, 178, 228, 282
Overbeek, Henk xix, 1, 4, 7f, 12n, 155,
169, 171, 180, 185, 193, 197, 213, 223,
229f, 233, 244, 263, 266, 269, 271–3,
279, 280, 282f, 286n

Palloix, Christian 5, 60f, 268, 287n
Passive revolution 170, 175f, 198, 267. *See
also* hegemony
Paulson, Henk 251, 253
Periodization **24–7**, 74, 76–7n, 185, 204,
208–9, 242, 265, 275, 277, **279–80**, 285
Perry, James 208
Peterson, V. Spike 218–21 passim
van der Pijl, Kees xix, 1, 4, 7f, 12n, 116,
121, 170f, 175, 180ff, 188, 198ff, 204f,
207f, 211, 212, 214, 219, 221, 224, 228,
231, 233–6 passim, 264, 266–74 passim,
277ff, 280, 283ff, 287n
Pillarization (Dutch politics) 35, 36f,
52, 55n
Polanyi, Karl 138, 209–10
Policy 33, 75, 86, 88, 279. *See also*
employment policy, foreign policy,
monetary policy, social policy,
trade policy
Political agency 121, 125, **127–30** (ERT),
146 (ECB), 177 (Hungary)
Political parties **31–4**, 39–43, 50–3, 68, 87,
122, 154, 177, 210, 279; confessional **52**
Populism 35, 145ff, **151–60**, 162ff, 194;
authoritarian 200; nationalist **207–12;**
right-wing xx, 10, 257, 281
Portfolio investment 45–6, 60, 62, 66,
82f, 224
Post-colonialism 217–21
Posthuma, Folkert E. 22, 39, 42
Poulantzas, Nicos 3ff, 59, 203f, 244, 268f

Predatory vs systemic neoliberalism 11,
199d, 242ff, **247–52**, 255ff, 272
Productive capital 8, **60–2**, **81–2**, 197, 203,
245ff, 271ff. *See also* industrial capital and
profit-producing capital
Profit-producing capital 229, 271–5. *See also*
industrial capital
Protectionism 27f, **33–41**, 37ff, 43f, 48, 50,
55, 66ff, 73–4, 86, 128ff, 133, 176, 208
Protestantism 33, 36f, 52
Proto-concept 229, 275, 277, 283–4
Pseudo-valorization 65

Race 10, 215–8
Racism 217
RECIPE (Research Center for International
Political Economy) 7, 268
Reductionism, class 21, 60, 219, 228
Regulation, asymmetrical **146–63** passim
Regulation (juridico-political) 34, 41, 43,
45, 47, 50, 53f, 88, 135, 149, 155f,
209, 225f
Regulation, financial 256
Regulation (governance) 37, 128, 183.
See also governance
Regulation, neoliberal 9; supranational
156, 160
Regulation approach 3, 11, 202, **263–6**, 274,
286; Parisian 3, 5, 263, 265f, 274, 287n;
German 266; grenoblois 3, 266, 287;
Religion **36–7**, 52; see also Catholicism;
Parties, confessional; Protestantism;
working class, religious divisions in
Reproduction, capitalist 30, 121, 138, 185,
209, 223–4, 265, 278, 285. *See also*
circuits of capital
Reproductive economy 219–21
Reregulation 146, 160, 162
Restructuring 22, 26, 28, 62, 81, 87ff, 92,
134ff, 149ff, 155, 160, 175ff, 211, 218ff,
271, 281; neoliberal 136f, **149–53**, **155**,
159, 177, 211, 281
Robinson, William I. 199, 205, 224
Ruling class, 5, 8, 29–30, 203f, 207, 242, 270,
278f; antagonisms in 29f, 76, 203, 205;
Atlantic 192, 204f; British 87; Dutch 21ff,
279; German 66, 205; transnational 5.
See also governing class
Runyan, Anne Sisson 218
Russia 250, 257f

Sassen, Saskia 218
School, criteria for defining 4–6, 10, 12n,
274f; Amsterdam School as distinct
school 4–6; heterodox vs mainstream 6;

research environment for school formation 6–7. *See also* regulation approach

Sève, Lucien 283

Shadow banking 244, **248–50**, 254–6, 258

Shareholders **101–4**, 114, 156f, 234

Self-regulation 207

Sexism 217

Single Currency 131

Single Market 146, 149, 160ff, 176

Social Democracy **50–3**, 68, 70, **128–9, 131ff**, 138, 163, 203–4

Social policy 51–4. *See also* austerity, welfare state

Societalization 65–6, 204, 228, 265, 269, 278, 282f

Soros, George 251, 253

Soviet bloc 11, 69, 75, 176, 208, 242ff, 247, 250

Space, transnational 2, 124, 186, 205, 266

State 4, **30–32**, 59, 276; modes of intervention 25, 30ff, 38f, 53, 64f, 71, 82, 84–8, 92, 185, 193f, 207f, **252–3**, 276; transnationalization 121, 199. *See also* civil society; governance; hegemony; Hobbesian contender 5; internationalization of the state; Lockean heartland; welfare state; world of states

State–capital nexus 194f, 199, 270, 273, 288n

State-centrism 169, 172, 181, 185–6, 203

State monopoly capitalism 21, 55n, 58, 65, 76n, 182, 243, 280

State-owned enterprise 193, 236

Stato allargato 270. *See also* state, modes of intervention

Stato integrale 285. *See also* civil society; hegemony

Strategic–relational approach 186, 198, 205

Streeck, Wolfgang 245, 247, 257

Structure–agency 8, 30, **120–1**, 180, 185f, 212–3, 222, 225, 229, 233, 276, 278–9, 282. *See also* class agency, ideological agency, political agency

Struggle, class 22, 51–2, 58–9, 85, 95, 211ff, 228–31, 277; fractional **29–39**, 47, 85–6, 128ff, 257f, 279, 283f; hegemonic 10, 121, 170ff, 181, 185, 197, 208, 211, 224, 235, 266, 277, 280; ideological 8, 119; political 20, 29–30, 51–2, 119, 128, 184; among ruling classes 8; subaltern 215

Subaltern groups 200, 213, 215, 267, 277, 281

Sum, Ngai-Ling 172, 213, 235, 266, 280

Super-state (EU) 145f

Supranationalism 120, 128, 147

Surplus value 30, 32, 46, 60, 62ff, 80–1; absolute 84, 86; relative 65–7, 73ff, 79, 85, 94, 207. *See also* pseudo-valorization; valorization; value

Sutherland, Peter 125–7, 130, 133, 142n, 256

Sweden 104, 170

Sweezy, Paul 5, 30

Tariffs, *see* free trade, protectionism

Third World 29, 218–9, 221, 247, 249

Ties, corporate 110–4

Toronto School 3, 7, 12n, 264; relation to Amsterdam School and transnational historical materialism 3

Trade capital, see commercial capital

Trade policy **33–40**, 43f, 48, 55, 71

Trade unions 69, 85, 88, 90, 93f, 125, 128, 136, 148f, 154, 156, 160, 209, 221. *See also* labour movement

Transnational capital **119–23**, 127ff, 132–42, 141n, 171–2, 175–8, 186, 192, 198–9, 204–5, 211–2, 234, 242, 281

Transnational historical materialism **3–4**, 223f, **263ff**, 268ff, 274, 282; as bridge between Marxism and critical IPE 4; *See also* historical materialism, Marxism; Toronto School

Treub, Willem 22–3, 35

Trias Politica **149–51**

Trilateral Commission 75, 171, 246, 257, 279

Trotsky, Leon 2

Trump, Donald 187, 194, 220, 256f

Ultra-imperialism 205

Uneven and combined development 10, 170, 172, 205, 281

United Kingdom 25, 40–5, 48, 61–2, 67, 76, 80, 83, **89–97**, 104, 204, 242–3, 246

United States of America 25, 29, 61, 63, 68, 71, **80–3**, 88–91, 96, 102ff, 113–4, 203–4, 246–50, 257–8

University of Amsterdam xix, 1, 4, 7, 11, 198, 234, 263f, 266

Use values 29, 273, 283

Valorization 79, 81, 277f. *See also* pseudo-valorization

Value 272; of labour power 95; law of 29. *See also* surplus value

Variegated capitalism 76, 186, 283

Varieties of capitalism 103, 138, 186, 198, 205, 265, 284f

Varieties of neoliberalism 264f, 271, 283–4

Volcker, Paul 247ff, 253ff
Vliegenthart, Arjun 268

Wallerstein, Immanuel 5, 12n, 284
Wang, Tiejun 181–2
Wang, Zhengyi 183
Washington Consensus 186–7, 286
Welfare state 80, 128, 133, 153, 157, 160, 163, 176, 203, 248f
Wigger, Angela 13n, 268, 281f, 287
Wilson, Angela 218, 220
Wilson, Harold 80, 92–3
Working class 29, 37, 71, 75, 92, 95; religious divisions 52f, 73. *See also* labour movement; trade unions

World Bank 176, 187–8
World of states 41, 59f, 63, 170, 172, 202, **269**, 273, 278ff, 284
World systems theory xix, 3, 5, 12n, 181, 185f, 223, 268, 271, 284f
World War I 22, 33, 35, 42, 84, 87, 152, 203, 243; post-WWI period 24, 26, 61, 84
World War II 27, 35–6, 53, 65, 243; post-WWII period 27, 55, 61f, 65, 80, 86, 148, 163, 204, 246

Yurchenko, Yuliya 199

Zhang, Jianxin 182–3